CLARENDON ANCIENT HISTORY SERIES

General Editors

Brian Bosworth   Miriam Griffin
David Whitehead   Susan Treggiari

The aim of the CLARENDON ANCIENT HISTORY SERIES is to provide authoritative translations, introductions, and commentaries to a wide range of Greek and Latin texts studied by ancient historians. The books will be of interest to scholars, graduate students, and advanced undergraduates.

EUSEBIUS

Life of Constantine

Introduction, translation,
and commentary by
Averil Cameron
and
Stuart G. Hall

CLARENDON PRESS · OXFORD
1999

This book has been printed digitally and produced in a standard specification in order to ensure its continuing availability

OXFORD
UNIVERSITY PRESS

Great Clarendon Street, Oxford OX2 6DP

Oxford University Press is a department of the University of Oxford.
It furthers the University's objective of excellence in research, scholarship,
and education by publishing worldwide in

Oxford New York

Auckland Bangkok Buenos Aires Cape Town Chennai
Dar es Salaam Delhi Hong Kong Istanbul Karachi Kolkata
Kuala Lumpur Madrid Melbourne Mexico City Mumbai Nairobi
São Paulo Shanghai Singapore Taipei Tokyo Toronto
with an associated company in Berlin

Oxford is a registered trade mark of Oxford University Press
in the UK and in certain other countries

Published in the United States
by Oxford University Press Inc., New York

ISBN 0-19-814971-4
ISBN 0-19-814924-7 pbk

PREFACE

The work known as the *Life of Constantine* is the most important source for the reign of Constantine the Great and particularly for his support of Christianity. It is, however, controversial. Its author, Eusebius, bishop of Caesarea in Palestine, is often, though mistakenly, regarded on the strength of it as Constantine's official propagandist; in contrast some have thought the work so distorted and unfair that they have denied that Eusebius could have written it. Surprisingly, however, while there is a long bibliography of studies devoted to the question of its authenticity, no English commentary exists, and no English translation has been attempted for over a century. It is the aim of the present work to make the *Life* accessible to students and scholars alike, and to make use of the large amount of recent work on Constantine's reign and especially on the particular aspects described there. We are fortunate in that there is an excellent recent critical edition of the Greek text by Friedhelm Winkelmann, and this is the basis of our translation and commentary, with only a few variations, all of which are discussed in the appropriate places. Eusebius' Greek is often obscure and equally often pretentious; we have not tried to gild the lily but to stay close to the original in the hope of conveying its very characteristic tone. The commentary seeks to explain and elucidate the content; it could of course have been very much more detailed.

The present work is the result of a collaboration between two scholars with somewhat differing approaches, drawn from the history of late antiquity and the history of the early Church respectively. We consider this to be a great advantage in understanding Eusebius' manner of writing, and while some parts of what follows may owe more to one of the authors than to the other, we have—perhaps surprisingly—succeeded in reaching agreement on all matters of substance. Perhaps the most striking result of working on the project has been the full realization of the complex relation between Eusebius' own writings, and between the *Life* and the ecclesiastical and theological context in which it was written.

Thanks and acknowledgements are due to colleagues and

friends. Several seminars have contributed to the work's gestation, at King's College London (where the authors were colleagues until Averil Cameron moved to Oxford and Stuart Hall retired to Scotland), the Institute of Classical Studies, the University of California at Berkeley, Macquarie University, the Collège de France, and the University of Warwick, as well as audiences at the Oxford Patristic Conference, and the Triennial Conference at Oxford and at the University of Bergen. Stuart Hall would also like to thank King's College London for a term's study-leave to work on the *Life*. Among individuals we would like to thank J. J. Arce, T. D. Barnes, whose important book *Constantine and Eusebius* (1981) has done so much to stimulate a new interest in the subject, Andrew Burnett, Paul Cartledge, Hal Drake, Jan Willem Drijvers, Sam Lieu, Raoul Mortley, Samuel Rubenson, Hans-Ulrich Wiemer, Brian Warmington and Anna Wilson. Richard Burgess kindly allowed us to see work in advance of publication and we are especially grateful to Martin Biddle for his advice, and for allowing us to see the proofs of his forthcoming book. Brenda Hall provided the excellent index. Finally, our grateful thanks are due to the various members of the seminars, especially Charlotte Roueché, Richard Price, Scott Bradbury, Judith Evans-Grubbs, and Michael Hollerich.

A.C., S.G.H.

Keble College, Oxford
Elie, Fife
July 1998

CONTENTS

LIST OF ILLUSTRATIONS

ABBREVIATIONS

I. Eusebius, Vita Constantini: Editions and Translations

Heikel   I. A. Heikel, *Eusebius Werke I. Über das Leben Constantins, Constantins Rede an die heilige Versammlung. Tricennatsrede an Constantin, GCS Eusebius*, i (Leipzig, 1902).

Winkelmann   F. Winkelmann, *Über das Leben des Kaisers Konstantins, GCS Eusebius*, 1/1 (Berlin, 1975, rev. 1992).

Bagster/   *The Life of Constantine by Eusebius, together with the Oration*
Richardson   *of Constantine to the assembly of the Saints and the Oration of Eusebius in Praise of* Constantine, rev. translation, with prolegomena and notes by E. C. Richardson, NPNF 2/1 (New York, 1890), 405–632.

Tartaglia   L. Tartaglia, *Eusebio di Cesarea, Sulla Vita di Costantino*, introd., trans., and notes, Koinonia, 8 (Naples, 1984).

Gurruchaga   M. Gurruchaga, *Eusebio de Cesarea, Vida de Costantino* (Madrid, 1994).

II. Other Works by Eusebius

Drake, *In Praise of*   H. A. Drake, *In Praise of Constantine: A Historical Study*
Constantine   *and New Translation of Eusebius's Tricennial Orations* (Berkeley and Los Angeles, 1976).

HE   *Historia Ecclesiastica*, ed. Theodor Mommsen, *Eusebius Werke*, ii. *Die Kirchengeschichte*, GCS *Eusebius*, 2 1–2 (Leipzig, 1903), English trans., H. J. Lawlor and J. E. L. Oulton, *Eusebius Bishop of Caesarea. The Ecclesiastical History and the Martyrs of Palestine, translated with Introduction and Notes* (London, 1927; repr. 1954); G. A. Williamson, *Eusebius: The History of the Church*, rev. with introduction by Andrew Louth (Harmondworth, 1989).

Mart. Pal. *Martyrs of Palestine*, ed. E. Schwartz, GCS 9/2 (Leipzig, 1908), trans. Lawlor and Oulton (s.v. *HE*).

PE   *Praeparatio Evangelica*, ed. K. Mras, GCS 43/1–2 (Berlin, 1954, 1956), trans. E. H. Gifford, *Eusebii Praeparatio Evangelica* (Oxford, 1903)

DE   *Demonstratio Evangelica*, ed. I. A. Heikel, GCS 23 (Leipzig, 1913), trans. W. J. Ferrar, *Eusebius, Proof of the Gospel* (London, 1926).

Contra Hieroclem	*Contra Hieroclem*, ed. E. des Places and M. Forrat (SC 333; Paris, 1986).
LC	*De Laudibus Constantini*, see Drake, *In Praise of Constantine*
SC	*De Sepulchro Christi* (chs. 11–18 of the *LC*), trans. Drake, *In Praise of Constantine*

III. Other Works

AE	*L'Année Épigraphique*
AGWG. PH	*Abhandlungen der königlichen Gesellschaft der Wissenschaften zu Göttingen, Phil.-hist. Klasse*
AJA	*American Journal of Archaeology*
AJP	*American Journal of Philology*
Alföldi	A. Alföldi, *The Conversion of Constantine and Pagan Rome*, 2nd edn. (Oxford, 1969).
Anon. *De Rebus Bellicis*	M. Hassall and R. Ireland, eds., *De Rebus Bellicis* (BAR Int. ser. 63; Oxford, 1979).
ANRW	*Aufstieg und Niedergang der römischen Welt*, ed. H. Temporini (Berlin, 1972–).
Barnes, 'Lactantius'	T. D. Barnes, 'Lactantius and Constantine', *JRS* 63 (1973), 29–46.
Barnes, *CE*	Timothy D. Barnes, *Constantine and Eusebius* (Cambridge, Mass., 1981).
Barnes, *NE*	Timothy D. Barnes, *The New Empire of Diocletian and Constantine* (Cambridge, Mass., 1982).
Barnes, 'Persia'	T. D. Barnes, 'Constantine and the Christians of Persia', *JRS* 75 (1985), 126–36.
Barnes, 'Panegyric'	T. D. Barnes, 'Panegyric, History and Hagiography in Eusebius' *Life of Constantine*', in R. Williams, ed., *The Making of Orthodoxy: Essays in Honour of Henry Chadwick* (Cambridge, 1989), 94–123.
Barnes, 'Two Drafts'	T. D. Barnes, 'The Two Drafts of Eusebius' *Vita Constantini*', in T. D. Barnes, *From Eusebius to Augustine* (Aldershot, 1994), xii.
Baynes	N. H. Baynes, *Constantine the Great and the Christian Church* (London, 1929, 1931; 2nd edn., Oxford, 1972).
Baynes, 'Eusebius'	N. H. Baynes, 'Eusebius and the Christian Empire', *Mélanges Bidez*, 2 (1934) 13–18; repr. *Byzantine Studies and Other Essays* (London, 1955), 168–72.
BF	*Byzantinische Forschungen*
BFChTh.M.	*Beiträge zur Förderung christliche Theologie*, 2nd ser., Sammlung wissenschaftlicher Monographien
BMGS	*Byzantine and Modern Greek Studies*

Bruun, 'Christian Signs'	P. Bruun, 'The Christian Signs on the Coins of Constantine', *Arctos*, NS 3 (1962), 5–35.
Bruun, 'Sol'	'The Disappearance of Sol from the Coins of Constantine', *Arctos*, NS 2 (1958), 15–37.
Burckhardt	J. Burckhardt, *The Age of Constantine the Great* (1852), trans. M. Hadas (London, 1949).
BZ	*Byzantinische Zeitschrift*
BZNW	*Beihefte zur Zeitschrift für die neutestamentliche Wissenschaft*
Calderone, 'Eusebio'	S. Calderone, 'Eusebio e l'ideologia imperiale', in *Le trasformazioni della cultura nella tarda antichità: Atti del Convegno tenuto a Catania, Università degli Studi, 27 sett.– 2 ott. 1982* (Rome, 1985), 1–26.
Cameron, 'Construction'	'Eusebius' *Vita Constantini* and the Construction of Constantine', in Simon Swain and M. Edwards, eds., *Portraits: Biographical Representation in the Greek and Latin Literature of the Roman Empire* (Oxford, 1997), 145–74.
Cameron, 'Form and Meaning'	Averil Cameron, 'Form and Meaning: the Vita Constantini and the Vita Antonii', in T. Hägg and P. Rousseau, eds., *Greek Biography and Panegyrics in Late Antiquity* (Berkeley and Los Angeles, forthcoming).
CCSL	Corpus Christianorum series latina
Chron. Min.	*Chronica Minora*, ed. T. Mommsen
CJ	*Codex Justinianus*
Coleman-Norton	R. Coleman-Norton and F. C. Bourne, eds., *Ancient Roman Statutes* (Austin, 1961).
CP	*Classical Philology*
CTh	*Codex Theodosianus*
Dodgeon and Lieu	Michael H. Dodgeon and Samuel N. C. Lieu, eds., *The Roman Eastern Frontier and the Persian Wars* AD 226–363: *A Documentary History* (London and New York, 1991).
DOP	*Dumbarton Oaks Papers*
Dörries, *Constantine the Great*	H. Dörries, *Constantine the Great* (New York, 1972).
Dörries, *Selbstzeugnis*	H. Dörries, *Das Selbstzeugnis Kaiser Konstantins* (*AGWG. PH* 3. 34; Göttingen, 1954).
Drake, *De laudibus*	H. A. Drake, 'When was the *De laudibus Constantini* Delivered?', *Historia*, 24 (1975), 345–56.
Drake 'True Cross'	H. A. Drake, 'Eusebius on the True Cross', *JEH* 36 (1985), 1–22.
Drake, 'Genesis'	H. A. Drake, 'What Eusebius Knew: The Genesis of the Vita Constantini', *CP* 83 (1988), 20–38.
Elliott, 'Conversion'	T. G. Elliott, 'Constantine's Conversion: Do We Really Need It?', *Phoenix*, 41 (1987), 420–38.

Elliott, 'Early Development'	T. G. Elliott, 'The Early Religious Development of Constantine', *JRelH*, 15 (1989), 283–91.
Farina	R. Farina, *L'impero e l'imperatore cristiano in Eusebio di Cesarea: La prima teologia politica del cristianesimo* (Zurich, 1966).
FGrH	F. Jacoby, ed., *Die Fragmente der griechische Historiker* (1923–).
Fowden, *Empire*	G. Fowden, *Empire to Commonwealth: Consequences of Monotheism in Late Antiquity* (Princeton, 1993).
Gager	J. Gager, *Moses in Greco-Roman Paganism* (Nashville, Tenn., 1972).
GCS	Die griechische christliche Schriftsteller der ersten Jahrhunderte
Grant	R. M. Grant, *Eusebius as Church Historian* (Oxford, 1980).
GRBS	*Greek, Roman and Byzantine Studies*
Grégoire, 'Eusèbe'	H. Grégoire, 'Eusèbe n'est pas l'auteur de la "Vita Constantini" dans sa forme actuelle et Constantin ne s'est pas "converti" en 312', *Byzantion*, 13 (1938), 561–83.
Grégoire, 'La Vision'	H. Grégoire, 'La Vision de Constantin "liquidé"', *Byzantion*, 14 (1939), 341–51.
Grünewald, *Constantinus*	T. Grünewald, *Constantinus Maximus Augustus* (Historia Einzelschriften, 64; Stuttgart, 1992).
Hall, 'Eusebian Material'	S. G. Hall, 'The Use of Earlier Eusebian Material in the *Vita Constantini*, I. 58–59', *Studia Patristica*, 24 (1993), 96–101.
Hall, 'Eusebian Sources'	S. G. Hall, 'Eusebian and Other Sources in Vita Constantini I', in *Logos. Festschrift für Luise Abramowski* (Berlin, 1993), 239–63.
Hall, 'Some Constantinian Documents'	S. G. Hall, 'Some Constantinian Documents in the *Vita Constantini*', in Samuel N. C. Lieu and Dominic Montserrat, eds., in conjunction with Bill Leadbetter and Mark Vermes, *Constantine. History, Historiography and Legend* (London, 1998), 86–103.
Hollerich, 'Religion and Politics'	M. Hollerich, 'Religion and Politics in the Writings of Eusebius: Reassessing the First "Court Theologian"', *Church History*, 59 (1990), 309–25.
HUT	Hermeneutische Untersuchungen zur Theologie
ILS	*Inscriptiones Latinae Selectae*
ILCV	*Inscriptiones Latinae Christianae Veteres*
JbAC	*Jahrbuch für Antike und Christentum*
JEH	*Journal of Ecclesiastical History*
JRelH	*Journal of Religious History*

JRS	*Journal of Roman Studies*
JThS	*Journal of Theological Studies*
Lact., *DMP*	Lactantius, *De Mortibus Persecutorum*, ed. and trans. J. L. Creed (Oxford, 1984).
Lane Fox	R. Lane Fox, *Pagans and Christians in the Mediterranean World from the Second Century A.D. to the Conversion of Constantine* (Harmondsworth, 1986).
Leeb	R. Leeb, *Konstantin und Christus* (Berlin, 1992).
Liebeschuetz, *Continuity and Change*	J. H. W. G. Liebeschuetz, *Continuity and Change in Roman Religion* (Oxford, 1976)
Liebeschuetz, 'Religion'	J. H. W. G. Liebeschuetz, 'Religion in the Panegyrici Latini', in F. Paschke, ed., *Überlieferungsgeschichtliche Untersuchungen* (TU 125; Berlin, 1981), 389–98.
MacCormack, 'Panegyrics'	Sabine MacCormack, 'Latin Prose Panegyrics: Tradition and Discontinuity in the Later Roman Empire', *REA* 22 (1976), 29–77.
MacCormack, *Art and Ceremony*	Sabine MacCormack, *Art and Ceremony in Late Antiquity* (Berkeley and Los Angeles, 1981).
MAMA	*Monumenta Asiae Minoris Antiquae*
MEFR	*Mélanges de l'École Française de Rome*
Moreau	Lactantius, *De Mortibus Persecutorum*, ed. and trans. J. Moreau (SC 39; Paris, 1954).
Nixon and Rodgers	C. E. V. Nixon and Barbara Saylor Rodgers, *In Praise of Later Roman Emperors. The* Panegyrici Latini. *Introduction, Translation and Commentary* (Berkeley and Los Angeles, 1994).
NPNF	A Select Library of Nicene and Post-Nicene Fathers
ODB	*The Oxford Dictionary of Byzantium*, ed. A. Kazhdan *et al.*, i–iii (New York, 1991).
Opitz, *Urkunden*	H. G. Opitz, *Athanasius Werke 3. 1, Urkunden zur Geschichte des arianischen Streites 318–328*, 1–2 Lieferung (Berlin and Leipzig, 1934–5).
Optatus, *App.*	*Optatus: Against the Donatists*, trans. and ed. Mark Edwards (Translated Texts for Historians, 27; Liverpool, 1997), Appendix.
Origo	*Origo Constantini: Anonymus Valesianus*, ed. I. König, i. *Text und Kommentar* (Trierer historische Forschungen, 11; Trier, 1987).
Pasquali, 'Die Composition'	G. Pasquali, 'Die Composition der *Vita Constantini* des Eusebius', *Hermes*, 46 (1910), 369–86.
Piganiol, *L'Empire chrétien*	A. Piganiol, *L'Empire chrétien*, 2nd edn. (Paris, 1972).

PG	*Patrologia Graeca*, ed. J.-P. Migne
PLRE	*Prosopography of the Later Roman Empire*, i
REA	*Revue des études augustiniennes*
REG	*Revue des études grecques*
RhM	*Rheinisches Museum*
RIC vii	*Roman Imperial Coinage*, vii: *Constantine and Licinius A. D. 313–337*, ed. P. Bruun (London, 1966).
RQH	*Revue des questions historiques* (Paris, 1866–1939).
SC	Sources chrétiennes
Sirinelli	J. Sirinelli, *Les Vues historiques d'Eusèbe de Césarée durant la période prénicéenne* (Dakar, 1961).
Soden, *Urkunde*	H. von Soden and H. Lietzmann, *Urkunden zur Entstehungsgeschichte des Donatismus*, 2nd edn. (Kleine Texte 122; Berlin, 1950).
Stevenson, *NE*	J. Stevenson, *A New Eusebius*, 2nd edn., rev. with additional documents by W. H. C. Frend (London, 1987).
Storch, 'Constantine'	R. Storch, 'The "Eusebian Constantine"', *Church History*, 40 (1971), 145–55.
Storch, 'Trophy'	R. Storch, 'The Trophy and the Cross: Pagan and Christian Symbolism in the Fourth and Fifth Centuries', *Byzantion*, 40 (1970), 105–17.
Studien	F. Winkelmann, *Studien zu Konstantin dem Grossen und zur byzantinische Kirchengeschichte* (Birmingham, 1993), ed. W. Brandes and J. F. Haldon.
TAPA	*Transactions of the American Philological Association*
TIR	*Tabula Imperii Romani/Judaea. Palaestina*, ed. Y. Tsafrir, L. Di Segni, and J. Green (Jerusalem, 1994).
TRE	*Theologische Realenzyklopädie*
TU	Texte und Untersuchungen zur Geschichte der altchristlichen Literatur
Wallace-Hadrill	D. S. Wallace-Hadrill, *Eusebius of Caesarea* (London, 1960).
Winkelmann, *Textbezeugung*	F. Winkelmann, *Die Textbezeugung der Vita Constantini des Eusebius von Caesarea* (TU 84; Berlin, 1962).
Winkelmann, 'Authentizitäts-problems'	F. Winkelmann, 'Zur Geschichte des Authentizitätsproblems der Vita Constantini', *Klio*, 40 (1962), 187–243 (= *Studien*, i).

NOTE TO TRANSLATION

The square brackets in the translation denote the page number of the Greek text in Winkelmann's edition.

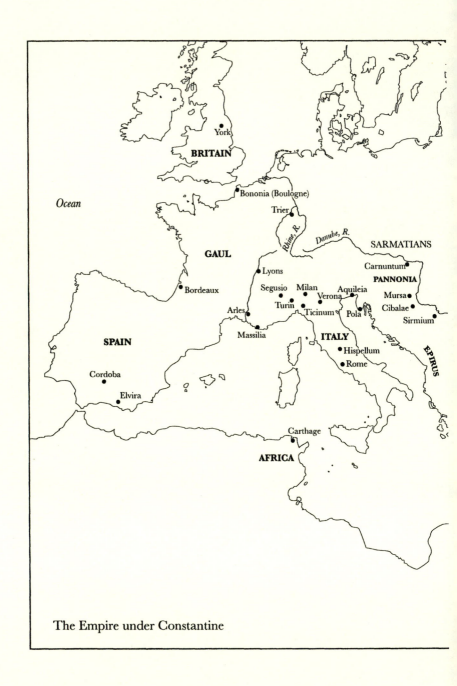

The Empire under Constantine

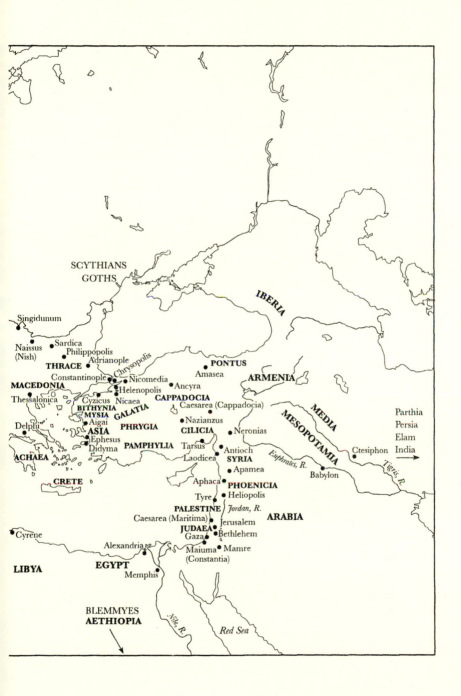

SCYTHIANS
GOTHS

IBERIA

Singidunum

Naissus
(Nish) Sardica
       Philippopolis
       Adrianople
THRACE   Chrysopolis   PONTUS
       Constantinople Nicomedia   Amasea   ARMENIA
MACEDONIA   Helenopolis   Ancyra
Thessalonica   Cyzicus Nicaea CAPPADOCIA
            BITHYNIA   Caesarea (Cappadocia)   MEDIA
            MYSIA GALATIA   MESOPOTAMIA   Parthia
Delphi   Aigai   Nazianzus   Persia
            ASIA   PHRYGIA   CILICIA   Elam
            Ephesus   Neronias   Ctesiphon   India
            Didyma   PAMPHYLIA Tarsus
ACHAEA   Laodicea Antioch   Euphrates, R.
                                   SYRIA
                              Apamea   Babylon   Tigris, R.
CRETE   Aphaca   PHOENICIA
                   Tyre   Heliopolis
            PALESTINE   Jordan, R.
            Caesarea (Maritima)   Jerusalem   ARABIA
Cyrene   JUDAEA   Bethlehem
                   Gaza
            Alexandria   Mamre
                   Maiuma   (Constantia)
LIBYA   EGYPT
            Memphis

BLEMMYES
AETHIOPIA   Nile, R.   Red Sea

INTRODUCTION

I. THE AUTHOR AND THE WORK

The *Life of Constantine* (*Vita Constantini*, henceforth *VC*) is the main source not only for the religious policy of Constantine the Great (ruled AD 306–37, sole Emperor 324–37) but also for much else about him. It is attributed in the manuscripts to Eusebius, bishop of Caesarea (d. AD 339), who was also the author of the first history of the Church (*Church History, Historia Ecclesiastica, HE*) and many other works of biblical scholarship, Christian apologetic, and contemporary religious debate.[1] The *VC* is divided into four books, with chapter headings by a later editor (see below, p. 24, § 5). The title by which it is generally known is somewhat misleading, in that while the work certainly has biographical elements, it is better described as an uneasy mixture of panegyric and narrative history (see below, § 6). Many of the details which it records are to be found only here, and since the *VC* presents a view of Constantine that is not only extremely pro-Christian but also, as we can see from comparison with some of his other works, particular to the interests of Eusebius himself, it is not surprising that it has proved extremely controversial. Some scholars are disposed to accept its evidence at face value while others have been and are highly sceptical (§ 2). Indeed, the integrity of Eusebius as a writer has often been attacked and his authorship of the *VC* denied by scholars eager to discredit the value of the evidence it provides, with discussion focusing particularly on the numerous imperial documents which are cited verbatim in the work. In contrast, T. D. Barnes's major book on Constantine, for example, makes substantial use of the *VC*, and the work remains the single most important source for Constantine. Strangely, in view of the amount of attention which has been devoted to it, and to the issues surrounding the reign and policies of Constantine, there is no

---

[1] There is a Penguin translation of the *HE* by G. A. Williamson, *Eusebius, The History of the Church* (Harmondsworth, 1965), revised with new material and introduction by Andrew Louth (1989). For Eusebius' other works see T. D. Barnes, *Constantine and Eusebius* (Cambridge, Mass., 1981) (*CE*), especially 164–88.

monograph devoted to the *VC* and only two short commentaries to date, in Italian and Spanish respectively. In what follows we accept the work's Eusebian authorship and aim in the commentary to show in detail how carefully crafted and how complex its construction actually is; only by adopting such a procedure can the whole be understood or the historical value of individual passages properly assessed.

Eusebius, bishop of Caesarea in Palestine, is one of the most prolific and important writers of the early Church.[2] He was much influenced by the theology of Origen, in whose tradition he followed, and whose library he inherited, and he was a major biblical scholar and interpreter.[3] He may have begun his *History of the Church* from the beginnings to his own day before the start of the Diocletianic persecution in AD 303. If so he soon found himself writing against a very different background, as Constantine first revealed himself as a supporter of Christianity and then attacked and defeated his remaining ally and co-emperor, Licinius. Having continued the narrative of the *HE* up to Constantine's victory over Maxentius in AD 312 he adapted it to changing circumstances by revising and updating it in successive editions, adding the final touches after Constantine's final victory over Licinius in AD 324 but apparently before the Council of Nicaea in the following year.[4] In addition to the genre of church history, Eusebius also established that of the Christian chronicle, beginning from creation, while others of his major works, especially the *Praeparatio Evangelica* (*Preparation for the Gospel*, *PE*) and *Demonstratio Evangelica* (*Demonstration of the Gospel*, *DE*), set out his providential arguments for the coming of Christianity, the defeat of paganism and God's plan of salvation.

For Eusebius, Constantine played a central role in this scheme, and the *VC* too is a highly apologetic work.[5] In books I–II he draws in detail on his earlier narrative of the same events

---

[2] See in addition to Barnes, *CE*, D. S. Wallace-Hadrill, *Eusebius of Caesarea* (London, 1960); G. Chesnut, *The First Christian Histories* (Théologie historique, 46; Paris, 1977); R. M. Grant, *Eusebius as Church Historian* (Oxford, 1980).

[3] For Eusebius as a scholar and a writer see Barnes, *CE*, part 2.

[4] The evidence is set out by T. D. Barnes, 'The Editions of Eusebius' Ecclesiastical History', *GRBS* 21 (1980), 191–201, at 196–201, with earlier references; see also A. Louth, 'The Date of Eusebius' *Historia Ecclesiastica*', *JThS* NS 41 (1990), 111–23; R. W. Burgess, 'The Dates and Editions of Eusebius' *Chronici Canones* and *Historia Ecclesiastica*', *JThS* NS 48 (1997), 471–504, at 483–86.

[5] For Eusebius as apologist see Burgess, 'Dates and Editions', esp. 489–91.

in the *HE*, heightening the apologetic tone still further (§4 below), and then takes up the story where he had left off, describing the campaign against Licinius in more detail; he then carries it on, though with thematic interruptions, until Constantine's death in AD 337. Eusebius seems to have left the *VC* unfinished or unrevised when he died himself in May 339, but he had recently written other works relating to Constantine, and closely connected with the *VC*. Chief among these are the speech delivered to commemorate the thirtieth anniversary of the Emperor's accession in AD 335–6, known as the *Tricennalian Oration*, or *Laus Constantini* (*LC*), and a surviving speech—not the only one he wrote—on the dedication of the church of the Holy Sepulchre in Jerusalem in 335 (*SC*). Views differ about when he started work on the *VC* (§3 below), but he may have begun collecting some of the material immediately after 324.

As a bishop in Palestine, Eusebius did not know Constantine personally until he attended the Council of Nicaea in 325, and even after that he had few personal dealings with the Emperor. Like that of other churchmen, however, his eagerness to enlist imperial support for the Church steadily grew as Constantine's own interest became clearer. Eusebius was regarded as essentially pro-Arian in sympathy and when he went to the Council of Nicaea he had been formally condemned by an Antiochene synod. His experience at Nicaea led him to support Constantine's formula, but the ecclesiastical politics of the rest of the reign proved complex and Eusebius' own position continued to dictate the manner of his writing and his presentation of the evidence. Even if some material had been collected earlier, his later work on the *VC* was done at a time when the future seemed uncertain so far as church politics were concerned, and one of the aims of the work in its final form was to urge the continuation of what Eusebius claimed to be Constantine's policies on the latter's three sons and successors, who had all been declared Augusti in September 337 after months of uncertainty and even bloodshed.[6] These circumstances must be carefully kept in mind when assessing the historical value of individual passages.

---

[6] See Averil Cameron, 'Eusebius' *Vita Constantini* and the Construction of Constantine', in S. Swain and M. Edwards, eds., *Portraits: Biographical Representation in the Greek and Latin Literature of the Roman Empire* (Oxford, 1997), 145–74.

2. AUTHENTICITY

By far the greater part of the large modern bibliography on the
VC is concerned with the question of its authenticity.[7] Nevertheless, few scholars today would attempt to deny that it is a work
of Eusebius, particularly in view of the similarities of thought and
style between the *VC* and his other works.[8] Recognition of its
authenticity invites a reconsideration of Eusebius' presentation of
Constantine, as well as of his methods of work. The fact that this
also reinstates the *VC* as the major source for Constantine makes
a thorough examination of the construction, sources and aims of
the work, not just its 'authenticity', long overdue.

Although the manuscripts ascribe the *VC* unequivocally to
Eusebius, the extent to which it was known or read during the
fourth century is uncertain, despite the fact that by the end of the
century the *HE* had been translated into Latin and become a
standard work.[9] The *VC* was known to the fifth-century Greek
church historians Socrates and Sozomen and others through the
lost work of Gelasius of Caesarea. However, it had been eclipsed by
the early Byzantine period by fanciful or legendary accounts of
Constantine, which served to create a mythical history for the city
of Constantinople. Despite this early lack of interest, however, the
scholarly attack on the authenticity of the *VC* is largely a modern
phenomenon. It was put most forcibly by H. Grégoire shortly
before the Second World War,[10] though many of the difficulties
had already been seen by others, and counter-arguments
advanced.[11] More recently, scholars have generally reacted against
this hyper-scepticism, and while recognizing the problems presented by the work, Barnes, for example, has no hesitation in using
it as the basis for his picture of a firmly Christian Constantine.[12]

---

[7] For a history of the problem see F. Winkelmann, 'Zur Geschichte des Authenti-
zitätsproblems der Vita Constantini', *Klio*, 40 (1962), 187–243 (= W. Brandes and J. F.
Haldon, eds., F. Winkelmann, *Studien zu Konstantin dem Grossen und zur byzantinische
Kirchengeschichte* (Birmingham, 1993), i); and for a summary see Tartaglia, 13–14.

[8] See Winkelmann, pp. lvii–lxiv.   [9] See § 11 below.

[10] H. Grégoire, 'Eusèbe n'est pas l'auteur de la "Vita Constantini" dans sa forme
actuelle, et Constantin ne s'est pas "converti" en 312', *Byzantion*, 13 (1938), 561–83; 'La
Vision de Constantin "liquidée"', *Byzantion*, 14 (1939), 341–51.

[11] See in particular N. H. Baynes, *Constantine the Great and the Christian Church*
(London, 1931; 2nd edn. Oxford, 1972), with Winkelmann, 'Authentizitätsproblems',
197; summary at Tartaglia, 13–14.

[12] On the *VC*, see Barnes, *CE* 265–71; the strength of Constantine's commitment to
Christianity is recognized for instance by R. Lane Fox, *Pagans and Christians in the*

Much of the older hostility to the evidence of the *VC* arose from prejudice. This took several forms, whether stemming from hostility to Eusebius as author or attempting to undermine the image of Constantine as the Emperor responsible for Christianizing the Roman Empire and bringing state and Church together. Some older scholars were suspicious of the work in the light of Eusebius' reputation for Arianism and the controversial place he held in later doctrinal disputes.[13] As a critic of Christianity, Edward Gibbon had already represented Constantine in unfavourable terms, and from the nineteenth century, and in particular after the appearance of Jacob Burckhardt's book on Constantine in 1853,[14] the Emperor came under frequent attack from rationalist criticism, not least via aspersions cast on the reliability and even the honesty of Eusebius. Burckhardt famously wrote that the latter was 'the most objectionable of all eulogists, who has utterly falsified his [i.e. Constantine's] likeness'.[15] This judgement was confirmed for many by the realization that Eusebius had indeed successively (and clumsily) altered what he had written about Constantine in the *HE* as the political situation developed, and in particular as Constantine turned on his erstwhile ally Licinius. It fostered an ultra-sceptical approach to the numerous Constantinian documents contained in the *VC*. But the documents differ in style and language from the main (Eusebian) body of the *VC*, and closer study reveals their similarity in tone and language to other Constantinian pronouncements; moreover, the earlier text preserved in the three *HE* manuscripts and in a London papyrus also confirms their authenticity.[16] Even so, hostility to the Christian Constantine

---

Mediterranean World from the Second Century A.D. to the Conversion of Constantine (Harmondsworth, 1986).

[13] Below, § 11.

[14] J. Burckhardt, *Die Zeit Constantins des Grossen* (Basel, 1853; 2nd edn. 1880); trans. M. Hadas, *The Age of Constantine the Great* (London, 1949). Cf. Edward Gibbon, *The Decline and Fall of the Roman Empire*, ii, chs. 18 and 20; Gibbon is well aware of the 'silences' and distortions in the *VC*.

[15] *Age of Constantine*, 260; cf. 261, 'odious hypocrisy'.

[16] Below, § 4*b*; for a good survey and defence of authenticity see also Charles Pietri, 'Constantin en 324: Propagande et théologie impériales d'après les documents de la *Vita Constantini*', in *Crise et redressement dans les provinces européennes de l'Empire (milieu du IIIe – milieu du IVe siècle ap. J.C.): Actes du colloque de Strasbourg (décembre 1981)* (Strasbourg, 1983), 63–90 (repr. in C. Pietri, *Christiana Respublica, Éléments d'une enquête sur le christianisme antique* (Collection de l'École française de Rome, 234, 3 vols.; Paris, 1998), i. 253–80.

continues to inform some modern historical writing.[17] The debate is of great historical importance, for the *VC* is frequently the only source for a particular document or a particular statement,[18] and the work as a whole is of primary importance for any judgement on Constantine's reign.

There are nevertheless real problems about the construction and content of the *VC*.[19] Many scholars have argued for a Eusebian core overlaid with later interpolations, dating either from the reign of Constantius II or from later in the fourth century. But most of the argument is inconclusive and fails to recognize Eusbius's apologetic aims. The many inconsistencies and irregularities of form (see below), are explained by Barnes by a modified version of the thesis put forward by G. Pasquali in 1910, according to which the work went through two distinct stages in the writing before being left unfinished by Eusebius on his death.[20] The fact that it frequently uses material from the *HE* and *LC*, especially in books I and II, taking over many extracts verbatim, has often been held to be an indication of a later compiler at work. However self-reference is very characteristic of Eusebius as a writer, and he clearly had the *HE* (as also the *LC*) to hand while writing this part of the *VC*, in order to revise his earlier narrative in the light of later experience.[21] The detailed account of Constantine's vision in 312 which is so prominent in

[17] See e.g. T. G. Elliott, 'Eusebian Frauds in the Vita Constantini', *Phoenix* 45 (1991), 162–71.

[18] For a defence of Eusebian reliability see T. D. Barnes, 'Panegyric, History and Hagiography in Eusebius' *Life of Constantine*', in R. Williams, ed., *The Making of Orthodoxy: Essays in Honour of Henry Chadwick* (Cambridge, 1989), 94–123', at 114–15, with 'The Two Drafts of Eusebius's *Vita Constantini*', in T. D. Barnes, *From Eusebius to Augustine: Selected Papers 1982–1993* (Aldershot, 1994), xii, and see below, § 10.

[19] For summaries see Winkelmann, pp. liv–lvi; Tartaglia, introd., 14–17, and see Barnes, 'Panegyric', 98–102 ('doublets and inconsistencies').

[20] G. Pasquali, 'Die Composition der *Vita Constantini* des Eusebius', *Hermes* 46 (1910), 369–86, developed by Barnes, 'Panegyric', supplemented by his 'Two Drafts'; see also Winkelmann, p. lvi–lvii, and Tartaglia, 17. Barnes argues (reversing the sequence proposed by Pasquali) that the work began as a continuation of the *Ecclesiastical History*, some time after 324, and subsequently took the form of a panegyric on Constantine's death in 337 (Barnes, 'Panegyric', 110–14), only to be expanded again and left unfinished by Eusebius at his death. For discussion see Averil Cameron, 'Construction', and see §§ 3 and 6 below.

[21] On the use of the *HE* in the *VC* see S. G. Hall, 'The Use of Earlier Eusebian Material in the *Vita Constantini*, I. 58–59', *Studia Patristica*, 24 (1993), 96–101; 'Eusebian and Other Sources in *Vita Constantini* I', *Logos. Festschrift für Luise Abramowski* (Berlin, 1993), 239–63, and cf. H. A. Drake, 'What Eusebius Knew: The Genesis of the *Vita Constantini*', *CP* 83 (1988), 24 on the *LC* and the *Theophany*.

the *VC* (I. 28. 9) is absent altogether from the *HE*. It is of course conceivable that the later narrative does, as Eusebius claims, derive from personal conversation with the Emperor himself,[22] but it is also important to realize that it represents the mature reflection of Eusebius on Constantine's divinely inspired rise to power and supplies a structural and ideological need at this point in the narrative. Similar considerations explain the differences of emphasis between the narrative in *HE* of Constantine's campaigns against Licinius and the account given in *VC* I. 48–II. 18; writing with apologetic purposes at the end of Constantine's reign, Eusebius has produced in the *VC* a version which justifies Constantine's action against his co-emperor, former ally and fellow supporter of Christians, and sharpens the allegations of Christian persecution against Licinius which had already been added to the *HE* when it was hastily reissued shortly after the final victory of Constantine in 324.[23] In so doing he defends Constantine against the accusation of having broken his alliance more than once,[24] and presents the whole narrative in heavily ideological and religious terms, stressing Constantine's role as the new Moses leading the Christian people out of the tyranny of persecution.[25] Acceptance of the date of 316 for the battle of Cibalae instead of 314 removes the problem perceived by some earlier scholars that *VC* I. 49 seems to make Constantine's war against Licinius start after his Decennalia in 315.[26] For similar reasons, Maxentius too emerges in the *VC* as an open persecutor, whereas at *HE* 8. 14 he is described as a counterfeit Christian. This part of the *VC* is less a sober historical account than a rhetorical justification of Constantine's rise to power written from the Christian point of view and with an eye to the political issues of the end of the reign. In the *VC*, Constantine's father, Constantius, emerges as a pious monotheist, indeed almost a Christian, in sharp contrast to his clearly pagan role in the Latin panegyrics which are much more closely contemporary with the events.[27]

A further difficulty stressed by Grégoire, namely the apparent confusion of Maximian and Maximin at *VC* I. 47,[28] can also be

---

[22] See on I. 28–32; cf. III. 12.

[23] *VC* I. 51–II. 2; cf. *HE* 10. 8–9.

[24] See on II. 9. 4 and below, § 9.

[25] § 7 below.

[26] § 9 below; see however II. 9. 4 and notes *ad loc.*

[27] See *VC* I. 13–18 and see on I. 13–18, 17. 2, 32.

[28] See Winkelmann, p. lvi; 'Authentizitätsproblems', 217, 230–1; and see note on I. 47.

explained on closer analysis of the relation of *VC* to *HE*. Like the *VC*'s modern critics, the author of the chapter headings has failed to see that these chapters are a patchwork drawn from different parts of the *HE*, with a logic of their own which makes a reference here to Maximian explicable even if apparently out of chronological context. These extracts from the *HE* are not therefore to be read as later interpolations[29] but as part of a deliberate reworking of his earlier version by Eusebius himself. While the theoretical possibility of interpolations into a Eusebian original either here or at other points in the text cannot indeed be entirely excluded, there are few if any certain examples. Thus at *VC* IV. 57, where there is a lacuna in the manuscripts, the Geneva edition contains a passage in square brackets concerning a peace treaty with Persia, and introducing the description of Constantine's mausoleum; this may be a later interpolation based on the brief information in the chapter heading.[30] The phrase 'even now', used of Constantine's tomb in IV. 71, has also given rise to suspicion.[31] But the doubts attached by some scholars to the alleged anti-pagan measures of Constantine described in books III and IV are less justified, as is the suggestion that the famous phrase 'bishop of [or for] those outside [the Church]' is not Eusebian.[32]

The case for most of the alleged interpolations has failed to take Eusebius' working methods sufficiently into account. We may accept that the *VC* as a whole is his work, and indeed Pasquali argued that he himself had altered and developed his own earlier draft as circumstances changed. In almost no case are real anachronisms demonstrable, while despite the general unevenness of the work, stylistic analysis shows a striking homogeneity of minor usages. Admittedly, the *VC* is often clumsy, repetitive,[33] and even at times contradictory, but it demands to be understood in the light of a close analysis of its structure and of Eusebius' writing practice. It is hardly possible to imagine another writer so closely in touch with the latter as to have been able to compose the *VC* and pass it off as Eusebian.

[29] See 'Authentizitätsproblems', 206, 217–18.
[30] Ibid. 233; see on IV. 56–7; for the MSS and editions of the *VC* see § 12 below.
[31] See on IV. 58–60.
[32] *VC* IV. 24; see 'Authentizitätsproblems', 234–46.
[33] For example, II. 20–1 seems to summarize the document cited in full at 23–42 but see note.

Moreover, the work closely fits the circumstances of the immediate aftermath of Constantine's death. We must find other reasons for its comparative obscurity after Eusebius' death than the hypothesis that it is substantially the work of a later author.

3. DATE AND CIRCUMSTANCES OF COMPOSITION

The structure of the *VC* has suggested either that Eusebius left it unfinished, or that it went through several stages of composition, or both. In Pasquali's view it started as an encomium, composed immediately after Constantine's death on 22 May 337, and was converted into an apologetic work of wider scope in response to the events which followed, which included the dynastic murders of summer 337, the restoration of Athanasius from exile, and the proclamation of Constantine's three sons as Augusti on 9 September. Left unfinished at Eusebius' death (probably May 339, but dated by Pasquali to 338), it was published with chapter headings by an editor, perhaps Eusebius' successor Acacius. Barnes proposes the reverse order of composition on the basis of the chronological range of the documents included, which begin after Eusebius has recounted Constantine's victory over Licinius in 324, and envisages Eusebius as collecting material for the 'narrative history' from soon after this date.[34] He rightly emphasizes that the present work must be read in close conjunction with the other writings of the later years of Eusebius. These included, besides the *LC* and *SC,* the polemical *Contra Marcellum* and the *Ecclesiastical Theology,* provoked by the return from exile of another of Eusebius' ecclesiastical opponents.[35] On the other hand, the need for a more formal panegyrical account came later, with the thirtieth anniversary and subsequent death of the Emperor, rather than at an earlier stage. Finally, H. A. Drake has argued (mainly on the basis of book IV) that the *VC* was first conceived in 335 and that Eusebius was collecting material for it with the Emperor's encouragement when he was in Constantinople in 336.[36]

VC IV. 60–72 describe Constantine's last illness, baptism, death, and burial, and on that basis it has often been supposed

---

[34] Barnes, 'Panegyric', 'Two Drafts', with Cameron, 'Construction'.
[35] Cf. Barnes, *CE* 264–5.   [36] Drake, 'Genesis'.

that the work as a whole was not written until after the Emperor's death.[37] However, while the references in the introduction and conclusion to Constantine's three sons as Augusti must indeed postdate 9 September 337, they could be additions to an already existing work or work in progress.[38] A *terminus ante quem* for Eusebius' composition is provided by his own death in May 339.[39]

Whatever the genre or genres of the *VC* (on which see below), books I–III at least are arranged in broadly chronological fashion, and despite its rather untidy arrangement of subject-matter, book IV continues the narrative up to Constantine's death and burial. It is noticeable that while standard panegyrical themes reappear in book IV, it is the earlier portion of the *VC*, covering Constantine's reign up to the victory over Licinius in 324, which shows the closest relation to Eusebius' earlier narrative in the *HE*, that is treated in the most formal panegyrical style, For these years, while Constantine ruled in the west, Eusebius had no personal knowledge of the Emperor or much access to official material, and his dependence on his own earlier narrative was therefore also the greater. Equally strong was his desire to correct and supplement it with new interpretations and rhetorical flourishes. From II. 19 on, however, the treatment broadens out considerably: the formal panegyrical elements diminish and the comparison of Constantine with Moses (see below) is no longer sustained; on the other hand the inclusion of documents, which is one of the most striking features of the *VC*, now begins. This change in the nature of the narrative coincides with Eusebius' account of the Council of Nicaea in 325, which was probably the first occasion on which Eusebius had encountered the Emperor personally. It is also worth noting that for the narrative of events after 325–6 all the documents included, with the exception of IV. 9–13, the letter to Shapur, have a direct connection with Eusebius himself, or would have come to him naturally as an eastern bishop.[40]

---

[37] Drake, 'Genesis', 20–1; cf. Averil Cameron, 'Eusebius and the Rethinking of History', in E. Gabba, ed., *Tria Corda: Scritti in onore di Arnaldo Momigliano* (Como, 1983), 71–88, at 87, corrected by Drake, 'Genesis', 28, and see Barnes, 'Panegyric', 113, with n. 66.

[38] *VC* I. 1. 3; IV. 69. 2; see Tartaglia, 15.

[39] See Barnes, *CE* 263.

[40] See B. H. Warmington, 'The Sources of Some Constantinian Documents in Eusebius' Ecclesiastical History and Life of Constantine', *Studia Patristica*, 18/1 (1986), 93–8, and below, § 4*b*.

The question of which parts were written first is not straight-forward. Drake argues for book IV,[41] but this seems unlikely, as books I–III, and in particular I–II are far more polished. Book IV shows traces of Eusebius' stays in Constantinople in 335 and 336. It contains several self-references (see below), and mentions the speeches which Eusebius wrote for the dedication of the church of the Holy Sepulchre at Jerusalem in 335 and for Constantine's Tricennalia in 335–6.[42] At IV. 32, 46 Eusebius announces his intention of attaching these speeches to the *VC*;[43] it is natural therefore to see these works as forming a group close in date to each other. *LC* 18. 1–3, 11. 7, together with *SC* fin., suggest that Eusebius was thinking of a historical work about Constantine when these passages were written. He also refers to personal observation in Constantinople at IV. 7 and 50, and anecdotal material in this book might come from personal experience, for example, IV. 30, 48 and the account of the marriage of Constantius II at IV. 49.[44] However, these provide no more than *termini post quem*, and show only that Eusebius' stays in Constantinople affected the nature of this part of the *VC* by providing him with the personal details that are so lacking in the early parts; compare the striking description of the Emperor's entry at the opening of the Council of Nicaea and the telling details about the dinner-party to which the bishops were invited when the Council ended, both of which for all their literary overtones clearly derive from Eusebius' own experience.[45] The Council of Tyre of 335 which exiled Athanasius under Eusebius' own presidency, and its aftermath in Constantinople, are passed over with barely a mention,[46] but it is clear that Constantine's policies (and his own) needed a defence, and Drake indeed argues that he had the Emperor in view in writing. In any case, the restoration of Athanasius after Constantine's death in 337 would have made a renewed apologia an absolute imperative.

---

[41] Drake, 'Genesis', 31; cf. 30, attributing the initiative to Eusebius himself, on his visit to Constantinople in the autumn of 335.   [42] See IV. 33, 45, 46.

[43] In the MSS the *VC* is followed by the *Oration to the Saints* (described as Bk. V in two of them), *LC* and *SC*; the speech described at *VC* IV. 46 is not however the one which is now attached; see IV. 33, 46 and notes; T. D. Barnes, 'Two Speeches by Eusebius', *GRBS* 18 (1977), 341–45.

[44] See Drake, 'Genesis', 25–7, 29, arguing for a further visit to Constantinople at Easter 337.

[45] III. 10, 15.   [46] IV. 41, with note.

IV. 68, at least, was clearly written after the dynastic murders of the summer months of 337, for it omits all reference to the promotions of the unfortunate Dalmatius and Hannibalianus which took place at the same time as the allocations to Constantine's sons,[47] and much of the ecclesiastical emphasis in the work, especially its stress on the validity of councils, can be explained in relation to the danger which the restoration of Athanasius and Marcellus in the same year represented to Eusebius and his ecclesiastical views. Most telling, however, are the opening and closing paragraphs of the work, which advocate the continuance of Constantine's policies under the new regime by representing him as still ruling from heaven through his three sons on earth, much as Constantine's father Constantius had been depicted in the Latin panegyrics as conscious and rejoicing in heaven at the rule of his sons.[48] If Eusebius began the *VC* as a panegyric of Constantine along more or less conventional, though Christian, lines, the events of summer 337 presented a drastically changed situation, and a real need to justify Constantine's policies and demonstrate the truth of Eusebius' interpretation.[49] The new Augusti had shown how ruthless they could be, and whatever personal misgivings he may have had about the chances for a tripartite reign, it was in Eusebius' interests to urge harmony and continuity with the policies of their father, at the same time presenting his own interpretation of what those policies had been. At the end of the year 337 the future of the Constantinian Empire must have seemed very far from certain.

The *VC* is a clearly a work of apologetic, but it may not have had a single object; rather, the various purposes which it might serve may only have become clear as events developed and as it underwent successive stages of writing. Eusebius is not a polished writer, and we should not suppose that all the infelicities can be accounted for simply by assuming that he left it unfinished. More likely, perhaps, in view of the way in which he made the work function as a 'Mirror for Princes', offering covert advice to the sons of Constantine, is the view that it was expanded in some haste to suit particular needs.

[47] *Origo*, 35; see §9 below.
[48] I. 1. 3; IV. 72; cf. *Pan. Lat.* 7 (6), AD 310, 14. 3–4.
[49] See §6.

4. SOURCES

Where did Eusebius find his material for the *VC*? Winkelmann's index (pp. clv–clvii) lists 'writings used'; the list contains forty biblical passages, eight legal texts, eight literary texts and thirty-nine passages from Eusebius' own works. His separate list (p. ccxxx) of sources for the documents attributed to Constantine in the *VC* adds six biblical, two Eusebian, and two other references. Eusebius was an old hand at documented history, as is shown by the *HE*, *PE*, and *DE*. In the *VC* he treats the Constantinian documents in a way directly comparable with his treatment of sources in these earlier works:[50] narrative is deduced from Constantine's words and then the document itself is presented. Much of his source-material, however, is embedded in narrative or in rhetorical prose without acknowledgement. This is conspicuously the case with his use of his own earlier writings and must be presumed for much else.

Winkelmann's lists, though invaluable, are in some respects misleading and incomplete. Some of the references are to texts possibly alluded to rather than positively used, or to biblical passages alluded to for conventional moralistic or rhetorical reasons rather than as sources for historical construction. Further, much more of the narrative is generated from the sources than such a list of quotations and allusions betrays, and there are clear cases where wording is derived from the earlier Eusebian writings but not recorded in Winkelmann's lists. We may classify the actual sources used by Eusebius as follows.

(a) Eusebius' own writings

Substantial passages are cited with little or no change, especially from *HE* and *LC*. At the same time important variations occur, of which we give some examples here.[51] *HE* included the campaigns against Maxentius, Maximin Daia, and (in the hurried last edition) Licinius. This material is freely drawn upon in the *VC*, but with adjustments. In the *VC* the campaign against Maxentius is led by the cross-shaped standard, not mentioned in the *HE*; this plays a leading part in the new reading of Constantine and leads Eusebius to adjust his earlier narrative in

---

[50] See Grant, 22–32.
[51] See for what follows Hall, 'Eusebian Material'; 'Eusebian and Other Sources'.

I. 37. 1. Similarly the campaign against Licinius is greatly expanded, with eyewitness material, legend and material about the standard.[52] More interestingly, features of the description of Maximin's activity, omitted in the account of Maximin in I. 58–9, now turn up in the account of Licinius: the advice of prophets and oracle-mongers in the account of Licinius in II. 4. 2–4 resembles *HE* 9. 10. 6; the retreat of Licinius to his homeland in II. 11. 1 also resembles *HE* 9. 10. 6; and the idea of a second more culpable and cowardly war is not attributed to Licinius in *HE* as it is in *VC* II. 11–12, but may derive from *HE* 9. 10. 13–14, which is concerned with Maximin. All this suggests both a thoughtful and meticulous use of Eusebius' earlier text, and a careful editing process. Again, the crimes of Licinius at *VC* I. 51–4 are largely derived from the hastily compiled list in *HE* 10. 8. 10–11, but the beginning is now altered to emphasize his ban on episcopal councils, which had been last and least in *HE* 10. 8. 14. This reflects the ecclesiastical concerns of 337–8, when the conciliar decisions of the eastern bishops were threatened by the restoration of Athanasius and Marcellus to episcopal sees from which they had been formally deposed, and matches Eusebius' high regard for councils in the *VC* generally. In III. 33 the recovery of the tomb of Christ and the building of a great church over it are described in words lifted from *LC* 9. 16. But the description is overlaid with the idea that this is the New Jerusalem prophesied in Scripture, and reflects Eusebius' intense concern with that complex of buildings (III. 25–40) and with the Council of Jerusalem (IV. 41–7); so much so, indeed, that the Eusebian source of the text in *LC* 9. 16 has not been noticed by Winkelmann or his predecessors.

Eusebius has wasted little of his previous work. On the other hand, he does not use passages twice, but on returning to a source picks up exactly where he left off. He does not use the material in the order in which it stood before, but appears to work through parts of *HE* 8–10 and *LC* 8–9 systematically extracting what is useful. Much of his apparently independent material can be understood as development of what he had written earlier. His omissions and variations can also often be understood in relation to his purposes in writing the *VC*. This

[52] II. 5, 6. 1, 6. 2, 10. 2.

use and manipulation of Eusebian material might seem to indicate that some other author was at work. But the procedures are not out of keeping with the way Eusebius uses his sources in the *HE*.[53]

The parts based wholly or partly upon *HE* and *LC* are as follows:

I. 13–18 and I. 22–4 use material from *HE* 8. 13. 10–14.

I. 33. 1 follows *HE* 8. 14. 1–2.

I. 33. 2 follows *HE* 8. 14. 14 (cf. *LC* 7. 7).

I. 34 follows *HE* 8. 14. 17.

I. 35–6 follow *HE* 8. 14. 3–6.

I. 37–40 follow *HE* 9. 9. 2–11.

I. 40–1 partly follow *LC* 9. 8–9.

I. 41. 3 is based on *HE* 10. 5. 2–17.

I. 42 is based on *HE* 10. 5–7 (cf. also *LC* 9. 14, 19).

I. 44–5 is based on documents in *HE* 10. 5. 15–17. 2.

I. 47. 1 follows closely *HE* 8. 13. 15.

I. 48–50.2 follow *HE* 10. 8. 1–6.

I. 50. 2–51. 1 follow *HE* 10. 8. 7–8.

I. 52, 54. 1 follow *HE* 10. 8. 10–12.

I. 54. 2–56. 1 follow *HE* 10. 8. 11–14.

I. 56. 2 follows *HE* 10. 8. 9.

I. 57. 1–2 follow *HE* 8. 16. 2–4 and 8. 17. 1.

I. 57. 3 is based on *HE* 8. 17. 1.

I. 58. 1–2 is based on *HE* 8. 14. 13–14 (cf. also 8. 14. 8–9 and *LC* 7. 7).

I. 58. 3 follows *HE* 9. 10. 2–4.

I. 58. 4–59. 1 is based on *HE* 9. 10. 14–15.

II. 1. 1–2 follows *HE* 10. 8. 2 (cf. 10. 9. 3).

II. 1. 2–3. 2 follow *HE* 10. 8. 14–9.3 (cf. 10. 9. 5).

II. 16–18 is based on *LC* 9. 8.

II. 4. 2–4, 11. 2 uses the theme of *HE* 9. 10. 6.

II. 11. 1 perhaps follows *HE* 9. 10. 6.

II. 11. 2, 15–16 may reflect *HE* 9. 10. 1–4.

II. 19. 1 may follow *HE* 9. 11. 1.

II. 19. 2–20. 1 follow *HE* 10. 9. 6–8.

---

[53] See e.g. the case of the paraphrase of the Martyrdom of Polycarp (*HE* 4. 15. 1–46), or the adjustments apparently made in the various stages of composition of *HE* itself, as when the name of Licinius is suppressed in the decree of toleration of Galerius, when the final chapters about Licinius' persecution are added (*HE* 8. 17. 3–4).

III. 26. 5–7 develops *HE* 10. 4. 26–7.

III. 33 develops *LC* 9. 16.

III. 41 follows *LC* 9. 17.

III. 50 follows *LC* 9. 14–15.

III. 54. 4–55. 4 follow *LC* 8. 1–7.

IV. 17–19 partly follow *LC* 9. 10–11.

IV. 40. 1 may develop *LC* 3. 2.

(b) Imperial documents

Eusebius had already included a number of earlier Constantinian documents in *HE* 10,[54] and in the *VC* he cites the Greek text of fifteen, beginning in book II in the year 324, after the account of Constantine's victory over Licinius.[55] Many of these are letters of Constantine addressed to bishops or churches, but they also include three letters addressed more widely, and a letter from Constantine to Shapur of Persia.[56] No less than seven of the letters were either addressed to Eusebius himself, or to him in company with other bishops, or concerned him directly;[57] these documents are of very varying import, ranging from the personal to matters of high policy. Eusebius sometimes claims to have by him originals signed by the Emperor,[58] and some of these presumably came to him in Greek. Documents were sometimes distributed in both Latin and Greek, or Eusebius might have a Latin copy which he translates.[59] Latinisms and signs of chancellery arrangement, especially in the documents cited in book II, and issued after Constantine's victory over Licinius in 324, confirm their official origin, even though the subject-matter and sentiments expressed by the

---

[54] *HE* 10. 5. 2–14 (cf. Lact., *DMP* 48), 15–17, 18–20, 21–4; 6; 7.

[55] II. 24–42, 46, 48–60, 64–72; III. 17–20, 30–2, 52–3, 60, 61, 62, 64–5, IV. 9–13, 35, 36, 42. For the documents in the *VC* see S. Corcoran, *The Empire of the Tetrarchs: Imperial Pronouncements and Government* AD 284–324 (Oxford, 1996), 20–1, who also discusses in detail the nature, provenance, and style of imperial documents and legislation, including those of Constantine, from 284 to the end of the tetrarchic period in 324.

[56] II. 24–42; 48–60; III. 64–5; these are listed by Corcoran, *Empire of the Tetrarchs*, Appendix D, 315–16, and see P. Silli, *Testi Costantiniani nelle fonte letterarie (Materiali per una Palengenesi delle Costituzioni Tardo-Imperiali* iii (Milan, 1987), nos. 16, 17, 19. For the similarities and differences between letters and edicts see Corcoran, *Empire of the Tetrarchs*, 198–203, and for the letter to Shapur (IV. 9–13) see ibid. 316, and Silli no. 34.

[57] Cf. III. 60–2, on the possibility of Eusebius moving to the see of Antioch.

[58] II. 23. 3; 47. 2.

[59] II. 23. 1 (Latin and Greek); II. 47. 2; cf. also *HE* 8. 17 and elsewhere (Latin copy).

Emperor must have seemed novel.[60] Some letters Eusebius received personally, or concerned matters in which he was intimately involved, like the episcopal election at Antioch.[61] Others would be sent to him as metropolitan of Caesarea, either because they were widely circulated to church leaders or because they affected his jurisdiction, which included Jerusalem.[62] Others he may have acquired from a friendly official.[63] He also quotes the inscription on Constantine's statue in Rome and the text of the prayer of the army, and refers to Constantine's speeches and letters.[64]

All but one of the letters are on religious or ecclesiastical subjects.[65] If they are not addressed to Eusebius personally, most touch so closely on church affairs that they would naturally fall into the possession of an active metropolitan bishop. There is also a fragment or extract from a letter to the Persian king in IV. 9–13. The absence of heading and formal greeting in this single case suggest that Eusebius obtained the extract from an unusual source, perhaps an imperial official, or perhaps a previous written account such as that apparently in use in IV. 1–7; the original, he says (IV. 8), was in Latin. Of the documents, eight belong to the period from 324 to 326, and the rest include six sent to Eusebius himself, hence needing no effort on his part to obtain them.[66] B. H. Warmington has named an imperial notarius called Marianus as the likely source of the imperial documents and of some information about them; he is the official enthusiastically praised by Eusebius in IV. 44, and probably also in II. 63, 73.[67] Eusebius also states or implies that he has more letters at his disposal than he presents in his present work,[68] and

---

[60] So Pietri, 'Constantin en 324', 71–2; Pietri envisages Eusebius making a selection carefully chosen to illustrate Constantine's religious views and policy in the tense atmosphere after his death.

[61] II. 46; III. 61; IV. 35, 36 (personal receipt); III. 60. 3 (Antioch).

[62] So presumably III. 17–20, 64–5; IV. 42. Jerusalem: III. 29. 2, 51. 1.

[63] II. 63; perhaps IV. 9–13.

[64] I. 40. 1 (inscription); IV. 20 (prayer); III. 12, 22–4; IV. 29, 32, and 55 (speeches and letters).

[65] The documents are listed by Barnes, 'Panegyric', 111–13, with the comment that Eusebius' selection is a very personal one (p. 111) and the suggestion that he was collecting them in 325 and 326, but not later.

[66] Ibid. 113.

[67] Warmington, 'Sources', 93–8, and see Barnes, 'Panegyric', 113.

[68] III. 24, cf. IV. 27. 3.

we have already noticed that some of the narrative in I. 44–5 depends on documents used in the *HE*.

The evidence for Constantine's documentary and literary output as a whole is presented and discussed in a fundamental study by H. Dörries.[69] He lists fifty-six letters and decrees gathered from a wide range of literary sources, especially the historical writings of Eusebius, polemical tracts of Athanasius, and the anti-Donatist collection of Optatus.[70] Of these fifty-one are attributed to Constantine personally, or are issued in his name. All except one are concerned with religious or ecclesiastical affairs. There would have been similar documents on other subjects, which did not interest these writers, which are lost. The letters and decrees exhibit an intense and personal involvement in the subjects they deal with. Constantine writes as one who is totally committed to the church and the Gospel, the brother and colleague of bishops, with a strong sense of personal mission and desire to satisfy God. While interpreters from Burckhardt onwards who denied that Constantine was a religious Christian regarded many of the documents as inauthentic, it is now more usual to accept the letters as mostly or entirely genuine (Baynes, Lietzmann, Jones, Barnes).[71] The unusually personal tone, seen by some as a sign of falsification, is remarkably similar over a range of documents from diverse sources, and it would be very strange if official documents were forged in so personal and improbable a style.[72] The ideas expressed and the literary style are generally consistent not only with the other letters but with the other documents, including for instance the Constantinian letters in Optatus' *Appendix*.[73] Moreover, they differ in style from the main text of the *VC*, while in several cases it is clear that Eusebius is using a document which does not precisely fit the interpretation which he puts on it. Finally, the authenticity of one of the most hotly contested documents, the

[69] H. Dörries, *Das Selbstzeugnis Kaiser Konstantins* (Abh. d. Akad. d. Wiss. in Göttingen, philol.-hist. Kl. 3. 34; Göttingen, 1954); see also H. Kraft, 'Kaiser Konstantins religiöse Entwicklung', *Beiträge zur historischen Theologie*, 20 (1955), 160–201.

[70] Dörries, *Selbstzeugnis*, 16–128; for the Constantinian documents collected in the appendix to Optatus's *History of the Donatist Controversy* see the annotated translation by Mark Edwards, *Optatus: Against the Donatists* (Translated Texts for Historians, 27; Liverpool, 1997).

[71] See Tartaglia, 17–21, with a survey of earlier opinions.

[72] See O. Seeck, 'Die Urkunden der Vita Constantini', *Zeitschr. für Kirchengeschichte*, 18 (1898), 321–45, at 330.

[73] See further Heikel, introd., pp. lxvi–ciii.

letter at II. 24–42, has been remarkably confirmed by the discovery of part of the text in an official papyrus contemporary with or earlier than the writing of the *VC*.[74]

In addition to citing the documents themselves, it is clear that Eusebius uses their content to generate his own account. For example, IV. 8 may contain nothing more than is deduced from IV. 9–13. The alleged embassy to Persia may be deduced from the mere existence of a letter, the exchange of gifts from its friendly tone, and the report of multitudes of Christians in the Persian domain follows directly from IV. 13. Constantine is described as being 'quite a young boy' at the tyrant's court (I. 12. 1), perhaps because this is implied by his own words in II. 51. 1. As Emperor, Constantine crosses from his father's domain to Britain, 'enclosed by the edge of Ocean', in I. 25. 2, perhaps only because he himself says that his campaign of liberation began 'from that sea beside the Britons' (II. 28. 2), and 'from the shores of Ocean' (IV. 9). The beneficial laws summarized in II. 20–1 appear to be described on the basis of Constantine's provisions in II. 30–41; though there is also the possibility that they come from a parallel letter to the churches, described but not cited at II. 23. 2. While I. 52 begins with an item of persecution derived from *HE*, most of it could be deduced from the decree of restitution (see II. 30–8). In such ways Constantine's letters may themselves have provided significant parts of Eusebius' surrounding text. Sometimes Eusebius claims to describe or summarize letters not presented in the text, and he may be telling the truth;[75] however, such claims should be treated with reserve, since he might base such statements on general probability without any specific information at his disposal. At III. 59. 3–5 he is disarmingly frank about the embarrassment which might be caused to living persons if the Emperor's words of eighteen years or so past were to be published, and he is no doubt to be believed.

150 Constantinian laws are collected by Dörries, chiefly from *CTh* but also from *CJ* and elsewhere, and there is a complete list of those known from literary sources by P. Silli.[76] Not all of

---

[74] A. H. M. Jones, and T. C. Skeat, 'Notes on the Genuineness of the Constantinian Documents in Eusebius' *Life of Constantine*', *JEH* 5 (1954), 196–200.

[75] See III. 22–3.

[76] *Selbstzeugnis*, 162–208; cf. Silli, *Testi Costantiniani*. For Constantine's legislation up to 324, the end of the tetrarchic period, see also Corcoran, *Empire of the Tetrarchs*.

Constantine's legislation has been preserved, for reasons to do with its transmission and with the compilation of the Codes. Inscriptions also record measures of Constantine, of which those from Hispellum and Orcistus are significant for his religious policies.[77]

In a number of places, all in *VC* IV, Eusebius refers specifically to laws without citing them directly. These concern Sunday rest (IV. 18. 2, 19–20; 23, cf. *CTh* 2. 8. 1; *CJ* 3. 12. 1, AD 321); the alleged ban on pagan sacrifice (IV. 23, cf. *CTh* 16. 10. 2 (Constantius II, AD 341); *CTh* 9. 16. 1–3, AD 318–20, prohibits magic and private use of *haruspices*); the abolition of gladiatorial games (IV. 25. 1, cf. *CTh* 15. 12. 1, AD 325); the repeal of the Augustan laws penalizing celibacy (IV. 26. 2–4, cf. *CTh* 18. 16. 1, AD 320), and the alleged ban on Christians being enslaved to Jews (claimed at IV. 27. 1, but cf. *CTh* 16. 9. 1, *Sirm.* 4, AD 335, which allow Jews to keep Christian slaves). Eusebius also records (IV. 2 6) that Constantine made informal wills binding (cf. *CTh* 16. 2. 4). What we read in the *VC* often does not correspond closely, or at all, to the text as we have it in the Codes; Eusebius may not have had the text available, or may have been basing his account on general awareness, or on a summary from someone else. If he was using the texts, he has given them a strongly Christian interpretation by selective quotation or other means.[78] Of the repeal of the Augustan marriage laws, he says that existing legislation penalized the childless and claims that Constantine wanted to benefit consecrated virgins of both sexes, i.e. Christian ascetics; however, it seems clear that the measure was only one part of a comprehensive edict on family law which has been split up under different titles in the Codes.[79] Eusebius does understand, however, that the law was about the important matter of inheritance. In general, he concentrates on Constantine's pronouncements in the form of letters, formal and informal, which

---

[77] See Dörries, *Selbstzeugnis*, 209–26; Hispellum: *ILS* 705, and see note on IV. 16; Orcistus: *MAMA* vii. 305.

[78] See in general B. H. Warmington, 'Eusebius of Caesarea's Versions of Constantine's Laws in the Codes', *Studia Patristica*, 24 (1993), 201–7. Warmington's general verdict is that Eusebius was 'a careless and perhaps tendentious reporter of recent legislation, even when it seems he had a text' (p. 205).

[79] See Judith Evans-Grubbs, *Law and Family in Late Antiquity: The Emperor Constantine's Marriage Legislation* (Oxford, 1995), 128–30, with Warmington, 'Eusebius of Caesarea's Versions', 204; Corcoran, *Empire of the Tetrarchs*, 194.

he saw as revealing Constantine's piety, and it is not his aim to give a complete or an impartial account of the Emperor's legislation.[80] Other allusions to Constantine's activity occur at I. 43, on Constantine's benefactions, on which cf. *CTh* 10. 8. 1; II. 45. 1, a decree banning the erection of idols, divination, magic, and sacrifice (see above); IV. 2–3, changes in land-tax law; IV. 26. 2–3, a ban on effeminate priests in Egypt; IV. 27. 2, the status of synodical decrees.

(c) *Secular histories*

In *HE* Eusebius refers to the authority of earlier historians, especially when writing of the disasters of the Jews in book II, with reference to Josephus, and there may be a reference to Dio Cassius and Appian at IV. 2. 1–5; but this material probably came to him through a secondary Christian source such as Origen. *VC* I. 10 seems to indicate acquaintance with secular historians who have written about bad emperors like Nero, but more probably reflects a stock theme.[81] *VC* I. 11. 1 suggests that Eusebius will privilege moral 'deeds' over military and secular history; however, IV. 1–6 (alone) suggests that he did have a secular source (for the order followed, cf. *Origo*, 30–2). He may have used such a source (possibly the lost pagan history by Praxagoras) also for the campaign against Licinius at II. 6. 2 and 10. 4–12. 2; for the letter to Shapur at IV. 8–13, and for legislation mentioned at IV. 18–26. It is not impossible that he drew on panegyrical speeches for his praise of Constantius I at I. 13–17 or for the benefactions mentioned at I. 43, but he shows no direct knowledge either of Lactantius or of the *Panegyrici Latini*.

(d) *Scriptural citations and models*

There are some forty citations or allusions to the Bible in the main text, and six more in the documents; they are evenly divided between the Old and New Testaments. Eusebius uses scriptural exemplars to provide a typological framework, especially in his comparison of Constantine with Moses (for discussion see § 7).[82] Further, the fulfilment of prophecy provides

---

[80] Warmington, 'Eusebius of Caesarea's Versions', 206–7.

[81] See Barnes, 'Panegyric', 109–10, with comments on the contents of the library at Caesarea at 108–9.

[82] For scriptural usage in the *LC* see S. Calderone, 'Eusebio e l'ideologia imperiale', *Le*

verification, first of Scripture itself and secondly of the divine providence which sends, directs, and inspires Constantine. Thus the battle with Maxentius answers the prophecies of Moses and the Psalmist at I. 38, while Constantine's emblem of the serpent pierced by the cross-shaped *labarum* and thrust downwards fulfils Isaiah's words (III. 3), and the church over the tomb of Christ is the New Jerusalem of Revelation 3: 12 and 21: 2. The majority of Eusebius' allusions are to the Old Testament, but the list of nations at the Council of Nicaea is modelled consciously on the list given in the Acts of the Apostles.[83] Eusebius also cites Scripture for moral or pious comment.[84] He adapts references to the Scriptures to the linguistic texture of the work by using symbolic and Platonizing language when referring to them.[85]

(e) Secular citations

There are occasional allusions to classical works.[86] At I. 7 Eusebius may be thinking of Xenophon's *Cyropaedia*, but the comparison with Cyrus was a rhetorical commonplace (see below and note *ad loc.*). At I. 17. 2 Eusebius refers to a saying 'that it is a blessed thing to have no troubles and to give none to another', possibly from Epicurus, unless merely proverbial. At I. 57. 2, the remark on the malady of Galerius may allude to Plato, *Laws* 959 c, but cf. also 2 Maccabees 9: 9; it is already found in *HE* 8. 16. 4, and Lact., *DMP* 33. There may be Homeric allusions at II. 16. 2, 43. 5; III. 15. 2, 54. 6; IV. 7. 1.

(f) Firsthand and oral evidence

Eusebius saw Constantine as a youth (I. 19), talked to an officer from Licinius' army (II. 5. 5), heard rumours of miracles (II. 6. 1), was deeply involved in the church controversies and councils described at II. 61–2; III. 4–15, 21; IV. 59, 63–6; IV. 41, and close enough to have information about the conversion of the

---

trasformazioni della cultura nella tarda antichitàe, Atti del Congresso tenuto a Catania, Università degl Studi, 27 sett.–2 ott. 1982 (Rome, 1985), 18–22.

[83] III. 7–8, cf. Acts 2: 1–13.

[84] E.g. Ps. 132 (131): 7 at III. 42. 2, or Phil. 1: 18 at III. 58. 4.

[85] See on I. 3. 4, 38. 1; II. 12. 1 and cf. *LC* pref., 5. In *LC* 1. 1, the clergy are *basilikoi paides;* see Calderone, 'Eusebio', 5–7, and see on I. 32. 1.

[86] Winkelmann, 156.

cities of Constantia and Constantine (IV. 37–9). Decrees of Licinius would affect his see of Caesarea (I. 53), and he knew personally the sacred buildings in Palestine (III. 41–7), and especially in Jerusalem (III. 25–40), where he attended the Council in AD 335 (IV. 43–7). Caesarea's status as a metropolitan see included Jerusalem, though the Jerusalem bishops were now led to aspire to independence or even to their own primacy, which they eventually attained. Several scholars (Rubin, Drake, Walker and others) have seen this tension in Eusebius' description of the building in Jerusalem, but see notes on III. 25–46. He was deeply concerned with the holy sites, and with the Empress Helena's work in Palestine, and would have had personal information about it, as perhaps also about the destruction of temples, though this does not prevent him from putting his own interpretation on what happened.[87] He notes and describes imperial portraiture on coins and statues (IV. 15, 73), and visited Constantinople,[88] whose architecture and statuary he describes (III. 3, 48–9, 54. 2–3), and where he observed foreign embassies (IV. 7), perhaps attended a public oration by the Emperor (IV. 29–32), and delivered one himself (IV. 33). He may have seen the mausoleum described in IV. 58–60. He was present at the palace for the Tricennalia (II. 1. 1), where he presumably observed Constantius' marriage (IV. 49–50), though his account of it is mingled with tendentious fiction about the sons of Constantine (IV. 51–2). Towards the end such material reflects the conditions and anxieties of the period after Constantine's death, notably in the critique at IV. 54 and the account of the succession of Constantine's sons at IV. 68. His version of the Emperor's baptism, lying-in-state, and funeral (IV. 60. 4–71) probably derives from the clergy of Constantinople, whose bishop Eusebius (formerly of Nicomedia) was an ally of his namesake; for the description of mourning at Rome at IV. 69 see note *ad loc.*

Eusebius was not an intimate of Constantine. He may have met him only at Nicaea and when he was in Constantinople for the Tricennalia. But he claims that he was shown a later version of the cross-shaped standard or *labarum* (I. 31), and that he heard from Constantine himself the story of the latter's vision (I. 27–30;

---

[87] See III. 54–8.   [88] See Drake, 'Genesis'.

see below and notes) and of the miraculous efficacy of the standard (II. 6–10); perhaps he also heard the related material about military prayers and ornaments (IV. 18. 3–21), however much this may have improved with the telling.[89]

5. PLAN OF THE *VC*

Any conception of the plan of the *VC* must be connected with the view one takes of its literary character, for which see § 6,[90] for the common division of the work into chapters varies between manuscripts and does not go back to Eusebius, while the traditional chapter headings are also inauthentic, though possibly close in date to Eusebius.[91] We must divine the structure of his thought from the text itself. This is not always clear, for Eusebius moves easily from one subject to another, not always indicating a clear break. Our own understanding of the work's structure is set out below; we have generally followed Winkelmann, but with some variations. The headings given below are also used in the translation and commentary, but it must be emphasized that they are not original. Rather, they have been provided by ourselves, with the aim here and in the body of the translation and commentary of helping the reader to understand what Eusebius wrote and how the *VC* is constructed. The Greek chapter headings (based on Winkelmann's edition) are translated at pp. 54–66 below.

Book I

1–11.	*Preface*
1–3.	Constantine's immortality
4–6.	God's achievement in Constantine
7–9.	Constantine superior to other Emperors
10–11.	Eusebius' purpose and plan
12–24.	*Birth, family, and youth*
12.	Childhood among the tyrants
13–18.	Career and character of Constantine's father
19–21.	Constantine joins his father
22–4.	Constantine declared Emperor
25–41. 2.	*Deeds in war I: The liberation of the West*

[89] For arguments against the common view of Eusebius as a 'court theologian', see Barnes, 'Panegyric', 114.

[90] For Barnes's view of its overall plan see 'Panegyric', 95–6 ('a messy structure').

[91] Winkelmann, p. xlix; see above, § 1.

6. THE LITERARY CHARACTER OF THE *VC*

The *VC* is a literary hybrid. But it is neither sufficient nor plausible to describe it as a mixture of two separate stages, imperial encomium and historical/hagiographic narrative.[92] Eusebius was an innovative writer in many other spheres, and the very task of writing about a Christian emperor presented new problems and called for new solutions. Even if Eusebius was not particularly successful in literary terms,[93] he should be given the credit for experimenting in the *VC* with new possibilities.

The introductory chapters (I. 1–11), while appealing to commonplaces, also place the work in a context of something

---

[92] Barnes, 'Panegyric', 104–8, aims to assign every passage either to a 'conventional commemoration of a dead monarch' (p. 102), 'a speech composed by Eusebius during 337, presumably begun when he heard of Constantine's death on 22 May' and revised after 9 Sept. (p. 104), or to 'a more grandiose and detailed exposition and. . . connected narrative' (p. 108); this aim is refined and taken further in Barnes, 'Two Drafts', 4–8. In contrast J. Moreau, 'Eusebius von Caesarea', *RAC* vi (Stuttgart, 1966), 1073–5, regards the whole work as a panegyric. For detailed criticism of Barnes's view see Cameron, 'Construction'.   [93] So Tartaglia, 22.

novel, and are the more striking in view of the references to the three Augusti, which show that the opening at least (like the conclusion) was written after September 337, no doubt after the composition of the main body of the work. The impulse behind the final stage of writing was highly political: Eusebius wished to urge the continuation of the Constantinian settlement on Constantine's sons.[94] Yet even if he left the work unfinished, Eusebius paid close attention to its literary presentation, and framed the *VC* in a literary as well as a political sense with these opening and closing chapters. At I. 1. 2–3 and again at 1. 9 and IV. 72 Constantine is claimed to live on in the reign of his three sons. At I. 1. 2–2. 3 the perplexity and incompetence of the author in face of his subject is expressed. At I. 3. 2 it is emphasized that art, sculpture, and inscriptions, though used to commemorate the dead, are perishable in comparison with God's rewards to Constantine. At I. 4–6 Eusebius describes Constantine's mission to overthrow the persecutors and their religion and to set an example of true godliness. In I. 7–8 we read how Constantine excelled the greatest conquerors of the past, Cyrus and Alexander, not only in the extent of his conquests, but in the godly manner of his life and death. I. 9 expresses the continuity of Constantine's virtue, received from his father and now passed to his sons. I. 10–11 are interesting, as describing Eusebius' purpose and plan. If bad emperors have books written about them, he says, the virtuous certainly should. I. 11, where Eusebius asserts that he will confine himself to matters relating to Constantine's Christian policies, has often seemed problematic, in view of the fact that he does not in practice so limit himself, and especially in the light of the war narrative in books I–II; however, that narrative is told as a religious war, and the comparisons of Constantine to Moses are prominent—the victory over Licinius represents the freedom of the Christians from persecution. I. 12 establishes the comparison with Moses (see below); we are to regard Constantine's reign as divinely ordained in the same way as Moses was chosen to lead his people out of Egypt and receive the law. In I. 10 Eusebius likens his task to that of a painter tracing a 'verbal portrait' of Constantine.[95] The work

---

[94] See Cameron, 'Construction'.
[95] See note *ad loc.* and cf. I. 11. 1. Here Eusebius is writing in the manner of Hellenistic ethical biography and universal history; his model may be Plutarch's *Life of*

is to be instructive, that is, it will not merely present a useful record of virtue, or be embellished with high style[96] but will give an account of Constantine guaranteed to be correct by Eusebius' claim to special knowledge. Its purpose is thus explicitly said to be didactic.[97]

Modern discussion has begun from a structural analysis of the work and centred round the *VC*'s perceived combination of biography and encomium.[98] However, when Eusebius sets out the nature of his own work (I. 10–11) it is clear that its antecedents are mixed. He compares it with previous histories (I. 10. 2), as well as with 'lives' (I. 10. 3) and accounts of *praxeis* (I. 10. 3) written for the purpose of *epideixis*. Thus Eusebius himself calls to mind the Acts of the Apostles and locates his work in a Hellenistic historiographical tradition.[99] Eusebius uses the verb *historein* here and of his own activity;[100] he does not himself call the *VC* a *bios*, nor do the manuscripts call it a *bios* but merely *eis ton bion*.[101] In the same chapter he professes to spurn classicizing rhetoric. Nevertheless, the whole introduction is indebted to the standard rhetorical *praefatio*, and is based on the requirements of a standard imperial panegyric or *basilikos logos*. Indeed, Eusebius makes effective use of the stock encomiastic comparisons even while introducing the theme of Moses as a type for Constantine.

We may agree with Pasquali, Barnes, and others that the *VC* is not unitary; it was probably not composed in a single stage, and later insertions were made by Eusebius himself. It is not clear, however, over what period the writing continued. Book IV is

---

Alexander; see R. Mortley, *The Idea of Universal History from Hellenistic Philosophy to Early Christian Historiography* (Lewiston, NY, 1996), 31–2; 174–7.

[96] I. 10. 3–4.

[97] F. Heim, *La Théologie de la victoire de Constantin à Théodose* (Théologie historique, 89; Paris, 1992), 90–1, analyses chs. 1–11 and concludes that their aim is to show how Constantine's success (I. 4–9, recapitulated in the closing chapters) depends on his piety.

[98] See Winkelmann, pp. xlix–liii; Tartaglia, 7–15; see also Cameron, 'Construction'; 'Form and Meaning'.

[99] See Mortley, *Universal History*, 31–2, 174–7.

[100] See III. 24. 2, 51. 2, with II. 23. 2, and cf. Tartaglia, 11. But he is generous with his terminology: other terms used are *diegema* (I. 23), *graphe* (II. 5), *diegesis* (II. 63), *hypothesis* (IV. 32) and *logos* (III. 59. 5).

[101] See Anna Wilson, 'Biographical Models: the Constantinian Period and Beyond', in Samuel N. C. Lieu and Dominic Montserrat, in conjunction with Bill Leadbetter and Mark Vermes, *Constantine: History, Historiography and Legend* (London, 1998), 107–35. See Barnes, 'Panegyric', 103.

neither clearly a panegyric nor clearly a narrative, showing elements of both, and Barnes admits that here as elsewhere the construction is 'messy'.[102] The many infelicities of structure are commonly explained on the hypothesis that the work was left unfinished.[103] Yet I. 1–11, together with IV. 71–5, which is surely Eusebian, relate to the work as a whole, and just as he allowed the final form of the *HE* to go out despite many remaining inconsistencies, and with only crude and hasty updating, Eusebius may have thought the *VC* as it stood good enough to release, particularly as the circumstances of the latter months of 337 made rapid publication desirable. There is in fact no certainty that Eusebius was still working on the *VC* up to the time of his own death, nor does the addition of chapter headings by another hand in itself require such an explanation.

Just as the *HE* was not like a standard classical history, so the *VC* is neither an encomium, nor a *bios*, nor yet a history, but a combination of all of these. That Eusebius could envisage panegyrical treatments of Constantine of quite different kinds is clear from a comparison with the *LC*. The *VC* taken as a whole is not a conventional encomium, for the rhetorical features characteristic of such a work, according to the precepts of Menander Rhetor,[104] which are followed closely in book I and the first part of book II, and which partially return in book IV, give way in the rest of books II and III to a much more expansive narrative and documentary treatment. Yet the work is also more than a *bios*, particularly in view of its inclusion of documents. Nor is it a straightforward history. There was as yet no precedent for a consciously Christian imperial encomium.[105] But by the early fourth century, *Lives*, both Christian and pagan, were becoming a popular vehicle for ideological messages; Eusebius had recent examples to note in the *Lives* of Pythagoras and Plotinus by the pagan Porphyry, whose work he had elsewhere been at pains to refute, and book 6 of his own *HE* contains what amounts to a *Life*

---

[102] Barnes, 'Panegyric', 95.   [103] Ibid. 104.
[104] Ed. D. A. Russell and N. G. Wilson, *Menander Rhetor* (Oxford, 1981); further below.
[105] See S. MacCormack, 'Latin Prose Panegyrics: Tradition and Discontinuity in the Later Roman Empire', *REA* 22 (1976), 29–77; H. Kloft, *Liberalitas Principis: Herkunft und Bedeutung. Studien zur Prinzipatsideologie* (Kölner historische Abhandlungen, 18, Cologne 1970), 170–7, discusses Eusebius' adaptation of standard motifs of imperial panegyric to Christian use.

of Eusebius' hero Origen; he also knew the *Life* of Apollonius of Tyana.[106] The *Life of Antony*, generally regarded as the first saint's life proper, was still to be written when Eusebius died.[107] In one sense the *VC* represents a 'political' as opposed to an ascetic *Life* (such as the *Lives* of Plotinus and Pythagoras); yet it too clearly constitutes a version of hagiography.[108] It presents Constantine as a 'divine man' or hero (*theios aner*), marked as such by divine signs. Just as Moses was granted the sign of the burning bush, so Constantine receives his vision. Hagiography and panegyric were to share many formal characteristics, and if the subject was an emperor the well-defined genre of imperial encomium meant that there was likely to be an even closer connection. However, the inclusion of documents on the scale to which Eusebius practises it in the *VC* was, like their use in the *HE*, an innovation and was not in the nature of things to become an established hagiographical feature.[109] Yet the documents too serve Eusebius as a guarantee of God's choice of Constantine, and affirm the authority of Eusebius' testimony as promised at I. 10. Eusebius' thinking about the role and mission of Constantine was to develop further in the years after 325, and his mature judgement on the Emperor is fully set out in the *LC*, close in date to the *VC* as he left it.

The features which the *VC* shares with the classic *basilikos logos*[110] are the following: I. 7–9 *synkrisis* (comparison with other rulers), I. 12–13 *genos* (birth, family, upbringing); I. 19–20 youth and accession; I. 25–40 deeds in war (despite Eusebius'

---

[106] Origen: *HE* 6. 1–36; see Patricia Cox, *Biography in Late Antiquity: A Quest for the Holy Man* (Berkeley and Los Angeles, 1983), 69–101; on Eusebius and Porphyry see below, § 7, and see Cameron, 'Construction'; 'Form and Meaning'. Fourth-century *Lives*: T. Hägg and Philip Rousseau, eds., *Greek Biography and Panegyrics in Late Antiquity* (Berkeley and Los Angeles, forthcoming).

[107] For a comparison, see Cameron, 'Form and Meaning'.

[108] Admitted by Barnes, 'Panegyric', 110 ('an experiment in hagiography'), comparing the *Life of Antony* (and pointing out at p. 103 that Eusebius did know the *Life of Apollonius of Tyana*), even while denying that it is a *Life;* cf. also 116 ('something. . . which hovers between ecclesiastical history and hagiography').

[109] Though compare the long speeches attributed to Antony in the *Life of Antony*.

[110] For these see Russell and Wilson, eds., *Menander Rhetor*, 77 ff.; C. E. V. Nixon and Barbara Saylor Rodgers, *In Praise of Later Roman Emperors. The Panegyrici Latini. Introduction, Translation and Commentary* (Berkeley and Los Angeles, 1994), 21–6; M. Mause, *Die Darstellung des Kaisers in der lateinischen Panegyrik* (Palingenesia, 50; Stuttgart, 1994); Heikel, pp. xlvi ff.; G. Pasquali, 'Die Composition der *Vita Constantini* des Eusebius', *Hermes*, 46 (1910), 369–86, at 384–5; Tartaglia, 8.

disclaimer, I. 11); I. 41–2 deeds in peace; 46 ff. deeds in war. II. 1–19 continues the narrative of Constantine's campaign against Licinius and his eventual victory. The similarities with imperial panegyric go deep, and extend to terminology, motifs, and types of argument; these are discussed in the notes, and see especially on I. 28–9, Eusebius' narrative of Constantine's vision. The *VC* also shows a preoccupation with the visual presentation of the Emperor and the appearance of Constantine himself which finds echoes in both the Latin panegyrics and the visual evidence.[111] From II. 20 Eusebius turns to Constantine's settlement and subsequent Christian policies; even this despite its length could fall under the category of deeds in peace, and it includes conventional subject-matter (legislation, building activity). Book IV contains panegyrical material interspersed with personal anecdote (cf. in particular IV. 1–4 philanthropy, *liberalitas*; 5–14. 1 foreign relations; 14–25 *pietas*; 29–39 *iustitia*; from IV. 40 onwards Eusebius mainly records events and anecdotes of the close of the Emperor's life. Barnes sees II. 24–60, 61–73; III. 5–22 as 'slabs of documentary history', while I. 26–46 (the war against Maxentius) is also taken to be a connected narrative interrupting the panegyrical sequence.[112]

Where did Eusebius acquire his familiarity with the rhetorical features of panegyric? He is unlikely to have known the *Panegyrici Latini*, where the broad categories of the *basilikos logos* are observed,[113] but the precepts laid down in the rhetorical treatises were standard fare in the system of higher education generally available. However, while the opening part of book I (unlike the *LC*) does indeed follow the broad scheme advocated by Menander Rhetor, elsewhere panegyrical and narrative or historical elements are intermingled in varying degrees, just as in so many later saints' *Lives*. A particular panegyrical feature adopted by Eusebius is the omission of proper names (Diocletian, Maximian,

---

[111] For a comparison of the *Panegyrici Latini* with the visual evidence see R. R. R. Smith, 'The Public Image of Licinius I: Portrait Sculpture and Imperial Ideology in the Early Fourth Century', *JRS* 87 (1997), 170–202, at 194–201.

[112] 'Panegyric', 105–6; compare 106–7 on I. 48–II. 19.

[113] Cf. Nixon and Rodgers, 10–14; for a structural and linguistic analysis of the *Panegyrici Latini* see M.-C. L'Huillier, *L'Empire des mots: Orateurs gaulois et empereurs romains, 3ᵉ et 4ᵉ siècles* (Paris, 1992), unfortunately without parallels from the *VC.*; L'Huillier notes the high proportion of space given to military narrative in the Latin panegyrics, as in *VC* I–II.

Maximin, Galerius, Arius, Athanasius: see on I. 26). The non-panegyrical features of the *VC* (in the strict sense) are the inclusion of connected narrative in chronological rather than thematic order, and the incorporation of lengthy documents. As has been noted, certain similarities can also be seen with Plutarchan biography: for instance the comparison between Constantine and the persecutors at III. 1.[114] This seems to have resulted in 'an uneasy juxtaposition of the scientific/ethical style *Life* and the encomium', a new genre which 'probably owes nothing to Roman sources'.[115] But it seems unlikely that Eusebius himself had as clear a view of genre as modern critics wish upon him.

The question of the intended audience of the *VC* is also contentious. Eusebius has attempted an elevated style,[116] and it seems likely that the work was aimed at a mixed audience of Christians and pagans, particularly those with influence at court and not least the sons of Constantine themselves; similarly the audience of *Pan. Lat.* 5 (8), 312 (composed for Constantine's Quinquennalia), had, we are told, consisted of Constantine, his *amici* and his high officials, together with visiting delegations from the cities of Gaul, and the *LC* was delivered in the palace at Constantinople during Constantine's Tricennalia, where pagan rhetors were also present.[117] Panegyrics were written for performance, and Eusebius is no exception in his consciousness of audience and occasion.[118] The language and general presentation of the *VC* are studiously neutral; the biblical allusions are neither frequent nor usually obvious, and the preface has pretensions to high style and a clear debt to classical rhetoric. The comparison of Constantine with Moses was one which pagans as well as Christians would understand, and which had featured in recent works; in several passages it is introduced in carefully classicizing language. At

[114] So Tartaglia, 9, with G. Ruhbach, *Apologetik und Geschichte: Untersuchungen zur Theologie Eusebs von Caesarea*, Diss. Theol. (Heidelberg, 1962), 201–3; cf. n. 44 above. Tartaglia draws attention to the special importance of biography for Christian writers and to the sense in which Constantine's life is seen by Eusebius as a model of Christian life (cf. I. 5).

[115] Mortley, *Universal History*, 180.

[116] Winkelmann, p. lvii–lviii.

[117] *LC* I. 2–3, cf. *VC* IV. 33, 46, with H. A. Drake, 'When was the *De laudibus Constantini* Delivered?', *Historia*, 24 (1975), 345–56.

[118] On these features in the Latin panegyrics see L'Huillier, *L'Empire des mots*, 119, 287–303.

IV. 54 Eusebius complains of the pseudo-Christians at Constantine's court; at IV. 29 he describes the Emperor's regular public sermons, while noting that the audience often came out of mere curiosity and remained unpersuaded. It is likely that court circles contained people of all persuasions as well as many who prudently kept their own counsel. The same is likely to be true of the first readership of the *VC*. In order to reach these varied groups, the *VC*, a fully Christian work, uses a language and literary manner which conform at least in general terms to classical expectations. We should not conclude from this any hesitation or equivocation about Christianity on Constantine's part.[119]

7. EUSEBIUS' PORTRAYAL OF CONSTANTINE

Together with the *LC*, the *VC* presents a distinctive view of Constantine and a conception of the Christian Empire which was to become standard in the Byzantine Empire.[120] Hellenistic ruler-theory was proposed as a source by Norman Baynes.[121] The Emperor is seen as specially marked out by God, and himself an imitator of God, beneficent ruler and lawgiver on earth, with the special task of ensuring the correct worship of God (as Constantine saw his role himself as early as 313: Optatus, *App.* 3). He was raised up by God to end the persecutions, and was a friend of the divine Logos. His duty was to further the Christian religion and to abolish the errors of polytheism. The *LC* puts into Platonic vocabulary and vague and symbolic language the ideas and actions more explicitly described in the *VC*: Eusebius also mentions in the *LC* (8) the destruction of the temple at Aphaca (*VC* III. 54, 55) and the confiscation of temple treasures. Many individual phrases descriptive of Constantine are shared by the *LC* and the *VC*, and both works develop the view of Constantine inherent in the closing parts of the *HE*. In all these works, Constantine's

---

[119] As supposed by H. A. Drake, *In Praise of Constantine* (Berkeley and Los Angeles, 1976), e.g. 79, with 'Genesis', 33–5.

[120] See F. Dvornik, *Early Christian and Byzantine Political Philosophy: Origins and Background*, ii (Washington, DC, 1966), 611–22; cf. J.-M. Sansterre, 'Eusèbe de Césarée et la naissance de la théorie "césaropapiste"', *Byzantion*, 42 (1972), 131–95, 532–94.

[121] N. H. Baynes, 'Eusebius and the Christian Empire', in *Byzantine Studies and Other Essays* (London, 1955), 168–72 (first published 1933).

religious role leads directly to political and military success.[122] This thinking is the Christian version of Roman imperial ideology, and especially of imperial encomia in verse and prose.

However, the influences of Middle Platonic ruler-theory and of Christian writers such as Clement and Origen are more immediate than Hellenistic models.[123] A key element in Eusebius' thought is the idea of *mimesis*, whereby the Christian ruler and his Empire are held to mirror or imitate God in heaven. In recent years the influence of biblical models and imagery on Eusebius' thought has also been stressed.[124] In fact, Eusebius was attempting something new, which would be very different from the conventional *basilikos logos*.[125] His developed political theory, or theology of empire, is set out in the group of later works to which the *VC* belongs.[126]

The most obvious device used by Eusebius in the *VC* to bring home his ideological message is the patterning of Constantine on Moses.[127] First appearing at I. 12, the comparison recurs explicitly at I. 20 and again at I. 38 in the context of the battle against Maxentius, where Eusebius develops the comparison with the crossing of the Red Sea which he had used at *HE* 9. 9; in the final campaign against Licinius Constantine's tabernacle (II. 12. 1) is based on that in Exodus (II. 12, 14). Moses is distinguished as the servant of God in Numbers 12: 7, 8, quoted in Hebrews 3: 5. Eusebius uses this biblical word of him ('the great Servant Moses',

---

[122] Cf. esp. *VC* I. 6 and 8.

[123] Tartaglia, 21; detailed discussion in R. Farina, *L'impero e l'imperatore cristiano in Eusebio di Cesarea: La prima teologia politica del cristianesimo* (Zurich, 1966).

[124] See Calderone, 'Eusebio', 1–2, against Baynes and Dvornik (on Platonism, see 10–11); and see M. Hollerich, 'Religion and Politics in the Writings of Eusebius: Reassessing the first "Court Theologian"', *Church History*, 59 (1990), 309–25, at 309–13; Ruhbach, *Apologetik und Geschichte*.

[125] Calderone, 'Eusebio', 2–3, also citing F. Taeger, *Charisma*, ii (Stuttgart, 1960), 686 ff. on the originality of the *LC*; for *VC* cf. Barnes, 'Panegyric', 116 ('something daringly original').

[126] See Cameron, *Tria Corda*; Calderone, 'Eusebio'; for Eusebius' earlier view of history see J. Sirinelli, *Les Vues historiques d'Eusèbe de Césarée durant la période prénicéenne* (Dakar, 1961); general and bibliograhy, Hollerich, 'Religion and Politics', 309–10.

[127] Discussed by Mortley, *Universal History*, ch. 5, and see Hollerich, 'Religion and Politics', 321–5; id., 'The Comparison of Moses and Constantine in Eusebius of Caesarea's *Life of Constantine*', *Studia Patristica*, 19 (1989), 80–95; Wilson, 'Biographical Models'; Claudia Rapp, *JThS* N.S 49 (1998), 685–95.

I. 38. 5), and likens Constantine to him almost immediately (I. 39. 1). Moses is also a prophet (I. 12. 1; II. 12. 1, following Deuteronomy 18: 15–18, cf. Acts 3: 22; 7: 37); when Constantine's gifts as visionary and prophet are described, he is called God's servant, using Moses' title (*therapon*). Moses' story is told in 'sacred books' and 'divine oracles' (I. 38. 1; II. 2. 1), which are verified by God's work in Constantine (I. 38. 1–4). This principle of fulfilment and verification of the 'ancient oracles of the prophets, transmitted in Scripture', is important, and has been clearly stated in the work's preface.[128]

The deliberateness of the sustained Moses image is striking in view of the close dependence of this part of the *VC* on the *HE*. Eusebius' method of working is extremely careful, and the Moses analogy, developing much further the use already made of it in *HE* 9. 9, is inserted very precisely into the fabric of the text. In *HE* 9. 9, whereas the fate of Maxentius is compared with that of Pharaoh, and the victors likened to those about Moses, no parallel is drawn between Constantine and Moses. In contrast, in the adaptation of this story in the *VC* the comparison is made explicit (I. 39. 1). The whole of Constantine's life as ruler of God's people is now to be read in terms of the figure of Moses.

Eusebius' explicit allusions to Moses are presented with some attention to linguistic detail; at I. 12. 1 he refers to 'an ancient report' (*pheme*) about the Hebrews, then summarizes the circumstances of Moses's youth, finally stating (I. 12. 2) that whereas the old story was 'framed as a myth' the wonders which God has revealed through Constantine are 'greater than in myths'. Eusebius retains the apologetic style evident in his reference to Moses in the *HE*, especially at I. 12 and I. 38, deflecting the likelihood that the stories in the Old Testament will not be believed. Yet he now develops the likeness further; thus Constantine spends his youth at the court of tyrants (I. 12), returns to lead his people to freedom from persecution, and then takes on the role of lawgiver. This was a threefold pattern, based on the three periods in the life of Moses, which was to have an important place in later hagiography.[129]

Moses was not only an Old Testament type for Constantine;

---

[128] I. 3. 4; cf. I. 2. 3–3. 1 and 1. 4.

[129] See M. Harl, 'Les trois quarantaines de Moïse', *REG* 80 (1967), 407–12.

he was also a figure known and respected by pagans as well as Christians and Jews, and featured in contemporary writing following a tradition going back to Josephus and to Philo's *Life of Moses*. Eusebius quoted Josephus on Moses in his *Praeparatio Evangelica* (8. 8. 1–55) as a means to refuting Porphyry, and in his life of Origen at *HE* 6. 19. 10 f. he cites a work called 'On the harmony of Moses and Jesus', again in the context of Porphyry's criticisms. Eusebius also states that the desire to refute Porphyry was the starting-point for the *Canones*, and the importance to him of the question of the antiquity of Moses is indicated in the work's opening.[130] Moses was thus a key figure in Christian apologetic, according to which Mosaic law prepared the world for the Christian dispensation, which reached its culmination in Constantine.[131] The Jewish and Christian tradition claimed that Moses had been the source for Greek philosophy, thus that he was the bringer of culture and learning as well as piety, and while some pagans were critical of Moses, more regarded him as the type of the wise lawgiver.[132] The sustained comparison of Constantine and Moses would have much more resonance for contemporaries than it has for us. It is fundamental to Eusebius' developed historical thinking, as expressed in the *Praeparatio Evangelica*, the *Demonstratio Evangelica*, and the *logos* theology of the *Theophany*, the latter a work of AD 335, used extensively in the *LC* and very close in date to the *VC*. In the *DE* Eusebius makes an explicit connection between Moses and Jesus.[133] In the *VC*, that association is not directly made; yet the comparison between Constantine and Moses, 'a secular application of biblical typology without precedent in Christian literature before Eusebius',[134] was perfectly suited to the work's apologetic purpose.

The Moses analogy is closely connected with a second theme

---

[130] See Burgess, 'Dates and Editions', 488–9 and app. II.

[131] Cf. ibid. 489: the preface to the *Canones* shows that Eusebius 'is clearly initiating a dialogue with Jewish, pagan, and even earlier Christian historians and apologists over what was probably the most fundamental chronological crux of Jewish and early Christian apologetic'.

[132] See J. G. Gager, *Moses in Greco-Roman Paganism* (New York, 1972); A. Droge, *Homer or Moses? Early Christian Interpretations of the History of Culture* (HUT 26; Tübingen, 1989); Mortley, *Universal History*, 112–20, 135–49, 167–70.

[133] *DE* 3. 2. 6–7; see Hollerich, 'Religion and Politics', 318–21.

[134] Hollerich, 'Religion and Politics', 321.

in the *VC*, that of the persecutors as tyrants.[135] In the first reference to Moses at I. 12, Eusebius makes it clear that he now equates Constantine's victories with the exodus from Egypt; the passage is very carefully structured so that no one will miss the fact that a major theme of the *VC* is here being announced. It is made more explicit in various ways, for example, by likening Constantine's youth and upbringing at the court of Diocletian and Galerius to that of Moses at the court of Pharaoh (I. 12. 1, 20. 2). Eusebius distances Constantine's father Constantius from the other tetrarchs (I. 13. 1–3 (cf. *HE* 8. 13. 12–13); I. 15–17) and portrays Constantine's opponents Maxentius and ultimately Licinius as unequivocal persecutors of Christians (I. 13. 1–3; 51–9). His father must be shown as pious and virtuous if Constantine is to have the right pedigree (I. 12. 3, 21, 22–7; cf. I. 18, 25).

The account of Constantine's vision, told at I. 28 and the source of so much modern dispute, falls within the panegyrical frame of the opening section and the chapters which work out the Moses analogy. Nevertheless, it is additional to the *HE* narrative, and great stress is laid upon it by Eusebius; whatever the source of Eusebius' information (allegedly Constantine himself: I. 28. 1), Eusebius also needed to explain the vision's absence from *HE* and the veracity of his new account. Preceded and followed by passages describing the thoughts of Constantine (I. 27, 29), the description carries guarantees of its own authenticity in the claim of personal information (I. 28. 1) and heavy emphasis on eye-witness testimony (I. 28. 2, 'with his own eyes'; I. 29, Constantine's dream; I. 30, Eusebius' sight of the *labarum*). The anachronism in the *labarum* description has often been noted; moreover, the timing of the vision, as well as (apparently) its nature, is quite different from the account of Constantine's dream told by Lactantius at *DMP* 1. 44.[136] At this point in the narrative, the story provides Constantine with a divine sign such as Moses was also given (with I. 27–9 compare Exodus 3: 1–6; Acts 7: 30–5), and it gives Eusebius the starting point for the emphasis which he is to lay henceforth on the 'saving sign' (*semeion*) or 'trophy' (*tropaion*), that is, the cross. In the description of the statue which Constantine erected in Rome after the victory

---

[135] Similarly, the *HE* is dominated by a number of Eusebian preoccupations which run through the whole work (Grant). [136] See notes *ad loc.*

soon after (I. 40. 2, cf. *HE* 9. 9. 10) it is now explicitly said to be 'in the shape of the cross'. What Constantine saw in the sky was a cross (I. 28. 2); the *labarum* is a version of this 'sign', of the cross (I. 29); in addition, Eusebius refers to the cross as a 'trophy' (I. 28. 2), making explicit the assimilation of the terms cross, sign and trophy which is so prominent in the rest of the *VC*, and in the *LC* (see especially *LC* 10).[137] The vision of the cross and description of the *labarum* at I. 28–31 underpin the thinking behind Eusebius' presentation of Constantine in *LC* and *VC*, and provide the essential explicit equation of cross/sign/trophy. The description of the making of the *labarum* (I. 29–31) also allows Eusebius to evoke the making of the Ark of the Covenant (Exodus 25–8), as later (II. 12) Constantine builds a tabernacle for use on campaign against Licinius, while the miraculous powers of the cross-shaped *labarum* (II. 6. 2–9. 2) evoke the rod of Moses (Exodus 4: 1–5; 14: 16; 17: 8–13, of which 14: 16 is the most important passage). No doubt the cross/sign/trophy theme became fully developed in Eusebius' mind with his reflections on the meaning of the building of the church of the Holy Sepulchre, on which he himself delivered an oration (IV. 45. 3) and which occupies so much space in *VC* III (III. 25–40). It also in part provides the rest of the *VC* with the structural framework which it otherwise lacks once Eusebius has passed the point of the victory of Licinius and his need to rewrite the *HE* diminishes.

8. THE CAREER OF CONSTANTINE

Constantine was the son of Constantius I (later known as Chlorus), Caesar AD 293, Augustus 305, d. 25 July 306, by Helena; six more children were born to Constantius by his second wife Theodora, the daughter of Maximian.[138] Constantine was born at Naissus (Nis), *c.*272–3.[139] He served under Diocletian and Galerius in the east from *c.*293 and was with Diocletian in Nicomedia when not on campaign until 305.[140] He

---

[137] See R. Storch, 'The Trophy and the Cross: Pagan and Christian Symbolism in the Fourth and Fifth Centuries', *Byzantion*, 40 (1970), 105–17; Calderone, 'Eusebio', 25–6.

[138] Barnes, *NE* 35–7, 60–1; *PLRE* I, Fl. Val. Constantius 12.

[139] See on I. 8; II. 51; IV. 53 and see Barnes, *NE* 39–41.

[140] Barnes, *NE* 41–2.

married first Minervina, the mother of his son Crispus, and in 307 Fausta, the daughter of Maximian and Eutropia; he had five more children, the three future Caesars and Augusti Constantine II, Constantius II and Constans, and two daughters, Constantina (m. Gallus, Caesar 351–4) and Helena (m. Julian, Augustus 361–3).[141] Constantine died on 27 May 337, at the age of 64 or 65.[142]

On his father's death Constantine was proclaimed Augustus by the troops at York, but received the title of Caesar from Galerius and that of Augustus only in 307 from Maximian, probably at Trier;[143] at this stage he bore his father's epithet Herculius.[144] On the news of Maximian's usurpation in 310 Constantine marched south to Massilia where he defeated him and caused him to commit suicide. The Latin Panegyric of 310 for the first time claims his descent from the third-century Emperor Claudius II Gothicus (268–70) and records an alleged vision of Apollo;[145] subsequently, and for many years afterwards, Constantine's coins featured the legend *Soli invicto* ('to the Unconquered Sun').[146] After the death of Galerius (311), Constantine marched against Maxentius, was victorious at Verona, and defeated Maxentius at the Milvian Bridge over the Tiber on 28 October 312, after which he entered Rome. A meeting with Licinius at Milan early in 313 resulted in the marriage of his sister Constantia to Licinius and an agreement on religious toleration, the so-called 'Edict of Milan'.[147] Constantine also began issuing laws in favour of Christians, thus encountering the problem of division between Christians in North Africa and the beginnings of Donatism,[148] a situation which he tried to deal with by summoning councils at Rome (313) and Arles (314; see on I. 44. 1–2). Licinius' defeat of Maximin and the latter's death,

---

[141] Barnes, *NE* 43.

[142] See in general Barnes, *NE* 5–8; 68–80; Hall, *TRE* xix. 489–500, Konstantin I; *PLRE* I, Fl. Val. Constantinus 4.

[143] Barnes, *NE* 5, 69; see *Pan. Lat.* 7 (6), AD 310.

[144] *Pan. Lat.* 7 (6), AD 310.

[145] *Pan. Lat.* 7 (6), AD 310, 21. 3–7; see B. Saylor Rodgers, 'Constantine's Pagan Vision', *Byzantion*, 50 (1980), 259–78, and see note on I. 28. 2. The Latin panegyrist introduces the genealogy as something new: *quod plerique adhuc fortasse nesciunt* (2. 1).

[146] P. Bruun, 'The Disappearance of Sol from the Coins of Constantine', *Arctos*, NS 2 (1958), 15–37.

[147] *HE* 10. 5; Lactantius, *DMP* 48.

[148] Laws: *HE* 10. 5. 15–17, 6. 1–5; Donatism: see note on I. 41–5.

also in 313, left Constantine and Licinius sole emperors. Church-building began in Rome, and Constantine celebrated his Decennalia there in 315 (I. 48). He intended to go to Africa himself to settle the Donatist quarrel in 315 (Opt., *App.* 6) but was prevented by renewed hostilities against Licinius.

Constantine invaded Licinius' territory in AD 316 and two battles were fought, the first at Cibalae (October 316), the second, in which he defeated Licinius, at Campus Ardiensis, early in 317. Peace was patched up and Constantine's sons Crispus and Constantine, and Licinius' son Licinius (two of them infants), were all proclaimed Caesars (317). The date of this war was 316 rather than 314;[149] it has often been thought that Eusebius omits it altogether in the *VC*, but this is not clearly so.[150] After this, Licinius soon began to be represented as a persecutor of Christians.[151] Constantine campaigned in Gaul against the Sarmatians (323) and in 324 prepared to confront Licinius, whom he defeated at Adrianople on 3 July, 324, aided by Crispus, who commanded his fleet and destroyed Licinius' ships. Licinius fled and, after being defeated a second time at Chrysopolis (18 September), abdicated, and was subsequently killed with his son.[152]

From 19 September 324 until his death Constantine was sole Emperor. He set in hand legislation to restore church property and regulate religious affairs,[153] visited Antioch and summoned and attended the Council of Nicaea (May-June 325), where he also celebrated his Vicennalia.[154] He was in Rome in July, 326; shortly before, his son Crispus was put to death at Pola and Fausta died, both in mysterious circumstances,[155] after which Constantine's mother Helena, declared Augusta in 324, received more prominence.[156] Helena founded churches in the Holy Land, and died soon after her return.[157] Constantine did not remarry. The new foundation of Constantinople, planned immediately after Constantine's defeat of Licinius,[158] was dedicated on

---

[149] See Barnes, *CE* 65–8, following P. Bruun; so also Grünewald, *Constantinus*, 109–12; the date of 314 is defended by König, *Origo*, 119–23.

[150] See notes on I. 50. 2; II. 9. 4.

[151] *HE* 10. 8; Lactantius, *Inst.* 1. 1; see notes on I. 49–59.

[152] See notes on II. 9. 4, 15–18.

[153] II. 20–2, 24–42, 45.   [154] III. 22.

[155] Pola: Barnes, *NE*, 84, and see *NE* 9; *CE* 220–1; *PLRE* i, F. Max. Fausta.

[156] See on III. 25.

[157] Churches: III. 41–3. 4; death: *PLRE* I, Fl. Iulia Helena 3, and see on III. 43. 5–7. 3.

[158] Barnes, *CE* 212.

11 May 330, in Constantine's presence. From then on, he spent much of his time there, though he campaigned against the Goths in 332 and the Sarmatians in 334 (see on IV. 5–6), and north of the Danube in 336. The church of the Holy Sepulchre in Jerusalem was dedicated in September 335, and Eusebius delivered one of the speeches (he later repeated it in the presence of Constantine in Constantinople).[159] Constantine made a settlement in 335 which assigned separate territorial spheres to his three surviving sons and to his half-nephews Dalmatius and Hannibalianus (see on IV. 51–2. 3; his nephews were killed during the months following Constantine's death). Also in 335, Constantine encountered Athanasius in Constantinople and called the Council of Tyre which condemned and exiled him.[160] During 336 Eusebius was in Constantinople and delivered the *LC*, which celebrated the Emperor's Tricennalia.[161] The Emperor fell ill and was baptized at Easter 337 by Eusebius of Nicomedia at a suburb of Nicomedia, where he died on 22 May, the day of Pentecost, while preparing a campaign against Persia.[162] His body was escorted to Constantinople, where he lay in state and was interred by his son Constantius in a Christian ceremony in his mausoleum; he also received the traditional honours of *consecratio* in Rome and was described as *divus*.[163]

9. CONSTANTINE'S MISSION

The letters of Constantine, and especially the documents in the *VC*, give an insight into his religious views and attitudes, which are inseparable from the public policy which they express. Constantine feels a divine calling to rescue the peoples of the Empire from tyranny, specifically from Maxentius and Licinius, and to unite them in the knowledge of God; his army fights under God's sign, achieving 'deeds of salvation', and he prays that God will through him bring healing to the eastern Empire.[164] God's cure for the tyranny of the persecutors was to

---

[159] See on IV. 33. 1–2, 46. [160] IV. 41–2.
[161] See on IV. 40; Drake, 'Genesis'. [162] IV. 64. 2; IV. 61–4, with notes.
[163] Constantinople: IV. 65–7, 71–3; Rome: IV. 69, 73, with notes.
[164] II. 64–5. 1; II. 55. 1, cf. *LC* 6. 21. This is also Eusebius' view: *LC* 5. 1.
Constantine's religious thought is discussed by H. Kraft, *Konstantins religiöse Entwicklung* (Tübingen, 1995) and see Dörries, *Selbstzeugnis*. For his vocabulary in relation to God see Heim, *La Théologie de la victoire*, 37–51.

examine and approve Constantine's service, so that he could dispel the horrors and so that 'the human race, taught by my obedient service, might restore the religion of the most dread Law, while at the same time the most blessed faith might grow under the guidance of the Supreme'; with God as ally he has 'raised up the whole world step by step with sure hopes of salvation'.[165] This salvation is an expression of providence, the divine government of the world both physical and moral, which leads to God's acts of reward and punishment in history and beyond. No intelligent and virtuous person can observe the divine laws operating in nature without rising to the knowledge of God.[166] God is often spoken of with a respectful periphrasis: 'Providence' (*pronoia*), 'the Supreme' (*to kreitton*), 'the Divinity' (*to theion, divinitas*). As supreme God he holds all things in his hand, and rules with fatherly kindness. It is his providence which raised up Constantine to save the world from evil.[167] Persecution of the Church is rebellion against God, and leads to calamity in this life and beyond.[168] The testimony of martyrs and confessors, by contrast, deserves greatest honour.[169] The evidence of judgement and saving providence is the foundation of Constantine's faith: 'I genuinely love your name, and dread your power, which you have revealed by many tokens, confirming the strength of my faith.'[170] God's truth can be described as Law (*nomos, lex*) a concept which embraces in varying mixtures the laws of nature, the books of the Bible, and the religious system of Christianity. In it is the truth: in contradiction to the polytheistic 'sanctuaries of falsehood' stands 'the shining house of your truth, which you have given in accordance with nature'.[171] The truth is a medicine, openly available in the Church for all to receive, which heresy distorts into deadly poison.[172]

The Church is not only the repository of this truth for the benefit of mankind; it also offers the worship due to God. Thus the Church ensures the peace and prosperity of the Empire; the unity of the Church and God's proper worship will ensure that his favour persists; the building and enlargement of churches facilitates both teaching and worship.[173] In this respect Constantine is

---

[165] II. 28. 2; IV. 9.   [166] II. 48, 58. 1.   [167] II. 28.
[168] II. 27. 2.   [169] II. 26. 1, 40.   [170] II. 55. 2.
[171] II. 56.   [172] II. 59; III. 64. 1, cf. II. 68. 1.
[173] II. 65. 2; *HE* 10. 7. 2; *VC* II. 46, III. 30 etc.

little different from his polytheistic predecessors. Purity of religion could even motivate a persecutor, and was held to preserve the divine favour, *pax deorum*, for the whole Empire. Constantine is therefore directly concerned with the people of the Church. He works hard to secure their unity and concord, in Egypt and Antioch as in North Africa, and in Tyre and Jerusalem; they are 'brothers . . . who are pledged to God by one and the same commitment to a right and just course of life as members of a sacred and holy family'.[174] He regularly addresses any bishop as 'brother', as if he were one of them, and in one place calls himself 'bishop appointed by God over those outside'.[175] His use of episcopal councils to resolve ecclesiastical disputes indicates a genuine sense of their spiritual power: he explicitly endorses the early Church's idea that assembled bishops speak with the voice of God, and legislated to allow episcopal decisions to be binding in civil law.[176]

Doubts have been expressed about the genuineness of Constantine's Christianity.[177] Once the letters are accepted as authentic, Constantine's conviction of divine calling and service must be accepted. But was he at heart a Christian, and if so, of what kind? Opinions differ as to the degree of his theological awareness, and as to his ultimate motives.[178] Some hold him to have been a syncretist; others that he had little belief in the saving work of the cross of Christ as generally understood by Christians.[179] He was in practice willing to tolerate polytheism, even if he could be at the same time personally hostile and

[174] II. 66–8; III. 20. 2; IV. 42; III. 60. 2.   [175] IV. 24, where see note.
[176] III. 20. 1; *CTh* I. 27. 1.
[177] Notably in the past Jakob Burckhardt and Eduard Schwartz. Modern thinkers produce sharply conflicting estimates, not always wisely based: compare the opposing views of Alistair Kee, *Constantine Versus Christ* (London, 1962), and Paul Keresztes, *Constantine: A Great Christian Monarch and Apostle* (Amsterdam, 1981). For a balanced estimate see Baynes or Dörries (whose assessment is distilled in English in Hermann Dörries, *Constantine the Great* (New York, 1972), though it lacks the accuracy and authority of his original work).
[178] See Øyvind Norderval, 'The Emperor Constantine and Arius: Unity in the Church and Unity in the Empire', *Studia Theologica*, 42 (1988), 113–50, arguing for religious unity as his primary aim, but for tolerance of a degree of pluralism; he was thwarted when others refused to cooperate (see on IV. 41).
[179] H. A. Drake, 'Constantine and Consensus', *Church History*, 64 (1995), 1–15, argues that his aim was rather to promote a moderate monotheism which both Christians and pagans could accept; this was not in Drake's view a matter of syncretistic belief but of policy. Cf. also id., 'Lambs into Lions: Explaining Early Christian Intolerance', *Past and Present*, 153 (1996), 3–36.

verbally abusive: the combination of insult and permission in
II. 56, 62 is typical. Eusebius' statement that he chiefly promoted
Christians to office is a clear exaggeration.[180] He continued to
honour the Unconquered Sun, and this deity figures on his coins
to the exclusion (with rare exceptions) of Christian symbols.
When he appoints the Day of the Sun for rest, he does not refer to
its Christian significance,[181] and even Eusebius' account of his
vision in 312 is loaded with solar symbolism. The best explanation however is not that Constantine was a half-informed
syncretist, so much as that the Sun could be a potent symbol
of the one God worshipped by Christians.[182]

It has also been argued that Constantine's understanding of
Christian doctrine is defective at a crucial point, the person and
work of Jesus Christ, to the extent that he is rather theist than
Christian. It is true that the death of Christ plays little apparent
part in his thinking—even in the *Oration to the Saints*, which was
delivered at the Easter festival, chapter 11 stresses the teaching
and resurrection of Christ, but not his suffering.[183] God is often
seen by Constantine as Saviour (*soter*), an idea which undoubtedly includes the giving of victory in war, and is not related
particularly to spiritual reconciliation with God by the saving
death of Jesus. Rather, the cross is a 'saving trophy' precisely
because it brings victory in battle over the powers of tyranny.
Similarly his engagement in the Arian, Nicene and post-Nicene
controversies with the theological question of the person of Christ
and his divinity may appear to be time-serving: he is more
interested in the unity and effectiveness of the Church than in the
truth of the doctrines it adopts. Many modern readers, including
earnest Christians, might sympathize with the Emperor's view
that the dispute over Arianism was out of all proportion, and that
the issues did not justify the drastic actions and divisions it
caused.[184] But it should be noted that even at this time, he was

---

[180] II. 44; see e.g. R. von Haehling, *Die Religionszugehörigkeit der hohen Amtsträger der
römischen Reiches von Constantins I. bis zum Ende der Theodosianischen Dynastie* (Antiquitas, 3
23; Bonn, 1978); R. MacMullen, *Christianizing the Roman Empire AD 100–400* (New
Haven and London, 1984), 43–8; see however T. D. Barnes, 'Statistics and the
Conversion of the Roman Aristocracy', *JRS* 85 (1995), 135–47.

[181] IV. 18 and notes.

[182] On this see the fundamental discussion of Baynes in his appendix (pp. 95–103).

[183] Just as his primary interest in the site of the church of the Holy Sepulchre was the
place of the resurrection rather than the rock of Golgotha.   [184] II. 69–71.

sure Arius was wrong.[185] Such favour as he later showed to Arius was in response to professions of orthodoxy, and his banishing of Athanasius, the arch anti-Arian, was on political and disciplinary grounds, not theological. It is best therefore to accept Constantine's attachment to the Christian God and to Christ as the response of one deeply committed to his imperial calling, who adopts and patronizes Christ precisely because he seems to bring 'salvation'—victory, that is, prosperity and peace. It is a doctrine which many of the best Christian intellectuals of the day (including both Eusebius and Lactantius) were not ashamed to approve and encourage.

10. THE HISTORICAL VALUE OF THE *VC*

The *VC* is the single most important source for the reign of Constantine. As such, it needs and deserves careful and detailed examination, and above all, a consideration of the nature of the *VC* *qua* literary composition. Historically, estimation of the quality of the *VC* has shared in the broader issue of the reputation of Eusebius.[186] Particularly in this century, it has been the object of repeated attack on grounds of authenticity and veracity (see § 2 above); however, much of this criticism arose from the application of the wrong criteria to the *VC* by interpreting it as a strictly historical work, rather than as a work of apologetic suffused with ideological and encomiastic themes and style in the manner of other works of Eusebius. Eusebius was a biblical scholar as well as a Christian apologist,[187] and the *VC* is to be read not as a 'scientific' history, but, like most of his works, from those points of view.

A number of specific features of the *VC* which seem to impair its historical value have also been adduced as grounds for doubting Eusebius' authorship. These include the omission of Crispus' role in the campaign against Licinius, originally included in the *HE*, the 'doctoring' of Constantine's settlement for the succession in 335[188] and the alleged omission of the battle

---

[185] II. 69. 1.

[186] For a brief statement see S. Calderone, 'Il pensiero politico di Eusebio di Cesarea', in G. Bonamente and A. Nestori, eds., *I cristiani e l'impero nel IV secolo* (Macerata, 1988), 45–54.

[187] So Calderone, 'Il pensiero', 51–4, and cf. Barnes, *CE* 106–25, 164–88.

[188] IV. 40 with note; on Crispus in the *HE*, see Burgess, 'Dates and Editions', 494, and note on II. 1. 2–3. 2.

of Cibalae (see above). But they can generally be explained (unless based on misunderstandings) by reference to Eusebius' apologetic aims in the *VC*, and to the circumstances when it was written. Since book I and II. 1–19 (and sections of the rest of the *VC*, especially in book IV) are written in the manner of panegyric, one should not expect sober historical reporting, and it is natural that Constantine's parentage is made the subject of encomiastic elaboration. His vision is also there for apologetic reasons (above, § 7). A number of scholars believe that Eusebius deliberately omitted the discovery of the True Cross at Jerusalem, but it would have been to his apologetic advantage to include it, and it is more likely that the discovery postdated the *VC*.[189] Surprisingly, the city of Constantinople does not receive much attention in the *VC*, but what attention it does receive is designed to promote the idea of it as a new Christian foundation.[190] Scholars have found it difficult that Eusebius claims that he will concentrate only on the Emperor's religious actions,[191] but then includes narratives of his military campaigns; yet for Eusebius (as for traditional imperial panegyrists) all Constantine's actions have a religious inspiration and a religious interpretation (see above). The Emperor's very success is the result of God's favour. On the other hand, some secular and anecdotal material about Constantine's policies and demeanour as Emperor is also included, especially in book IV, where there are sometimes similarities with other sources such as the *Origo Constantini*. At times, for instance in his remarks on the senatorial order at IV. 1 or on wills at IV. 26. 1, Eusebius provides information on secular matters not to be found elsewhere.

For all its religious and personal bias, the *VC* is the fullest and most important source for the reign of Constantine; the other most important sources are the account in Lactantius's pamphlet *On the Deaths of the Persecutors* (*De Morte Persecutorum, DMP*), the *Origo Constantini*, and Zosimus' *New History* 2. 8–39. Of these, the account in the *Origo* is largely neutral in religious terms, though some Christian elements are present, derived from Orosius, while Zosimus' version is aggressively pagan and

---

[189] See on III. 28.

[190] See III. 48, 54; IV. 58. 1. B. H. Warmington suggests that Eusebius was conscious of the criticisms of extravagance directed at the foundation of the new city (e.g. Zosimus, 2. 32).   [191] I. 11. 1.

hostile.[192] Constantine is also the subject of five contemporary Latin panegyrics, covering the period AD 307–21, contained in the surviving collection of *Panegyrici Latini*.[193] Aside from the Latin panegyrics, no contemporary pagan account has survived, although Praxagoras is known to have composed a laudatory history in Greek of Constantine's rise.[194] We do however have the collection of learned and effusive poems in Constantine's honour sent to the Emperor from exile by Publilius Optatianus Porfyrius in 324–5.[195] But the hostile versions seem to have started early, and some of that tradition can be detected in surviving fourth-century accounts (see also § 11 below).[196]

11. THE LATER TRADITION OF THE *VC*

Later testimonia to the *VC* are few.[197] It was known to the church historian Gelasius of Caesarea (d. 395) and after him in varying degrees to the fifth-century church historians Socrates, Sozomen, Theodoret, and Gelasius of Cyzicus.[198] It has often been claimed that it was not known or at least not cited during the fourth century, but Libanius' panegyric on Constantius II and Constans, which naturally enough also praises their father Constantine, contains a number of similarities with the *VC* even though Libanius entirely omits any reference to Constantine's

---

[192] For the *Origo* see the commentary by I. König, *Origo Constantini. Anonymus Valesianus, i. Text und Kommentar* (Trier, 1987); an English translation of Zosimus with brief notes exists by R. T. Ridley, *Byzantina Australiensia*, 2 (Canberra, 1982). König accepts a late 4th-cent. date for the *Origo*, with later additions, but the original work may be earlier: see T. D. Barnes, 'Jerome and the *Origo Constantini imperatoris*', *Phoenix*, 43 (1989), 158–61 (*c*.340).

[193] See Nixon and Rodgers, reproducing the Latin text by R. A. B. Mynors.

[194] *FGrH* 219; it is summarized by Photius.

[195] Ed. G. Polara (Turin, 1973). On Porfyrius see T. D. Barnes, 'Publilius Optatianus Porfyrius', *AJP* 96 (1975), 173–86; he was released during Constantine's Vicennalia, 325–6.

[196] For discussion in relation to Constantine's Persian expedition, his baptism, and his death see G. Fowden, 'The Last Days of Constantine: Oppositional Versions and their Influence', *JRS* 84 (1994), 146–70.

[197] Winkelmann, pp. xxvii–xxxiii; id., 'Die Beurteilung des Eusebius von Cäsarea und seiner Vita Constantini im griechischen Osten', in J. Irmscher, ed., *Byzantinische Beiträge* (Berlin, 1964), 91–119 (= *Studien*, 15), at 107.

[198] See Winkelmann, pp. xxvii–xxx; id., *Textbezeugung*, 71–88; id., *Untersuchungen zur Kirchengeschichte des Gelasios von Kaisareia* (Berlin, 1966); see also A. Linder, 'The Myth of Constantine the Great in the West: Sources and Hagiographic Commemoration', *Studi Medievali*, 3rd ser. 16 (1975), 43–95, and see on IV. 56.

Christianity.[199] However, neither Julian in his *Caesares* nor Ammianus Marcellinus is likely to have used the strongly Christian and partisan *VC* when writing of Constantine,[200] and even Eusebius' *HE* was not available in Latin until it was translated and continued by Rufinus in 402 or 403. Moreover, Eusebius himself was regarded as suspect in many quarters for his sympathy for the Arian cause.[201] From the fifth century on the *VC* seems to have been unknown or neglected until Photius read it in the ninth century (see below).

From an early stage (probably as early as the fifth century) Constantine himself entered the realm of legend and hagiography, as the saintly Christian founder of Constantinople; in the Byzantine period, some twenty-five *Vitae* and *encomia* are known, with extant manuscripts beginning *c.*800, and from the ninth century onwards the various legendary features in these works pass into historical writing on Constantine.[202] Constantine's vision of the cross, and Helena as the finder of the True Cross, also passed into the highly ideological manuscript illustrations of the

---

[199] *Or.* 59, AD 344–5; see H.-U. Wiemer, 'Libanius on Constantine', *CQ* 44 (1994), 511–24, at 513–14; cf. P. Petit, 'Libanius et la Vita Constantini', *Historia* 1 (1950), 562–80 (*contra*, J. Moreau, 'Zum Problem der Vita Constantini', *Historia*, 4 (1955), 234–45). The speech is translated with introduction and notes in Lieu and Montserrat, eds., *From Constantine to Julian* (London, 1996), 147–209 (see p. 206 on possible use of the *VC*); Libanius himself says that his interpretations are familiar ones: *Or.* 59. 20. Contrast his emphasis on religious elements in the case of Julian, *Or.* 13 (362) and 12 (363), which give a pagan version of Eusebius' imperial theory.

[200] Nor does it seem to have been used in Julian's *Oration* 1, his panegyric of Constantius (AD 355), which praises Constantine.

[201] See Winkelmann, 'Die Beurteilung', 108–12. For an explicit statement as to Eusebius' orthodoxy see Germanos I of Constantinople (715–30), *De Haeresibus et Synodis*, *PG* 98. 53A.

[202] For these developments see F. Winkelmann, 'Ein Ordnungsversuch der griechischen hagiographischen Konstantinviten und ihrer Überlieferung', in J. Irmscher and P. Nagel, eds., *Studia Byzantina*, ii, (Berliner Byzantinsche Arbeiten, 44; Berlin, 1973), 267–84 (= Winkelmann, *Studien*, 12); 'Die älteste erhaltene griechische hagiographische Vita Konstantins und Helenas (BHG Nr. 365z, 366, 366a)', in J. Dummer, ed., *Texte und Textkritik* (TU 133; Berlin, 1987), 623–38 (*Studien*, XIII); Fowden, 'Last Days of Constantine'; G. Dagron, *Empereur et prêtre: Étude sur le "césaropapisme" byzantin* (Paris, 1996), 154–8; see also E. T. Brett, 'Early Constantine Legends: A Study in Propaganda', *Byzantine Studies*, 10 (1983/4), 52–70; H. J. Cowdrey, 'Eleventh-Century Reformer's Views of Constantine', *BF* 24 (1997), 63–91 (Constantine in the *Actus Silvestri*); Lieu and Montserrat, eds., *From Constantine to Julian*, 97–146 (translation of BHG 364, the 'Guidi-Vita', with notes); M. Van Esbroeck, 'Legends about Constantine in Armenian', *Classical Armenian Culture* (Chico, Calif., 1982), 79–101. They are seen as beginning at a later date by A. Kazhdan, '"Constantine imaginaire": Byzantine Legends of the Ninth Century about Constantine the Great', *Byzantion*, 57 (1987), 196–250.

ninth century.[203] These developments show how far the interest in the genuine historical record for Constantine, in so far as it is represented in the *VC*, had already receded, and indeed the hagiographic *Vitae* do not use the *VC* directly, although there seems to have been a Syriac translation of the *VC* which has not survived, and whose date is uncertain.[204] During the early Byzantine and Iconoclast periods, therefore, the *VC* was eclipsed by the hagiographical *Lives* of Constantine, and Eusebius himself regarded as suspect;[205] the Iconoclasts were, however, responsible for renewed interest in Eusebius, whom they regarded as an opponent of images.[206] This revival seems to have led to the rediscovery of the *VC*. After the ending of Iconoclasm in 843, Photius records in his *Bibliotheca* an encomiastic work on the life of Constantine by Eusebius in four books.[207] He goes on to criticize Eusebius' style, points out that the work includes many passages from the *HE*, and comments that it says that Constantine was baptized at Nicomedia, without naming the bishop who baptized him; Photius also criticizes Eusebius' position on Arius and Arianism. Photius' entry shows a renewed awareness of the *VC* in Constantinople with the revival of learning and the ending of Iconoclasm; equally, his unfavourable verdict demonstrates the reasons for its earlier neglect. V, the earliest surviving manuscript (Vat. gr. 149), dates from the tenth century. In the fourteenth century Nikephoros Kallistos Xanthopoulos knew of the *VC* as a work in five books.[208]

12. TRADITION AND EDITIONS

This new translation and commentary is based on the critical edition of the *VC* by Winkelmann, whose introduction discusses

---

[203] See Leslie Brubaker, 'To Legitimize an Emperor: Constantine and Visual Authority in the Eighth and Ninth Centuries', in P. Magdalino, ed., *New Constantines* (Aldershot, 1994), 139–58, for Par. gr. 510, and see especially 142–9.

[204] Winkelmann, p. xxxii; 'Die Beurteilung', 109.

[205] The legendary Constantine predominates in the 8th cent.: see Averil Cameron and Judith Herrin *et al.*, eds., *Constantinople in the Eighth Century: The Parastaseis Syntomoi Chronikai* (Leiden, 1984). This composite work is dated to *c.*800 by A. Berger, *Untersuchungen zu den Patria Konstantinupoleos* (Poikila Byzantina, 8; Bonn, 1988); it shows no knowledge of the *VC*.

[206] See S. Gero, 'The True Image of Christ: Eusebius' Letter to Constantia Reconsidered', *JThS* NS 32 (1981), 460–70.   [207] Phot., *Bibl.*, cod. 127.

[208] He is apparently dependent on Socrates: Winkelmann, p. xxxi.

the manuscripts in detail.[209] Winkelmann's fundamental work on the textual history of the *VC* provides an indispensable basis for study.

The textual transmission of the *VC* is complex; the present brief account is based on the full discussion by Winkelmann, pp. ix–xvi and his longer discussion published in Texte und Untersuchingen, 84. Among the principal manuscripts containing the *Life* the oldest and best (though by no means error-free) is *Cod. Vat. gr.* 149 (V, 10th cent.), in which the *VC* is followed by the *Oratio ad Sanctos,* presented as book V of the *VC* (cf. *VC* IV. 32).[210] The chapter headings are written twice in uncials, once at the beginning of each book and again in the margins of the main text, and the documents also appear with uncial headings. Next in importance come *Cod. Mosq. gr.* 50, also containing the *HE* and *LC* (J, 12th cent.), *Cod. Mosq gr.* 340 (N, 12th cent.), *Cod. Par. gr.* 1437 (A, 13th cent.) and *Cod. Par. gr.* 1432 (B, 14th cent.). In addition, some manuscripts of the *HE* (*Codd. Laur. gr.* LXX.29, 10th cent.; *Paris gr.* 1431, 11th cent.; *Paris gr.* 1433, 11th/12th cent.) also contain the document given at *VC* II. 24–42, addressed by Constantine in Eusebius' copy to the provincials of Palestine, but sent to all the eastern provinces, and offer a better text than that given by the main manuscripts of the *VC*. Part of the same document (II. 27–9) also appears in P. Lond. 878, written very shortly after the promulgation of the edict and in close agreement with the version of the three *HE* manuscripts.[211] In addition, the many places where Eusebius has drawn from his own earlier works (especially *HE, LC,* and *SC*) sometimes allow comparisons with the text of those works. Finally, the *VC* is used by the church historians of the fifth century, especially Socrates; because of the separate transmission of their works, these can sometimes be of limited use in editing the *VC*.

The text has therefore been transmitted both directly, through its own manuscript tradition, and indirectly, via its use by later writers, while Eusebius' habit of drawing on his own works

[209] See also his discussion in *Die Textbezeugung der Vita Constantini des Eusebius von Caesarea* (TU 84, Berlin, 1962).

[210] See Winkelmann, p. xxxi.

[211] See A. H. M. Jones and T. C. Skeat, 'Notes on the Genuineness of the Constantinian Documents in Eusebius' *Life of Constantine*', *JEH* 5 (1954), 196–200.

sometimes means that they too can be used to correct our text. We have a better text of II. 24–42 than for the rest of the work, thanks to the London papyrus and the manuscripts of the *HE* cited above. But though in the main body of the text V is generally the best guide, it is not always correct and it is always necessary to consider the witnesses to an individual passage in their entirety.

The chapter division also varies between the different manuscripts; in general, we follow Winkelmann's edition, just as for convenience we also give the page numbers of his Greek text. The style of the chapter headings differs materially from that of the rest of the work, they supply names not in the main text, and they use the third person when referring to Eusebius. It seems most likely therefore that they were supplied by a contemporary soon after Eusebius' death, no doubt the editor whom many scholars believe to have been responsible for publishing the work.[212] The arrangement of the *VC* in four books may also be attributable to the posthumous editor.[213] Here, as in Winkelmann's edition, the chapter headings are given together before the *VC* itself, so as not to disturb the continuity of the main text. In order to help the reader, the present translators have introduced at suitable points headings and subheadings which correspond with their understanding of the structure as the author saw it (see above, § 5). These headings and subheadings, which are are not in the manuscripts, are distinguished by italic type from words translated from the Greek text. The numbers in square brackets in the translation refer to the pages of Winkelmann's edition.

The first printed edition of the Greek text of the *VC* was that of Stephanus (Paris, 1544). The Geneva edition of 1612 reproduced this text together with the *LC* and the Latin translation of the *VC* by John Christopherson, bishop of Chichester (d. 1558); however, the Greek text offered in J.-P. Migne's *Patrologia Graeca*, 20 (Paris, 1857) is that of Valesius, who re-edited the *VC* in 1659 with full notes and a Latin translation. The first modern critical edition of the *VC* was that of Heikel, with very full and useful introduction. All previous editions are now superseded by that of Winkelmann.

---

[212] See Winkelmann, pp. xlvi–xlvix.   [213] Barnes, 'Panegyric', 104.

Older English translations exist by S. Bagster (London, 1845), revised by E. C. Richardson (NPNF 1, Oxford and New York, 1890). The Italian translation by L. Tartaglia includes short notes and a useful introduction, as does the Spanish version by M. Gurruchaga.

Italic type is used in what follows, not only for the editors' headings and subheadings, but to distinguish the documents attributed to Constantine from the rest of Eusebius' text.

CHAPTER HEADINGS

In the manuscripts the whole *VC* is divided into chapters, the numbering of which is still used for reference. The headings of these chapters go back to an early editor or copyist, and not to Eusebius himself (see Introd., § 1). Since they have their own historic interest, and occasionally provide useful information, a translation of them is presented here, on the basis of the Greek text in pp. 3–13 of Winkelmann's edition. The headings and subheadings in the Plan (Introd., § 5) and in the translation itself have been made by the present translators, who believe they are a better guide to Eusebius' plan and thought.

CHAPTERS OF THE GODLY LIFE OF
THE BLESSED EMPEROR CONSTANTINE

Book I

---

[1] *Ekphrasis*, the technical term for a rhetorical description.

---

[2] Lit. 'was catechized', i.e. received Christian instruction.
[3] Following Valesius's emendation. The MSS have 'Maximin'. See notes at I. 47.

59. That blinded by disease Maximin wrote in favour of Christians

Chapters of the first Book

The Chapters of the Second Book

1. The secret persecution of Licinius destroying bishops in Amasea in Pontus
2. Destruction of churches and butchery of bishops
3. How Constantine was roused on behalf of Christians destined for persecution
4. That Constantine made military preparations with prayer, but Licinius with divination
5. What Licinius said as he sacrificed in the grove about the idols and Christ
6. Visions in the cities ruled by Licinius, as if Constantine's armies were marching through
7. That in battle, wherever the cross-shaped sign appeared, victorious events ensued
8. That fifty were selected to carry the cross
9. That of the cross-bearers, the one who fled fell, while the one who stood faithfully by it survived
10. Various engagements and Constantine's victories
11. Flight and trickery of Licinius
12. How Constantine would win victories by praying in his tent
13. Generous treatment of prisoners of war
14. Further on the prayers in the tent
15. Licinius' cunning over friendly relations and his idolatry
16. How Licinius urged his troops not to engage the cross in battle
17. Constantine's victory
18. Licinius' death and celebrations of victory for it
19. Joy and festivals
20. Constantine's legislation on behalf of confessors
21. On behalf also of martyrs and ecclesiastical property
22. How he also revived the spirits of the people
23. That he proclaimed God as the source of good things; and on copies of laws

---

[4] Literally 'Hellenes'.

Chapters of the second book

The Chapters of the Third Book

---

[5] See n. 1.

---

[6] See n. 4.

[7] i.e. Goths; see note *ad loc.*   [8] Lit. *ethnici*, 'from the nations'.

20. Words of the prayer given to the soldiers by Constantine
21. The signs of the Saviour's cross on the armour of the soldiers
22. Earnestness in prayer and respect for the Easter feast
23. How he prohibited idolatry but honoured martyrs and festivals
24. That he said he was a kind of bishop of non-Christian affairs[9]
25. Further on prohibition of sacrifices and initiation rites and single-combat shows and the former obscene persons by the Nile
26. Reform of the existing law against the childless, and similarly further reform of that pertaining to wills
27. That he made laws that a Christian might not be slave to Jews, that the decisions of synods are legally binding, and so on
28. Gifts to churches and grants to virgins and the poor
29. Written works and speeches of Constantine
30. That to one covetous person he measured out a grave to shame him
31. That he was mocked for his excessive generosity
32. On the work which Constantine wrote 'To the assembly of the saints'
33. How he stood to listen to Eusebius' speeches about the tomb of the Saviour
34. That he wrote to Eusebius on Easter and sacred books
35. Constantine to Eusebius, praising his work on Easter
36. Constantine to Eusebius on the making of sacred books
37. How the books were manufactured
38. How the port of Gaza was designated a city because of Christianity and named Constantia
39. That in Phoenicia one place was made a city, and in the other cities there was destruction of idol-shrines and building of churches
40. That having in his thirtieth year proclaimed three sons as Emperors he proposed to carry out the dedication of the Martyrion in Jerusalem

---

[9] The chapter heading puts in the word 'affairs', which is missing in the main text; see note *ad loc.*

---

[10] See n. 1.
[11] See n. 1.

The chapters of the fourth book

---

[12] 'Religious service'.

TRANSLATION

Eusebius Pamphili
On the Life of the Blessed Emperor Constantine

BOOK I

1–11. *Preface*

1–3. *Constantine's immortality*

[15] **1** (1) It was but recently the whole human race celebrated various ten-year periods for the great Emperor with festive banquets. It was but recently we ourselves hymned the conqueror with praises for his twenty years, taking the floor at the Council of God's ministers. Just now we wove garlands of words also for his thirty years, in the very palace hardly yesterday to crown his sacred head. (2) But today our thought stands helpless, longing to express some of the conventional things, but at a loss which way to turn, stunned by the sheer wonder of the amazing spectacle. Wherever it casts its gaze, whether east or west, whether all over the earth or up to heaven itself, every way and everywhere it observes the Blessed One present with the Empire itself. (3) On earth it perceives his own sons like new lamps filling the whole with his radiance, and himself powerfully alive and directing the whole government of affairs more firmly than before, as he is multiplied in the succession of his sons. If previously they still shared the honour of Caesars, now that they have put on his whole mantle of Godfearing virtue, they have been declared Imperatores Augusti, singled out with their father's honours.

2 (1) When our thought observes the one who was recently visible in a mortal body, and amazingly present with us even after his life is ended, when Nature rejects over-prolongation as alien— when our thought observes him endowed with the imperial palaces and properties and honours and panegyrics, it is utterly disconcerted. (2) But now that it reaches upward to the very vaults of heaven, it pictures there too the thrice-blessed soul in the presence of God, [16] stripped of all mortal and earthly attire, and brilliant in a flashing robe of light. (3) Then perceiving that soul no longer confined in mortal occupations for long periods of time, but honoured with the ever-blooming garland of endless life and the immortality of a blessed eternity, thought in its mortality stands agape, uttering not a word, but convicted by itself of its impotence; it condemns itself to silence, and concedes to the superior and universal Thought the right to utter worthy praises. For him and him alone who is the immortal Thought of God is it possible to confirm his own words, 3 (1) by which he predicted that those who give him glory and honour would excel in generous recompense, while those who set themselves up as his enemies and foes would bring on themselves the destruction of their lives. Hence he has now proved the promises of his own words to be unfailing, showing the ends of the lives of godless tyrants who attack God to be abominable, but making even the death of his servant as well as his life to be enviable and worthy of much praise, so that this too became memorable and worthy not of mortal but of immortal record.

(2) Mortal nature, finding consolation for a mortal and fragile end, appeared to glorify the tombs of our predecessors with immortal honours by dedicating portraits; some by devising pictures in coloured encaustic painting, or statuary figures carved from lifeless material, and others by incising deep lettering on blocks and pillars, supposed they could entrust the merits of those they honoured to everlasting monuments. Yet those were all mortal things which are destroyed by the passage of time, since they were the configurations of corruptible bodies, and did not portray the shapes of an immortal soul. Nevertheless they seemed to satisfy those who had nothing else to set their hopes upon after the termination of mortal life. (3) But God, God the universal Saviour of all, who has stored up benefits beyond mortal imagination for the lovers of true piety, gives even here as a first instalment a foretaste of his rewards, somehow guaranteeing immortal hopes to mortal eyes. (4) This is what ancient oracles of prophets, transmitted in Scripture, predict; this is what lives of Godbeloved men in ancient times illustrious with every kind of virtue attest when they are recounted to the new generation; this is what our own age also has proved to be true, when Constantine, alone among all those who have ruled the Roman Empire, [17] became a friend of the all-sovereign God,

and was established as a clear example to all mankind of the life
of godliness.

4–6. *God's achievement in Constantine*

4 This is also what God himself, whom Constantine honoured, by standing at Constantine's side at the beginning, the
middle and the end of his reign, confirmed by his manifest
judgement, putting forward this man as a lesson in the pattern of
godliness to the human race. As the only one of the widely
renowned Emperors of all time whom God set up as a huge
luminary and loud-voiced herald of unerring godliness, he is the
only one to whom God gave convincing proofs of the religion he
practised by the benefits of every kind which were accorded him:
5 (1) he honoured his imperial reign with three complete
decades, and circumscribed his human life with twice that
number. Making him the model of his own monarchical reign,
he appointed him victor over the whole race of tyrants and
destroyer of the God-battling giants, who in mental frenzy raised
weapons against the Sovereign of the universe himself. (2) They,
you might say, appeared briefly and were at once extinguished,
while God, who is one and only, fortified with divine armour his
servant as one against many. By him he cleansed humanity of the
godless multitude, and set him up as a teacher of true devotion to
himself for all nations, testifying with a loud voice for all to hear,
that they should know the God who is, and turn from the error of
those who do not exist at all. 6 As a loyal and good servant, he
would perform this and announce it, openly calling himself a
slave and confessing himself a servant of the All-sovereign, while
God in recompense was close at hand to make him Lord and
Despot, the only Conqueror among the Emperors of all time to
remain Irresistible and Unconquered, Ever-conquering and
always brilliant with triumphs over enemies, so great an Emperor
as none remembers ever was before in reports of those of old, so
Godbeloved and Thriceblessed, so truly pious and complete in
happiness, that with utter ease he governed more nations than
those before him, and kept his dominion unimpaired to the very
end.

7–9. Constantine superior to other emperors

7 (1) Among the Persians of [18] old, ancient story indeed relates that Cyrus was declared more illustrious than those before him. Yet one ought to have regard not just to that, but to the end of a long life, and they say that he suffered a death which was not fitting, but vile and shameful at a woman's hand. From among the Macedonians Alexander, so the sons of Greece relate, overthrew countless tribes of diverse nations, but before he reached full manhood he died an early death, carried off by revelry and drunken orgies. (2) He reached two years past thirty, and of this the period of his reign measured one-third; he waded through blood, a man like a thunderbolt, mercilessly enslaving entire nations and cities, young and old alike. But while his youth had barely blossomed, and he still mourned his lost childhood, fate fell deadly upon him, and childless, rootless, homeless, in a foreign and hostile land, that he might harm the human race no more, removed him. At once his empire was divided, as each of his servants tore off a portion and seized it for himself.

For such deeds as these he is hymned in choruses; **8** (1) but our Emperor began where the Macedonian ended, and doubled in time the length of his life, and trebled the size of the Empire he acquired. (2) With mild and sober injunctions to godliness he equipped his troops, then campaigned against the land of the Britons and the dwellers at the very Ocean where the sun sets. He annexed the whole Scythian population, which was in the far north divided into numerous barbarian tribes; (3) and once he had also extended his Empire in the extreme south as far as the Blemmyes and Aethiopians, he did not treat the acquisition of what lay in the orient as beyond his scope, (4) but illuminating with beams of the light of true religion the ends of the whole inhabited earth, as far as the outermost inhabitants of India and those who live round the rim of the whole dial of earth, he held in subjection all the toparchs, ethnarchs, satraps and kings of barbarian nations of every kind. These spontaneously saluted and greeted him, and [19] sent their embassies with gifts and presents, and set such store by his acquaintance and friendship, that they honoured him at home with pictures of him and dedications of statues, and alone of emperors Constantine was recognized and acclaimed by them all. For his part he used imperial addresses to announce his own God openly and boldly even to the people of those lands.

9 (1) Yet it was not in words he did these things whilst failing in deeds. He travelled every virtuous road and took pride in fruits of piety of every kind. By the magnanimity of his helpful actions he enslaved those who knew him, and ruled by humane laws, making his government agreeable and much prayed for by the governed. Then finally the God he honoured, after he had struggled for a long period of years in the divine athletic contest, crowned him with the prizes of immortality, and removed him from a mortal reign to that endless life which he has reserved for holy souls, having raised up a threefold offspring of sons to succeed to his Empire. (2) Thus also did the throne of Empire descend from his father to him, and by natural law it was stored up for his sons and their descendants, and extended to unaging time like a paternal inheritance. So may God himself, since he both exalted the Blessed One when he was still among us with divine honours, and dying adorned him with exquisite perfections from himself, become also his recorder, inscribing his successful conflicts on tablets of heavenly monuments for long eternities.

10–11. *Eusebius' purpose and plan*

10 (1) As for me, even though to say anything worthy of the blessedness of the man is beyond my power, while to be silent would be safe and peril-free, yet one must model oneself on the human painter, and dedicate a verbal portrait in memory of the Godbeloved, if only to escape the charge of sloth and idleness. I would be ashamed of myself if I did not put together what I can, little though it be and poor, for the one who out of his extraordinary devotion to God honoured us all. (2) I consider that the book which deals with the deeds of the great imperial mind, deeds bestowed by God, will in any case be edifying and necessary for me. Would it not be a disgrace if the memory of Nero and of those others far worse than Nero, vicious and godless tyrants, were to find ready authors, who have [20] embellished their accounts of wretched deeds with stylish expression and stored them in many-volumed histories, while we are silent, when God himself has vouchsafed to bring us together with an

Emperor so great that all history has not reported his like, and to see him, to know him, and to share his company? It therefore behoves us, above all others, to give to every one whose desire is stimulated to divine affection by the representation of noble deeds our own unreserved account of good things.

(3) Those writers who have composed lives of worthless characters which are of no use for moral improvement, whether from partisanship or animosity towards certain persons, or possibly also as a demonstration of their own personal skill, by flaunting their fluency with words have unnecessarily expanded their narrative of shameful actions, setting themselves up, before people whose good fortune under God is to escape those evils, as teachers not of good deeds, but of deeds fit for the silence of oblivion and darkness. (4) For my part, may the account which I give, feeble though it is when compared with the greatness of the subject of our discourse, yet derive lustre from the mere reporting of good deeds; and the recording of actions dear to God shall provide reading not unprofitable, but of practical benefit to well-disposed minds.

11 (1) The greatest, the imperial parts of the history of the Thriceblessed, his encounters and battles in war, his valiant deeds and victories and routing of enemies, and how many triumphs he won, his peacetime decrees for the welfare of the state and the benefit of the individual, and the legal enactments which he imposed for the improvement of the life of his subjects, and most of his other acts as Emperor, and those which everybody remembers, I intend to omit. My purpose in the present work is to put into words and write down what relates to the life which is dear to God. (2) Since even these events are innumerable, I shall pick out from those which have reached us the most significant and worth recording for those who come after us, and even of these I shall set out the narrative as briefly as possible, since the occasion demands that I offer unrestrained praises in varied words of the truly Blessed One. It was not possible to do this in the past, for we are forbidden to call any man blessed before his death in view of the uncertainty of life's changes. Let God be called upon for aid, and as fellow-worker let our inspiration be the heavenly Word.

12–24. *Birth, family, and youth*

12. *Childhood among the tyrants*

[21] Let us begin our story with our subject's early youth. 12 (1) An ancient report relates that terrible generations of tyrants once oppressed the Hebrew people, and that God, disclosing himself as gracious to the oppressed, provided for Moses, a prophet still in his infancy, to be reared in the heart of the palace and family circle of the tyrants, and to learn to share the wisdom they possessed. When the passage of time summoned him to manhood, and Justice who helps the injured began to pursue those who injured them, it was time for the prophet of God to leave that home of the tyrants and serve the will of the Supreme, diverging in actions and words from the tyrants who had brought him up, and acknowledging as his own those who were his true kith and kin. God then raised him up as leader of the whole nation, and he liberated the Hebrews from bondage to their enemies, while through him he pressed the tyrannical race with the torments of divine pursuit. (2) This ancient report, which most people regard as a kind of myth, was previously in everybody's ears, but now the same God has vouchsafed to us also to be eyewitnesses of public scenes, more certain than any myth because recently seen, of wonders greater than those in story. Tyrants who in our time set out to make war on the God over all oppressed his Church, while in their midst Constantine, soon to be the tyrant-slayer, still a tender young boy and blooming with the down of youth, like that very servant of God, sat at the tyrants' hearth, yet though still young he did not share the same morality as the godless. (3) With the aid of the divine Spirit a virtuous nature drew him away from that way of life towards one of piety and the favour of God, while at the same time imitation of his father was a motive which challenged the son to imitate what was good. For he had a father—since at this point his memory also deserves to be revived—most distinguished among the Emperors of our time. It is necessary to give a brief account of him where it touches on the merit of his son.

13–18. *Career and character of Constantine's father*

[22] **13** (1) When four men shared power in the Roman Empire, this man was the only one who adopted an independent policy and was on friendly terms with the God over all. (2) They besieged and ravaged the churches of God and demolished them from top to bottom, removing the houses of prayer right to their foundations; he kept his hands clean of their sacrilegious impiety, and did not resemble them at all. They stained their provinces with civic massacres of godfearing men and women; he kept his soul unstained with their defilement. (3) By the confusion of evils of unnatural idolatry they enslaved first themselves and then all their subjects to the deceits of evil demons; he led those under his rule in the way of utter tranquillity, and determined that for his people what affected devotion to God should be unharmed. While the others held the threat of very heavy taxation over all men and threatened them with a life unliveable and worse than death, Constantius alone provided sound and peaceable government, and supplied aid from his resources no less than a father would provide. (4) Since this man's countless other virtues are universally celebrated, having mentioned one or two achievements and used these as illustrations of those omitted, I shall pass on to the proper subject of my work.

14 (1) Since many stories about this Emperor were in circulation, that he was kind and good and extremely attached to what pleases God, and that because he was extremely sparing of his subjects he had not assembled any financial reserves, the Emperor who then exercised supremacy sent and rebuked him for neglect of the public interest and reproached him for penury, giving as evidence for his allegation the fact that he had nothing in reserve in his treasury. (2) He asked those who came from the Emperor to wait where they were, while he summoned those persons from all the provinces under his rule who had abundant wealth and told them that he needed money, and that now was the time for each of them to demonstrate his spontaneous loyalty to their Emperor. (3) When they heard this, as if it had been their long-felt desire to demonstrate their good [23] will, quickly and eagerly they filled the treasuries with gold and silver and other financial resources, vying with each other in their effort to give more, and they did this with happy smiling faces. (4) When this happened Constantius invited those who had come from the senior Emperor to be eyewitnesses to his wealth. Then he ordered them to transmit the testimony of what their eyes had seen to the one who had accused him of poverty. He further added to his remarks that these funds had not been acquired from tricksters or by fraud, and that whereas he had now gathered them under his own hand, they had formerly been kept for him in the care of the owners of the money who acted as faithful depositaries. (5) They were overcome with amazement at what had happened, and it is reported that after their departure the most generous Emperor sent for the owners of the money, and told them they should take it all and go home, commending these persons for their obedience and ready loyalty.

(6) That was one action which illustrates the generosity of the man in question. The other might provide manifest evidence of his holy concern for divine things. 15 Provincial governors were throughout the world persecuting the godly by the decree of those in power. Starting first of all from the imperial palaces themselves the Godbeloved martyrs endured the trials of true religion, facing with eager fortitude fire and iron, deep sea and every kind of death, so that the whole imperial service might soon be stripped of Godfearing men, a policy which had the chief effect of depriving its perpetrators of God's protection; for by persecuting the Godfearers they also expelled their prayers. 16 (1) To Constantius alone a wise counsel born of a pious mind occurred. He performed an act which is remarkable to hear of, and astonishing to have done. A choice was offered to all the imperial servants under him, from lowly domestics to those with commissions as governors: he proposed that either they sacrifice to the demons and be permitted to stay with him enjoying the customary advancement, or if they did not comply they should be excluded from all access to him and be removed and dismissed from his acquaintance and intimacy. (2) When they had divided two ways, some to the latter group and some to the former, and the nature of the decision of each was clearly demonstrated, the amazing man then finally revealed his secret trick: he condemned the one group for cowardice and self-concern, and warmly commended the others for their sense of duty to God. Thereupon he declared those who had betrayed

God not worthy of imperial service either: how could they keep faith with the Emperor if they were found to have no conscience about the Supreme? He therefore decreed that they were to be banished far from the palace, while those, he said, who for their truth had been attested worthy of God, would be the same where the Emperor was concerned; he appointed them as bodyguards and watchmen for the imperial house, saying that he ought to employ such men among his chief and closest friends and servants, and to prize them above stores of great treasure.

17 (1) This brief account shows how Constantine's father is remembered. What sort of end ensued for him, when he had shown himself so disposed towards God, and how far the God whom he had honoured made clear the difference between him and his partners in Empire, might be easily discovered by anyone who applies his mind to what actually happened. (2) When he had for a long time given proofs of his merit as an emperor, recognizing only the God over all and condemning the polytheism of the godless, and had fortified his house all around with the prayers of holy men, he finally finished the course of his life serenely and undisturbed, exactly as in the saying that it is a blessed thing to have no troubles and to give none to another. (3) Thus directing the whole period of his reign in peace and tranquillity, he consecrated his whole household to the one God of the Universe, with his children and wife, and including the domestic servants, so that the body of persons assembled within the imperial quarters was in all respects a church of God; with it were present also ministers [25] of God, who conducted constant rituals on behalf of the Emperor. These things were done only under him, at the time when under the others it was not permitted to mention the race of the godly by so much as their name.

18 (1) Close on this followed his reward from God, so that he now came to share the supreme imperial power. Those who were advanced in years managed somehow to withdraw from power, frequent changes having afflicted them from the first year of their onslaught on the churches; finally Constantius alone was entitled First Augustus. Originally he had been distinguished by the crown of the Caesars and had been appointed senior among them; after proven service among them he was promoted to the rank most highly regarded by the Romans, and was given the title of First Augustus of the four appointed to succeed. (2) But he excelled the other emperors also by the singularity of his large family, assembling a great band of sons and daughters. But when he was about to complete his mellow old age by paying the debt our common nature exacts and finally departing his life, God once more became for him a doer of marvellous works, by arranging that the first of his sons, Constantine, should be present to take over his Empire.

19–21. *Constantine joins his father*

19 (1) This son was with his imperial colleagues; and in their midst, as has been said, he conducted himself in the same way as that ancient prophet of God. Now that he had passed from childhood to youth he was granted highest honour among them. As such we knew him ourselves as he travelled through the land of Palestine in company with the senior Emperor, at whose right he stood, a noble sight for those with eyes to see, able already [26] to display an imperial quality of mind. (2) In handsome physique and bodily height no other could bear comparison with him; in physical strength he so exceeded his contemporaries as even to put them in fear; he took pride in moral qualities rather than physical superiority, ennobling his soul first and foremost with self-control, and thereafter distinguishing himself by the excellence of his rhetorical education, his instinctive shrewdness and his God-given wisdom.

20 (1) As a result of this those then in power observed with envy and fear that the young man was fine, sturdy and tall, full of good sense. They reckoned that his stay with them was not safe for them, and devised secret plots against him, though out of respect for his father they avoided inflicting public death upon him. (2) The young man was aware of this, and when once and again the plottings were with God-given insight detected by him, he sought safety in flight, in this also preserving his likeness to the great prophet Moses. In the whole affair God was working with him, intending that he should be present to succeed his father.

21 (1) Immediately he had escaped the schemes of the plotters he made all speed to get to his father, and he arrived after so long away at the very moment when his father's life was reaching its final crisis. When Constantius saw his son quite unexpectedly

standing there, he rose from his couch, flung his arms round him, and declared that his mind had been relieved of the only grief which had prevented him from setting life aside, which was the absence of his son; and [27] he sent up a prayer of thanks to God, saying that he now considered death better than deathlessness, and duly set his affairs in order. (2) He gave instructions to his sons and daughters, who gathered round him like a choir, and in the palace itself, on the imperial couch, he handed over his part of the Empire by natural succession to the senior in age among his sons, and expired.

22–4. *Constantine declared Emperor*

22 (1) The Empire however was not left ungoverned. Arrayed in his father's own purple robe Constantine emerged from his father's halls, showing to one and all that, as though revived, his father reigned through him. Then he led the cortège, and with his father's friends about him he formed the escort for his father. Enormous crowds of people and military guards, some before and some following behind, attended the Godbeloved in full state. All of them honoured the Thriceblessed with acclamations and laudations, and with unanimous consent praised the accession of the son as a new life for the dead; and immediately from the first word in their cries of acclamation they proclaimed the new Emperor Imperator and Venerable Augustus. (2) They lauded the deceased with their acclamations for the son, and they blessed the son as appointed to succeed such a father; all the provinces under his rule were full of happiness and unutterable joy, because not even for the briefest moment had they been deprived of orderly imperial rule. This was the end of a pious and devout life which God displayed to our generation in the case of the Emperor Constantius.

23 As to the others who used the methods of war to persecute the churches of God, I have decided that it is not proper to report the way their lives ended in the present account, nor to stain the record of good deeds by presenting their contrary. Experience of the events is sober warning enough to those whose own eyes and ears have known the story of what happened to each one.

24 In such a way then did God, the President of the whole world, of his own will select Constantine, sprung from such a

father, as universal ruler and governor, that no man could claim the precedence which he alone possessed, since the rest owed the rank they held to election by others.

25–41. 2. Deeds in War I: The Liberation of the West

25. 1. Constantine settles his father's domain

[28]   25 (1) Once he was established in imperial power, he first attended to the needs of his father's portion, supervising with loving care all the provinces which had previously been allotted to his father's government; if any barbarian tribes living beside the River Rhine and the Western Ocean dared to rebel, he subdued them all and turned their savagery to gentleness, while others he repulsed and chased off his territory like wild beasts, when he saw that they were incurably resistant to change to a gentle life.

25.2–26. Constantine observes the plight of Rome

(2) When these things were settled to his satisfaction, he turned his attention to the other parts of the inhabited world, and first crossed to the British nations which lie enclosed by the edge of Ocean; he brought them to terms, and then surveyed the other parts of the world, so that he might bring healing where help was needed.   26 When he then perceived that the whole earthly element was like a great body, and next became aware that the head of the whole, the imperial city of the Roman Empire, lay oppressed by bondage to a tyrant, he first gave opportunity for those who governed the other parts to rescue it, inasmuch as they were senior in years; but when none of these was able to give aid, and even those who did make the attempt had met a shameful end, he declared that his life was not worth living if he were to allow the imperial city to remain in such a plight, and began preparations to overthrow the tyranny.

27–32. Constantine seeks divine aid and receives the labarum

27 (1) Knowing well that he would need more powerful aid than an army can supply because of the mischievous magical

devices practised by the tyrant, he sought a god to aid him. He regarded the resources of soldiers and military numbers as secondary, for he thought that without the aid of a god [29] these could achieve nothing; and he said that what comes from a god's assistance is irresistible and invincible. (2) He therefore considered what kind of god he should adopt to aid him, and, while he thought, a clear impression came to him, that of the many who had in the past aspired to government, those who had attached their personal hopes to many gods, and had cultivated them with drink-offerings, sacrifices and dedications, had first been deceived by favourable predictions and oracles which promised welcome things, but then met an unwelcome end, nor did any god stand at their side to protect them from divinely directed disaster; only his own father had taken the opposite course to theirs by condemning their error, while he himself had throughout his life honoured the God who transcends the universe, and had found him a saviour and guardian of his Empire and a provider of everything good. (3) He judiciously considered these things for himself, and weighed well how those who had confided in a multitude of gods had run into multiple destruction, so that neither offspring nor shoot was left in them, no root, neither name nor memorial among mankind, whereas his father's God had bestowed on his father manifest and numerous tokens of his power. He also pondered carefully those who had already campaigned against the tyrant. They had assembled their forces with a multitude of gods and had come to a dismal end: one of them had retreated in disgrace without striking a blow, while the other had met a casual death by assassination in his own camp. He marshalled these arguments in his mind, and concluded that it was folly to go on with the vanity of the gods which do not exist, and to persist in error in the face of so much evidence, and he decided he should venerate his father's God alone.

28–32. *The vision of Constantine*

28 (1) This God he began to invoke in prayer, beseeching and imploring him to show him who he was, and to stretch out his right hand to assist him in his plans. As he made these prayers and earnest supplications there appeared to the Emperor a most

remarkable divine sign. If someone else had reported it, it would perhaps not be easy [30] to accept; but since the victorious Emperor himself told the story to the present writer a long while after, when I was privileged with his acquaintance and company, and confirmed it with oaths, who could hesitate to believe the account, especially when the time which followed provided evidence for the truth of what he said? (2) About the time of the midday sun, when day was just turning, he said he saw with his own eyes, up in the sky and resting over the sun, a cross-shaped trophy formed from light, and a text attached to it which said, 'By this conquer'. Amazement at the spectacle seized both him and the whole company of soldiers which was then accompanying him on a campaign he was conducting somewhere, and witnessed the miracle.

29 He was, he said, wondering to himself what the manifestation might mean; then, while he meditated, and thought long and hard, night overtook him. Thereupon, as he slept, the Christ of God appeared to him with the sign which had appeared in the sky, and urged him to make himself a copy of the sign which had appeared in the sky, and to use this as protection against the attacks of the enemy. **30** When day came he arose and recounted the mysterious communication to his friends. Then he summoned goldsmiths and jewellers, sat down among them, and explained the shape of the sign, and gave them instructions about copying it in gold and precious stones.

This was something which the Emperor himself once saw fit to let me also set eyes on, God vouchsafing even this. **31** (1) It was constructed to the following design. A tall pole plated with gold had a transverse bar forming the shape of a cross. Up at [31] the extreme top a wreath woven of precious stones and gold had been fastened. On it two letters, intimating by its first characters the name 'Christ', formed the monogram of the Saviour's title, *rho* being intersected in the middle by *chi*. These letters the Emperor also used to wear upon his helmet in later times. (2) From the transverse bar, which was bisected by the pole, hung suspended a cloth, an imperial tapestry covered with a pattern of precious stones fastened together, which glittered with shafts of light, and interwoven with much gold, producing an impression of indescribable beauty on those who saw it. This banner then, attached to the bar, was given equal dimensions of length and breadth. But the upright pole, which extended upwards a long way from its lower end, below the trophy of the cross and near the top of the tapestry delineated, carried the golden head-and-shoulders portrait of the Godbeloved Emperor, and likewise of his sons. (3) This saving sign was always used by the Emperor for protection against every opposing and hostile force, and he commanded replicas of it to lead all his armies.

32 (1) That was, however, somewhat later. At the time in question, stunned by the amazing vision, and determined to worship no other god than the one who had appeared, he summoned those expert in his words, and enquired who this god was, and what was the explanation of the vision which had appeared of the sign. (2) They said that the god was the Onlybegotten Son of the one and only God, and that the sign which appeared was a token of immortality, and was an abiding trophy of the victory over death, which he had once won when he was present on earth. They began to teach him the reasons for his coming, explaining to him in detail the story of his self-accommodation to human conditions. [32] (3) He listened attentively to these accounts too, while he marvelled at the divine manifestation which had been granted to his eyes; comparing the heavenly vision with the meaning of what was being said, he made up his mind, convinced that it was as God's own teaching that the knowledge of these things had come to him. He now decided personally to apply himself to the divinely inspired writings. Taking the priests of God as his advisers, he also deemed it right to honour the God who had appeared to him with all due rites. Thereafter, fortified by good hopes in him, he finally set about extinguishing the menacing flames of tyranny.

33–41. 2. The campaign against Maxentius

33–6. The crimes of Maxentius

33 (1) Indeed, the one who had thus previously seized the imperial city was busily engaged in abominable and sacrilegious activities, so that he left no outrage undone in his foul and filthy behaviour. He parted lawful wives from husbands, and after misusing them quite disgracefully returned them to their husbands. He did this not to obscure or insignificant persons, but

insolently to those who held highest positions in the Roman Senate. So he misused disgracefully innumerable free-born women, yet found no way to satisfy his unrestrained and insatiable appetite. (2) But when he turned his hand also to Christian women, he was no longer able to devise convenient means for his adulteries. They would sooner yield their life to him for execution than their body for immoral use. 34 One woman, the wife of one of the senators with the office of prefect, when she learnt that those who procured such things for the tyrant had arrived—she was a Christian—and knew that her own husband out of fear had ordered them to seize her and take her away, [33] having requested a little time to put on her customary attire, went into her room and once alone plunged a dagger into her breast. Dying at once, she left her body to the procurers, but by her actions, which spoke louder than any words, she shewed to all mankind both present and future that the only thing that is invincible and indestructible is the chastity acclaimed among Christians. Such then did she prove to be.

35 (1) Before the one who committed such outrages all men cowered, peoples and princes, high and low, and were worn down by savage tyranny. Even if they kept quiet and endured the harsh servitude there was still no respite from the tyrant's murderous cruelty. On one occasion on a slight pretext he gave the people over to slaughter by his escorting guards, and there were killed countless multitudes of the people of Rome right in the middle of the city, by the weapons and arms, not of Goths or barbarians, but of their own countrymen. (2) The number of senators whose murder was encompassed as a means to acquire each one's property it would not be possible to calculate, since thousands were put to death, sometimes on one fictitious charge, sometimes on another. 36 (1) At their peak the tyrant's crimes extended to witchcraft, as for magical purposes he split open pregnant women, sometimes searched the entrails of new-born babies, slaughtered lions, and composed secret spells to conjure demons and to ward off hostilities. By these means he hoped he would gain the victory. (2) Ruling by these dictatorial methods in Rome he imposed on his subjects unspeakable oppression, so that [34] he brought them finally to the utmost scarcity and want of necessary food, such as our generation never remembers happening in Rome at any other time.

37–8. *Constantine's victory*

37 (1) Constantine meanwhile was moved to pity by all these things, and began making every armed preparation against the tyranny. So taking as his patron God who is over all, and invoking his Christ as saviour and succour, and having set the victorious trophy, the truly salutary sign, at the head of his escorting soldiers and guards, he led them in full force, claiming for the Romans their ancestral liberties. (2) Maxentius put his confidence more in the devices of sorcery than in the loyalty of his subjects, and did not even dare to go beyond the gates of the city, but fortified every place and territory and city which was under his dominion with an immense number of soldiers and countless military units. But the Emperor who relied upon the support of God attacked the first, second, and third formations of the tyrant, overcame them all quite easily at the very first onslaught, and advanced to occupy most of the land of Italy.

38 (1) He was now very near to Rome itself. Then, so that he should not be forced because of the tyrant to fight against the people of Rome, God himself drew the tyrant out, as if with chains, far away from the gates; and those ancient words against the wicked, widely disbelieved as mere legend, though in sacred books believably recorded for believers, by his divine actions he proved to be true for every single eye which saw his marvels, believing and unbelieving alike. (2) Accordingly, just as once in the time of Moses and the devout Hebrew tribe 'Pharaoh's chariots and his force he cast into the sea, and picked rider-captains [35] he overwhelmed in the Red Sea' (Exodus 15: 4), in the very same way Maxentius and the armed men and guards about him 'sank to the bottom like a stone' (Exodus 15: 5), when, fleeing before the force which came from God with Constantine, he went to cross the river lying in his path. When he himself joined its banks with boats and bridged it perfectly well, he had built an engine of destruction for himself, intending thus to catch the friend of God. (3) But the latter had his God present at his right hand, while Maxentius constructed in his cowardice the secret engines of his own destruction. Of him it could also be said that 'he dug a hole and excavated it, and will fall into the pit he made. His labour will return on his head, and on his pate will his wickedness fall' (Psalm 7: 16–17). (4) Thus then by God's will

the mechanism in the link and the device concealed in it gave
way at a time which was not intended, the crossing parted, and
the boats sank at once to the bottom with all their men, the
coward himself first of all, and then the infantry and guards
about him, just as the divine oracles had previously proclaimed:
'They sank like lead in much water' (Exodus 15: 10). (5) So
even if not in words, yet surely in deeds, in the same way as those
who accompanied the great Servant Moses, these who won this
victory from God might be thought thus to have raised the same
hymn against the ancient wicked tyrant and said: 'Let us sing to
the Lord, for he is gloriously glorified; horse and rider he threw
into the sea; he became a succour and shelter for my salvation'
(Exodus 15: 1–2); and, 'Who is like you among the gods, Lord,
who is like you? Glorified among the saints, wonderful, gloriously doing miracles' (Exodus 15: 11).

39–41. 2. *Celebrations and monument to victory*

[36] **39** (1) These and other praises akin to them Constantine
expressed in deeds to the universal Captain, the timely Giver of
his victory, in the same way as the great Servant, and then rode in
triumph into the imperial city. (2) Immediately all the members
of the Senate and the other persons there of fame and distinction,
as if released from a cage, and all the people of Rome, gave him a
bright-eyed welcome with spontaneous acclamations and
unbounded joy. Men with their wives and children and countless
numbers of slaves with unrestrained cheers pronounced him
their redeemer, saviour and benefactor. (3) He, however, being
possessed of inward fear of God, was not inflated by their cries
nor over-exuberant at their praises, but was conscious of the help
of God; so he immediately offered up a prayer of thanksgiving to
the Giver of his victory. **40** (1) He announced to all people in
large lettering and inscriptions the sign of the Saviour, setting this
up in the middle of the imperial city as a great trophy of victory
over his enemies, explicitly inscribing this in indelible letters as
the salvific sign of the authority of Rome and the protection of the
whole empire. (2) He therefore immediately ordered a tall pole
to be erected in the shape of a cross in the hand of a statue made
to represent himself, and this text to be inscribed upon it word
for word in Latin: 'By this salutary sign, the true proof of valour, I
liberated your city, saved from the tyrant's yoke; moreover the

Senate and People of Rome I liberated and restored to their ancient splendour and brilliance.'

41 (1) The Godbeloved Emperor, proudly confessing in this way the victory-bringing cross, was entirely open in making the Son of God known to the Romans. (2) All the city's population together, including the Senate and all the people, as they recovered from bitter tyrannical repression, seemed to be enjoying beams of purer light and to be participating in rebirth to a fresh new life. All the nations which bordered on the Ocean where the sun sets, set free from the evils which formerly oppressed them, kept rejoicing in happy gatherings as they hymned the mighty Victor, the Godfearing, the general Benefactor, and with one single voice they all acknowledged the common good of mankind which by God's grace had dawned in Constantine.

41. 3–48. *Emperor of the West*

41. 3–43. *Generosity to Christians and others*

(3) An imperial letter was also published everywhere, granting the enjoyment of their goods to those whose property had been confiscated, and recalling to their own homes those who had suffered unjust exile. It also released from imprisonment and every kind of liability or threat at law those subjected to them by the tyrant's savagery.

42 (1) The Emperor personally called together the ministers of God, regarding them honourably and cherishing them with highest consideration, since he favoured those men by deed and word as consecrated to his God. Thus he had as his table-companions men whose appearance was modest as to style of dress, but by no means modest in the consideration he gave them, because he thought he should have regard not to the man as most people see him but to the God honoured in each. He took them with him also wherever he set out on campaign, [38] trusting that in this too the one they worshipped would be present at his right hand. (42. 2) Indeed he also supplied rich help from his own resources to the churches of God, enlarging and elevating the places of worship, while beautifying the grander ecclesiastical sacred buildings with many dedications.

43 (1) He made all sorts of distributions to the poor, and apart from them showed himself compassionate and beneficent to those outside who approached him. For some poor desperate wretches who publicly solicited alms he would provide not only money or necessary food, but decent clothing for the body. For those who were originally of higher birth but had run on hard times he made more generous provision, with imperial magnanimity providing munificent benefactions to such persons: to some he made grants of land, others he promoted to various offices. (2) Those unfortunate enough to be orphaned he cared for in the father's stead, and repaired the vulnerability of widowhood for women by personal concern, so far as to find them husbands from his acquaintance, and rich men for orphaned girls deprived of parents. He managed this by supplementing the dowry needed for the brides to bring to those who were receiving them in the bond of marriage. (3) Just as the sun rises and spreads the beams of its light over all, so also Constantine shone forth with the rising sun from the imperial palace, as though ascending with the heavenly luminary, and shed upon all who came before his face the sunbeams of his own generous goodness. It was not possible to come near him without receiving some benefit, nor would the good hopes of those who looked to him for support ever be disappointed.

44–5. *Constantine deals with Church disputes*

44 (1) Towards all people in general he was such a man. But to the Church of God he paid particular personal attention. When some were at variance with each other in various places, like a universal bishop appointed by God he convoked councils of the ministers of God. [39] (2) He did not disdain to be present and attend during their proceedings, and he participated in the subjects reviewed, by arbitration promoting the peace of God among all; and he took his seat among them as if he were one voice among many, dismissing his praetorians and soldiers and bodyguards of every kind, clad only in the fear of God and surrounded by the most loyal of his faithful companions. (3) Then such as he saw able to be prevailed upon by argument and adopting a calm and conciliatory attitude, he commended most warmly, showing how he favoured general unanimity, but

the obstinate he rejected. 45 (1) There were even some who spoke harshly against him, and he tolerated them without resentment, with a gentle voice bidding them to behave reasonably and not be contentious. Some of them respected his rebukes and desisted, while those who were past curing and could not be brought to a sound mind he left in the hands of God, being unwilling himself to devise anything whatever to any person's hurt.

(2) For this reason it came about that those in Africa reached such a pitch of dissension that crimes were committed, some evil demon apparently resenting the unstinted present prosperity and driving those men on to criminal actions, in order to provoke the Emperor's fury against them. (3) His envy however did not prosper: the Emperor treated what was being done as ridiculous and said he understood the provocation of the Evil One; the crimes were not done by sane men, but by those either out of their minds or goaded to frenzy by the evil demon; they ought to be pitied rather than punished; he was in no way harmed by their lunatic folly, except in so far as he felt pain for them out of extreme kindness of heart.

46–7. *Victories abroad, plots unmasked, and divine favours*

46 Thus then the Emperor, serving God the overseer of all with his every action, took untiring care of his churches. God repaid him by putting all the barbarian nations beneath his feet, so that always and everywhere he raised trophies over his foes, and [40] by proclaiming him Victor among them all, and making him a terror to foes and enemies, though he was not naturally such, but the gentlest, mildest, and kindest man there ever was.

47 (1) While he was thus engaged, the second of those who had retired from power was caught organizing an assassination plot, and met a shameful death. He was the first whose honorific inscriptions and statues and whatever else of the kind had been accorded him anywhere in the world to acknowledge his rank, were removed because of his profane impiety. (2) After him others of the same family were caught organizing secret conspiracies against him, God miraculously disclosing the plots of all these to his servant by supernatural signs. (3) Indeed, he often vouchsafed him manifestations of deity, when divine visions were

miraculously displayed to him and provided him with all sorts of foreknowledge of future events. It is not possible to describe in words those unspeakable marvels from God's grace which God himself saw fit to bestow on his servant. (4) By these he was safely hedged about to the end as he lived his life, pleased at the loyalty of his subjects, and pleased also that he saw all those under him passing their lives in contentment, and utterly over-joyed at the happiness of the churches of God.

48. *Decennalia celebrations*

48 Such was he until the tenth anniversary of his accession was reached. For that he celebrated popular festivals everywhere, and offered up prayers of thanksgiving to God the King of all like sacrifices without fire and smoke.

49–59. *The crimes of Licinius*

49–50. *Breaking faith*

While these things continued to give him joy, what he heard about the distress of the eastern provinces certainly did not. **49** (1) There also, so it was reported to him, a wild beast threatened the Church of God and the rest of the provincials. The Evil Demon, as if [41] to compete, was working for the opposite of what was being done by the Godbeloved, so that it seemed that the whole Roman domain had been left in two parts and resembled night and day, with darkness spread over those who lived in the east, and brilliant daylight illuminating the inhabitants of the other part. (2) Because innumerable benefits from God were supplied to the latter, the sight of what was happening was not tolerable to Envy, which hates good, nor to the tyrant who was oppressing the other part of the world. While his government was successful he had been privileged with a connection by marriage to so great an Emperor as Constantine, but he ceased to imitate the Godbeloved and was beginning to follow the evil of the policy of the ungodly: his own eyes had seen their lives brought to an end, yet he attempted to follow their policy rather than terms of friendship with his superior. **50** (1) He therefore waged constant war against his benefactor, and had no regard in his mind for laws of friendship, oaths, kinship, or treaties. That most generous man had provided him with tokens of true good will by granting him the privilege of sharing his paternal descent and the ancestral imperial blood by joining him in marriage to his sister, and allowed him the right to enjoy authority over those who live in the east, while he with the opposite in mind constructed all manner of schemes against his superior, adopting first one kind of plot and then another, in order to repay his benefactor with evil. (2) At first he did everything craftily and deceitfully under the guise of friendship, hoping that his crimes would remain undetected; but the other's God exposed to him the darkly devised plots. When he was detected in his first crimes, he went on to a second deception; sometimes he offered the hand of friendship, sometimes he confirmed treaties with oaths. Then he suddenly breaks the agreement, once more seeks terms through [42] an embassy, yet again tells shameful lies, and ends up declaring open war; in his mindless folly he finally began a campaign against the very God whom he knew the Emperor worshipped.

51–54.1. *Measures against Christians*

51 (1) First of all he began an investigation, for the time being discreet, of the servants of God under his control, who had never been involved in any offence against the state, hunting for some malicious pretext to accuse them. Not finding any fault, however, or any way of charging those men, he issued a law decreeing that the bishops should never communicate actively with each other at all, that none of them be permitted to visit his neighbour's church, and that no synods, councils, or discussions of common interest be held. (2) That was just a pretext for ill-treating us: one either had to defy the law and be liable to punishment, or submit to the decree and break the Church's canons. There was no other way of resolving important issues except by synodical meetings; divine canons prescribe that episcopal ordinations may only take place in this way.

The Godhater issued such decrees because he knew that he was acting contrary to the Godbeloved. While the one promoted peace and concord by assembling the priests of God in obedience to the divine law, the other schemed to disable what was good and tried to shatter harmonious concord. 52 Furthermore, because the friend of God saw fit to receive the servants of God within the imperial court, the Godhater chose the converse and drove all the godly men under him from the imperial court, and sent into exile the very persons around him who were most faithful and loyal, and those who for their former noble deeds had achieved honour and high rank in his service he ordered to become slaves to others, and to perform menial tasks. All their goods he grabbed as if they were no one's, and even threatened with death those who claimed the saving name.

This same person, who possessed a soul passionate and unbridled, and committed countless adulteries and unmentionable atrocities, could not believe in chastity as a virtue in human nature, taking himself as the wretched standard. 53 (1) Hence he made a second law, requiring that men and women should not be present together at prayers to God, nor women attend the sacred schools of virtue, nor bishops give instruction to women in devotional addresses, but that women should be appointed as teachers of women.

(2) When everybody treated these rules as ridiculous, he devised another scheme to destroy the churches. He said that the normal assemblies of lay people should be held outside the gates in open country, since the air outside the gates was much fresher than that in the urban places of worship.

54 (1) As not many were obedient in this either, he finally came into the open and ordered that members of the army in each city were to be demoted from ranks of command, if they would not sacrifice to the demons. The ranks of officers in every province were thus deprived of Godfearing men, and the creator of these laws was himself deprived of prayers, since he had robbed himself of holy men.

54. 2–55. General policy and character

(2) What need is there to recall secular affairs, and how he ordered that those suffering imprisonment should not be permitted charitable distributions of food, nor pity be shown to those in bonds perishing with hunger, nor any kindness be allowed at all, nor any kind deed be done by those drawn by natural feeling to compassion for their neighbours? In legislation

this man was shocking and quite wicked, absolutely extreme in harshness of character, inasmuch as the penalty was also imposed, that those exercising charity should suffer the same as those who received it, and that those who provided philanthropic ministrations should undergo the same as those already in misery.

55 (1) Such were the decrees of Licinius. What need is there to list his innovations about marriage, or his alterations about those passing from life, in which he criminally annulled long established good and wise laws of Rome and substituted foreign ones of harsh effect, inventing countless pretexts to harm his subjects? Thus he devised new land measurements, so that the smallest plot should be reckoned greater in size, out of greed for extra taxation. (2) Thus also he registered persons who were no longer on estates but long since dead and buried, making this a source of further profit to himself. [44] His miserliness had no limit, and his greed was insatiable. Hence when he had filled all his treasuries with an enormous quantity of gold and silver and money, he complained bitterly of poverty, his soul oppressed with Tantalus-like passion. (3) The barbaric punishments he invented for persons who had done no wrong, the confiscations of goods, the executions of noble and respected men, whose lawful spouses he handed over to filthy menials to be foully abused, and the number of married women and young virgins whom despite the physical deterioration of old age he himself raped, there is certainly no need to dwell upon, since his final extremes have made the early ones appear small and negligible.

56–9. Licinius ignores the fate of Galerius and Maximin

56 (1) His final madness was to take up arms against the churches, and attack whichever of the bishops he regarded as chiefly opposing him, and reckoned as hostile the friends of the Godbeloved and great Emperor. (2) Hence his anger with us became very intense, and he stopped thinking rationally and his mind became completely deranged. He did not let the memory of those who before him had persecuted the Christians enter his mind, nor of those whom he had himself been established to destroy and punish for the evil of their policies, nor of those he had himself witnessed, when he saw with his own eyes the first initiator of the evils, whatever his name was, smitten with divinely inflicted illness.

57 (1) When this person began the assault on the churches, and became the first to stain his soul with the blood of just and godfearing men, God-sent punishment pursued him, beginning with his very flesh and extending to his mind. (2) A general inflammation arose in the middle of his bodily private parts, then a deeply fistulous ulcer; these spread incurably to his intestines, from which an unspeakable number of maggots bred and a stench of death arose; his whole bodily bulk having been converted by excess eating into a vast quantity of fat, which then, as it decomposed, is said to have caused an intolerable and frightful spectacle to those nearby. (3) As he wrestled with so many evils he did indeed ultimately become aware of his crimes against the Church. He then made confession to God and stopped the persecution of Christians, by laws and imperial rescripts he encouraged the building of churches, and ordered them to do as they were accustomed and pray for him.

58 (1) Such was the penalty paid by the originator of the persecution. But though he was witness of these things and knew them well from experience, the person our story is describing forgot them all completely, neither reminding himself of the punishment imposed on the first nor the avenging judgement against the second. (2) The latter had even striven to outdo his predecessor in a sort of competition in evil, and prided himself on the invention of novel punishments to use on us. He was not satisfied with fire and iron and crucifixion, wild beasts and deep seas, but went on to invent a new form of torture in addition to all these, and decreed that the organs of sight should be mutilated. So great throngs not only of men, but of women and children, the sight of their right eyes and their ankle-joints maimed by iron and branding, were committed to forced labour in mines. (3) For these things he also was soon pursued by the judgement of God, when, drawing confidence from his hopes in demons, whom he supposed to be gods, and in his countless thousands of soldiers, he went to war. At that time, his hope of divine help gone, he took off the imperial dress, for which he was not fit, timidly and cowardly slipped into the crowd, and planned to survive by flight; and then, going into hiding in one estate and village after another, [46] he supposed he could escape detection dressed as a menial.

(4) But he did not also elude the great eye which supervises everything. Just when he finally hoped that his life was safe, he was struck down by a fiery shaft from God, his whole body consumed with the fire of divine vengeance, so that his whole physical appearance as he had been before became unrecognizable, dry skeletonized bones like mere phantoms being all that was left of him. **59** (1) As the chastisement of God became more severe his eyes began to protrude and fell from their sockets leaving him blind, as he was subjected by the most just verdict of God to the very punishment which he had been first to introduce for God's martyrs. Still living despite such great afflictions, he too in the end acknowledged the God of the Christians and renounced his own war against him; he too composed recantations just as his predecessor had done. In published laws and decrees he confessed his own error in the matter of those he had supposed to be gods, testifying that by personal experience he had come to recognize only the God of the Christians.

(2) Though Licinius had learnt all this from the facts, and not by hearsay from others, he still got involved in the same things, as though his mind had been blacked out by a moonless night.

BOOK II

1–22. Deeds in War II: The Victory over Licinius

1–2. Licinius attacks the Church

[47]   1 (1) We have described how this person began his headlong fall into the pit where God's enemies lie. The policies of those, whose destruction for irreligion he had seen with his own eyes, he now began to emulate to his own hurt, and he rekindled the persecution of Christians like the blaze of a long-extinguished flame, stirring up the fire of irreligion to fiercer heat than had those before him. (2) Like some wild beast, or a twisting snake coiling up on itself, breathing wrath and menace of war with God, he dared not yet, for fear of Constantine, openly assail the churches of God subject to him. Rather he disguised the poison of his evil, and planned insidiously and gradually his policies against the bishops, and began to remove the most distinguished of them by a conspiracy of the provincial rulers. Even the method of slaughter used against them was grotesque,

of a kind quite unheard of before. The actions taken at Amasea in Pontus surpassed all extremes of cruelty.

2 (1) Some of the churches now suffered complete demolition for the second time, following their previous devastation. Others were shut by the local officials, to prevent their regular members from congregating and rendering to God the authorized services. The one who gave this command did not believe that these services were performed for his benefit, his judgement being affected by a bad conscience, but [48] he was convinced that we were carrying them out and propitiating God for Constantine. (2) Certain persons, who were his fawning lackeys, convinced that what they did was congenial to his profanity, imposed death sentences on the most respectable church leaders, and they were taken away and punished without excuse like bloody murderers, though they had done no wrong. Some now faced a quite new form of execution: their bodies were gradually chopped with a sword into many pieces, and after this harsh torment, shocking beyond the tales of tragedy, they were thrown into the deep sea as food for fish. (3) Furthermore, as so recently before, once more there were banishments of Godfearing men, and again the countryside and again the desert received the worshippers of God. When these policies of the tyrant were also progressing in this way, he began finally to think about launching a general persecution; he had taken the decision and there would have been nothing to prevent his putting it into immediate effect, had not the Champion of his own people anticipated the event, and lit a great lantern in the darkness and blackest night, when he guided to these parts his servant Constantine.

3–5. *Preparations for a war of religion*

3 (1) Constantine regarded the report of the matters described as no longer tolerable. He arrived at a considered conclusion, and combining firm determination with his innate kindness he set out to the defence of the oppressed. He reckoned that it must be a pious and holy act by removing one man to rescue most of the human race: as long as he kept using great kindness, and was merciful towards one undeserving of sympathy, the latter was gaining nothing, since he did not turn away from the practice of evil at all, but merely increased his rage

against his subjects, while for those injured by him no further hope of rescue remained. (2) With these considerations in mind the Emperor unhesitatingly [49] determined to extend his hand to save those who had reached extremes of misery. He began the normal preparations of military equipment, his whole force of infantry and cavalry formations was assembled, and leading all were the tokens of his hope in God for success.

4 (1) If ever he needed prayers, he was sure that he needed them now. He therefore provided himself with priests of God, supposing that these must be in his company and be present as sure guardians of his soul. (2) Predictably, the one who sheltered behind tyranny, learning that victories over enemies had been won by Constantine only because God worked with him, and that the priests just mentioned were in his company and constantly present, and that the emblem of the saving passion went before him and his whole army, dismissed these things as ridiculous, mocking them and abusing them with insulting words. For his part he kept about him seers and diviners, Egyptian druggists and wizards, sacrificial interpreters and prophets of what he thought of as gods. Then having appeased those he thought of as gods with sacrifices, he enquired what the final outcome of his campaign was likely to be. (3) With long prophecies in elegant verses from all the oracles they unanimously promised him that he would soon be victorious over enemies and win the war. Augurs announced that favourable results were signalled by the flight of birds, and *haruspices* declared that the arrangement of entrails gave similar indications. (4) Borne up by such deceptive promises as these he advanced with great confidence to resist to the best of his ability the onslaughts of the Emperor.

5 (1) As he was about to begin the war, [50] he called together the select members of his bodyguard and valued friends to one of the places which they consider sacred. It was a grove, well-watered and thickly growing, and all sorts of images of those he thought were gods were erected in it, carved in stone. He lit candles to them, and made the usual sacrifices, and then is said to have delivered such a speech as this:

(2) 'Friends and comrades, these are our ancestral gods, whom we honour because we have received them for worship

from our earliest forefathers. The commander of those arrayed against us has broken faith with the ancestral code and adopted godless belief, mistakenly acknowledging some foreign god from somewhere or other, and he even shames his own army with this god's disgraceful emblem. Trusting in him, he advances, taking up arms not against us, but first and foremost against the very gods he has offended. (3) Now is the moment which will prove which one is mistaken in his belief: it will decide between the gods honoured by us and by the other party. Either it will declare us victors, and so quite rightly demonstrate that our gods are true saviours and helpers, or else, if this one god of Constantine's, whoever he is and wherever he sprang from, defeats our troops, who are very numerous and perhaps numerically superior, let no one hereafter be in doubt which god he ought to worship, since he should go over to the winner and offer to him the prizes of victory. (4) If the foreign god whom we now mock should prove superior, let nothing stop us from acknowledging and honouring him too, saying goodbye to these, whose candles we light in vain. But if ours prevail, which is not in doubt, after our victory here let us launch the war against the godless.'

(5) Such was his speech to those present. The author of the present work was given this information shortly afterwards by those who personally heard his words. Addressing them in these terms he gave orders to his armies to begin the action.

6–10. *Licinius' attack repelled by God's aid*

6 (1) While this was being done a manifestation beyond description is said to have been seen among those subject to the tyrant. Various battalions of the armed men serving Constantine [51] were apparently seen in broad daylight marching through the cities as if they had won the battle. They were seen even though no such thing was in reality happening; by a divine and superior power the vision which was seen revealed in advance what was going to happen.

(2) When the armies engaged, the first act of war came from the one who had broken the compact of friendship. It was after that that Constantine, calling upon the Saviour God who is over all, and making this the signal to the soldiers around him,

defeated the first attacking force. Then soon afterwards he got the better of a second engagement, and now achieved yet greater successes with the saving trophy leading his own contingent. 7 Where this was displayed, there ensued a rout of the enemy, and pursuit by the victors. The Emperor became aware of this, and wherever he saw a unit of his own army in difficulties, he would give orders for the saving trophy to give support there as a sort of victorious antidote. Victory would at once ensue, as courage and strength by some divine favour braced up the strugglers.

8 (1) For this reason he ordered some of his personal guards, distinguished for physical strength, personal courage, and pious habits, to attend solely to the service of the standard. These men numbered at least fifty; their sole task was to escort and guard with their weapons the standard, taking it in turns to carry it on their shoulders. (2) These things the Emperor himself recounted to the present writer in a moment of leisure long after the events, adding a noteworthy miracle to his account. 9 (1) He said that in the middle of one engagement in the war, when the army was suffering massive noise and confusion, the soldier carrying the standard on his shoulder [52] got into a panic and handed it over to another man, so that he could escape from the battle. As soon as the other had received it, and he withdrew from the protection of the standard, a flying javelin pierced his midriff and ended his life. (2) Meanwhile, as he lay there dead, paying the penalty for cowardice and disloyalty, to the one who lifted up the saving trophy it became a life-saver; frequently the bearer was saved when javelins were aimed at him, and the staff of the trophy caught the missiles. It was a quite extraordinary miracle, how the enemy javelins when they reached the narrow circumference of the pole would stick fast in it, while the bearer was saved from death, as if nothing could ever strike those who perform this service. (3) The story comes not from us, but once again from the Emperor himself, who in our hearing reported this too in addition to other matters.

(4) When by the power of God he had won the first battles, he finally began to move forward, advancing his troops in good order. 10 (1) Those in the forefront of the enemy position were unable to withstand their first onslaught; dropping their weapons from their hands they surrendered at the Emperor's feet. He

received them all unharmed, delighted that the men's lives were saved. (2) Others stood to their arms and tried to give battle. When the Emperor was sure that they would not accept the friendly terms which he had offered, he sent in his army. They immediately turned and fled in rout. Some of them were then caught and killed according to the law of war, while others fell upon each other and died by their own swords.

11–14. *Constantine's religious and merciful conduct*

11 (1) Their commander was appalled by these events. When he perceived that he was stripped bare of the support of his own people, that the vast numbers of his own picked forces and confederacy were lost to him, and that [53] his hope in those he thought were gods had in the event proved worthless, he thereupon suffered the ignominy of flight. He fled, and with a few men crossed to the interior of his territory and reached safety, the Godbeloved having instructed his men not to pursue hard, so that the fugitive might reach safety. He hoped that, when he realized what evil he had come to, he might yet forsake his manic impetuosity, and come by a change of heart to a better frame of mind. (2) He conceived this idea out of excessive kindness of heart, and was ready to forget the past and to grant pardon to the unworthy. The other, however, did not desist from depravity, but piling evil upon evil committed yet worse crimes; he even dared to meddle again in the malignant arts of the sorcerers. It could be said of him, as well as of the ancient tyrant, that 'God hardened his heart' (Exodus 9: 12).

12 (1) While he was getting involved in things of such a kind, and pushing himself down into the pits of perdition, the Emperor, seeing that he would need to organize another campaign, dedicated the respite to his Saviour: he pitched his tent outside the camp a long way off, and there he observed a chaste and pure rule of life, offering up his prayers to God, just like that ancient prophet of God, who, so the divine oracles assure us, pitched the tent outside the encampment. There attended him a few men, whose faith and religious loyalty had been proved in his company. His habitual practice, on every other occasion when he was setting out to engage in battle, had been this. He would move slowly for the sake of caution, and

aimed to do everything at God's behest. (2) While taking his time in making supplications to his God he would sooner or later receive a revelation from God, and then as if moved by a divine inspiration he would rush suddenly from the tent, immediately rouse his troops, and urge them not to delay, but to draw their swords at once. In a massed assault they would strike vigorously, until in a brief moment of time they won the victory, and set up monuments to their enemies' defeat.

[54] 13 (1) Such then had been for a long time past the practice of the Emperor in conducting military operations: he always kept his God before his mind and endeavoured to conform his actions to God's purposes, and he was anxious to avoid great slaughter. (2) He was therefore as careful to preserve the enemy's men as his own. So he also urged his men when they had won a battle to spare their prisoners, and as men themselves not to forget their common humanity. If sometimes he saw that the fury of the soldiers was out of control, he would restrain them with gold, ordering that the one who captured one of the enemy should be paid a fixed sum in gold. The Emperor's ingenuity invented this incentive to save human life, so that already countless numbers even of barbarians were saved because the Emperor purchased their lives with gold.

14 (1) Such deeds and countless others akin to them were favoured by the Emperor at other times. At this time too he set up the tent for himself in his accustomed manner before the battle, and devoted his time to prayer to God. He gave up all ease and comfortable life, subjecting himself to fasts and harsh treatment of the body, and in this way winning God's favour for his prayerful pleas that he might have God at his right hand to succour him, and might do those things which God was putting into his mind. (2) Thus he took unsleeping care for the general welfare, interceding for the safety not only of his own men, but also of his enemies.

15–18. *Renewed war and final victory*

15 When the one so recently a fugitive deceitfully pretended to sue again for terms of amicable settlement, he was even prepared to allow him this, offered on treaty conditions which were beneficial and conducive to the general good. This person

pretended to accede to the treaty with good will, confirming his good faith with oaths. Yet he again began to assemble a military force in secret, once more he initiated war and battle, called barbarian men to his support, and went about looking for other gods, since he had been deceived by the previous ones. He let no memory of what he had so recently said about the gods sink into his mind, nor was he willing to acknowledge the God who championed Constantine, but absurdly went to look for more and stranger gods. [55]   **16** (1) Then, knowing from experience what great divine and secret power lay in the saving trophy by which Constantine's army had learnt to conquer, he urged his officers not to come into conflict with it, nor even incautiously to let their eyes rest upon it: its power was terrible, it was inimical and hostile to him, and they ought therefore to avoid battle with it. After giving these instructions, he launched his offensive against the one who out of humanity was holding back and postponing the death sentence on himself.

(2) Thus one side advanced confident in a great throng of gods and with a large military force, protected by shapes of dead people in lifeless images. The other meanwhile, girt with the armour of true religion, set up against the multitude of his enemies the saving and life-giving sign as a scarer and repellent of evils. For a while he exercised restraint, and was at first sparing, so that, because of the treaty he had made, he should not be first to initiate hostilities.   **17** But when he saw his opponents persisting, already with sword in hand, the Emperor then became very angry and with one blow put to flight the whole opposing force, and won victories over enemies and demons alike.   **18** He then judged the Godhater himself, and afterwards his supporters, according to the law of war, and imposed on them appropriate punishment. With the tyrant those who conspired in the war against God paid the just penalty and died. Those who so recently had been buoyed up by hope from diviners found themselves in fact accepting the God of Constantine as he truly was, and confessing that they acknowledged him the true and only God.

19. *Victory celebrations*

19 (1) Now that the evil men were removed, the sunlight shone, purified at last of dictatorial tyranny. The whole Roman dominion was joined together, the peoples of the east being united with the other half, and the whole body was orderly disposed by the single universal government acting as its head, the authority of a single ruler reaching every part. Bright beams of the light of true religion brought shining days to those who before had 'sat in darkness and the shadow of death' (Luke 1: 79/Isaiah 9: 1). There was no more memory of former evils, as all people everywhere sang praise to the Victor and professed to know only his Saviour God. (2) And he, famous for every godly virtue, the Emperor Victor (he created this title personally for himself as his most appropriate surname because of the victory which God had given him over all his enemies and foes) took over the east. He brought under his control one Roman Empire united as of old, the first to proclaim to all the monarchy of God, and by monarchy himself directing the whole of life under Roman rule. (3) All fear was removed of those evils by which all had been formerly oppressed. The people in every province and city celebrated merry feasts, and those who before were sad looked on each other with smiling faces and bright eyes. Their choruses and hymns spoke first of all of God the universal King, as he truly is, and then with unrestrained voices celebrated the Conqueror and his most virtuous and Godbeloved sons the Caesars. There was a forgetting of ancient ills, oblivion of every wickedness, enjoyment of present good and expectation of more to come.

20–2. *Persecution and tyranny ended*

20 (1) There were now promulgated among us, as previously among those who occupy the other half of the civilized world, decrees full of the generosity of the Emperor. Laws with an odour of piety towards God offered all kinds of promises of good, giving what was useful and beneficial to the inhabitants of each regional prefecture, and announcing measures appropriate for the churches of God.

(2) In the first place these summoned home those who for refusing to worship idols had been sentenced to banishment and expulsion by the governors of provinces. Next they released from their obligations those who had on the same grounds been enrolled among the *curiales*, and [57] summoned those deprived

of property to resume it. (3) Those who at the time of trial distinguished themselves by their fortitude in the cause of God, and had been sent to hard labour in mines, or sentenced to live on islands, or compelled to servile labour on public works, enjoyed absolute release from them all. (4) The imperial indulgence recalled from disgrace those also who had been stripped of military ranks for their determined religious devotion, offering them the free choice either of recovering what was theirs and resuming the honours of their former station, or if they were attracted by civilian life, to receive permanent immunity from public duties. (5) Those sentenced to the disgrace and humiliation of servile work in clothing factories they released along with the rest.

21 Such provision did the Emperor's letter prescribe for those who had suffered these things. On the question of property belonging to the same persons the law made thorough provision. Where holy martyrs of God had finally laid down their life in their confession, he ordered that those related to them by kindred should receive their property, but if there were no relatives, the churches should receive the inheritance. Property also which had previously been transferred from the Treasury to third parties either by sale or by gift, and what still remained there, the deed of indulgence directed to be restored to its owners.

So much did the published indulgences provide for the churches. 22 On the people outside the churches and all the provinces the Emperor's magnanimity bestowed gifts of other kinds in great abundance. Because of them, all those in our part saw before their eyes those things which they had previously heard were being done in the other half of the Roman Empire, and had called the beneficiaries happy, praying that they too might some time enjoy the same; and now they also could deem themselves blessed, confessing that a strange new thing, such as the whole history of the world on which the sun shines had never told before, had illuminated the mortal race in so great an Emperor. Such were their feelings.

23–43. *Constantine's Confession of God: The Letter to the East*

23 (1) When everything had been brought under the Emperor by the power of the Saviour God, he made it plain to

everyone who it was that supplied good things to him, and he would insist that he considered him to be the cause of his triumphs, and not himself; and he proclaimed this very thing in both Latin and Greek in a document sent to every region. (2) The excellence of his statement may be observed by looking at the actual texts. There were two of these, one [58] sent to the churches of God, the other to the outsiders in each city. It would in my opinion be relevant to our present theme to include the latter, both so that the actual text of this decree may survive through our history and be preserved for those after us, and in order to confirm the truth of our narratives. (3) It is taken from the original copy of the imperial law in our possession, in which also the signature written with his own hand attests as with a seal the truth of the words.

24 (1) *Victor Constantinus Maximus Augustus to the provincials of Palestine.*

For a long time past it has been obvious to those of right and sound views about the Supreme, and to the absolute exclusion of all doubt, how great that difference is which distinguishes the correct observance of the most sacred cult of Christianity from those who are violently hostile and adopt a contemptuous attitude to it. (2) *But now there have been even more clearly demonstrated, by more manifest deeds and more brilliant achievements, both the absurdity of doubt and the magnitude of the power of the great God, when, to those who faithfully honour the most dread Law and are not so rash as to break any of its injunctions, the benefits have been unstinted, and strength for their undertakings has been superb, with an outcome to match their good hopes; while for those who adopted the irreligious policy the consequences have also corresponded with their designs.* (3) *For who is likely to meet with any good, if he neither acknowledges the God who is the source of good things, nor is willing to worship him properly? The facts themselves provide confirmation of what has been said.*

25 *Anyone who casts his mind back over the times which stretch from the beginning to the present, and lets his thoughts dwell upon all the events of history, would find that those who have first laid a just and good foundation for their affairs have also brought their undertakings to a good conclusion, and as it were from a pleasant root have also gathered a sweet fruit; whereas those who have engaged in criminal outrages, and either vented senseless fury against the Supreme, or [59] have not taken a holy* *attitude towards human kind, but criminally caused exiles, disgrace, confiscations, massacres and many such things, never repenting or turning their mind towards better things—they too have met condign retribution. These results are perhaps neither untoward nor unreasonable.*

26 (1) *Those who embark with righteous purpose on certain actions and continually keep in mind the fear of the Supreme, holding firm their faith in him, and do not allow the present terrors and perils to outweigh their future hopes, even though for a time they suffer hardships, yet, because they believed greater honours to be in store for them, they did not even take what had befallen them as hardship, but the fame they won was the more brilliant, the harder the severities they suffered.* (2) *Those, however, who either contemptuously ignored the right, or did not acknowledge the superior realm, who flagrantly subjected to outrages and savage punishments those who in faith pursued it, and who failed to recognize that they were themselves wretched for having punished them on such pretexts, or that those who had gone to such lengths to preserve religious respect for the Supreme were fortunate and blessed indeed, many of their armies have fallen, many have been turned to flight, and their whole military organization has collapsed in shame and defeat.*

27 (1) *From such policies arise harsh wars, from such policies, destructive spoliation. Hence arise shortages of necessary supplies, and a host of impending disasters. Hence the champions of such great wickedness have either met their final doom in the calamity of deadly destruction, or in spinning out a life of shame have found it harder than death. They have received punishments to fit their crimes.* (2) *For the extent of the disasters each one has suffered shows how far he was swept on by folly in his idea that he could even defeat the divine Law; so that not only do they suffer hardship in this life, but also have the prospect of more horrible terrors in the places of torment below the earth.*

[60] 28 (1) *When such and so grave a wickedness oppresses humanity, and when the state is in danger of utter destruction from a sort of pestilential disease and needs much life-saving medical care, what relief does the Divinity envisage, what escape from horrors? And that is surely to be considered divine, which alone really exists, and holds power continuously through all time; it is surely not mere bombast to use solemn words to acknowledge the benefit received from the Supreme.* (2) *He examined my service and approved it as fit for his own purposes; and I, beginning from that sea beside the Britons and the parts where it is appointed by a superior constraint that the sun should set, have repelled and scattered the horrors that held everything in subjection, so that on the*

one hand the human race, taught by my obedient service, might restore the religion of the most dread Law, while at the same time the most blessed faith might grow under the guidance of the Supreme. 29 (1) *I could never fail to acknowledge the gratitude I owe, believing that this is the best of tasks, this a gift bestowed on me. Now my advance reaches the eastern lands, which, oppressed with graver calamities, cried out for the cure from us to be greater also. Indeed my whole soul and whatever breath I draw, and whatever goes on in the depths of the mind, that, I am firmly convinced, is owed by us wholly to the greatest God.*

(2) *I am quite well aware that no human favour will be required by those who have rightly pursued the heavenly hope and have made it their firm and settled choice in the divine realm; the honours they enjoy are so much the greater, the more they have freed themselves from liability to earthly losses and fears.* [61] (3) *I deem it proper nevertheless that we should remove as far away as possible the constraints which have been from time to time imposed upon them, and the undeserved tortures, from those in no way guilty or culpable. It would be quite absurd if, under those who were anxious to persecute these men on account of their cult of the Deity the steadfastness and firmness of their soul should be sufficiently discerned, whereas under the servant of God their glory should not be elevated to a higher and more blessed level.*

30 (1) *Therefore all such as exchanged their native land for exile because they did not despise that faith in the Deity to which they had consecrated themselves with their whole souls, being subjected to harsh sentences of judges, at whatsoever time it happened to each, or such as were included in curial registers, not having been reckoned in their number previously, let them be restored to their ancestral place and customary contentment, and give thanks to God the liberator of all.* (2) *Or such as were deprived of their goods and, afflicted by the loss of all their existing wealth, have hitherto been living in straitened circumstances, let them be given back their old dwellings and birthright and properties, and enjoy to the full the beneficence of the Supreme.*

31 (1) *Furthermore, as to those held against their will in islands, we order that they enjoy the benefit of this provision, so that, whereas they are confined by the rigours of mountains and surrounding seas, they may be set free from the ugly and desolate wilderness and take themselves back to their loved ones, fulfilling their eager desire;* (2) *they have lived for a long time a life of poverty in unremitting squalor, and* [62] *may seize the opportunity to return, and be free from anxieties in future. It would be quite absurd if under us, who claim and believe ourselves to be God's*

servants, it were to be so much as reported that they live in fear, let alone that it should be believed, when it is our practice to correct even the wrongs done by others.

32 (1) *Those also who were condemned either to labour under harsh conditions in mines, or to perform menial tasks at public works, let them exchange incessant toils for sweet leisure, and now live an easier life of freedom, undoing the infinite hardships of their labours in gentle relaxation.* (2) *But if any have been deprived of their civil liberty and suffered public dishonour, then let them, with the gladness appropriate considering they have been parted by a long exile, take up again their former rank and make haste back to their native lands.*

33 *Those furthermore who were once appointed to military ranks, and were removed from them on the harsh and unjustified ground that they confessed to acknowledging the Supreme, and prized him above the rank they held; let them have the choice either, if they like military service, of remaining in the status they had before, or else with honourable discharge of enjoying retirement. For it would be right and proper that one who has exhibited such valour and resolution in the face of pressing perils should enjoy retirement, if he so wishes, and rank in accordance with his choice.*

34 (1) *Those moreover who were forcibly deprived of their noble rank and subjected to a judicial sentence of such a kind that they were sent to women's quarters or linen factories and endured unwonted and shameful toil, or were reckoned Treasury slaves, their former gentle birth notwithstanding, these* [63] *are to rejoice in the honours they previously enjoyed and in the benefits of liberty; they are to claim their ancestral rank and to live henceforth in complete happiness.* (2) *He who has exchanged liberty for slavery through what was surely an ungodly and inhuman madness, and has often deplored his unwonted servile tasks, and quite suddenly found himself a bondservant instead of a free man; let him obtain his former freedom in accordance with our decree, and let him return to his forebears and pursue occupations befitting a free man, erasing from his memory the unsuitable menial tasks at which he previously toiled.*

35 (1) *Property must not be overlooked; individuals were deprived of it on various pretexts. But any who while undergoing the highest and divine conflict of martyrdom with fearless and courageous resolution were deprived of their property, and any who standing firm in confession prepared eternal hope for themselves, and those who were compelled to go abroad because they did not despise the faith and yield to their persecutors, and thus were also deprived of their goods, and any who without even being sentenced to death suffered deprivation of their goods, we decree that* *their estates should attach to their next of kin.* (2) *And since the laws expressly refer to the closest among those related, it is easy to determine to whom the inheritances belong; and also because those should rightfully inherit who would have been the nearest kin if the deceased had met a natural death.* 36 *But if no relative of any of the aforesaid should remain to become the rightful heir, whether of the martyrs, I mean, or of the confessors, or indeed of those who lived abroad after moving for such a reason, let the Church in every particular place be appointed to receive the inheritance. It will surely be no injustice to those who went away, if she for whom they underwent all their labours enjoys this inheritance.* [64] *It is moreover necessary to add this also, that if any of the aforesaid made any bequest of their property to persons of their choice, it is reasonable that their ownership remain valid.*

37 (1) *To the end that no ambiguity appear in this decree, and that all may be readily informed about what is lawful, be it known to all, that if any be possessed of any land or house or orchard or anything else belonging to the aforementioned, it is honourable and in their best interest for them to confess them and make restitution with all speed.* (2) *For even though in a great many cases certain persons should appear to have profited considerably from their unlawful possession, and we judge their excuse for these things inadmissible, yet nevertheless, if they themselves acknowledge the extent and the source of what they have amassed, they are to petition us for pardon for this offence, so that their possessive greed may be cured by such correction, and at the same time the supreme God, allowing this as a sort of reformation, may be indulgent to the sin committed.* 38 *It may be that the existing owners (if it is appropriate or possible to apply that term in their case) of such property will put forward as a defence that it was not possible to refuse in the circumstances, when the aspect of all the atrocities was so multiform, when there were people being savagely exiled, mercilessly ruined, indiscriminately expelled, when there were frequent confiscations from innocent persons, insatiable persecutions, sales of property. But if any insist on such arguments and persist in their possessive designs, they will discover that this kind of thing will not be without penalty to themselves, especially when what issues from us in this respect is a service to the supreme God. Such things as in the past a deadly necessity compelled one to accept, it is now dangerous to keep. Besides, it is necessary in every way to use arguments and examples to minimize acts of acquisitiveness.*

[65] 39 *Not even the Treasury, should it be in possession of any of the aforementioned, shall be permitted to confirm its title; but as not daring*

even to answer back the holy churches, from those things which for a time it has unlawfully possessed it shall lawfully withdraw, . . . to the churches. And everything which may appear rightly to belong to the churches, whether the property be houses or any fields and orchards or anything else whatsoever, with no diminution of property right, but completely unimpaired, shall by this our decree be restored.

40 *Furthermore the places themselves which are honoured by the bodies of the martyrs and stand as monuments to their glorious decease, who could doubt that they belong to the churches, or would not so decree? Since no gift could be better nor other labour more agreeable and rich in advantage, than at the instigation of the divine will to take active steps about such things, and that what was on evil pretexts of lawless and foul men taken away, should be rightfully restored to the holy churches and conserved.*

41 *But since complete provision would forbid us to pass over in silence such persons as by lawful purchase acquired anything from the Treasury, or received it by public grant, if they also vainly extend their possessive desires to such things, be it known to such persons, however much they have endeavoured by their rash purchase to alienate our good will towards them, nevertheless they shall enjoy that good will in whatever way is possible and fitting. Let that be sufficient provision for such things.*

42 *But since the most obvious and manifest demonstrations have revealed that, by the goodness of Almighty God and by the frequent acts both of encouragement and of assistance which he has seen fit to perform on my behalf, the harsh regime which formerly gripped all humanity has been driven away from every place under the sun,* [66] *let each and every one of you observe with close attention what that authority is which has been established, and what grace: it has eliminated and destroyed the seed, so to speak, of the most evil and wicked men, and spreads unstintingly to all lands the newly recovered happiness of good men; it gives back again full authority for the divine Law itself to receive with all reverence the accustomed cult, and for those who have consecrated themselves to this to perform the due rites. If they have as it were looked up out of deepest darkness and take clear cognizance of what is happening, they will henceforward manifest towards him appropriate religious reverence and corresponding worship.*

    To be published in our oriental regions.

43 Such were the dispositions made in the first communication of the Emperor to us. The things referred to in the law were immediately implemented. There was a complete reversal of policy from the violence done shortly before by the tyrants' cruelty, and those for whom they were decreed enjoyed imperial bounties.

44–61. 1. *Constantine Promotes the Church and Restrains Paganism*

44–45. 1. *General measures*

44 From this the Emperor went on to take practical steps. He first sent governors to the peoples in their various provinces, for the most part men consecrated to the saving faith; those who preferred paganism he forbade to sacrifice. The same applied also to the ranks above provincial government, the highest of all, who held office as prefects. If they were Christians, he permitted them to make public use of the name; if otherwise disposed, he instructed them not to worship idols.   45 (1) Next, two laws were simultaneously issued. One restricted the pollutions of idolatry which had for a long time been practised in every city and country district, so that no one should presume to set up cult-objects, or practise divination or other occult arts, or even to sacrifice at all. The other dealt with erecting buildings as places of worship and extending in breadth and length the churches of God, as if almost everybody would in future [67] belong to God, once the obstacle of polytheistic madness had been removed.

45. 2–46. *Church buildings*

(2) That the Emperor both held such views and was writing then to the authorities in each place was indicated by his sacred decree about God, and the law provided that no financial cost should be spared, but the expenses actually furnished from the imperial funds. Those in charge of the churches in each place were also written to in terms similar to those in which he deigned to write to us, sending this first letter to the present writer personally:

46 (1) *Victor Constantinus Maximus Augustus to Eusebius.*
Until the present time, well-beloved brother, while the impious policy and tyranny persecuted the servants of the Saviour God, I believe, and have through careful observation become convinced, that all the church

buildings have either become delapidated through neglect, or through fear of the prevailing iniquity have fallen short of their proper dignity. (2) *But now, with liberty restored and that dragon driven out of the public administration through the providence of the supreme God and by our service, I reckon that the divine power has been made clear to all, and that those who through fear or want of faith have fallen into sins, and have come to recognize That which really Is, will come to the true and right ordering of life.* (3) *Where therefore you yourself are in charge of churches, or know other bishops and presbyters or deacons to be locally in charge of them, remind them to attend to the church buildings, whether by restoring or enlarging the existing ones, or where necessary building new. You yourself and the others through you shall ask for the necessary* [68] *supplies from the governors and the office of the Prefect, for these have been directed to cooperate wholeheartedly with what your holiness proposes.*

God preserve you, dear brother.

46 (4) These then were the terms of letters to those in charge of the churches in every province. The provincial governors were ordered to act accordingly, and the legislation was implemented with great speed.

47–61. 1. *Letter against polytheistic worship*

47 (1) Carrying yet further his piety towards God, the Emperor sent to the provincials in every national area an instructive decree refuting the idolatrous error of his predecessors in power; he urged that it was more rational for his subjects to acknowledge the God over all and expressly to adopt his Christ as Saviour. (2) This document too, which bears his autograph but is translated from the Latin, is highly relevant to quote in our present study, so that we may feel that we are listening to the voice of the Emperor himself as he makes this proclamation for all mankind to hear:

48 (1) *Victor Constantinus Maximus Augustus to the provincials of the east.*

Everything embraced by the sovereign laws of nature provides everybody with sufficient evidence of the providence and thoughtfulness of the divine ordering; nor is there any doubt among those whose intellect approaches that topic by a correct scientific method, that accurate apprehension by a healthy mind and by sight itself rises in a single impulse of true virtue to the knowledge of God. Hence no wise man would ever be disturbed at seeing the majority swept along by contrary attitudes. (2) *For the merit of virtue would lie unobserved, if vice had not on the other side exposed the life of perverse unreason. That is why a crown is promised for virtue, and judgement is exercised by the most high God. For my part I shall as far as I can try to acknowledge openly to you all what my hopes are.*

[69] **49** (1) *I held the previous Emperors as exceedingly harsh because of their savage ways, and only my father engaged in gentle deeds, with wonderful reverence calling upon the Saviour God in all his actions.* (2) *All the rest were mentally sick and embraced savagery rather than gentleness; they cultivated it unremittingly, perverting the truth for their own advantage. Their terrible wickedness reached such intensity that when all divine and human affairs were alike at peace, civil wars were rekindled by them.*

50 *Apollo at the time declared, it was said—from some cavern or dark recess and not from heaven—that the righteous on earth prevented him from speaking truly, and that that was why he was composing false oracles from the tripods. That was what his priesthood, letting their long hair droop down and driven on by madness, deplored as the evil among mankind. But let us see to what ultimate disaster this led.* **51** (1) *I invoke you now, Most High God! I heard then, when I was still just a boy, how he who at that time held first rank among the Roman Emperors, fearful coward that he was, his mind deceived by error, anxiously enquired of his guards who the 'righteous on earth' might be. One of the sacrificial officers of his court answered, 'Christians, I suppose.'* (2) *He swallowed the answer greedily like a drop of honey, and the swords designed to punish crimes he raised against unimpeachable holiness. Without delay he wrote, as it were with bloody dagger-blades, the edicts of carnage, and urged the magistrates to apply their native ingenuity to the invention of unprecedented tortures.*

52 *Then, then indeed, could be seen the power with which that sacred practice of godly piety every day withstood extraordinary abuses inflicted with sustained cruelty. Chastity, which no enemy had ever injured, became a toy for the drunken violence of frenzied fellow-citizens. What fire is there, what ordeal, what form of torture, which was not* [70] *applied to all persons of all ages without distinction? Then surely did the earth shed tears, and the order that sustains the universe wept aloud at being stained with the blood, and the day itself hid its face for grief at the sight.*

53 *But there is more. Those events are now the boast of the barbarians* *who at that time welcomed the refugees from among us, and kept them in humane custody, for they provided them not only with safety but with the opportunity to practise their religion in security. And now the Roman race bears this indelible stain, left on its name by the Christians who were driven at that time from the Roman world and took refuge with barbarians.*

54 *But why should I dwell further on those sorrows and the general world-wide grief? Gone now are the very authors of the abomination, devoted to everlasting punishment in the pits of Acheron, after a shameful death; they became embroiled in fratricidal wars and have left themselves neither name nor progeny. This would not have happened to them, had not that wicked prophecy of the Pythian oracles achieved fraudulent currency.*

55 (1) *Now I call upon you, the supreme God. Be merciful and gracious to your Orientals, and to all your provincials who have been crushed by protracted calamity, and proffer healing through me your servant. This petition is not unreasonable, Master of the Universe, Holy God. For by your guidance I have undertaken deeds of salvation and achieved them; making your seal my protection everywhere, I have led a conquering army. Whatever the public need may anywhere require, following the same tokens of your merit I advance against the enemy.* (2) *Because of this I have consecrated to you my own soul, purely blended with love and fear; for I genuinely love your name, and dread your power, which you have revealed by many tokens, confirming the strength of my faith. I strive therefore, putting my own shoulders to the task, to restore again your most holy house, which those polluted and vicious men have mutilated with wicked destruction.*

56 (1) *For the general good of the world and of all mankind I desire that your people be at peace and stay free from strife. Let those in error, as well as the believers, gladly receive the benefit of peace and quiet. For this sweetness of fellowship* [71] *will be effective for correcting them and bringing them to the right way. May none molest another; may each retain what his soul desires, and practise it.* (2) *But persons of good sense ought to be convinced that those alone will live a holy and pure life, whom you call to rely on your holy laws. Those who hold themselves back, let them keep if they wish their sanctuaries of falsehood. To us belongs the shining house of your truth, which you have given in accordance with nature. This we pray also for them, that by means of the general concord they too may enjoy what they desire.*

57 *Our policy is neither new nor revolutionary, but ever since the*

structure of the universe was, as we believe, solidly made, you have required this with the worship due to you; but the human race fell, led astray by various errors. But you through your Son, lest the evil press down still more, held up a pure light and put all men in mind of yourself. 58 (1) *Your deeds attest these things. Your power makes us innocent and faithful. The sun and moon have their lawful path; nor is it without order that the stars make their circuit of the cosmic wheel. The changes of the seasons revolve with regularity, the solid base of earth has been constituted by your word, the wind stirs in accordance with the decree imposed upon it, and the surge of welling waters issues abundantly in ceaseless flow; the sea is contained within fixed limits, and the whole extent of land and ocean is furnished with marvellous and serviceable resources.* (2) *If it were not by the decree of your will that this was done, so much diversity and the great division of power would have disabled all life and every thing; for those engaged in mutual conflict would have very severely injured mankind, something which they do, even if unseen.*

59 *But to you be utmost thanks, Lord of the Universe, supreme God! For the more humanity is perceived as diverse in its goals, the more* [72] *the doctrines of the divine word are confirmed for those who think aright and who are concerned with genuine merit. Nevertheless if any prevents himself from being cured, let him not blame it on someone else; for the healing power of medicines is set out, spread openly to all. Only let no one harm that which the facts guarantee to be undefiled. Let mankind, all of us, take advantage of the common heritage of good bequeathed us, that is the blessing of peace, but keeping our conscience clear of everything contrary.* 60 (1) *However let no one use what he has received by inner conviction as a means to harm his neighbour. What each has seen and understood, he must use, if possible, to help the other; but if that is impossible, the matter should be dropped. It is one thing to take on willingly the contest for immortality, quite another to enforce it with sanctions.* (2) *I have said these things and explained them at greater length than the purpose of my clemency requires, because I did not wish to conceal my belief in the truth; especially since (so I hear) some persons are saying that the customs of the temples and the agency of darkness have been removed altogether. I would indeed have recommended that to all mankind, were it not that the violent rebelliousness of injurious error is so obstinately fixed in the minds of some, to the detriment of the common weal.*

61 (1) Such words the Emperor, like a loud-voiced herald of God, addressed to all those in the provinces through a personal

letter, protecting his subjects from demonic error, while encouraging the pursuit of true godliness.

61. 2–73. *The Disputes in Egypt*

61. 2–62. *The two disputes*

(2) While he was cheered by these things, word was brought to him of no small disturbance afflicting the churches. He was shocked to hear of this, and tried to think of a cure for the evil. (3) The trouble was this. The people of God were in a splendid state, flourishing by imperial benefactions. There was no external terror to disturb, so newly did serene and deepest peace by God's grace protect the Church on every side. Envy therefore laid its snare against our prosperity, creeping inside and openly flaunting itself in the very assemblies of the saints. (4) Indeed it set even the bishops against each other, imparting divisive quarrels with divine doctrines as the excuse. Then it broke out like a great fire from a little spark. [73] It began from the summit of the Alexandrian church and spread through all Egypt and Libya and the further Thebaid. (5) It had already reached the other provinces and cities, so that it was possible to see not only the leaders of the churches sparring with words, but the multitudes also fragmented, some inclining to one side, some to the other. The spectacle of these events reached such absurdity that sacred points of divine doctrine were now subjected to disgraceful mockery publicly in the theatres of the unbelievers. 62 While those in Alexandria itself were sparring like juveniles over the highest matters, those around Egypt and the upper Thebaid were at variance on a previous long-standing issue, such that the churches were everywhere divided. The whole of Libya was labouring under these things like a diseased body, and with it the other parts, the provinces beyond, were catching the disease. Those in Alexandria sent delegations to the bishops of each province, while those who took the other side shared the same contentious spirit.

63–73. *Constantine's letter to Alexander and Arius*

63 When he heard about this the Emperor was cut to the quick, and took the matter as a personal calamity. He dispatched

one of the godly men of his court, one whom he knew well to be of proven moderation of life and faithful virtue, a man very famous for his religious confessions in earlier times, as a mediator to reconcile the disputants in Alexandria. By him he sent to those responsible for the quarrel a most apposite letter, which, as itself providing evidence of the Emperor's concern for the people of God, could well be presented in our account of him. It reads as follows:

[74] . **64** *Victor Constantinus Maximus Augustus to Alexander and Arius.*

I call God himself to witness, as I should, the helper in my undertakings and Saviour of the Universe, that a twofold purpose impelled me to undertake the duty which I have performed. **65** (1) *My first concern was that the attitude towards the Divinity of all the provinces should be united in one consistent view, and my second that I might restore and heal the body of the republic which lay severely wounded.* (2) *In making provision for these objects, I began to think out the former with the hidden eye of reason, and I tried to rectify the latter by the power of the military arm. I knew that if I were to establish a general concord among the servants of God in accordance with my prayers, the course of public affairs would also enjoy the change consonant with the pious desires of all.*

66 *Indeed, when an intolerable madness had seized the whole of Africa because of those who had dared with ill-considered frivolity to split the worship of the population into various factions, and when I personally desired to put right this disease, the only cure sufficient for the affair that I could think of was that, after I had destroyed the common enemy of the whole world, who had set his own unlawful will against your holy synods, I might send some of you to help towards the reconciliation of those at variance with each other.* **67** *For since the power of the light and the law of holy religion by the beneficence of the Supreme were reared, one might say, in oriental nurseries, and lit up the whole world at once with a sacred lantern, it was reasonable that, believing that you would be a kind of pioneers of the salvation of the nations, I should try to seek you both by the intention of my heart and by actual sight. So together with the great victory and the veritable triumph over my enemies, I chose to make the subject of my first enquiry that which* [75] *I considered to be of first and greatest importance to me.*

68 (1) *But (O best, divine Providence!) what a deadly wound my* *ears suffered, or rather my very heart, for the information that the division originating among you was much graver than those I had left behind there, so that your regions, from which I had hoped medicine would be supplied to others, were now in greater need of healing.* (2) *As I considered the origin and occasion for these things, the cause was exposed as extremely trivial and quite unworthy of so much controversy. Being driven therefore to the need for this letter, and addressing myself to that discretion which you have in common, and calling first on the divine Providence to support my action, I offer my modest services as a peaceful arbitrator between you in your dispute.* (3) *With the help of the Supreme, even were the cause of the dispute of greater moment, I would still be able without difficulty to entrust the discussion to the holy intentions of my hearers, and so to shift each of them towards a more helpful position. The same approach, when the issue constituting a general obstacle is small and utterly trivial, must surely guarantee me a more manageable and far easier settlement of the affair.*

69 (1) *I understand then that the first stages of the present dispute were as follows. When you, Alexander, demanded of the presbyters what view each of them took about a certain passage from what is written in the Law—or rather about some futile point of dispute—you, Arius, thoughtlessly replied with that opinion which either ought not to have been even conceived in the first place, or once conceived ought to have been consigned to silence. The dispute having thus arisen between you, fellowship was repudiated, and the most holy people were divided in two and forsook the concord of the common body.* (2) *Accordingly, let each of you extend pardon equally, and* [76] *accept what your fellow-servant in justice urges upon you. It is this. It was neither right to ask about such things in the first place, nor to answer when asked.*

With disputes of this kind, which no necessity of any law demands, but are promoted by argument in unprofitable idleness, even if they take place as some sort of gymnastic exercise, still it is our duty to shut them up inside the mind and not casually produce them in public synods, nor incautiously commit them to the hearing of the laity. (3) *For how great is any individual that he can either correctly discern or adequately explain the meaning of matters so great and so exceedingly difficult? And even supposing someone manages this easily, how many of the people is he likely to convince? Or who could sustain precise statements in such disputes without risk of dangerous mistakes? We must therefore avoid being talkative in such matters; otherwise, whether because by our natural limitations we cannot explain properly what is propounded, or because with their slower intellect the audience is incapable of reaching a correct understanding of what is said, one way or the other the people may be brought inevitably to either blasphemy or schism.*

70 *Both unguarded question therefore and incautious answer require a mutual exchange of pardon equal on both sides. For the impulse of your quarrel did not arise over the chief point of the precepts in the Law, nor are you faced with the intrusion of a new doctrine concerning the worship of God, but you have one and the same mind, so that you should be able to come together in compact of fellowship.* **71** **(1)** *That so many of God's people, who ought to be subject to the direction of your minds, are at variance because you are quarrelling with each other about small and quite minute points, [77] is deemed to be neither fitting nor in any way legitimate.*

(2) *But so that I may bring to the attention of your intelligences a slight comparison, you surely know how even the philosophers themselves all agree in one set of principles, and often when they disagree in some part of their statements, although they are separated by their learned skill, yet they agree together again in unity when it comes to basic principle. If this is so, surely it is far more right that we, who are the appointed servants of the great God should, in a religious commitment of this kind, be of one mind with each other?* **(3)** *Let us reconsider what was said with more thought and greater understanding, to see whether it is right that, through a few futile verbal quarrels between you, brothers are set against brothers and the honourable synod divided in ungodly variance through us, when we quarrel with each other over such small and utterly unimportant matters. These things are vulgar and more befitting childish follies than suitable to the intelligence of priests and informed men.* **(4)** *Let us consciously avoid all devilish temptations.*

Our great God, the Saviour of all, has extended the light to all alike; under his providence make it possible for me, the worshipper of the Supreme, to bring this effort to a conclusion, so that I may lead back his congregations themselves by my own address and ministration and earnest admonition to synodical fellowship. **(5)** *For since, as I said, there is one faith in us and one understanding of the belief we hold, and since the commandment of the Law in its every part throughout confines its totality to a single disposition of the heart, this which has raised a slight quarrel between you, since it does not refer to the meaning of the Law as a whole, must surely not import any division or faction among you.*

(6) *I do not say these things as though I were forcing you to come to agreement on every aspect of this very silly question, whatever it actually* *is. It is possible for the honour of the synod to be preserved intact by you, and one and the same fellowship to be kept generally, even though on detail some serious disagreement may arise between you over a tiny matter, since* [78] *we neither all agree among ourselves in wanting the same thing, nor does one single being and mind operate in us.* (7) *On the subject of divine Providence therefore let there be one faith among you, one understanding, one agreement about the Supreme; the precise details about these minimal disputes among yourselves, even if you cannot bring yourselves to a single point of view, ought to remain in the mind, guarded in the hidden recesses of thought.*

(8) *But let the excellence of general love, and faith in the truth, and reverence for God and the religion of the Law, remain undisturbed among you. Return to mutual love and kindness, restore to the whole people the proper bonds of affection, and you yourselves, as having purified your own souls, recognize each other again. Often love becomes sweeter when it returns again in reconciliation after hostility is set aside.*

72 (1) *Give me back therefore peaceful days and undisturbed nights, so that I too may still have some pleasure left in the clear light and happiness of a quiet life. Otherwise I must weep and constantly break down in tears, and not even face the rest of my life with equanimity. If the peoples of God, my own fellow-servants I mean, are so divided by wicked and damaging strife between themselves, how can my thoughts any longer be collected?* (2) *To let you appreciate how much this distressed me, when I recently set foot in the city of Nicomedia, my intention was to press on eastward straight away; I was already intent on visiting you and a large part of me was already with you, when the news of this business put a stop to my plans, so that I might not be obliged to see with my eyes what I had not thought it possible I would even hear reported verbally.* (3) *By the concord among you open to me now the road to the east, which you have shut by the the controversies between you, and make it quickly possible for me to look with pleasure both on you and on all the other congregations, and* [79] *in pleasing terms to express to the Supreme my debt of thanks for the general concord and liberation of all.*

73 While the Godbeloved thus provided for the peace of the Church through the letter which he issued, fine and noble service was done by the one who cooperated not only in the matter of the letter, but also in expressing the intention of its sender; he was in all respects a godly man, as has been said. But it was too great a matter to be dealt with by the letter, so that the ferocity of the quarrel increased, and the spreading evil reached every province in the east. This then was the effect of jealous Envy and a malignant demon resenting the prosperity of the churches.

BOOK III

1–3. Constantine Superior to the Tyrants through Piety

[80] 1 (1) In such a way then did Envy, the hater of good, resenting the prosperity of the Church, at a time of peace and happiness contrive storms and internal dissensions for her. The Emperor however, dear to God, certainly did not neglect his responsibilities; but, doing all the things opposite to those crimes committed shortly before by the savagery of the tyrants, he was superior to every enemy and foe.

(2) First, with every kind of constraint they enforced the worship of gods who are not, forsaking him who is; but he, by acts and words convicting of non-existence those who are not, urged recognition of the one who alone is. Next, they mocked the Christ of God with blasphemous words; but the very thing the godless chiefly aimed their slanders at he endorsed as his victorious protection, taking pride in the trophy of the Passion. They drove away the servants of God, depriving them of home and hearth; he called them all back, and restored them to their familiar hearths. (3) They inflicted humiliations on them; he made them honoured and the envy of all. They seized the livelihoods of the Godfearing and confiscated them unjustly; he restored them, and made many lavish gifts. They published their calumnies against church leaders in written decrees; he, on the other hand, elevating and promoting these men with the honours at his disposal, gave them nobler titles in announcements and laws. (4) They completely destroyed the places of worship, demolishing them from roof to floor; he decreed that the existing ones be augmented, and new ones erected on a grand scale at the expense of the imperial treasuries. They ordered that the divinely inspired oracles should be put to the flames and destroyed; [81] he commanded that these too should become abundant in multiple copies magnificently prepared at the expense of the imperial treasuries. (5) They ordered that synods of bishops should never dare to meet anywhere; he

assembled them from every province to his presence, and allowed them to enter the palace, to proceed into its inner chambers, and to share the imperial hearth and table. They honoured the demons with dedications; he stripped error bare, constantly distributing the materials wasted on dedications to those able to use them. They ordered the temples to be splendidly adorned; of these same buildings he completely destroyed those most highly prized by the superstitious. (6) They subjected the martyrs of God to the foulest penalties; he pursued those who had done this, and chastised them with proper punishment from God, while he never ceased honouring the memorials of the holy martyrs of God. They drove the Godfearing men out of the imperial courts; he constantly placed especial confidence in those very men, knowing them to be well-disposed and faithful towards him above all others. (7) They were mastered by wealth, their souls enslaved to the passion of Tantalus; he, with imperial magnificence opening wide all treasuries, made his distributions with rich and lavish hand. They effected countless murders in order to seize and confiscate the property of those destroyed; but, during the entire reign of Constantine, every sword hung down unused by the judges, while the peoples and city-dwellers of every province were ruled by their ancestral laws rather than constrained by duress.

(8) Observing these things, one might well say that a fresh, new-made way of life seemed to have appeared just then, as a strange light after thick darkness lit up the mortal race; and one might confess that the whole achievement belonged to God, who had advanced the Godbeloved Emperor to counter the horde of the godless.   2 (1) For, since men whose like had never been seen before had committed crimes against the Church such as had never been heard of since time began, God rightly produced a new thing himself, and by it achieved what had been known to no ear and seen by no eye. (2) And what could be more novel than the marvel of the Emperor's virtue, bestowed by God's wisdom on mankind? For he continually announced the Christ of God with complete openness to all, in no way concealing the Saviour's title, but rather taking pride in the practice. He made himself quite plain, at one time [82] marking his face with the Saviour's sign, at another proudly delighting in the victorious

trophy. 3 (1) This he displayed on a very high panel set before the entrance to the palace for the eyes of all to see, showing in the picture the Saviour's sign placed above his own head, and the hostile and inimical beast, which had laid siege to the Church of God through the tyranny of the godless, he made in the form of a dragon borne down to the deep. For the oracles proclaimed him a 'dragon' and a 'crooked serpent' in the books of the prophets of God (cf. Isaiah 27: 1); (2) therefore the Emperor also showed to all, through the medium of the encaustic painting, the dragon under his own feet and those of his sons, pierced through the middle of the body with a javelin, and thrust down in the depths of the sea. In this way he indicated the invisible enemy of the human race, whom he showed also to have departed to the depths of destruction by the power of the Saviour's trophy which was set up over his head. (3) This was what the colour of the paints indicated through the medium of the picture; but I was filled with wonder at the highmindedness of the Emperor, and at the way he had by divine inspiration portrayed what the words of the prophets had proclaimed about this beast: 'God will bring', they said, 'the great and fearful sword against the crooked dragon-serpent, against the dragon-serpent who flees, and will destroy the dragon that is in the sea' (cf. Isaiah 27: 1). The Emperor certainly portrayed images of these things, setting true representations in pictorial art.

4–24. *The Council of Nicaea*

4–9. *The calling of the Council*

4 These things then were done as he desired. But the effects of the resentment of Envy dreadfully agitating the churches of God in Alexandria, and the evil schism in the Thebaid and Egypt, disturbed him considerably. The bishop of one city was attacking the bishop of another, populations were rising up against one another, and were all but coming to physical blows with each other, so that desperate men, out of their minds, were committing sacrilegious acts, even daring to insult the images of the Emperor. But this did not so much rouse him to anger as to mental anguish, as he grieved at the [83] senseless conduct of the deranged.

5 (1) There was already another very dire sickness of longer standing than these, which had been a nuisance to the churches for a long time: the disagreement over the Feast of the Saviour. Some claimed that one ought to follow the practice of the Jews, and some that it was right to observe the exact time of the season, and not to err by following those who were outside the grace of the Gospel. (2) So in this matter too the congregations everywhere had already for a long time been divided, and the divine ordinances were in disarray, since for one and the same festival the divergence of date caused the greatest difference between those keeping the festival: some were disciplining themselves with fasting and mortification, when others were devoting leisure to relaxation. No human being was able to find a cure for the evil, since both parties were equally vehement in their disagreement; but for almighty God alone it was easy to cure even this, and alone of those on earth Constantine appeared as his agent for good.

(3) Once he received news of what has been described, and perceived that the letter which he had sent to those in Alexandria had failed, he applied his own mind to the matter, and said that this was another war which he must struggle to win against the invisible enemy disturbing the Church.   6 (1) Then, as if to march against him, he marshalled a legion of God, a world-wide Council, with respectful letters summoning the bishops to hasten from every place. It was not a simple command, but the Emperor's will reinforced it also with practical action; to some it offered the right to use the public post, to others a generous supply of pack-animals. A city was also designated which was appropriate for the Council, one bearing the name of victory, Nicaea in the province of Bithynia. (2) So as the announcement circulated everywhere, they all dashed like sprinters from the starting-line, [84] full of enthusiasm. They were drawn by the hope of good things, the opportunity to share in peace, and the spectacle of that strange marvel, to see such a great Emperor. So when all had come together, what was happening was seen already to be the work of God. For those who were furthest separated from each other, not only in spirit, but in physical presence and territories and places and provinces, were brought together, and one city received them all: a huge ring of priests was to be seen, a crown colour-woven with lovely flowers.

7 (1) From all the churches which filled all Europe, Libya, and Asia the choicest of the servants of God were brought together; and one place of worship, as if extended by God, took them in all together: Syrians with Cilicians; Phoenicians and Arabians and Palestinians; besides these, Egyptians, Thebans, Libyans, and those who came from between the rivers. Even a Persian bishop was present at the council, nor was a Scythian lacking from the assembly. Pontus and Galatia, Cappadocia and Asia, Phrygia and Pamphylia provided their chosen men. Thracians too and Macedonians, Achaeans and Epirotes, and among them those who lived far up-country, were present; and even of the Spaniards the very famous one was among those joining the assembly with all the rest. (2) The one in [85] charge of the imperial city was absent because of his old age, but his presbyters were present and deputized for him. Alone in all of history one emperor, Constantine, wove such a crown for Christ with the bond of peace, and to his Saviour dedicated a thank-offering fit for God for his victory over enemies and foemen, gathering among us this replica of the apostolic assembly. 8 For in their case also the word is that there were gathered 'from every nation under heaven' 'devout men' (Acts 2: 5), among whom were 'Parthians and Medes and Elamites, and dwellers in Mesopotamia, Judaea and Cappadocia, Pontus and Asia, Phrygia and Pamphylia, Egypt and the parts of Libya around Cyrene, the resident Romans, both Jews and proselytes, Cretans and Arabians' (Acts 2: 9–11)—except that they were inferior in that not all consisted of the ministers of God. In the present band the number of bishops exceeded 250 and the number of presbyters and deacons and of the many other attendants who accompanied them was beyond calculation. 9 Among the ministers of God some were outstanding for the word of wisdom, others for their severity of life and patient endurance, others were adorned by their moderation. Some among them were honoured for their length of years, others shone with youth and spiritual energy, some had just reached the road of priestly ministry. For all of these the Emperor had arranged that meals should be generously provided every day.

10–14. *The proceedings of the Council*

10 (1) On the day appointed for the Council, on which it was to reach a resolution of the issues in dispute, every one was present to do this, in the very innermost [86] hall of the palace, which appeared to exceed the rest in size. Many tiers of seating had been set along either side of the hall. Those invited arrived within, and all took their appointed seats. (2) When the whole council had with proper ceremony taken their seats, silence fell upon them all, as they awaited the Emperor's arrival. One of the Emperor's company came in, then a second, then a third. Yet others led the way, not some of the usual soldiers and guards, but only of his faithful friends. (3) All rose at a signal, which announced the Emperor's entrance; and he finally walked along between them, like some heavenly angel of God, his bright mantle shedding lustre like beams of light, shining with the fiery radiance of a purple robe, and decorated with the dazzling brilliance of gold and precious stones. (4) Such was his physical appearance. As for his soul, he was clearly adorned with fear and reverence for God: this was shown by his eyes, which were cast down, the blush on his face, his gait, and the rest of his appearance, his height, which surpassed all those around him . . . by his dignified maturity, by the magnificence of his physical condition, and by the vigour of his matchless strength. All these, blended with the elegance of his manners and the gentleness of imperial condescension, demonstrated the superiority of his mind surpassing all description. (5) When he reached the upper end of the rows of seats and stood in the middle, a small chair made of gold having been set out, only when the bishops assented did he sit down. They all did the same after the Emperor.

11 The bishop who was first in the row on the right then stood up and delivered a rhythmical speech, addressing the Emperor, and offering a hymn of gratitude for him to God the ruler of all. When he too had sat down, silence [87] fell on all as they gazed intently at the Emperor. He with shining eyes looked kindly on them all, and then, collecting his thoughts, in a soft and gentle voice he gave a speech somewhat like this:

12 (1) 'It was the object of my prayers, my friends, to share in your company, and now that I have received this, I know I must express my gratitude to the King of all, because in addition to everything else he has allowed me to see this, which is better than any other good thing; I mean, to receive you all gathered together and to observe one unanimous opinion shared by all. (2) Let no jealous enemy ruin our prosperity; now that the war of the tyrants against God has been swept away by the power of God the Saviour, let not the malignant demon encompass the divine law with blasphemies by other means. For to me internal division in the Church of God is graver than any war or fierce battle, and these things appear to cause more pain than secular affairs. (3) When therefore I won victories over enemies through the favour and support of the Supreme, I considered that nothing remained but to give thanks to God, and to rejoice also with those who had been liberated by him through our agency. When contrary to all expectation I learnt of your division, I did not defer attention to the report, but, praying that this too might be healed through my ministration, I immediately sent for you all. (4) I rejoice to see your gathering, and I consider that I shall be acting most in accordance with my prayers, when I see you all with your souls in communion, and one common, peaceful harmony prevailing among you all, which you, as persons consecrated to God, ought yourselves to be announcing to others. (5) So do not delay, my friends, ministers of God, and good servants of the common Lord and Saviour of us all, to begin now to bring the causes of the division between you into the open, and to loosen all shackles of dispute by the laws of peace. Thus [88] you will both achieve what is pleasing to the God of all, and you will give extreme gratification to me, your fellow servant.'

13 (1) When he had spoken these words in Latin, with someone interpreting, he made way for the leaders of the Council to speak. Some then began to accuse their neighbours, while the others defended themselves and made countercharges. A great many proposals were made by each side, and there was at first much controversy. The Emperor listened to all, without resentment, and received the proposals with patient flexibility; he took up what was said by each side in turn, and gently brought together those whose attitudes conflicted. (2) He addressed each person gently, and by speaking Greek—for he was not ignorant of that language either—he made himself pleasant and agreeable, persuading some and shaming others with his words, praising those who were speaking well, urging all towards agreement, until he had brought them to be of one mind and one belief on all the matters in dispute. 14 Thus the Faith prevailed in a unanimous form, and the same timing for the Festival of the Saviour was agreed on all sides. The general decisions were also ratified in writing through the individual signatures. When these things were finished, the Emperor said that this was the second victory he had won over the enemy of the Church, and held a victory-feast to God.

15. *Vicennalia celebrations*

15 (1) At the same time, the twentieth year of his rule was completed, [89] for which general celebrations took place in the other provinces. But for the ministers of God it was the Emperor himself who opened the celebrations, drinking with the reconciled and offering this, like a fitting sacrifice to God, through them; not one of the bishops was missing from the imperial banquet. (2) The event was beyond all description. Guards and soldiers ringed the entrance to the palace, guarding it with drawn swords, and between these the men of God passed fearlessly, and entered the innermost royal courts. Some then reclined with him, others relaxed nearby on couches on either side. It might have been supposed that it was an imaginary representation of the kingdom of Christ, and that what was happening was 'dream, not fact' (Homer, *Od.*, 19. 547).

16–20. *Constantine's report to the churches*

16 While the celebrations were proceeding splendidly, the Emperor went still further and received those who were present, magnanimously honouring every one according to his rank with gifts from himself. He transmitted the record of this Council also to those who were not present by a personal letter, which I will attach to this present account of him as a permanent record. It went like this:

17 (1) *Constantinus Augustus to the churches.*
Having learnt from experience of the prosperity of public affairs how great is the grace of the divine Power I have judged it appropriate for me

*that my aim before all else should be that among the most blessed
congregations of the universal Church a single faith and a pure love and a
religion that is unanimous about Almighty God be observed. (2) This
however could not achieve [90] an irreversible and secure settlement
unless, after all or the great majority of the bishops had gathered in the
same place, a decision were taken upon each of the points affecting the
most holy religion. For this reason when most had been assembled, and I
myself as one of you was also among those present (for I would not wish to
deny that in which I most delight, that I am your fellow-servant), all
topics were subject to proper discussion until the point was reached where
the doctrine pleasing to the all-seeing God of all was brought to light as
the basis for unanimous agreement, so that nothing remained to cause
further difference of opinion or dispute about faith.*

*18 (1) Thereupon, since a controversy had broken out on the subject of
the most holy day of Easter, it was unanimously decided that it would be
best for everyone everywhere to celebrate it on the same day. For what
could be better for us, and more reverent, than that this festival, from
which we have acquired our hope of immortality, should be observed
invariably in every community on one system and declared principle?*

*(2) In the first place it was decreed unworthy to observe that most
sacred festival in accordance with the practice of the Jews; having sullied
their own hands with a heinous crime, such bloodstained men are as one
might expect mentally blind. It is possible, now that their nation has been
rejected, by a truer system which we have kept from the first day of the
Passion to the present, to extend the performing of this observance into
future periods also. Let there be nothing in common between you and the
detestable mob of Jews! (3) We have received from the Saviour another
way; a course is open to our most holy religion that is both lawful and
proper. Let us with one accord take up this course, right honourable
brothers, and so tear ourselves away from that disgusting complicity. For
it is surely quite grotesque for them to be able to boast that we would be
incapable of keeping these observances without their instruction. (4) What
could those people calculate correctly, when after that murder of the Lord,
after that parricide, they have taken leave of their senses, and are moved,
not [91] by any rational principle, but by uncontrolled impulse, wherever
their internal frenzy may lead them? Hence it comes about that in this
very matter they do not see the truth, so that nearly always they get it
wrong, and instead of the proper calculation they observe the Pascha a
second time in the same year. Why then do we follow those who are by
common consent sick with fearful error? We would never allow the Pascha*

to be kept a second time in the same year. But even if that argument were absent, your Good Sense ought to make it the continual object of your effort and prayer, that the purity of your soul should not by any resemblance appear to participate in the practices of thoroughly evil persons.

(5) It is furthermore easy to see that in such an important matter, and for such a religious feast, it is wrong that there should be a discrepancy. Our Saviour has passed on the day of our liberation as one, the day, that is, of his holy passion, and it is his purpose that his universal Church be one. However much its parts may be separated in many different places, nevertheless it is cherished by the one Spirit, that is, by the divine will. (6) But let your Holiness's good sense reflect how dreadful and unseemly it is, that on the same days some should be attending to their fasts while others are holding drinking parties, and that after the days of Pascha some should be busy with feasts and recreations while others are dedicating themselves to the prescribed fasts. That is the reason therefore why divine Providence intends that this matter should achieve the proper settlement and be brought under one regulation, as I presume all are aware.

19 *(1) Since therefore it was proper that the matter should be adjusted in such a way that nothing be held in common with that nation of parricides and Lord-killers, [92] and since a decent system exists, which all the churches of the western, southern and northern parts of the world observe, and also some of the churches in the eastern areas, and as a consequence all have at this time judged that it is right (and I have personally given my word that it will please your Good Sense), that what is observed with one harmonious will in the City of Rome, in Italy and all Africa, in Egypt, the Spains, the Gauls, the Britains, the Libyas, the whole of Greece, the administrative region of Asia, Pontus and Cilicia, your Intelligence also will gladly embrace, when you reflect that not only is the number of the churches in the places mentioned greater, but also that it is a supremely holy thing for all to hold in common what seems both to be required by correct computation and to have nothing to do with Jewish perjury; (2) and to put the most important point concisely, by unanimous verdict it was determined that the most holy feast of Easter should be celebrated on one and the same day, since it is both improper that there should be a division about a matter of such great sanctity, and best to follow that option, in which there is no admixture of alien error and sin.*
20 *(1) In these circumstances, then, accept gladly the heavenly grace and this truly divine command; for all the business transacted in the holy assemblies of bishops has reference to the divine will.*

(2) *So once you have explained to our beloved brothers what is written above, you ought now to accept and institute the stated method of computation and the strict observance of the most holy day, so that when I come, as I have long desired, to see the state of your affairs, I may be able to celebrate the holy festival with you on one and the same day, and I may share with you my satisfaction on every count, as I observe* [93] *that devilish savagery has by the divine power and through our actions been obliterated, while our faith and peace and concord are everywhere flourishing.*

God preserve you, dear brothers.

(3) The Emperor sent out a text to the same effect as this letter to each of the provinces, enabling his readers to see reflected in his thinking the utter purity of his holy devotion to the Divinity.

21–2. *The bishops dismissed*

21 (1) When the Council was finally about to dissolve, he gave a farewell address to the bishops. He summoned them all together on one day, and took it as his theme that they should earnestly cultivate peace with each other. They should avoid contentious quarrels. They should not be envious if any among the bishops had a reputation for the word of wisdom, but regard the benefit of one man's skill as common to all. Those who were more proficient should not despise those of more modest gifts, for it is for God to decide who are on a true reckoning more proficient. To the weaker ones appropriate concessions should be made, since perfection is always a rarity. (2) They should therefore be tolerant with each other when they offend in minor matters, and be generous and forgive human weaknesses, all regarding harmonious concord as precious, so that no ground should be given by their mutual strife for mockery by those who are always ready to speak ill of the divine Law; those persons should be kept seriously in mind in every matter, since they can be saved if what we have seems to them worth while. One thing they should be in no doubt about was that not everybody gets benefit from intellectual ability. (3) There are some who are happy to be provided with a living, others who by habit fawn upon those in authority; some gladly greet those who affably hold out their hand, others feel affection when they are honoured with presents; but few are those with a passion for true ideas, and rare indeed the lover of Truth. So it was necessary to adapt oneself to all, providing like a doctor what would help to save each one, so that by every means the saving doctrine might be held in regard by all.

[94] (4) Such were his principal exhortations to them. Finally he urged them to offer fervent supplications to God for him. Thus bidding them farewell, he send them all off to go back where they belonged. They went back with joy, and there at last prevailed among them all a unanimity, which had been arrived at in the Emperor's presence, those who had been far apart being joined together as in a single body.

22 The Emperor, delighted at his success, had by means of letters distributed rich fruit among those who had not been present at the council; and he ordered ample grants of money to be made among the congregations both in the country and in the urban areas, thus celebrating the festival of the twentieth anniversary of his accession.

23–4. *Further conciliatory negotiations and letters*

23 When all were at peace, however, among the Egyptians alone the mutual bitterness remained undiluted, so that the Emperor was troubled yet again, though still not roused to anger. So with every deference he addressed them as 'fathers' or rather as 'prophets of God', summoned them a second time, again mediated tolerantly between the same people, and again honoured them with gifts. He also announced the arbitration through a letter, and to ratify the decrees of the Council he set his seal upon them. He urged them to cling to peaceful harmony, and not to split and splinter the Church, but to bear in mind the judgement of God. The Emperor gave these injunctions too in a letter of his own.

24 (1) He also wrote countless other things of the same kind, and composed a great many letters. In some he gave instructions to bishops about what affected the churches of God; but on occasion he also addressed the congregations themselves, and then the Thrice-blessed would call the laity of the Church his own 'brothers' and 'fellow-servants'. (2) But there may be an opportunity to assemble these in a special collection, so as not to disrupt the sequence of our present account.

25–47. 3. Buildings on Three Most Sacred Sites

25–8. Excavation of the Holy Sepulchre

25 Such was the situation when another memorable work of great importance [95] was done in the province of Palestine by the Godbeloved. It was this. He decided that he ought to make universally famous and revered the most blessed site in Jerusalem of the Saviour's resurrection. So at once he gave orders for a place of worship to be constructed, conceiving this idea not without God, but with his spirit moved by the Saviour himself.

26 (1) Once upon a time wicked men—or rather the whole tribe of demons through them—had striven to consign to darkness and oblivion that divine monument to immortality, at which, brilliant with light, the angel who had descended from heaven had rolled away the stone of those whose minds were set like stone in their assumption that the Living One was still with the dead, when he announced the good news to the women and removed the stone of disbelief from their minds by the information that the one they sought was alive. (2) It was this very cave of the Saviour that some godless and wicked people had planned to make invisible to mankind, thinking in their stupidity that they could in this way hide the truth. Indeed with a great expenditure of effort they brought earth from somewhere outside and covered up the whole place, then levelled it, paved it, and so hid the divine cave somewhere down beneath a great quantity of soil. (3) Then as though they had everything finished, above the ground they constructed a terrible and truly genuine tomb, one for souls, for dead idols, and built a gloomy sanctuary to the impure demon of Aphrodite; then they offered foul sacrifices there upon defiled and polluted altars. They reckoned there was one way alone and no other to bring their desires to realization, and that was to bury the Saviour's cave under such foul pollutions. (4) The wretches could not understand that it would be against nature for the one who had crowned his brow with the conquest of death to leave his accomplishment hidden. No more could the sun remain unnoticed by the whole world inhabited by man, as it shines after rising above the earth and drives its proper chariot-course across the sky; but brighter than this the Saviour's power as it illuminates the souls, though not the bodies, of men [96] was filling the entire world with his own beams of light.

(5) Nevertheless the devices of these godless and wicked men against truth lasted for long ages, and no one was ever found—no governor, no commander, no Emperor even—competent to clear away what had been perpetrated but one alone, the friend of God the universal King. (6) Possessed therefore by the divine Spirit he did not negligently allow that place which has been described to remain smothered by all sorts of filthy rubbish through the machination of enemies consigned to oblivion and ignorance, nor did he yield to the malice of the guilty; but calling upon God to be his collaborator, he ordered it to be cleared, thinking that the very space which enemies had sullied should especially benefit from the great work being done through him by the All-good. (7) At a word of command those contrivances of fraud were demolished from top to bottom, and the houses of error were dismantled and destroyed along with their idols and demons.

27 His efforts however did not stop there, but the Emperor gave further orders that all the rubble of stones and timbers from the demolitions should be taken and dumped a long way from the site. This command also was soon effected. But not even this progress was by itself enough, but under divine inspiration once more the Emperor gave instructions that the site should be excavated to a great depth and the pavement should be carried away with the rubble a long distance outside, because it was stained with demonic bloodshed. **28** This also was completed straightaway. As stage by stage the underground site was exposed, at last against all expectation the revered and all-hallowed Testimony (*martyrion*) of the Saviour's resurrection was itself revealed, and the cave, the holy of holies, took on the appearance of a representation of the Saviour's return to life. Thus after its descent into darkness it came forth again to the light, and it enabled those who came as visitors to see plainly the story of the wonders wrought there, testifying by facts louder than any voice to the resurrection of the Saviour.

29–40. *The church of the Holy Sepulchre*

[97] **29** (1) With these things thus completed, the Emperor next gave orders by the stipulations of pious laws and by

generous grants for a place of worship worthy of God to be built with rich and imperial munificence around the Saviour's cave, as if he had intended this for a long time and had looked into the future with superior foreknowledge. (2) He instructed those who governed the eastern provinces by generous and lavish grants to make the building out of the ordinary, huge, and rich, and to the bishop of the church who then presided in Jerusalem, he sent the following document. By it he displayed in clear terms the love for God in his own soul and the purity of his faith in the Saviour's Word, writing in this fashion:

30 (1) *Victor Constantinus Maximus Augustus to Macarius.*

So great is our Saviour's grace, that no words seem enough to match the present miracle. For the evidence of his most sacred passion, long since hidden under the ground, to have remained unknown for such a long period of years, until through the removal of the enemy of the whole republic it was ready to be revealed, once they were set free, to his servants, truly surpasses all marvels. (2) *If all those from every part of the world with a reputation for wisdom were to gather together in one place and try to say something worthy of the event, they would not be able to compete with the least part of it. The evidence of this miracle surpasses every natural capacity of human thought in the same degree that heavenly things are by common consent mightier than human.* (3) *That is why* [98] *it is always my first and only goal, that, just as the evidence for the truth manifests itself with newer wonders every day, so all our souls may by utter seriousness and unanimous endeavour also become more earnest about the holy law.* (4) *The thing therefore which I consider clear to everybody is what I want you in particular to believe, namely that above all else my concern is that that sacred place, which at God's command I have now relieved of the hideous burden of an idol which lay on it like a weight, hallowed from the start by God's decree, and now proved yet holier since it brought to light the pledge of the Saviour's passion, should be adorned by us with beautiful buildings.*

31 (1) *It is thus for your own Good Sense to make such order and provision of what is needed that not only a basilica superior to those in all other places, but the other arrangements also, may be such that all the excellences of every city are surpassed by this foundation.* (2) *As to the building and decoration of the walls, be advised that our friend Dracillianus, who exercises his office among the* praefecti illustrissimi, *and he who is governor of the province have been entrusted*

by us with its care. For my Religious Care has ordered that craftsmen and labourers and everything they may learn from your Good Sense to be needed for the building work should forthwith be supplied by their provision. (3) As to the columns or marble, you should after a survey yourself write promptly to us about what you may consider to be of most value and use, so that whatever quantity and kind of materials [99] *we may learn from your letter to be needful may be competently supplied from all sources. It is right that the world's most miraculous place should be worthily embellished.* **32** (1) *As to the vault of the basilica, whether you decide that it be coffered or in another style of construction I would wish to learn from you. If it were to be coffered, it might also be decorated with gold. (2) In short, in order that your Holiness may make known with all speed to the aforementioned magistrates how many labourers and craftsmen and what other expenditures are required, take care to refer immediately also to me not only the matters of the marble and pillars, but also the lacunary panels, should you judge that best.*

    God preserve you, dear Brother.

   33 (1) Thus did the Emperor write. No sooner had he written than the commands were put into effect. New Jerusalem was built at the very Testimony to the Saviour, facing the famous Jerusalem of old, which after the bloody murder of the Lord had been overthrown in utter devastation, and paid the penalty of its wicked inhabitants. (2) Opposite this then the Emperor erected the victory of the Saviour over death with rich and abundant munificence, this being perhaps that fresh new Jerusalem proclaimed in prophetic oracles, about which long speeches recite innumerable praises as they utter words of divine inspiration.

   (3) As the principal item he first of all decked out the sacred cave. It was a tomb full of agelong memory, comprising the trophies of the great Saviour's defeat of death, a tomb of divine presence, where once an angel, radiant with light, proclaimed to all the good news of the rebirth demonstrated by the Saviour. **34** This then was the first thing, like a head of the whole, which [100] the Emperor's munificence decorated with superb columns and full ornamentation, brightening the solemn cave with all kinds of artwork. **35** He then went on to a very large space wide open to the fresh air, which was decorated with a pavement of

light-coloured stone on the ground, and enclosed on three sides by long surrounding colonnades.

36 (1) On the side opposite the cave, which looked towards the rising sun, was connected the royal temple, an extraordinary structure raised to an immense height and very extensive in length and breadth. Its interior was covered with slabs of varied marble, and the external aspect of the walls, gleaming with hewn stone fitted closely together at each joint, produced a supreme object of beauty by no means inferior to marble. (2) Right up at the top the material which encased the outside of the roofs was lead, a sure protection against stormy rain; while the interior of the structure was fitted with carved coffers and like a vast sea spread out by a series of joints binding to each other through the whole royal house, and being beautified throughout with brilliant gold made the whole shrine glitter with beams of light. **37** Round each of the sides extended twin ranges of double colonnades, in upper and lower storeys, their tops also decorated with gold. Those at the front of the house rested upon huge pillars, while those inside the front were raised under blocks plentifully decorated all round their surfaces. Three doors well placed to face the sunrise received the crowds flowing in. **38** Facing these as the chief point of the whole was the hemisphere attached to the highest part of the royal house, ringed with twelve columns to match the number of the Apostles of the Saviour, their tops decorated with great bowls made of silver, which the Emperor himself had presented to his God as a superb offering.

39 For those going on from there to the entrances situated at the front of the shrine, another open space awaited them. Arcades stood there on either hand, a first court and colonnades beyond, and finally the gates of the court. Beyond these, right in the middle of the open square, the porticoes forming the entrance to the whole, beautifully wrought, offered to those passing outside a striking view of what was to be seen within.

[101] **40** This then was the shrine which the Emperor raised as a manifest testimony of the Saviour's resurrection, embellishing the whole with rich imperial decoration. He adorned it with untold beauties in innumerable dedications of gold and silver and precious stones set in various materials. In view of their size, number and variety, to describe in detail the skilled craftsman-

ship which went into their manufacture would be beyond the
scope of the present work.

41–43. 4. *Churches at Bethlehem and the Ascension*

41 (1) He took in hand here other sites venerated for their two
mystic caves, and he adorned these also with rich artwork. On the
cave of the first divine manifestation of the Saviour, where he
submitted to the experience of birth in the flesh, he bestowed
appropriate honours; while at the other he dignified the monument on the mountain-top to his ascension into heaven. (2) These
also he artistically honoured, perpetuating the memory of his
own mother, who had bestowed so much good on human life.
42 (1) This lady, when she made it her business to pay what
piety owed to the all-sovereign God, and considered that she
ought to complete in prayers her thank-offerings for her son, so
great an Emperor, and his sons the most Godbeloved Caesars
her grandchildren, came, though old, with the eagerness of
youth to apply her outstanding intellect to enquiring about the
wondrous land and to inspect with imperial concern the
eastern provinces with their communities and peoples. (2) As
she accorded suitable adoration to the footsteps of the Saviour,
following the prophetic word which says, 'Let us adore in the
place where his feet have stood' (Ps 132/131: 7), she forthwith
bequeathed to her successors also the fruit of her personal
piety.
43 (1) She immediately consecrated to the God she adored
two shrines, one by the cave of his birth, the other on the
mountain of the ascension. For the God with us allowed himself
to suffer even birth for our sake, and the place of his birth in the
flesh was announced among the Hebrews by the name of Bethlehem. [102] (2) Thus then the most devout Empress beautified
the Godbearer's pregnancy with wonderful monuments, in various ways embellishing the sacred cave there. The Emperor
himself shortly afterwards honoured this too with imperial
dedications, supplementing his mother's works of art with
treasures of silver and gold and embroidered curtains.
(3) Again the Emperor's mother erected on the Mount of
Olives the monument to the journey into heaven of the Saviour
of the Universe in lofty buildings; up by the ridges at the peak of

the whole mountain she raised the sacred house of the church, and constructed just there a shrine for prayer to the Saviour who chose to spend his time on that spot, since just there a true report maintains that in that cave the Saviour of the Universe initiated the members of his guild in ineffable mysteries. (4) There also the Emperor bestowed all kinds of offerings and ornaments on the great King.

43. 4–47. 3. *The death of the Empress Helena*

These then were the two everlastingly memorable, noble and utterly beautiful dedications to her Saviour at two mystic caves, which Helena Augusta, the Godbeloved mother of the God-beloved Emperor, founded as tokens of her pious intent, her son providing her with the right arm of imperial authority. (5) But the lady not long after reaped the due reward. She had traversed a whole lifespan amid everything good to the very portal of old age; by words and deeds she had produced luxurious growth from the Saviour's commandments; and then she had completed in full vigour of mind a life so orderly and calm in both body and soul, that as a result she also met an end worthy of her religion and a good reward from God even in this present life.

44 As she visited the whole east in the magnificence of imperial authority, she showered countless gifts upon the citizen bodies of every city, and privately to each of those who approached her; and she made countless distributions also to the ranks of the soldiery with magnificent hand. She made innumerable gifts to the unclothed and unsupported poor, to some making gifts of money, to others abundantly supplying what was needed to cover the body. Others she set free from prison and from mines where they laboured in harsh conditions, she released the victims of fraud, and yet others she recalled from exile.   45 Brilliantly though she shone in such things, she did not despise the other aspects of devotion to God. [103] She allowed herself to be seen continually making personal visits to the church of God. She adorned the places of worship with shining treasures, not neglecting the shrines in even the smallest of towns. One might see the wonderful woman in dignified and modest attire joining the throng and manifesting reverence towards the divinity by every kind of practice dear to God.

46 (1) When she had finally completed the course of a long enough life, and was called to the higher sphere, having lived to something like 80 years of age, when she was very near the end she made arrangements and dispositions, drawing up her last will in favour of her only son the Emperor, the monarch and world-ruler, and his sons the Caesars, her own grandchildren, bequeathing to each of her issue part of her estate, everything she possessed in the whole world. (2) Having settled her affairs in this way, she finally came to the end of her life. So great a son was present and stood by her, ministering and holding her hands, so as to make it seem likely to right-thinking people that the thrice-blessed one was not dead, but had in reality undergone a transformation and removal from earthly life to heavenly. Her very soul was thus reconstituted into an incorruptible and angelic essence as she was taken up to her Saviour.   **47** (1) Even the temporal dwelling of the blessed one deserved no ordinary care, so with a great guard of honour she was carried up to the imperial city, and there laid in the imperial tombs.

Thus passed away the Emperor's mother, one worthy of unfading memory both for her own Godloving deeds and for those of the extraordinary and astonishing offspring which arose from her. (2) He deserves to be blessed, all else apart, for his piety to the one who bore him. So far had he made her Godfearing, though she had not been such before, that she seemed to him to have been a disciple of the common Saviour from the first; and so far had he honoured her with imperial rank that she was acclaimed in all nations and by the military ranks as *Augusta Imperatrix*, and her portrait was stamped on gold coinage. (3) He even remitted to her authority over imperial treasuries, to use them at will and to manage them at her discretion, in whatever way she might wish and however she might judge best in each case, her son [104] having accorded her distinction and eminence in these matters too. It was therefore right that while recording his memory we should also record those things wherein, by honouring his mother for her supreme piety, he satisfied the divine principles which impose the duty of honouring parents.

47. 4–53. *Other Churches Built*

47. 4–49. *Constantinople*

47 (4) The Emperor thus constructed the fine buildings described in the region of Palestine in the aforesaid manner. But throughout all the provinces he also furnished newly built churches, and so made them far higher in public esteem than their predecessors. **48** (1) In honouring with exceptional distinction the city which bears his name, he embellished it with very many places of worship, very large martyr-shrines, and splendid houses, some standing before the city and others in it. By these he at the same time honoured the tombs of the martyrs and consecrated the city to the martyrs' God. (2) Being full of the breath of God's wisdom, which he reckoned a city bearing his own name should display, he saw fit to purge it of all idol-worship, so that nowhere in it appeared those images of the supposed gods which are worshipped in temples, nor altars foul with bloody slaughter, nor sacrifice offered as holocaust in fire, nor feasts of demons, nor any of the other customs of the superstitious.

49 You would see at the fountains set in the middle of squares the emblems of the Good Shepherd, evident signs to those who start from the divine oracles, and Daniel with his lions shaped in bronze and glinting with gold leaf. So great was the divine passion which had seized the Emperor's soul that in the royal quarters of the imperial palace itself, on the most eminent building of all, at the very middle of the gilded coffer adjoining the roof, in the centre of a very large wide panel, had been fixed the emblem of the saving Passion made up of a variety of precious stones and set in much gold. This appears to have been made by the Godbeloved as a protection for his Empire.

50. *Nicomedia and Antioch*

50 (1) With these things he beautified his own city. But he likewise honoured the chief city of Bithynia with the dedication of a very large and splendid church, raising there to his Saviour from his personal funds a [105] monument of victory over his enemies and the foes of God. (2) The most pre-eminent cities of the other provinces he made to excel in the artistic buildings of their places of prayer, just as he did in the case of the metropolis of the Orient, which was named after Antiochus. In it, as if to crown the provinces there, he consecrated a church unique for its size and beauty, surrounding the whole shrine with great precincts outside, and raising the hall of worship to an enormous height. It was constructed in an octagonal shape, with a ring of bays built right round at ground-floor and first-floor levels, and he encircled it with decorative features rich in abundant gold and bronze and all kinds of precious stuff.

51–3. *Mamre*

51 (1) These were the most important of the Emperor's dedications. But when he learnt that the self-same Saviour who had recently appeared to mankind had also in ancient times divinely manifested himself to Godloving men in Palestine near the oak called Mamre, there also he ordered a place of worship to be built in honour of the God who was seen there. (2) To the governors of provinces an imperial mandate was circulated through letters sent to each of them, commanding them to fulfil his instructions completely. But he also dispatched to the author of the present history a reasoned admonition, a copy which I should, I think, add to the present work to enable the concern of the Godbeloved to be accurately appreciated. He took us to task for what he had heard was going on here, and wrote in these exact terms:

52 *Victor Constantinus Maximus Augustus to Macarius and the other bishops of Palestine.*

The greatest single service to us of my most saintly mother-in-law has been [106] *to inform us through her letters to us of the mad folly of evil men, which has so far escaped attention among you, so that the neglected fault may receive appropriate corrective and restorative action from us, late perhaps but yet necessary. It is certainly a monstrous evil that the holy sites should be marred by sacrilegious abominations. What then is it, wellbeloved brothers, which has escaped your Intelligence, and the aforesaid lady's reverence for the divine would not let her suppress?*
53 (1) *The place by the oak which is known as Mamre, where we understand Abraham made his home, has been completely spoiled, she*

says, by superstitious persons. Idols fit only for absolute destruction have been set up beside it, she explains, and an altar stands nearby, and foul sacrifices are constantly conducted there. (2) Since therefore this appears to be both alien to our times and unworthy of the sanctity of the site, I would have your Reverences know that a letter has been written by us to Acacius our most distinguished comes *and Friend, directing that without delay such idols as he may find on the aforementioned site be consigned to the flames, the altar completely demolished, and in short, when all such things there have been got rid of, he should devote all possible effort and endeavour to clearing the whole area. After that, according to such instructions as you yourselves may give, he is to have built on the spot a basilica worthy of the catholic and apostolic Church. It will then be for your Wisdom and Reverence, as soon as you learn that all the defilements there have been completely removed, to meet with the bishops from Phoenicia, whom you will be able to summon on the authority of this letter, and to design a basilica worthy of my munificence, so that in accordance with my orders and with all speed the splendour of the building can be brought to completion under the supervision of our aforesaid* comes *in a manner fitting the antiquity and sacredness of the site.*

Above all I wish you to take particular care that in future none of those accursed and foul people dare to come near the place. It is to us quite intolerable and for all the culprits [107] *a punishable crime if any sacrilege is committed in such a place after our order, when we have given instructions that it is to be adorned with a pure basilica church in order to become a meeting-place fit for holy persons. Should anything occur contrary to this order, it is well that without any hesitation it should be reported to our Clemency by letters from you, so that we may order the person apprehended be subjected to the severest punishment as having broken the law.*

(3) You are surely aware that there first God the Lord of the universe both appeared to Abraham and spoke with him. It was there therefore that the religion of the holy Law first had its beginning, there that the Saviour himself with the two angels first vouchsafed the manifestation of himself to Abraham, there that God began to reveal himself to mankind, there that he spoke to Abraham about his future seed and instantly fulfilled his promise, and there that he predicted that he would be the father of very many nations. (4) In these circumstances it is right, so it seems to me, that by our provision this site should be both kept clear of every defilement and restored to its ancient holy state, so that no other activity goes on there except the performance of the cult appropriate to God the Almighty, our

Saviour and the Lord of the Universe. It is your duty to protect it with the necessary care, if indeed the fulfilment of my desires, which particularly accord with godly religion, so I firmly believe, is the wish of your Reverences.

God preserve you, dear brothers.

54–8. Pagan Temples

54. Removal of valuables

54 (1) In all these undertakings the Emperor worked for the glory of the Saviour's power. While he continued in this way to honour his Saviour God, he confuted the superstitious error of the heathen in all sorts of ways. (2) To this end he stripped the entrances to their temples in every city so that their doors were removed at the Emperor's command. In other cases the roofs were ruined by the removal of the cladding. In yet other cases the sacred bronze figures, of which the error of the ancients had for a long time been proud, [108] he displayed to all the public in all the squares of the Emperor's city, so that in one place the Pythian was displayed as a contemptible spectacle to the viewers, in another the Sminthian, in the Hippodrome itself the tripods from Delphi, and the Muses of Helicon at the palace. (3) The city named after the Emperor was filled throughout with objects of skilled artwork in bronze dedicated in various provinces. To these under the name of gods those sick with error had for long ages vainly offered innumerable hecatombs and whole burnt sacrifices, but now they at last learnt sense, as the Emperor used these very toys for the laughter and amusement of the spectators.

Another fate awaited the golden statues. (4) When he perceived that the masses in the manner of silly children were pointlessly terrified by the bogeys fashioned from gold and silver, he decided to get rid of these as one would stumbling-blocks dropped before the feet of people walking in the dark, and to open wide for all hereafter, clear and level, the royal way. (5) With this in mind he reckoned that he did not need armed men and a military force to confute these: one or two only of his familiar circle sufficed for the operation, and he sent these to every province at a single command. (6) Confident in the Emperor's piety and their own reverence for the Divinity, they visited populous communities and nations, and city by city, country by country, they exposed the long-standing error, ordering the consecrated officials themselves to bring out their gods with much mockery and contempt from their dark recesses into daylight, and then depriving them of their fine appearance and revealing to every eye the ugliness that lay within the superficially applied beauty. They then scraped off the material which seemed to be usable, purifying it by smelting with fire; as much useful material as was deemed to belong to them they collected and stored in a safe place, while conversely what was superfluous and useless they allowed the superstitious to keep as a souvenir of their shame. (7) 'Such wrought he also this' (Homer, *Od.*, 4. 242), the amazing Emperor. While he stripped the precious materials in the manner described from the dead idols, he collected the remaining statues made of bronze. These too were led captive, gods of stale legends dressed in hair cloth.

55. *The shrine at Aphaca demolished*

[109] **55** (1) The Emperor, having in these ways kindled a sort of radiant lamp, lest any secret relic of error might lie undetected, cast an imperial eye about him. As some high-soaring sharp-eyed eagle might from high above see things far off upon the earth, so as he patrolled his imperial home in his own fair city, he perceived from afar a dire trap for souls lurking in the province of Phoenicia. (2) This was a grove and precinct, not at a city centre nor among squares and streets, such as frequently adorn the cities for decoration, but it was off the beaten track away from main roads and junctions, founded for the hateful demon Aphrodite in a mountainous part of Lebanon at Aphaca. (3) This was a school of vice for all dissolute persons and those who had corrupted their bodies with much indulgence. Womanish men, who were not men but had rejected the dignity of their nature, propitiated the spirit with their sick effeminacy, and unlawful intercourse with women, stolen and corrupt sexual relations, and unspeakable, infamous practices went on at this shrine as in some lawless and ungoverned place. There was no one to find out what was being done because no respectable man dared to set foot there. (4) But what was practised there could not also escape the notice of the great

Emperor. Having observed even these things for himself with imperial forethought, he decided that such a shrine was not fit to see the sun's light, and ordered the whole to be entirely demolished, dedications and all. (5) On the Emperor's command the devices of licentious error were at once destroyed, and a detachment of soldiers saw to the clearing of the site. Those who had hitherto indulged themselves learned chastity from the Emperor's menace.

55. 5–56. *The temple of Asclepius in Cilicia demolished*

It was the same for the superstitious persons among the Greeks with scientific pretensions, who were also to learn their own folly by practical experience. [110] 56 (1) Since much error arose from the purported science associated with the Cilician spirit, and countless people got excited about him as a saviour and healer, because he sometimes manifested himself to those who slept near him, and sometimes healed the diseases of those physically ill—though when it came to souls he was a destroyer, drawing the gullible away from the true Saviour and attracting them to godless error—he did the proper thing, and protected by the jealous God as his veritable Saviour, he ordered this shrine to be demolished. (2) At one command the vaunted wonder of the noble philosophers was razed to the ground, pulled down by a military force, and with it the one who skulked within, no spirit, and surely no god, but a deceiver of souls who had practised fraud for many long years. Then the one who used to promise others a way to avoid evils and disasters could find no spell to protect himself, any more than when in the myth he was struck by lightning. (3) But there was nothing mythical about the successes bestowed by the God of the Emperor on our side, but by the manifest power of his Saviour the shrine there also was utterly destroyed, so that no trace remained there of the former madness.

57. *General campaign against idolatry*

57 (1) When all those who formerly were superstitious saw with their own eyes the exposure of what had deceived them, and observed the actual desolation of shrines and establishments

everywhere, some took refuge in the saving Word, while others, though they did not do that, still condemned the folly of their ancestors and laughed and mocked at those anciently held by them to be gods. (2) This was their inevitable reaction, when they saw hidden within the external form of the images a huge amount of foul matter. Inside were either bones and dry skulls from dead bodies which had been used for the devious magic arts of sorcerers, or foul rags full of disgusting filth, or a litter of hay and straw. (3) When they saw that these had been stuffed inside the lifeless objects they became very critical of the great intellectual folly of themselves and their fathers, especially when they realized that there was no resident in their dark sanctuaries, no spirit, no oracle, no god, no prophet, as they had previously supposed, and not even a vague, shadowy ghost. (4) This was why every dark cave and [111] every secret recess was readily accessible to the Emperor's emissaries, and forbidden innermost sanctuaries of temples were trodden by soldiers' feet, so that from this it was manifestly demonstrated to everyone that for a very long time the peoples had all been in the grip of mental paralysis.

58. The shrine of Aphrodite at Heliopolis demolished

58 (1) These things might well be regarded as among the Emperor's great achievements, as indeed might the local dispositions he made in particular provinces. Such a case was Heliopolis in Phoenicia, where those who worshipped unbridled pleasure under the title of Aphrodite had in the past allowed their wives and daughters without restraint to act as prostitutes. (2) Now however a fresh and chastening law was issued by the Emperor forbidding as criminal any of the old customs; for these persons also he provided written instructions, showing how he had been brought forward by God for this very purpose, of educating all mankind in laws of chastity; hence he did not disdain to communicate even with them through a personal letter, and he urged them to turn earnestly to the knowledge of the Supreme. (3) There also he supported his words with matching actions, setting in their midst also a very large church building for worship, so that what had never yet from the beginning of time been heard of now became for the first time

a fact, and the pagan city was granted presbyters and deacons of the Church of God, and a bishop consecrated to the God over all was appointed to oversee the people there. (4) Planning there also for large numbers to approach the Word, the Emperor made plentiful provision for the poor, using that too as an incentive to turn to the Saviour's teaching: he was almost using the same words himself as the one who said, 'Whether in pretence or in truth let Christ be preached' (Philippians 1: 18).

59–66. Church Disputes Settled

59–63. Constantine's letters about Antioch

59 (1) While all were enjoying a happy life under these conditions, and the Church of God was everywhere in every way and in every province increasing, once more Envy, who seeks opportunity against good things, was limbering up to attack the prosperity so rich in benefits. He perhaps hoped that the Emperor would himself change his attitude to us in irritation at our troubles and disorders. [112] (2) He therefore lit a great flame and plunged the church of Antioch into disasters of tragic proportions, so that the whole city was all but completely destroyed. The church people were split into two factions, while the general population of the city including the magistrates and military personnel were stirred up to warlike attitudes, and even swords might well have been used, had not God's oversight and fear of the Emperor quelled the passions of the mob, (3) and once more the Emperor's patience, in the manner of a saviour and physician of souls, applied the medicine of argument to those who were sick.

He negotiated very gently with the congregations, sending the most loyal of his proven courtiers who held the rank of *comes*, and he exhorted them in frequent letters to adopt a pacific attitude. He taught that they should behave in a manner befitting godliness, and used persuasion and pleading in what he wrote to them, pointing out that he had personally listened to the one who caused the sedition. (4) These letters of his too, which are full of helpful instruction, we would have produced at this point, but they might bring discredit on the persons accused. (5) I will therefore set these aside, determining not to renew the memory of evils, and will include in my work those which he composed in satisfaction at the unity and peace of the rest. In these he urged them not to try to obtain a leader from outside, inasmuch as they had achieved peace, but by the rule of the Church to choose as pastor that person whom the universal Saviour of the world would himself designate. He wrote to the laity themselves and to the bishops separately as follows:

60 (1) *Victor Constantinus Maximus Augustus to the laity at Antioch.*

As the concord among you is pleasing to the intelligence and wisdom of the world, I also recognize, brothers, that I love you with an undying affection, moved by the principles, the mode of life, the earnestness you show. In truth therefore the right way to enjoy good things is to [113] *adopt a right and healthy attitude of mind.* (2) *What could suit you so well? I wonder therefore whether I might say that the truth is a reason for you to look for salvation rather than hatred. Among brothers then, who are pledged to God by one and the same commitment to a right and just course of life as members of a sacred and holy family, what could be more precious than the unanimity which goes with the blessing of prosperity for all?—the more so when your education from the Law directs your purpose towards a better resolution, and we desire to reinforce the decision we make with sound doctrines.*

(3) *You may perhaps be wondering what is the purpose of the first paragraph of my letter. I shall not shirk the question or refuse to explain the reason. I acknowledge that I have read the reports in which, from the noble praises and testimonials which you bestow on Eusebius, presently bishop of Caesarea, a man I myself also have known well for a long time for his learning and integrity, I see that you are pressing to get him for yourselves.* (4) *What plan do you think I have formulated in my effort to find exactly the right solution? What view do I take of your earnest wish? O holy Faith, you who through the word and teaching of our Saviour present a sort of model for living, how difficult it would be even for you to resist sins, if you did not refuse to serve for gain! To me indeed it seems that the one who aims rather at peace has done better than victory itself; for where someone can do the fitting thing, there is nobody who would not be pleased.* (5) *I ask you therefore, brothers, for what reason do we take such decisions as to inflict injury on others by the choice we make? Why do we try to obtain things which will destroy belief in our reputation? I certainly praise the man whom you also judge worthy of rank and*

placement; yet what [114] *ought to remain in every congregation valid and assured should not be so enfeebled that each person cannot be satisfied with his own election, and all enjoy what belongs to them, and not merely one but several candidates be found who deserve equal consideration alongside this man.* (6) *There will thus be no trouble with disorder and violence if it transpires that appointments in the Church are on a par and in all cases equally attractive. It is not right to make consideration of these things a matter of defeating others, since all are equally committed to receiving and preserving the divine doctrines, whether they appear to be fewer or larger in number, so that one party is in no way less than the other with regard to the common principle.*

(7) *If now we are to state frankly the plain truth, it would be regarded not as retaining the man so much as stealing him, and the deed done as an act of force and not of justice, whichever way the majority votes. I myself state explicitly and emphatically that this act is liable to the charge of provoking the disorder of large-scale civil strife. Teeth appear in the character and strength even of sheep, when the attention and care of the shepherd disappears and they are deprived of the direction they had before.* (8) *If this is the case, and we are not mistaken, then you must first observe, brothers (for many serious matters will confront you from the start), in the first place whether your sincerity and loyalty towards each other will be perceived to be in no respect diminished; and secondly, that the one who came to give correct advice is reaping his due reward from the divine judgement, having received an exceptional testimonial in the large vote which you have given him for integrity. In these circumstances, as is your custom, with a fair mind make every proper effort to identify the man you need, setting aside all riotous and disorderly clamour; that sort of thing is always wrong, and it is from the striking together of conflicting materials that sparks and flames are kindled.*

(9) *May I thus be pleasing to God and live for you in accordance with your prayers, since I love you and the haven of your calm: drive from it that filth, and by good behaviour put in its place* [115] *concord, making your sign secure, and steering a course towards the heavenly light, your rudder (so to speak) iron-fast. You should therefore reckon even your cargo disposable: everything that spoiled the ship has been discharged from the holds. You must now plan for the benefit from all these things to be such that we do not a second time through rash and inexpedient haste appear to have either finally settled, or even started out on, an undesirable course.*

God preserve you, dear brothers.

61 (1) *Victor Constantinus Maximus Augustus to Eusebius*

I have read with great pleasure the letter which your Intelligence has written, and I take note that the principle of ecclesiastical canonical discipline has been strictly kept. May you abide by those things which appear both pleasing to God and consonant with the apostolic tradition. You should certainly consider yourself blessed in this respect, that by the testimony of practically the whole world you have been judged worthy to be bishop of any and every church. If they all desire you to be with them, undoubtedly they thereby increase that happiness you enjoy. (2) *But your Intelligence, which knows how to keep the commandments of God and the apostolic rule of the Church, has done exceptionally well in declining the episcopate of the church in Antioch, preferring to remain in that church in which by God's will you received the bishopric in the first place.* (3) *On this subject we have written a letter to the people. As to your colleagues in the ministry, who had themselves written to me on the subject in terms which your Purity will readily understand when you read it, since justice spoke against them, I have written to them at the instigation of God; your Intelligence will have to attend their council, so that what is decided at the church in Antioch* [116] *may be deemed entirely right both by God and by the Church.*

God preserve you, dear brother.

62 (1) *Victor Constantinus Maximus Augustus to Theodotus, Theodorus, Narcissus, Aetius, Alpheius and the other bishops who are at Antioch.*

I have read what was written by your Intelligence, and I welcome the wise resolve of Eusebius who shares your consecrated ministry. Having been apprised of all that has happened on the one hand by your letter and on the other by that of Acacius and Strategius the comites clarissimi, *I have, after making the necessary enquiries, written to the people of Antioch what is pleasing to God and fitting for the Church, and have also ordered a copy to be subjoined to this present letter, so that you may yourselves know what, stimulated by consideration of what is right, I have decided to write to the people. Your letter contained the proposal that, in accordance with the mind and purpose of the people and of your own determinate choice, Eusebius the most sacred bishop of the church of Caesarea should be installed as bishop of Antioch and take it under his care.* (2) *Eusebius' letter however, which appeared fully to preserve the rule of the Church, propounded the opposite view, that he should in no wise forsake the church entrusted to him by God. It is therefore decreed that his very just determination, which should be upheld by you all, be confirmed, and that he be not torn away from his church.*

My own judgement ought also to be made plain to your Intelligence. It is reported to me that Euphronius the presbyter, a citizen of Caesarea in Cappadocia, and George of Arethusa, also a presbyter, who was appointed to that order by Alexander of Alexandria, are of thoroughly proven faith. (3) It is therefore proper to indicate to your Intelligence [117] *these aforementioned and others, whom you may think worthy of the office of bishop, so that you may make decisions in accordance with the tradition of the Apostles. When such matters have been put in hand, your Intelligence will be able to arrange the ordination in accordance with the Church's canon and the Apostolic tradition in such manner as the principle of ecclesiastical discipline prescribes.*

God preserve you, beloved brothers.

63 (1) In giving such instructions to the leaders of the churches the Emperor urged them to conduct all their business for the honour of the divine Word.

63–6. *Suppression of sects*

When he had removed the divisions and brought the whole Church of God into harmonious concord, he went on to decide that another kind of men ought to be eliminated like a poison from humanity. (2) These were some destructive pests who under a cloak of sanctity were harming the cities. The Saviour's voice calls them false prophets or ravening wolves in one of his sayings, 'Beware of the false prophets, who will come to you in sheep's clothing, but inwardly they are ravening wolves; by their fruits you shall know them' (Matthew 7: 15–16). (3) An order to the provincial governors expelled the whole tribe of such persons, and in addition to the decree he also composed an admonition addressed to the persons themselves, urging them to come quickly to repentance: the Church of God would be for them a safe haven. Listen to the way he preaches to them too through his letter to them:

64 (1) *Victor Constantinus Maximus Augustus to heretics.*

Be it known to you by this present decree, you Novatians, Valentinians, Marcionites, Paulians and those called Cataphrygians, all in short who constitute the heresies by your private assemblies, how many are the falsehoods in which your idle folly is entangled, and how venomous the poisons with which your teaching is involved, so that the healthy are brought to sickness and the living to everlasting death through you. (2) You opponents of truth, enemies of life and counsellors of ruin! Everything about you is contrary to truth, [118] in harmony with ugly deeds of evil; it serves grotesque charades in which you argue falsehoods, distress the unoffending, deny light to believers. By continually sinning under a pretext of godliness you make all things foul, you wound innocent and pure consciences with deadly blows, you all but rob human eyes of daylight itself. (3) Why should I go into detail, when to speak about your villainies as they deserve is more than a short time and our business permits? The crimes done among you are so great and immense, so hateful and full of harshness, that not even a whole day would suffice to put them into words; and in any case it is proper to shut the ears and avert the eyes, so as not to impair the pure and untarnished commitment of our own faith by recounting the details. (4) Why then should we endure such evils any longer? Protracted neglect allows healthy people to be infected as with an epidemic disease. Why do we not immediately use severe public measures to dig up such a great evil, as you might say, by the roots?

65 (1) Accordingly, since it is no longer possible to tolerate the pernicious effect of your destructiveness, by this decree we publicly command that none of you henceforward shall dare to assemble. Therefore we have also given order that all your buildings in which you conduct these meetings are to be confiscated, the purport of this extending so far as to prohibit the gathering of assemblies of your superstitious folly not only in public but also in houses of individuals or any private places. (2) The best thing would be for as many as are concerned for true and pure religion to come to the Catholic Church and share in the sanctity of that by which you will also be able to attain the truth. But let there be wholly removed from the prosperity of our times the deception of your perverted thinking, by which I mean the polluted and destructive deviance of the heretics and schismatics. It is in keeping with our present blessedness, which under God we enjoy, that those who live in good hopes should be led from all disorderly error into the right path, from darkness to light, from vanity to truth, from death to salvation.

(3) To ensure that [119] this curative measure may also be enforced I have commanded, as already stated, all the meeting places of your superstition, I mean all the places of worship of the heretics, if indeed it is proper to call them places of worship, be confiscated and handed over incontestably and without delay to the Catholic Church, and other sites become public property; and that hereafter no opportunity be left for you to

meet, so that from this day forward your unlawful groups may not dare to
assemble in any place either public or private.

To be published.

66 (1) Thus were the secret conspiracies of the heterodox
destroyed by the Emperor's command, and the wild beasts, the
captains of their sacrilege, were driven off. Of those deceived by
them there were some who through fear of the imperial warning
crept into the Church with fraudulent purpose, dissembling as
occasion required, since the decree also required the books of
these persons to be hunted out, and they were caught carrying out
forbidden evil practices; this showed that they did it all to procure
safety by pretence. Others perhaps with genuine intent went over
to hope in the Supreme. (2) The presidents of churches made
careful distinction between these persons: those who tried to join
on fictitious grounds they warded off from the flock of God as
wolves hiding in sheep's fleeces; those who did so with a pure
heart they tested over a period and after sufficient trial included
them among the number of those allowed entry. (3) This then
was the policy towards the infamous heretics. Those who had no
sacrilegious doctrinal teaching, but were in other ways separated
from the common fellowship by reason of schismatic individuals,
they received without delay. They came flocking back like those
returning from exile to their native land, and acknowledged their
mother the Church, from which they had wandered off, but now
with joy and gladness made their return to her. The parts of the
common body were united together and joined in a single
harmony, and alone the Catholic Church of God shone forth
gathered into itself, with no heretical or schismatic group left
anywhere in the world. For this great achievement also, among
those that ever were, only the Emperor who cared about God
could claim responsibility.

BOOK IV

1–14. 1. *The Prosperous Empire*

1–4. *Philanthropy*

[120] 1 (1) While the Emperor was doing so much to build up
and honour the Church of God, and was performing all that
would bring the Saviour's teaching into good repute, he did not

neglect secular affairs, but in those also was persistently providing repeated and continuous good works of every kind for all the inhabitants of every province alike. On the one hand he showed general fatherly concern for all, while on the other he would honour each of those known to him with special promotions, bestowing everything on everyone with generosity of heart. One who sought favour of the Emperor could not fail to obtain his request, nor was anyone who hoped for generous treatment disappointed in his expectations. (2) Some received money in abundance, others goods; some acquired posts as prefects, others senatorial rank, others that of consuls; very many were designated governors; some were appointed *comites* of the first order, others of the second, others of the third. Similarly many thousands more shared honours as *clarissimi* or with a wide range of other titles; for in order to promote more persons the Emperor contrived different distinctions.

2 The way in which he planned for the happiness of the mass of mankind might be observed from one generally beneficial example, which has reached all parts ever since and is still recognized today. He removed a fourth part of the annual tax charged on land, and allowed this to the landlords, so that the one calculating the annual deduction found every four years that the landowners were not liable to tax. This was confirmed by law and remained in force in the subsequent period, and made the imperial bounty unforgettable and permanent, not only for those then living, but for their children and successors.   3 When others complained about the land measurements made under previous rulers, [121] alleging that their estates were overburdened, once again in this case by a decree he sent adjustment officers (*peraequatores*) to provide relief to the petitioners.

4 In settling disputes for others, so that the losing party in his court might not come off less pleased than the successful litigants, the Emperor would grant to the defeated party from his own resources sometimes property, sometimes money, ensuring that the loser was just as pleased as the winner, inasmuch as he had been admitted to his presence; for it seemed wrong that anyone who had stood before such an Emperor should depart disappointed and bitter. Thus both would leave court with happy smiling faces, and every one was full of admiration for the Emperor's magnanimity.

5–6. *Foreign relations I: Pacification of Goths and Sarmatians*

5 (1) What need is there for me to mention even incidentally how he subjected barbarian races to Roman rule, how he was the first to subjugate the Gothic and Sarmatian tribes which had never before learnt to serve, compelling them to accept the Romans as their masters even against their will? Previous rulers had even paid tribute to the Goths, and Romans served barbarians with yearly payments. (2) Such a reckoning was not acceptable to the Emperor, nor did it seem good enough to the Victor to make the same payments as his predecessors. Confident in his Saviour and brandishing the victorious trophy over them too, he very soon subdued them all, sometimes taming the refractory with the military arm, sometimes pacifying the rest by reasonable negotiations, converting them from a lawless animal existence to one of reason and law. In this way the Goths learnt at last to serve Rome.

6 (1) As to the Sarmatians, it was God himself who thrust them under the feet of Constantine, defeating men who gloried in their barbaric mentality in the following way. When the Goths attacked them, the masters armed their servants to repel their enemies. But when the slaves had won, they turned their arms against their masters and drove them all from their own land. The masters found no other safe refuge than Constantine alone. (2) He knew the meaning of rescue, and received them all as subjects in Roman territory. Those who were suitable he enrolled in his own forces; to the rest he apportioned land for cultivation of the means of subsistence, so that they acknowledged that the disaster had turned out good for them [122] in that they enjoyed Roman liberty instead of barbaric bestiality. Thus God bestowed upon him victories over all the nations, so that of their own accord all sorts of barbarian tribes were willing to submit to him.

7. *Foreign relations II: Foreign tributes*

7 (1) There were constant diplomatic visitors who brought valuable gifts from their homelands, so that when we ourselves happened to be present we saw before the outer palace gates waiting in a line remarkable figures of barbarians, with their exotic dress, their distinctive appearance, the quite singular cut

of hair and beard; the appearance of their hairy faces was foreign and astonishing, their bodily height exceptional. The faces of some were red, of others whiter than snow, of others blacker than ebony or pitch, and others had a mixed colour in between; for men of Blemmyan race, and Indian and Ethiopian, 'who are twain-parted last of men' (Homer, *Od.* 1. 23), could be seen in recounting those mentioned. (2) Each of these in turn, as in a picture, brought their particular treasures to the Emperor, some of them golden crowns, some diadems of precious stones, others fair-haired children, others foreign cloths woven with gold and bright colours, others horses, others shields and long spears and javelins and bows, showing that they were offering service and alliance with these things to the Emperor when he required it. (3) The Emperor received these from those who brought them and recorded them, and responded with equal gifts, so as to make the bearers very rich all at once. He honoured the most distinguished of them also with Roman titles, so that very many now longed to remain here, forgetting any thought of returning to their homes.

8–14. 1. *Foreign relations III: Peace with Persia*

8 When the Persian emperor also saw fit to seek recognition by Constantine through an embassy, and he too dispatched tokens of friendly compact, the Emperor negotiated treaties to this end, outdoing in lavish munificence the initiator of honorific gesture by what he did in return. Certainly, when he learnt that the churches of God were multiplying among the Persians and that many thousands of people were being gathered into the flocks of Christ, he rejoiced at the report, and, [123] as one who had general responsibility for them everywhere, there too he again took prudent measures on behalf of them all. This also he shall explain for himself in his own words through the letter which he dispatched to the Persian emperor, commending these people to him with utmost tact and discretion. This document also is in circulation among us, written by the Emperor personally in Latin, which may be more readily understood by the reader when translated into Greek. It runs like this:

9 *Guarding the divine faith I participate in the light of truth. Led by*

the light of truth I recognize the divine faith. By these things therefore, as events confirm, I acknowledge the most holy religion. I confess that I hold this cult to be the teacher of the knowledge of the most holy God. Having the power of this God as ally, beginning from the shores of Ocean I have raised up the whole world step by step with sure hopes of salvation, so that all those things, which under the slavery of such great tyrants yielded to daily disasters and had come near to vanishing, have enjoyed the general restoration of right, and have revived like a patient after treatment. The God I represent is the one whose sign my army, dedicated to God, carries on its shoulders, and to whatever task the Word of Justice summons it goes directly; and from those men I get immediate and happy recompense in marks of signal victory. This is the God I profess to honour with undying remembrance, and him I clearly perceive with unsullied and pure mind to take highest place.

10 (1) *Him I call upon with bended knee, shunning all abominable blood and foul hateful odours, and refusing all earthly splendour, since by all these things that lawless and unmentionable error is tainted, which has overthrown many of the nations and whole peoples, dropping them in the nethermost depths.* (2) *Those things which the God of the Universe, out of concern for* [124] *human welfare and because of his own love for mankind, has made available for use, should certainly not be diverted to suit the desire of individuals; he requires of men only a pure mind and soul unblemished, making these the measure of deeds of virtue and piety.* (3) *He takes pleasure in works of kindness and gentleness, befriending the meek, hating the violent, loving faithfulness, punishing unfaithfulness, shattering all ostentatious power, taking vengeance on overweening arrogance; those who proudly exalt themselves he utterly destroys, while he gives what they deserve to the humble and forgiving.* (4) *So because he also values highly righteous empire, he strengthens it with his own resources, and guards the imperial mind with the calm of peace.*

11 (1) *I believe I am not mistaken, my brother, in confessing this one God the Author and Father of all, whom many of those who have reigned here, seduced by insane errors, have attempted to deny. But such punishment finally engulfed them that all mankind since has regarded their fate as superseding all other examples to warn those who strive for the same ends.* (2) *Among them I reckon that one, who was driven from these parts by divine wrath as by a thunderbolt and was left in yours, where he caused the victory on your side to become very famous because of the shame he suffered.*

12 *Yet it would appear that it has turned out advantageous that even*

in our own day the punishment of such persons has become notorious. I have myself observed the end of those next to me, who with vicious decrees had harassed the people devoted to God. All thanks therefore are due to God, because by his perfect providence the entire humanity which reveres the divine Law, now that peace has been restored to them, exults triumphantly. Consequently I am convinced that for ourselves also everything is at its best and most secure [125] *when through their pure and excellent religion and as a result of their concord on matters divine he deigns to gather all men to himself.*

13 *With this class of persons—I mean of course the Christians, my whole concern being for them—how pleasing it is for me to hear that the most important parts of Persia too are richly adorned! May the very best come to you therefore, and at the same time the best for them, since they also are yours. For so you will keep the sovereign Lord of the Universe kind, merciful and benevolent. These therefore, since you are so great, I entrust to you, putting their very persons in your hands, because you too are renowned for piety. Love them in accordance with your own humanity. For you will give enormous satisfaction both to yourself and to us by keeping faith.*

14 (1) Thus finally, all nations of the world being steered by a single pilot and welcoming government by the Servant of God, with none any longer obstructing Roman rule, all men passed their life in undisturbed tranquillity.

14. 2–39. *Constantine's Sanctity*

14. 2–16. *Personal piety*

(2) The Emperor judged that the prayers of the godly made a great contribution to his aim of protecting the general good, so he made the necessary provision for these, becoming himself a suppliant of God and bidding the leaders of the churches make intercessions for him.   **15** (1) The great strength of the divinely inspired faith fixed in his soul might be deduced by considering also the fact that he had his own portrait so depicted on the gold coinage that he appeared to look upwards in the manner of one reaching out to God in prayer. (2) Impressions of this type were circulated throughout the entire Roman world. In the imperial quarters of various cities, in the images erected above the entrances, he was portrayed standing up, looking up to heaven,

his hands extended [126] in a posture of prayer.   16 Such was
the way he would have himself depicted praying in works of
graphic art. But by law he forbade images of himself to be set up
in idol-shrines, so that he might not be contaminated by the error
of forbidden things even in replica.

17–21. *Staff and military personnel*

17 One might observe the more solemn aspects of these
things by noting how he conducted matters even in the imperial
quarters in the manner of a church of God, being himself the
leader in earnestness of those constituting the church there. He
would take the books in his hands and apply his mind to the
meaning of the divinely inspired oracles, and would then render
up lawful prayers with the members of the imperial household.
18 (1) He also decreed that the truly sovereign and really first
day, the day of the Lord and Saviour, should be considered a
regular day of prayer. Servants and ministers consecrated to God,
men whose well-ordered life was marked by reverent conduct
and every virtue, were put in charge of the whole household, and
faithful praetorians, bodyguards armed with the practice of
faithful loyalty, adopted the Emperor as their tutor in religious
conduct, themselves paying no less honour to the Lord's saving
day and on it joining in the prayers the Emperor loved.
(2) The Blessed One urged all men also to do the same, as if
by encouraging this he might gently bring all men to piety. He
therefore decreed that all those under Roman government
should rest on the days named after the Saviour, and similarly
that they should honour the days of the Sabbath, in memory, I
suppose, of the things recorded as done by the universal Saviour
on those days.
(3) The Day of Salvation then, which also bears the names of
Light Day and Sun Day, he taught all the military to revere
devoutly. [127] To those who shared the divinely given faith he
allowed free time to attend unhindered the church of God, on the
assumption that with all impediment removed they would join in
the prayers.   19 To those who did not yet share in the divine
Word he gave order in a second decree that every Lord's Day
they should march out to an open space just outside the city, and
that there at a signal they should all together offer up to God a

form of prayer learnt by heart; they ought not to rest their hopes on spears or armour or physical strength, but acknowledge the God over all, the giver of all good and indeed of victory itself, to whom it was right to offer the lawful prayers, lifting up their hands high towards heaven, extending their mental vision yet higher to the heavenly King, and calling on him in their prayers as the Giver of victory and Saviour, as their Guardian and Helper. He was himself the instructor in prayer to all the soldiery, bidding them all to say these words in Latin:

20. (1) *'You alone we know as God,*
You are the King we acknowledge,
You are the Help we summon.
By you we have won our victories,
Through you we have overcome our enemies.
To you we render thanks for the good things past,
You also we hope for as giver of those to come.
To you we all come to supplicate for our Emperor
*   Constantine and for his Godbeloved Sons:*
That he may be kept safe and victorious for us in long,
*   long life, we plead.'*

(2) Such were the things he decreed should be done by the military regiments every Sunday, and such were the words he taught them to recite in their prayers to God.   **21** Furthermore he caused the sign of the saving trophy to be marked on their shields, and had the army led on parade, not by any of the golden images, as had been their past practice, but by the saving trophy alone.

22–3. *Domestic religion*

[128]   **22** (1) He himself, like someone participating in sacred mysteries, would shut himself at fixed times each day in secret places within his royal palace chambers, and would converse with his God alone, and kneeling in suppliant petition would plead for the objects of his prayers. On days of the Feast of the Saviour, intensifying the rigour, he would perform the divine mysteries with his whole strength of soul and body, on the one hand wholly dedicated to purity of life, and on the other initiating the festival for all. (2) He transformed the sacred

vigil into daylight, as those appointed to the task lit huge wax tapers throughout the whole city; there were fiery torches that lit up every place, so as to make the mystic vigil more radiant than bright day. When dawn interposed, in imitation of the beneficence of the Saviour he opened his beneficent hand to all provinces, peoples, and cities, making rich gifts of every kind to them all. (3) Such then was his religious practice towards his own God.

23–5. *Christianity promoted and idolatry suppressed*

23 For all those under Roman rule, both civilian and military, access was universally blocked to every form of idolatry, and every form of sacrifice banned. A decree went also to the governors of each province directing that they should similarly reverence the Lord's Day. These same persons at the Emperor's behest honoured the days of martyrs as well, and adorned the times of festival with public gatherings. Such things were all carried out as the Emperor desired. 24 Hence it is not surprising that on one occasion, when entertaining bishops to dinner, he let slip the remark that he was perhaps himself a bishop too, using some such words as these in our hearing: 'You are bishops of those within the Church, but I am perhaps a bishop appointed by God over those outside.' In accordance with this saying, he exercised a bishop's supervision over all his subjects, and pressed them all, as far as lay in his power, to lead the godly life.

25 (1) Hence it is not surprising that in successive laws and ordinances he prohibited everyone from sacrificing to idols, from practising divination, from having cult-figures erected, from performing secret rites, and from defiling the cities by the carnage of gladiatorial combat. (2) To those in Egypt and especially Alexandria, who had a custom of worshipping their river through the offices of effeminate men, another law was [129] sent out, declaring that the whole class of homosexuals should be abolished as a thing depraved, and that it was unlawful for those infected with this gross indecency to be seen anywhere. (3) Whereas the superstitious supposed that the river would no longer flow for them in its customary way, God cooperated with the Emperor's law by achieving quite the opposite of what they

expected. For although those who defiled the cities by their abominable practice were no more, the river, as though the land had been cleared for it, flowed as never before, and rose in abundant flood to overflow all the arable land, by its action teaching the senseless that one should reject polluted men and attribute the cause of prosperity to the sole giver of all good.

26–8. *Legislation and public charity*

26 (1) Indeed, with countless such measures taken by the Emperor in every province, there would be plenty of scope for those eager to record them. The same applies to the laws which he renewed by transforming them from their primitive state to a more hallowed one. It will be easier to explain briefly the nature of these reforms also.

(2) Ancient laws had punished those without children by stopping them inheriting from their kinsmen. This was a harsh law against the childless, since it punished them as criminals. By repealing this he permitted the proper persons to inherit. The Emperor made this change towards sacred justice, saying that it was those who offended deliberately who ought to be corrected with fitting punishment. (3) Nature has made many childless, when they have prayed to be blessed with large families, but have been disappointed through bodily infirmity. Others have become childless, not through rejecting the natural succession of children, but through abstaining from intercourse with women, an abstinence which they chose through a passion for philosophy, and women consecrated to the sacred service of God have practised a chaste and absolute virginity, consecrating themselves by a pure and all-holy life of soul and body. (4) Ought this then to be thought to deserve punishment, and not admiration and approval? Their zeal is highly deserving, their achievement surpasses nature. Those therefore who are disappointed in their desire for children by bodily infirmity should be pitied rather than penalized, and the lover of the Supreme deserves the highest admiration and not punishment. Thus the Emperor with sound reasoning remodelled the law.

(5) Furthermore for those near death ancient laws prescribed that even with their last breath the [130] wills they made must be expressed in precise verbal formulae, and that certain phrases

and terminology must be used to state them. This led to much malicious manipulation to circumvent the intentions of the deceased. (6) The Emperor noted this, and changed this law too, saying that the dying person should express what he had in mind in plain simple words and everyday speech, and compose his will in an ordinary document, or even unwritten if he wished, provided he did this in the presence of trustworthy witnesses, able to preserve accurately what is entrusted to them.

27 (1) He also made a law that no Christian was to be a slave to Jews, on the ground that it was not right that those redeemed by the Saviour should be subjected by the yoke of bondage to the slayers of the prophets and the murderers of the Lord. If any were found in this condition, the one was to be set free, the other punished with a fine.

(2) He also put his seal on the decrees of bishops made at synods, so that it would not be lawful for the rulers of provinces to annul what they had approved, since the priests of God were superior to any magistrate.

(3) He made countless decrees like these for those under his rule. It would need leisure to commit them to a separate work for the precise analysis of the Emperor's policies in those also. What need is there now to set out in detail how, having attached himself to the God over all, he pondered from dawn to dusk on which of mankind to benefit, or how he was fair to all and impartial in his benefits?

28 But to the churches of God in particular he was exceptionally generous in his provision, in one place bestowing estates, and elsewhere grain allowances to feed poor men, orphan children, and women in distress. Then with great concern he also provided huge quantities of clothing for the naked and unclad. He singled out as worthy of special honour those who had dedicated their lives to godly philosophy. He would all but worship God's choir of those sanctified in perpetual virginity, believing that in the souls of such as these dwelt the God to whom they had consecrated themselves.

29–33. *Speaking and listening*

29 (1) Indeed in order to enlarge his understanding with the help of the divinely inspired words, [131] he would spend the hours of the night awake, and repeatedly made public appearances without calling upon speechwriters; he thought that he ought to rule his subjects with instructive argument, and establish his whole imperial rule as rational. (2) Consequently when he gave the invitation, countless multitudes rushed to join the audience to hear the Emperor's philosophy. If while speaking he had occasion to mention God, standing quite straight with intense face and subdued voice, he would seem to be initiating the audience with deep awe in the inspired doctrine, and then when the hearers let out favourable exclamations he would indicate that they should look to heaven and save the adulation and honour of their reverent praises for the King over all.

(3) In planning his addresses, he would at one point set out refutations of polytheistic error, showing that the religion of the heathen is a deception and a façade for atheism; at another point he would recommend that the sole Godhead should be acknowledged, and would systematically expound providence both in general and in particular cases. Thence he would proceed to the Saviour's dispensation, demonstrating the necessity for it to happen in terms of what is appropriate. He would then go on to deal with the doctrine of divine judgement. (4) Next he would touch on things which struck the audience most forcefully, rebuking thieves and frauds and those who committed themselves to greedy profiteering. Striking them, and as if actually flogging them, with his argument, he made some of his courtiers bow their heads as their conscience was smitten. Testifying in plain words he announced to them that he would give an account to God of their activities; for the God over all had given him sovereignty over things on earth, and he in imitation of the Supreme had committed particular administrative regions of the Empire to them; all however would in due course be subject to scrutiny of their actions by the Great King. (5) Such were the constant themes of his affirmation, his admonition, his teaching.

With the assurance of the authentic faith he held and expressed such views, but they were slow to learn and deaf to what is good; they would cheer his words with cries and acclamations of approval, but in practice they ignored them through greed. 30 (1) So in the end he tackled one of those round him and said, 'How far, my man, do we make greed stretch?' Then on the ground he drew with the staff which he had in his hand the measure of the height of a man, and said, 'If all the wealth in the world and all the land there is becomes yours, [132] you will still not possess more than this plot here marked out—assuming you even get that.' (2) But in spite of what he said and did, not one was restrained by the blessed one; yet events have manifestly convinced them that the pronouncements of the Emperor were like divine oracles and not mere words. 31 But since the fear of death failed to deter the wicked from their evil ways, the Emperor being wholly given to clemency, and none of those who governed the various provinces took any steps anywhere at all against the offenders, this certainly brought no small reproach upon the whole regime. Whether that was fair or not is for each to judge as he sees fit, and I content myself with recording the truth.

32 However that may be, Latin was the language in which the Emperor used to produce the text of his speeches. They were translated into Greek by professional interpreters. By way of example of his translated works I shall append immediately after this present book the speech which he entitled, 'To the assembly of the saints', dedicating the work to the Church of God, so that none may think our assertions about his speeches to be mere rhetoric.

33 (1) One other thing seems to me to be unforgettable, a deed which the marvellous man did in our own presence. On one occasion, emboldened by his devotion to divine things, we asked permission to deliver an address about the Saviour's tomb for him to hear. He listened with rapt attention, and where a large audience was standing round right inside the palace he stood up and listened with the others. When we begged him to rest on the imperial throne which was nearby, he would not do so, but made a shrewdly considered critique of the speech, and affirmed the truth of its doctrinal theology. (2) Since it took a long time and the speech still continued, we suggested breaking off; he however would not allow it, but urged us to go on to the end. When we asked him to sit he kept refusing, saying at one time that when the doctrine of God was being discussed, it was wrong for him to relax while he listened, and at another that it was good and beneficial for him to stand: it was a holy thing to listen to divinity standing up. When [133] this too came to an end, we returned home and took up our regular business.

34–7. Letters on Christian topics

34 He meanwhile in his prudent care for the future of the churches of God wrote a letter to us personally on the copying of divinely inspired Scriptures. With it he appended another on the most holy feast of Pascha. After we had addressed to him a mystical explanation of the account of the festival, the reply with which he honoured us in response may be learnt by reading the letter itself, as follows:

35 (1) *Victor Constantinus Maximus Augustus to Eusebius.*

It is a major undertaking, greater than words can describe, to speak worthily of the mysteries of Christ and to interpret in a suitable way the dispute about and origin of Pascha, and its beneficial and painful bringing to fulfilment. Worthily to express the divine to human beings is impossible even for those of able intellect. (2) *Nevertheless with great admiration for your learning and endeavour I have gladly read the book myself, and as you desired I have ordered it to be published for the large number who are sincerely attached to the worship of God.* (3) *Now that you are aware how cordially we enjoy receiving such gifts from your Intelligence, do make every effort to give us the pleasure of more frequent literary works, in which you allow you are well trained. We are urging you 'already sprinting', as the saying goes, to your habitual studies. Such great confidence certainly shows that the one who renders your efforts into the Latin tongue has not been found by you to be unworthy of what you have written, true though it is that it is impossible for such a translation satisfactorily to represent the elegance of the words.*

May God preserve you, beloved brother.

Such was his letter on that subject. The one on the provision of divine Scriptures runs as follows:

36 (1) *Victor Constantinus Maximus Augustus to Eusebius.*

[134] *In the City which bears our name by the sustaining providence of the Saviour God a great mass of people has attached itself to the most holy Church, so that with everything there enjoying great growth it is particularly fitting that more churches should be established.* (2) *Be ready therefore to act urgently on the decision which we have reached. It appeared proper to indicate to your Intelligence that you should order fifty volumes with ornamental leather bindings, easily legible and convenient for portable use, to be copied by skilled calligraphists well trained in the art, copies that is of the Divine Scriptures, the provision and use of which*

you well know to be necessary for reading in church. (3) *Written instructions have been sent by our Clemency to the man who is in charge of the diocese that he see to the supply of all the materials needed to produce them. The preparation of the written volumes with utmost speed shall be the task of your Diligence.* (4) *You are entitled by the authority of this our letter to the use of two public vehicles for transportation. The fine copies may thus most readily be transported to us for inspection; one of the deacons of your own congregation will presumably carry out this task, and when he reaches us he will experience our generosity.*

God preserve you, dear brother.

37 These then were the Emperor's instructions. Immediate action followed upon his word, as we sent him threes and fours in richly wrought bindings ⟨. . .⟩

37–9. Conversion of cities

This may be confirmed by another rescript of the Emperor, in which he explains that he was pleased to learn that our neighbouring city of Constantia, which formerly consisted of absurdly superstitious men, had in a movement of godly religion turned from its former idolatrous error, and that he welcomed what they had done ⟨. . .⟩

38 At this time then in the province of Palestine Constantia endorsed the saving religion, and achieved higher honour both with God and with the Emperor. It was designated a city, which it had not been before, and exchanged its name for the superior title of the Emperor's religious sister.

39 (1) The same action was taken by many other places, like that with the Emperor's name in Phoenicia, where the citizens committed to the flames a barely countable number of wooden cult-figures, adopting instead the Saviour's Law. (2) In other provinces whole crowds changed sides and came to the knowledge of the Saviour; in every territory and city they got rid of the things they formerly held sacred, made of all kinds of wood, as if they were nothing. Temples and built-up precincts they demolished without orders from anyone, and building churches on their foundations they changed from their former error.

(3) To describe one by one the deeds of the Godbeloved is not so much our task as that of those who were privileged to spend the whole time with him. We have put down briefly in this work

the information we have received, and shall now go on to the last period of his life.

40–52. 3. *Final Achievements*

40. *Tricennalia and promotion of sons*

40 (1) Thirty years of his reign were nearing completion. His three royal sons, most illustrious Caesars, were appointed at different times as co-emperors. The one with the same name as his father, Constantine, was first to share the honour at the time of his father's tenth anniversary; the second, adorned with the same name as his grandfather, Constantius, about the time of the twenty-year celebrations; and the third, Constans, who by the name applied to him signifies firmness and constancy, was promoted about the end of the third decade. (2) So like a trinity having acquired a triple Godbeloved offspring of sons, [136] and having honoured his offspring with adoption into imperial rank at the end of each decade, he reckoned his own thirtieth anniversary an auspicious occasion for thanksgivings to the universal King of all, and decided that it would be fitting to carry out the consecration of the *martyrion* which had been constructed with all artistic endeavour in Jerusalem.

41–2. *The Council at Tyre*

41 (1) Envy however, resentful of this too, like a dark cloud opposing the sun's bright beams, tried to disturb the brilliance of the festival, once more confusing the Egyptian churches with his disputes. (2) But the one who cared about God again armed a full synod of bishops as God's army and mobilized them against the mean demon, ordering them to hasten from all Egypt and Libya, from Asia and Europe, first to resolve the dispute, and then to conduct the consecration of the shrine referred to. (3) On their way he commanded them to settle their quarrels at the metropolis of Phoenicia, since it was not right to attend the worship of God with divided counsels, when the divine Law forbids those in dispute to present their offerings before they are reconciled in friendship and are at peace with each other. (4) Those salutary commands the Emperor personally vitalized with his own intellectual effort, and directed them to go about their business in total concord and harmony, writing as follows:

42 (1) *Constantinus Victor Maximus Augustus to the Holy Synod at Tyre.*

It would perhaps be apt and very much in keeping with the prosperity of our times [137] *that the universal Church should be free from strife and that the servants of Christ should refrain from all verbal attacks. But since some persons, spurred on by unhealthy rivalry (for I could not say they live up to their own standards) are trying to turn everything upside down, something which I consider an extreme disaster, I therefore urge you, 'already sprinting' (as the saying is), to come together without delay, to constitute the Synod, to defend those in need of help, to bring healing to brothers at risk, restore to concord members at variance, and to correct what is wrong, while time permits, so that you may restore to so many provinces that proper harmony which quite monstrously the arrogance of a few persons has destroyed. (2) That this purpose is pleasing to God the Sovereign of the universe, to me the supreme object of every prayer, and for yourselves, if you do re-establish peace, a cause of not inconsiderable fame, I am sure all men will agree. So do not delay further, but use your best endeavours straight away, and bring your business to a swift and proper conclusion, meeting of course in the absolute sincerity and good faith, which everywhere, almost uttering the words audibly, that Saviour whom we worship requires especially of you.*

(3) Nothing that falls to my particular care will be lacking to you. Everything you mentioned in your letter has been done by me. I have written to the bishops you wished me to, that they should come and take part in your deliberations; and I have sent Dionysius, a man of consular rank, who will also notify those who ought to attend the synod with you, and will be present to observe the proceedings, with a particular eye to good order. (4) Should any one (which I do not expect) attempt even now to thwart our command and refuse to attend, somebody will be sent from me from here to expel him by imperial mandate, and [137] *to make it clear that it is not right to oppose decrees of the Emperor promulgated on behalf of the truth.*

(5) Finally it shall be your Holiness' task, by unanimous verdict, pursuing neither enmity nor favour but in accordance with the ecclesiastical and apostolic canon, to discover the proper remedy for the offences committed or mistakes if they have been made, so that you may free the

Church of all malicious criticism, relieve my anxiety, and, by restoring the blessing of peace to those now at variance, win for yourselves highest fame. God preserve you, dear brothers.

43–8. The assembly in Jerusalem

43 (1) While these orders were being put into effect, another imperial officer intervened, pressing the Council with an imperial letter, and urging them to go at once and not defer their journey to Jerusalem. (2) So they all set off from the province of Phoenicia and came by public transport to their destination. All the space there was then filled with a vast divine chorus, as notable bishops from every province gathered together in Jerusalem. (3) The Macedonians sent the bishop of their metropolis, the Pannonians and Mysians fair blossoms from among them of God's younger generation; a sacred member of the Persian bishops was present, a man very learned in the divine oracles; the Bithynians and Thracians enhanced the dignity of those attending the Synod. (4) The more important Cilicians were not missing, and the leading Cappadocians also excelled among the rest for their scholarly learning. All Syria and Mesopotamia, Phoenicia and Arabia with Palestine itself, Egypt and Libya, the inhabitants of the Theban area, all together made up the great divine band, and innumerable laity from all the provinces accompanied them. An imperial staff attended all these, and leading officials from the palace were sent to enhance the splendour of the festival with imperial supplies.

44 (1) There was also the one in charge of all these things, a man close to the Emperor, famous for his faith and piety, and for his expertise in divine Scripture; [139] being famous for his religious confession at the time of the tyrants, he was rightly entrusted with making these arrangements. This person, in accordance with the Emperor's wish, fulfilling his duties to perfection, honoured the synod with a friendly reception, with brilliant banquets and merry parties. (2) To the unclad poor and to the untold multitudes of indigent men and women, and to those who were in want of food and other necessities, he made lavish distributions of money and clothing, and furthermore beautified the whole shrine with rich imperial dedications.

45 (1) While he performed this service, God's ministers

enriched the feast with both prayers and sermons. Some praised the Godbeloved Emperor's devotion to the Saviour of all, and recounted in detail the magnificent work connected with the *martyrion*; some with festive sermons based on divine doctrines provided a variety of intellectual delights for all to hear. (2) Others gave expositions of the divine readings, disclosing hidden meanings, while others incapable of this propitiated God with bloodless sacrifices and mystic ceremonies; for the general peace and for the Church of God, for the Emperor himself, who was responsible for such great things, and for his Godbeloved sons, they offered up prayers of supplication to God. (3) This was the occasion when we also, being honoured with favours beyond us, graced the feast with various addresses to those assembled, at one time interpreting in a written work the elaborate descriptions of the Emperor's philosophical ideas, at another making figurative thoughts from the prophets apply to the symbolic rites presently in hand. In this way the festival of dedication was carried out with joyful celebrations in the thirtieth year of the Emperor's reign.

46 A description of the Saviour's church, of the salvific cave, of the Emperor's works of art and large number of offerings made of gold, silver and precious stones, all of this we have set down to the best of our ability in a separate work addressed to the Emperor himself. In due course, after the present book is finished, we shall publish that work, joining to it the speech on the thirtieth anniversary. The latter [140] we delivered a little later, having made the journey to the city named after the Emperor, in the Emperor's own hearing, thus having a second opportunity to praise God, the universal Emperor, in the imperial palace. The friend of God, while he listened to it, was like a man overjoyed; he said so himself after the hearing, when he dined with the bishops present and received them with every kind of honour.

47 This second synod, the greatest of those we know, the Emperor assembled in Jerusalem, following that first synod, which he had brilliantly celebrated in the capital of Bithynia. That one however was a celebration of victory, which offered prayers of thanksgiving in the twentieth year of his reign for the defeat of enemies and foes at the very Place of Victory (Nicaea); this one beautified the third decade, as the Emperor consecrated

the *martyrion* to God, the Giver of all good things, as a peace-time dedication around the Saviour's tomb.

48 When all these things were being done by the Emperor, and his great valour on God's behalf was being praised by the mouths of all, one of God's ministers in an excess of boldness declared in his presence that he was 'Blessed', because in this present life he had been judged worthy of universal imperial power, and in the next he would rule alongside the Son of God. He was annoyed on hearing these words, and told him he should not say such rash things, but should rather pray for him, that in both this life and the next he might be found worthy to be God's slave.

49–50. *The universal Empire*

49 During the course of his thirtieth year of reign he celebrated the marriage of his second son, having earlier done the same for the eldest. Parties and festivals were held, with the Emperor himself acting as bridegroom's friend to his son. He gave splendid banquets and receptions, the men celebrating in one place, the ladies in separate parties elsewhere, and rich distributions of gifts were bestowed on both peoples and cities.

50 On that occasion embassies from the Indians, who live near the rising sun, presented themselves, bringing gifts. These were all sorts of sparkling jewels, and animals of breeds differing from those known among us. These they brought to the Emperor showing that his power extended as far as the Ocean itself, and also how the [141] rulers of the land of India, by honouring him with painted pictures and the dedication of statues, recognized and confessed him as Sovereign and Emperor. So when he began his reign the first to be subjected to him were the Britons near where the sun sets in the Ocean, and now it was the Indians, whose land lies near the sunrise.

51–2. 3. *Sons prepared for succession*

51 (1) Now that he was in control of both ends of the entire inhabited world, he divided the government of the whole Empire among his three sons, as though disposing a patrimony to those he loved best: he allocated to the eldest his grandfather's portion,

to the second the government of the east, and that between them
to the third. (2) To provide them with a good inheritance that
would also save their souls, he planted in them the seeds of
godliness, introducing them to sacred studies, and appointing as
their teachers men of proven piety. For secular studies too he set
over them other teachers of first-class scholarship. Others introduced them to military science, another group educated them in
politics, and yet others trained them in legal skills. (3) An
imperial retinue was allocated to each of the sons, soldiers,
praetorians, and bodyguards, and military officers of various
ranks, generals, centurions, commanders, and tribunes whom
their father had previously tried for their expertise in war as well as
for their loyalty to him.   52 (1) While they were still of a tender
age the staff attached to the Caesars were obliged to accompany
them and administer public affairs. But when they reached
manhood their father by himself was all the instruction they
needed. Sometimes he encouraged them while they were with
him with personal admonitions to copy him and taught them to
make themselves imitators of his godly piety. Sometimes when
communicating with them in their absence about imperial
matters he would express his exhortations in writing, the greatest
and most important of these being that they should prize the
knowledge of God the King of all and devotion to him above all
wealth and even above Empire. (2) By now he had also given
them authority to take action for the public good by themselves,
and he urged them that one of their prime concerns should be the
Church of God, instructing them to be frankly Christian. So for
his part the Emperor [142] guided his sons, and they, not simply
obeying orders but of their own free will, exceeded their father's
exhortation: they applied their own efforts strenuously to sancti-
fication under God, and fulfilled the precepts of the Church in the
palaces themselves along with all their households. (3) Another
effect of the father's planning was that his children were given as
household companions only Godfearing men, and even of the
highest officials who were in charge of public affairs some were
such. So with men faithful before God, like a strong perimeter
wall, he protected them.

52. 4–73. *Baptism and Death*

52. 4–55. *Constantine's physical health and faith in immortality*

52 (4) When these matters had been duly settled by the Thriceblessed, God the Disposer of all good decided, since affairs universally had been well arranged by him, that it was now the right time to transfer him to better things, and exacted from him his debt to nature. **53** He was completing the thirty-second year of his reign, short of only a few months and days, and about twice that number of years of life. At that age his body remained sound and unimpaired, free from any defect and more youthful than any young man's, handsome to look at, and fit enough to do whatever needed physical strength, such as training, riding, and travelling, engaging in wars, raising monuments over defeated enemies and winning his usual bloodless victories over his opponents.

54 (1) His spiritual qualities had also advanced to the peak of human perfection. He was outstanding in all virtues, but especially for kindness. Most people considered this reprehensible because of the base conduct of selfish men, who attributed their own wickedness to the Emperor's forbearance. (2) It is true that we ourselves during these particular years noticed two difficulties. There was a relaxation of censure against wicked rapacious men, who damaged the whole course of affairs; and there was also an unspeakable deceit on the part of those who slipped into the Church and adopted the false façade of the Christian name. (3) His kindness and generosity, however, the straightforwardness of his faith, and the sincerity of his character led him to trust the outward appearance [143] of those reputed to be Christians, who with a faked attitude contrived to keep up the pretence of genuine loyalty to him. By entrusting himself to them he came to be blamed for their misdeeds, as Envy fastened this smear on his virtues. **55** (1) These men were, however, before long overtaken by divine punishment.

Meanwhile the Emperor's own mind was so far advanced in rhetorical skill that to the very end he continued to compose speeches, and continued to make public appearances and to deliver divinely edifying instructions to his audiences. He continued to legislate for both civil and military matters and to plan all things beneficially for the affairs of mankind. (2) It is worthy of record that as he reached the very end of his life he recited a kind of funeral speech before his regular audience. Speaking at length he discoursed in it upon the soul's immortality, on those who passed this present life devoutly, and on the good things stored up by God for those dear to him; and with long demonstrations he made it clear what end those on the other side will meet, as he included in his script the overthrow of the godless. By asserting this point very emphatically he appeared to be getting at some of those around him, so that he even asked one of those with pretensions to wisdom how the argument struck him, and he testified to the truth of what had been said, and though reluctant gave emphatic praise to the condemnation of polytheists. (3) In giving such a sermon to his acquaintance before his death he was like one making ready for himself a smooth and easy journey to the higher realm.

56–7. Preparations for war against Persia

56 (1) It also worthy of record that about the time in question, when there were reports of disturbances among the eastern barbarians, he said that this victory over them was what he had still to achieve, and he started military moves against Persia. (2) Once the decision was made he set the military officers to work, and also discussed the campaign with the bishops at his court, planning that some of those needed for divine worship should be there with him. (3) They said that they would only too gladly accompany him as he wished, and not shrink back, but would soldier with him and fight at his side with supplications to God. He was delighted with their promises and [144] made arrangements for their journey . . .

57 [Thereupon with much embellishment he also equipped for the conduct of that war the tent to form the church in which he intended to make supplications to God the Giver of victory together with the bishops. Meanwhile the Persians, learning of the Emperor's preparations for war, and being much afraid of doing battle with him, asked him by an embassy to make peace. At this the most pacific Emperor received the Persian embassy, and gladly came to friendly terms with them. And now the great

feast of the Pascha arrived, in which the Emperor kept vigil with the others, offering up prayers to God.

58 Thereupon he made preparations to build the *martyrion* in memory of the Apostles in the city named after him.]

58–60. *The shrine of the Apostles*

. . . He himself built up the whole shrine to an unimaginable height, and made it glint with various stones of every kind, facing it from the ground up to the roof. He divided the ceiling into delicate coffers and plated the whole with gold. Up above this on the roof itself he provided copper instead of tiling to protect the building securely against rain. Round this too glittered much gold, so that by reflecting back the rays of the sun it sent dazzling light to those who looked from afar. Trellised relief-work wrought in bronze and gold went right round the building.   59 Such was the eager care the shrine enjoyed as the Emperor greatly enriched it. Round it was a spacious court wide open to the fresh air, and round this quadrangle ran porticoes which faced the middle of the court where the shrine stood, and official houses, washrooms, and lampstores extended along the porticoes, and a great many other buildings suitably furnished for the custodians of the place.

60 (1) All these things the Emperor dedicated to perpetuate for all mankind the memory of our Saviour's Apostles. But he had another object also in mind when he built, which though secret at first was towards the end surmised by everybody. (2) He had prepared the place there for the time when it would be needed on his decease, intending with supreme eagerness of faith that his own remains should after death partake in the invocation of the Apostles, so that even after his decease he might benefit from the worship which would to be conducted there in honour of the Apostles. He therefore gave instructions for services to be held there, setting up a central altar. (3) So [145] he erected twelve repositories like sacred monuments in honour and memory of the company of the Apostles, and put his own coffin in the middle with those of the Apostles ranged six on either side. This too, then, as I said, he planned with careful thought, a place where after his life was over his remains would find a proper resting place.

(4) So having planned these things in his mind long in advance he dedicated the shrine to the Apostles, in the belief that their memorial would become for him a beneficial aid to his soul; and God did not disappoint him of the very things he looked for in his prayers. (5) Even as he was finishing the first disciplines of the paschal festival, and was enjoying the Day of Salvation in light and joy, having brightened the festival for himself and everyone, while he was spending his time in this way to the very end and was actually engaged in these things, God with whose aid he performed them vouchsafed at a propitious time to translate him to higher things.

61–4. *Illness, baptism, and death*

61 (1) First a bodily indisposition came upon him, then illness supervened, and thereupon he went out to the hot water baths of his city, and from there to the city named after his mother. There he spent his time at the chapel of the martyrs, and offered up supplicatory prayers and petitions to God. (2) But when he became aware that his life was ending, he perceived that this was the time to purify himself from the offences which he had at any time committed, trusting that whatever sins it had been his lot as mortal to commit, he could wash them from his soul by the power of the secret words and the saving bath. (3) Having perceived this, he knelt on the floor and made himself a suppliant to God, making confession in the *martyrion* itself, where also he was first accorded the prayers that go with laying-on of hands.

He left there and reached as far as the suburbs of Nicomedia. There he called together the bishops and addressed them thus:

62 (1) 'This is the moment I have long hoped for, as I thirsted and yearned to win salvation in God. It is our time too to enjoy the seal that brings immortality, [146] time to enjoy the sealing that gives salvation, (2) which I once intended to receive at the streams of the river Jordan, where our Saviour also is reported to have received the bath as an example to us. But God who knows what is good for us judges us worthy of these things here and now. (3) So let there be no delay. If the Lord of life and death should wish us to live again here, even so it is once and for all

decided that I am hereafter numbered among the people of God, and that I meet and join in the prayers with them all together. I shall now set for myself rules of life which befit God.'

(4) Such were his words. They in their turn performing the customary rites fulfilled the divine laws and imparted the secret gifts, giving such preliminary instruction as is required. Alone of all the Emperors from the beginning of time Constantine was initiated by rebirth in the mysteries of Christ, and exulted in the Spirit on being vouchsafed the divine seal, and was renewed and filled with divine light, rejoicing in his soul because of his intense faith, awestruck at the manifestation of the divinely inspired power.

(5) When the due ceremonies were complete, he put on bright imperial clothes which shone like light, and rested on a pure white couch, being unwilling to touch a purple robe again. **63** (1) Then he lifted up his voice and offered up a prayer of thanksgiving to God, after which he went on to say, 'I know that now I am in the true sense blessed, that now I have been shown worthy of immortal life, that now I have received divine light.' He went on to call those persons wretched, and said they were pitiable, who did not share those good things. (2) When the tribunes and senior officers from the armies filed in and lamented, bewailing their own imminent bereavement, and wished him extension of life, he answered them too by saying that he enjoyed true life now, and only he knew the good things he had received; they were therefore to hasten his journey to God and not postpone it. (3) Thereupon he made disposition of his property. The Romans who lived in the imperial city he honoured with annual grants. On his sons he bestowed as a father's estate the inheritance of Empire, having arranged everything as he desired.

64 (1) Each of these events took place during the greatest festival, the utterly sacred [147] and holy Pentecost, honoured with seven weeks and sealed up with a single day, during which divine words describe the ascension into Heaven of the universal Saviour and the descent of the Holy Spirit upon mankind. (2) Being granted these things during the festival, on the last day of all, which one might not inaccurately call the Feast of Feasts, about the time of the midday sun the Emperor was taken up to his God; he bequeathed to mortals what was akin to them, but he himself, with that part of him which is the soul's intelligence and love of God, was united to his God. That was the end of the life of Constantine.

65–7. Mourning and lying-in-state

We now go on to the sequel.   **65** (1) Immediately the praetorians and the whole company of personal guards tore their clothes, threw themselves on the ground, and started beating their heads, uttering wails of lamentation with groans and cries, calling him Master, Lord, and King, not so much Master as Father, just as if they were trueborn children. (2) Tribunes and centurions wept aloud for their Saviour, Protector, and Benefactor, and the rest of the troops suitably attired mourned like flocks for their Good Shepherd. (3) The populace similarly wandered all round the city, expressing their inward anguish of soul with groans and cries while others were thrown into a sort of daze, as each one mourned personally and smote himself, as if their life had been deprived of the common good of all.

66 (1) The military took up the remains and laid them in a golden coffin. They wrapped this in imperial purple, and bore it into the city named after the Emperor; then in the most superb of all the imperial halls they laid it on a high pedestal, and by kindling lights all round on golden stands they provided a wonderful spectacle for the onlookers of a kind never seen on earth by anyone under the light of the sun from the first creation of the world. (2) Within the palace itself, [148] in the central imperial quarters, the Emperor's remains, adorned with imperial ornaments, with purple and crown, was guarded day and night by a huge circle of people keeping vigil.

67 (1) The commanders of the whole army, the *comites* and all the ruling class, who were bound by law to pay homage to the Emperor first, making no change in their usual routine, filed past at the required times and saluted the Emperor on the bier with genuflections after his death in the same way as when he was alive. After these chief persons the members of the Senate and all those of official rank came and did the same, and after them crowds of people of all classes with their wives and children came to look. (2) These proceedings continued for a long time, the military having decided that the remains should stay there and be watched until his sons should arrive and pay respects to their father by personally attending to the rites. (3) Alone of mortals the Blessed One reigned even after death, and the customs were maintained just as if he were alive, God having granted this to him and no other since time began. Alone therefore among Emperors and unlike any other he had honoured by acts of every kind the all-sovereign God and his Christ, and it is right that he alone enjoyed these things, as the God over all allowed his mortal part to reign among mankind, thus demonstrating the ageless and deathless reign of his soul to those with minds not stony-hard.

68–73. *Succession and funeral*

While this was going on, **68** (1) the tribunes sent men chosen from the military officers, long known to the Emperor for faithfulness and loyalty, to report the events to the Caesars. (2) They did this, and as if by supernatural inspiration all the troops everywhere, when they learnt of the Emperor's death, came to one determination, as if the great Emperor were still alive for them to recognize no other than his sons alone as sovereigns of Rome. (3) Soon they saw fit to designate them, not Caesars, but from that time onwards each one an Augustus, which might be taken as the supreme and highest token of the original imperial authority. They did these things, announcing their individual votes and voices to each other in writing, and in a single moment of time the concord of the armies was made known to all people everywhere.

69 (1) The inhabitants of the imperial city and the Senate and People of Rome, when they learnt of the Emperor's decease, [149] regarding the news as dreadful and the greatest possible disaster, fell into unrestrained grief. Baths and markets were closed, as were public spectacles and all the customary leisure activities of happy people. The previously easygoing went about dejected, and together they all praised the Blessed One, the Godbeloved, the one who truly deserved the Empire. (2) Not only did they voice such cries, but took steps to honour him in death as if he were alive with dedications of his portrait. They depicted heaven in coloured paintings, and portrayed him resting in an aetherial resort above the vaults of heaven. These also named his sons alone and no others as Emperors and Augusti, and with suppliant cries begged that the remains of their own Emperor should be kept by them and laid in the imperial City.

70 (1) But those here were also paying respect to the one honoured before God. The second of his sons arrived at the city and brought his father's remains, himself leading the cortège. The military officers went in front in close order, and a throng of many thousands followed, and lancers and infantry escorted the Emperor's body. (2) When they reached the shrine of the Saviour's Apostles they laid the coffin to rest there. The new Emperor Constantius, honouring his father in this way, by his presence and by the respects paid to him fulfilled the things which the obsequies required.

71 (1) When he had withdrawn, together with the military officers, the ministers of God took the central position among the crowds and the assembled Godfearing laity, and they performed with prayers the rites of divine worship. Then tributes were paid to the Blessed One as he rested above on his high platform, while the people in their multitudes with those consecrated to God, not without tears but with plentiful weeping, offered prayers to God for the Emperor's soul, doing all that would most please the Godbeloved. (2) God showed his favour towards his servant also in this, that even his end bestowed the Empire upon his cherished and trueborn sons as his successors, and that [150] he was accorded the place he earnestly desired alongside the monument to the Apostles, as one may see even today that the mortal dwelling of the thriceblessed soul shares the honour of the invocation of the Apostles and is numbered among the people of God, having divine rites and mystic liturgies bestowed upon it, and enjoying participation in sacred prayers, he himself even after death holding on to empire. As if brought back to life he manages the whole administration, and Victor Maximus Augustus by his very name commands the government of Rome.

72 He is not like the Egyptian bird, which they say has a unique nature, and dies among aromatic herbs, making itself its own sacrifice, then revives from the ash and, as it flies up, turns into what it was before. He is more like his Saviour, who after the manner of seeds of corn multiplied with the blessing of God, and instead of one grain produced an ear and filled the whole wide world with his fruit. Just like him the Thriceblessed instead of one became manifold by the succession of his sons, so that he is honoured also by the setting up of portraits among all the provinces along with those of his sons, and the name of Constantine is familiarly heard even after the end of his life.

73 At the same time coins were struck portraying the Blessed One on the obverse in the form of one with head veiled, on the reverse like a charioteer on a quadriga, being taken up by a right hand stretched out to him from above.

74–5. *Conclusion: The Unique Emperor*

74 Having shown these things to our very eyes in the case of Constantine alone in all time, who was transparently displayed as a Christian, God who is over all exhibited how great was the difference for him between those who have seen fit to worship him and his Christ and those who choose the opposite. They, by setting out to attack his Church, made him their own enemy and adversary, and the disastrous end of the life of each one indicated the manifest punishment for their hostility to God, just as the end of Constantine made plain to everybody the rewards of the love of God. 75 He alone of all the Roman emperors [151] has honoured God the All-sovereign with exceeding godly piety; he alone has publicly proclaimed to all the word of Christ; he alone has honoured his Church as no other since time began; he alone has destroyed all polytheistic error, and exposed every kind of idolatry; and surely he alone has deserved in life itself and after death such things as none could say has ever been achieved by any other among either Greeks or barbarians, or even among the ancient Romans, for his like has never been recorded from the beginning of time until our day.

COMMENTARY

BOOK I

1–11. *Preface*

1–3. *Constantine's immortality*

Eusebius begins with an elaborate preface in high style, explaining his enterprise and justifying his praises of the dead Constantine (1. 2, *makarion*, 'the Blessed One'; 2. 1–3), who yet lives on and rules through his three sons (cf. IV. 71. 2), who are now Augusti (1. 3). Great men in the past have been honoured with portraits or inscriptions (3. 2), but God himself has shown favour and given victory to Constantine, the 'friend of God', and set him as an example of the godly life (3–6). In victorious kingship, Constantine surpasses Cyrus and Alexander (4–8); in domestic policy he was humane and magnanimous, and was granted legitimate successors by God (9). Eusebius calls for divine aid in his own attempt to draw a verbal portrait of the Emperor (9. 2–10. 1), in a composition which will be far more edifying than the lives of Nero and other tyrants (10. 2–4). Eusebius claims that he will omit the Emperor's deeds in war and his legislation in time of peace; he will record only the Christian aspects of Constantine's life, and will be selective and brief in the narrative (11. 1–2), in the interests of giving more space to the Emperor's praises, which could not be written during his lifetime in view of the unpredictability of life (11. 2).

The introduction demonstrates the awareness of and distancing from standard rhetorical panegyric that is found more overtly stated in the prologue to *LC*; but whereas the latter adopts a highly theoretical, yet self-conscious tone, and mystical language, the *Life*, being more biographical in format, is nearer to textbook panegyric (for the problem of the literary genre see Introduction, § 6).

1. 1. various ten-year periods. Modern editors delete as a scribal addition the words 'twice-ten' and 'thrice-ten' which follow in the manuscripts.

we ourselves hymned the conqueror. Eusebius delivered

orations both for Constantine's Vicennalia, after the Council of Nicaea in 325 (III. 15; the speech does not survive) and his Tricennalia (*LC*, see Drake, *In Praise of Constantine*). The date of the latter, delivered in Constantine's presence in the palace at Constantinople, was 25 July 336 (IV. 46–7; see Drake, *De laudibus*). The Emperor's Decennalia was celebrated in Rome in 315 (I. 48); Eusebius was in the east and did not meet him until 325. He telescopes the chronology for more vivid effect, though Constantine did die only a year after his Tricennalia, on 22 May 337.

garlands of words. Eusebius evokes the well-used imagery of games and festivals; cf. e.g. *LC* 6. 1.

1. 2. our thought stands helpless. Modesty is a standard topos of the panegyrist. *Logos* ('thought') cannot be translated adequately. In Greek it has two broad meanings: (*a*) '(ordered) thought', 'mind', 'reason', and (*b*) '(articulate) speech', 'word'. A development of (*a*) among philosophers applies it to the principle of order or the ordering providence of God in the universe, which Christian thinkers (starting with John 1: 1–14) identify with the Son of God, Jesus Christ; Eusebius plainly alludes to this in 2. 3 below, 'the superior and universal Thought (*logos*)'. A common development of (*b*) is to call a whole speech or literary work a *logos*; the Bible as 'word of God' is one important special case, and again Jesus Christ is perceived as God's spoken 'Word' in that sense. Here Eusebius says that his own thought/speech is silenced; he goes on nevertheless, invoking God's *Logos* to his aid. Constantine's relationship to the *Logos* is a main theme of *LC* (cf. e.g. 2. 3–5).

whether east or west. The theme of world-wide empire recurs later (I. 8; IV. 5–7).

1. 3. like new lamps. Light imagery is standard in panegyric; light in heaven, *LC* 1. 6. Constantine's sons are called 'beacons and lamps of the brilliance emanating from himself' at *LC* 3. 4.

himself powerfully alive. Eusebius stresses the continuity between Constantine and his three sons in order to defuse potential hostility towards or between them, and probably also to urge them to continue Constantine's policies; the same image of Constantine ruling through the succession (*diadoche*) of his sons recurs at IV. 71. The imagery of the *LC* is more fanciful still: the four Caesars are 'yoked . . . like colts beneath the single yoke of the imperial chariot', and controlled by Constantine with the 'reins of holy harmony and concord' (*LC* 3. 4). The Emperor 'rides along, traversing all lands alike that the sun gazes upon, himself present everywhere and watching over everything'. Caesars: see below. The fourth mentioned in *LC* was Dalmatius, killed after Constantine's death in 337; Eusebius writes him out at *VC* IV. 51 (on which see n.), when describing Constantine's division of the Empire among them in 335.

whole government of affairs. Literally 'the whole of life'; the notion of 'governing' is in the participle (*diakubernonta*).

Caesars . . . Augusti. Constantine (b. 316) was created Caesar at Serdica on 1 March 317, as part of his father's truce with Licinius (Barnes, *CE* 67), Constantius (b. later in 317), became Caesar in 324, Constans (b. 323 or 320) on 25 December 333 (Barnes, *NE* 8). The three Caesars were hailed as Augusti on 9 September 337, after eliminating possible rivals, including Dalmatius (for the background, Barnes, *CE* 262, and further on **IV. 51**).

2. 1. panegyrics. The word used is *hymnoi*; *LC* is a panegyric, as is *SC*, delivered at the dedication of the church of the Holy Sepulchre in 335 (see on **IV. 45–6**; Eusebius delivered more than one) and the speech on the dedication of the church at Tyre (*HE* 10. 4, *c.*315; Eusebius refers to his *panegyrikos logos*, *HE* 10. 12, and to the many panegyrics delivered at the dedication, 10. 3. 2; his own professed modesty, 10. 4. 1).

2. 2–3. 1. the immortal Thought of God. Only the divine Logos can properly praise Constantine, in whom his own promises had been shown to be true. The divine Word constantly promises rewards for the righteous and destruction for the wicked (frequently in the Psalms, e.g. Ps. 18, 52, 58).

3. 1. godless tyrants. Eusebius has in mind especially the biblical Pharaoh who oppressed the Israelites, and goes on to liken Constantine to Moses (I. 12) and his ending of the persecution to the deliverance of the children of Israel. His rivals Maxentius and Licinius are presented as persecutors and tyrants themselves (I. 26, 33–6; II. 1–18; Constantine's divinely inspired victory: II. 19).

the death of his servant. Constantine's death is implicitly contrasted with those of the persecutors (Lact., *DMP*, esp. 33, 49); the horrible deaths of Galerius (called Maximian by Lactantius) and Maximin are recounted at I. 57–8, and see I. 27. 3; cf. the same terminology in *HE* 8–9, and for the model, see 2 Macc. 9: 8–9 on the death of Antiochus Epiphanes. While the term 'servant' (*therapon*) is quite common in Christian writings, including the *VC*, with reference to those who worship or serve God, Eusebius often applies it to Constantine to indicate his likeness to Moses: see especially I. 6, 39. 1, and cf. Num. 12: 7; Heb. 3: 2.

3. 2. Mortal nature . . . Eusebius lists the various kinds of conventional imperial commemoration: portraits, pictures in encaustic, statues, inscriptions, all ultimately useless attempts at permanent commemoration in perishable materials.

3. 3. stored up . . . gives even here as a first instalment. The language is of money and banking.

3. 4. ancient oracles of prophets. Eusebius refers to the Scriptures in vague and literary terms. 'Ancient oracles': cf. *LC* prologue 5, 'the oracles of learned men' (see Calderone, 'Eusebio', 7; cf. *SC* 17. 7, 'prophetic voices . . . sacred books'; *LC* 1. 1 'the lessons of sacred writings'; *VC* I. 12. 1 'an ancient report'). The authenticity of Christian prophecy was of vital concern to Eusebius, and he was particularly anxious to prove the inefficacy of pagan oracles; this is to be found especially in *PE*, in answer to Porphyry's *Against the Christians* drawing on the latter's *Philosophy from Oracles*.

lives of Godbeloved men. Eusebius uses the terminology of biography—*bioi*. He had himself written about Origen and Pamphilus in this way (*HE* 6. 1–32; *Apology*, 6. 33. 4; Pamphilus, *HE* 6. 32); however, he surely refers here to biblical figures such as Abraham and Moses (cf. 'in ancient times').

Constantine. The Emperor is named for the first time.

a friend of the all-sovereign God. Constantine as the 'friend' of the Logos is a central theme in *LC*, e.g. 2. 1–3, 5. 1, 4; Calderone, 'Eusebio', 18. So also of Abraham, Isa. 41: 8, Jas 2: 23.

clear example to all.   Again the language of biography; cf. 4. 1
'a lesson in the pattern (*hypodeigma*) of godliness'; 5. 2 'teacher of
piety'.

4–6. *God's achievement in Constantine*

4.   God has set up Constantine to be his herald to promote
godliness, and has proved his favour with the benefits of long reign,
long life. and victory over his enemies. Constantine's mission and
his election by God are similarly emphasized at *LC* 6. 21.

5. 1. twice that number.   Constantine was probably born in
272 or 273 (Barnes, *NE* 39); his age at death is variously given in
later historical sources as between 60 and 65; Eusebius elsewhere
says that he began to reign at the age when Alexander died, i.e. at
the age of 32, and lived twice as long (*VC* I. 8), and that his life
was about twice as long as his reign, which is counted at nearly
thirty-two years (IV. 53). Against this, *VC* I. 19. 1, Lactantius, the
Panegyrici Latini, and Constantine himself quoted at *VC* II. 51 use
words like *adulescens, iuvenis,* or *pais* when referring to his
accession and first years, or in reference to 301–2 and 303;
however, this was part of his official propaganda to emphasize his
youth (Barnes, *NE* 39–41, and cf. *Pan. Lat.* 4 (10). 16. 4, AD 321.
For a date of birth *c.*280, see C. E. V. Nixon, 'Constantinus
Oriens Imperator: Propaganda and Panegyric. On Reading
Panegyric 7 [307]', *Historia*, 42 (1993), 229–46, at 239–40).
For the idea of youth as a panegyrical topos in relation to
Constantine: see R. R. R. Smith, 'The Public Image of
Licinius I', *JRS* 87 (1997) 200, and below, I. 19.

the model of his own monarchical reign.   Eusebius draws the
analogy between the one God and the one Emperor. The word,
eikon, for which cf. also *LC* 1. 1, is the standard word for 'image';
that the earthly kingdom is a copy or model of the heavenly one
(by *mimesis*) is a basic tenet of Eusebian political theory which he
shared with Philo and with Hellenistic and Platonic traditions
(Calderone, 'Eusebio', 10, in answer to Baynes, 'Eusebius', 169–
70, and with bibliographical refs.; see also 12–13). Monarchy is
contrasted with polyarchy at *LC* 3. 6, even while Eusebius praises
the partnership of Constantine and his sons, by which he is
spared the burden of sole rule (3. 1).

6. The section concludes with a typically fulsome panegyrical flourish. Eusebius does not report official imperial titulature, but 'unconquered' recalls the title *invictus*, and the piling up of praises recalls the long catalogues of imperial epithets and titles. For the significance of 'servant' see on **3. 1.**

7–9. Constantine superior to other Emperors

7. 1. ancient story. Alexander is recommended by Menander Rhetor for a rhetorical comparison in a *basilikos logos* (see D. A. Russell and N. J. Wilson, eds., *Menander Rhetor* (Oxford, 1981), 92 and cf. below, I. 8), and Cyrus is another standard *exemplum* for use in praise of rulers; Maximian is compared with Alexander at *Pan. Lat.* 10 (2). 10, AD 289, and Constantine at 6 (7) 17, AD 310, and 9 (12) 5, AD 313; Nazarius compares him with all other rulers, past and present, including Alexander (see M.-C. L'Huillier, *L'Empire des mots: Orateurs gaulois et empereurs romains, 3ᵉ et 4ᵉ siècles* (Paris, 1992), 203). There is no trace here of the argument in Eusebius' *Commentary on Isaiah* in which he had expounded the scriptural presentation of Cyrus as the Lord's anointed, given the task of freeing the Jews from Babylon and returning them to Jerusalem (Isa. 44: 8–45: 13; see Hollerich, 'Religion and Politics', 315; Barnes, *CE* 249, sees this as a late work). The term 'ancient story' disguises Eusebius' actual source, which was more probably the rhetorical tradition than Xenophon's *Cyropaedia*. Cyrus's death is differently reported in Xen., *Cyrop.* 8. 7. 2, Hdt. 1. 204 and Diod. 3. 11.

Alexander . . . so the sons of the Greeks relate. Again Eusebius is deliberately vague in giving his source; cf. 'ancient story'; for the use of 'sons' (*paides*) cf. *LC* 1. 1, on which see Calderone, 'Eusebio', 5–6. Eusebius gives a very hostile view of Alexander, and in both cases it is the deaths of these two kings that he compares unfavourably with Constantine's own; moreover, while Alexander subdued nations with blood, Constantine did so 'with utter ease' and was the 'gentlest of men' (IV. 46). Nevertheless, Plutarch, *Alexander*, may have been a source, see on I. 11. The 'servants' of Alexander (*therapontes*, a term often used by Eusebius for Constantine in relation to God; see on **3. 1** above) are the Successors; the comparison (soon to be proved unfortunate when Eusebius wrote) is with the sons of Constantine, who, he implies, peacefully inherited an undivided empire. *Pan. Lat.* 9 (12). 5, AD 313, also compares Constantine with Alexander.

8. 1. began where the Macedonian ended. Constantine succeeded (25 July 306) at the age at which Alexander died, lived twice as long (see on **5.** 1), and trebled the amount of territory he had inherited, namely his father Constantius's portion in the west, Britain, Gaul, and Spain.

8. 2. mild and sober injunctions. The language is that of the standard imperial virtues, Latin *clementia* and *prudentia*. For imperial virtues in the Latin panegyrics see Nixon and Rodgers, 22; L'Huillier, *L'Empire des mots*, 331–2.

8. 2–4. campaigned against the land of the Britons . . . illuminating . . . the ends of the whole inhabited earth. Constantine's world-wide dominion (see above) recurs as a theme in bk. IV, with the topos of foreign embassies (IV. 5–7, 50; see Barnes, *CE* 253). Constantine was in Britain in 305–6, 307, 310, and apparently also in 313 (based largely on coin evidence, though *VC* I. 25 seems to place his last campaign before that against Maxentius). **Scythian population** (Goths): IV. 5, cf. *Origo* 31; **Blemmyes and Aethiopians:** IV. 7; **India:** IV. 50. No mention is made of the Sarmatians (IV. 6), or of Persia (IV. 8, 56) (see notes *ad locc.*). Apart from Britain, the campaigns belong to the last period of Constantine's life; the introduction looks back from the perspective of his last years and his death. The passage seems to contradict Eusebius' intentions as stated at 11. 1–2 below, but as with the references to Cyrus and Alexander, it draws on one of the stock themes of panegyric (cf. Porfyrius, *Carm.* 5. 1 ff., 14. 9–10, written in exile, and so before 325). Eusebius emphasizes throughout that these conquests bring the 'light of true religion' and enable Constantine to announce the truth of God to the nations.

8. 4. gifts and presents. Cf. **IV. 7** and **I. 43** below. Generosity (*liberalitas*) is a mark of a good ruler: see H. Kloft, *Liberalitas Principis. Herkunft und Bedeutung: Studien zur Prinzipatsideologie* (Kölner historische Abhandlungen, 18; Cologne, 1970).

recognized and acclaimed by them all. For universalism and dominion in relation to Constantine, see G. Fowden, *Empire to*

Commonwealth: Consequences of Monotheism in Late Antiquity (Cambridge, 1993), ch. 4.

imperial addresses. These *(prosphonemasi)* were not so much Constantine's harangues (IV. 29–32) as written documents (so *prosphonein* at II. 61. 1, III. 24. 1, and elsewhere). Eusebius is probably thinking of the letter to Shapur (IV. 9–13). He ascribes to Constantine the freedom of speech, or 'boldness' *(parrhesia)* of the Apostles (Acts 4: 29, 28: 31).

9. 1–2. Eusebius stresses God's favour to Constantine, his translation to heaven and the blessing of his three sons and their smooth accession in unbroken line from Constantine's father, Constantius. The language is that of athletic contests, routinely applied by Christian writers from St. Paul onwards.

9. 1. The opening words seem to be modelled on Isocrates, *Evagr.* 45 and Xen., *Hier.* 11. 14; see Kloft, *Liberalitas Principis*, 19.

holy souls. Eusebius explicitly places Constantine in the class of *hosioi*, holy men.

9. 2. may God . . . become . . . his recorder *(grapheus)*. Eusebius is fond of the imagery of drawing, painting and inscribing; see 10. 1 and 3. 2, and cf. 2. 2–3: only the divine Logos can properly praise Constantine. The notion of God as an artist already had a long tradition and had been used by Philostratus, *Life of Apollonius of Tyana*, and by Methodius of Olympus (Sr. Charles Murray, 'Art and the Early Church', *JThS* NS 28 (1977), 321 n.).

10–11. *Eusebius' purpose and plan*

10. 1. verbal portrait. Eusebius likens his work to that of an artist drawing a picture *(eikon)* of Constantine. For the idea in earlier biography cf. also Plutarch, *Alex.* 1. 2, and later, Greg. Nyss., *Life of Moses* 3. 15, where the author says that his aim is to 'trace out in outline . . . the perfect life'; for the Plutarchan model see on 10. 3–4, and 11.

10. 2. Nero and . . . those others far worse than Nero. Eusebius has in mind the persecuting emperors, of whom he had written himself in the *HE*. His reference to 'authors who have embellished their accounts', 'stylish expression', and 'many-volumed histories' is not likely to be based on his own reading of secular works, but is part of the contrast he draws between supposedly corrupt secular histories and his own work.

to see him, to know him, and to share his company. Despite the reliance of many earlier scholars on this phrase in order to present Eusebius as Constantine's 'court theologian' (e.g. Storch, 'Constantine', 149–50), Barnes has argued that their contact was more distant and much less frequent; this is important for evaluating the claims he makes in the *Life* and the sources of his documents. What Eusebius claims here is in fact a modest acquaintance.

10. 3–4. Eusebius claims a moral and edifying purpose and invites a comparison with Plutarch's *Lives*: for a discussion of *VC* I. 10 see Raoul Mortley, *The Idea of Universal History from Hellenistic Philosophy to Early Christian Historiography* (Lewiston, NY, 1996), 174–81 (see p. 177 also with reference to the language of drawing, cf. 10. 1 above).

11. 1. Eusebius claims that he will omit both Constantine's deeds in war and his deeds in peace (the two standard components of conventional panegyric) in favour of his religious character and actions, being selective even there; similarly Plut., *Alex.* 1. 11, on which this passage may be based (see Mortley, *Universal History*, 175–7, referring to the *VC* as 'concerned with characterology of the Plutarchan type', and citing as examples of details about character *VC* I. 14 and 42–5; other passages, e.g. about legislation, are also interpreted by Eusebius for the light they shed on Constantine's character). A similar aim is announced at *LC* pref., 2–3. Since some of what follows seems to ignore what is said at *VC* 11, the passage has been taken by many scholars as evidence for a change of plan on Eusebius' part (e.g. Barnes, 'Panegyric', 99). It may be an indicator of the unrevised or unfinished state of the *Life*, but Eusebius is not a tidy writer and often left loose ends, as in his revisions to the *HE*. He constantly brings out the Christian significance of Constantine's military and civil actions, as he sees it, and Constantine's victories are an important indication for him of God's favour in recognition of his faith (so F. Heim, *La Théologie de la victoire de Constantin à Théodose* (Théologie historique, 89; Paris, 1992), 91–2). He is here partly excusing himself to the

reader for what might otherwise be regarded as culpable omissions, but equally, he himself interprets in a religious light what
might seem otherwise to be secular. L'Huillier, *L'Empire des mots*,
214 and 248, points out the high proportion of space in the Latin
panegyrics devoted to military narrative, and the religious
language used of Constantine in *Pan. Lat.* 6 (7), 9 (12), and 4
(10). Eusebius was writing in the same tradition.

11. 2. forbidden to call any man blessed before his death.
Eccles. 11: 28.

12–24. *Birth, Family, and Youth*

12. *Childhood among the tyrants*

12. 1. Moses. Eusebius first sets out here the typology he will
apply to Constantine: brought up like Moses in an enemy court
(that of Diocletian at Nicomedia), like him he freed his people
from tyrants (the persecutors) and led them to freedom and their
inheritance (Christianity). See Introduction, § 7. He draws the
analogy between Maxentius and Pharaoh at *HE* 9. 9. 5–8, based
on Exod. 15, and cf. below, 20. 2; 38. 2, 5; 39. 1 (cf. *HE* 9. 9. 9);
Constantine's victory in 312 is explicitly compared with that of
Moses at *VC* I. 39. 1. Here Eusebius uses Exod. 1–14 and Acts
7: 20–36; the implication in 12. 1 is that Constantine learnt
wisdom at the court of Nicomedia (for his education see on 19.
2). The apologetic argument implied in the passage is that the
miracles shown to Constantine demonstrate the truth of the
stories about Moses (12. 1–2, cf. *HE* 9. 9. 4, a passage used at *VC*
I. 38. 1). See Hollerich, 'Religion and Politics', and 'Moses and
Constantine', with Mortley, *Universal History*, 172–4.

Moses played an important role in Eusebius' thought: the *HE*
begins with Moses as the foremost of the prophets of Israel who
spoke of Christ (*HE* 1. 2. 4 ff.), and the comparison of Moses and
Christ occurs at length in *DE* 3. 2. 1–30, where Eusebius says
that Jesus was like Moses in that he too liberated his people,
though he was also greater than Moses. The role of Moses in
relation both to Judaism and to Christianity features both in *PE*
and *DE*. Thus, while Eusebius is careful not to say so directly,
the application of the Moses typology to Constantine stands in

direct comparison to its earlier use by Eusebius in relation to Christ (see further Hollerich, 'Religion and Politics', 317–24).

An ancient report. Almost the same phrase that is used of Cyrus (*palaios logos*, 7. 1), but in this case referring to Scripture, which Eusebius does not cite directly. It is repeated below, 12. 2. Moses's upbringing at the court of Pharaoh: Exod. 1: 22–2: 10, and esp. Acts 7: 18–23.

12. 2. which most people regard as a kind of myth. Eusebius seems to go out of his way to write as if for non-Christians, though see below, on 38. 1. Moses was well-known to them in the context of Jewish apologetic in the guise of wise lawgiver; it was argued by some that Plato was influenced by Moses and that he was the teacher of Orpheus (see J. Gager, *Moses in Greco-Roman Paganism* (New York, 1972); A. Droge, *Homer or Moses? Early Christian Interpretations of the History of Culture* (HUT 26; Tübingen, 1989); Mortley, *Universal History*). In this debate the *Life of Moses* by Philo, a writer influential on both Origen and Eusebius, played a central role. In the *HE*, Eusebius had also defended Origen's interpretation of Moses from the criticisms of Porphyry, and mentions a work of Origen's 'On the harmony of Moses and Jesus' (6. 19). The explicit analogy with Moses in the *VC* extends only through the campaign against Licinius narrated in bk. II (in II. 12 Constantine builds a tabernacle for himself where he can retire to pray), but the structure of the *VC* can be seen nevertheless as reflecting the three phases of forty years each in the life of Moses: (*a*) birth and upbringing at the Egyptian court, (*b*) leading the Israelites out of Egypt, and (*c*) Moses the lawgiver, making the tabernacle and overthrowing idolatry. These divisions were exploited in later works such as Gregory of Nyssa's *Life of Moses* (see M. Harl, 'Les trois quarantaines de Moïse, *REG* 80 (1967), 407–12, and 'Moïse figure de l'évêque', in A. Spira, ed., *The Biographical Works of Gregory of Nyssa* (Philadelphia, 1984)).

eyewitnesses of public scenes. Eusebius lays stress throughout on the 'proofs' and signs which demonstrate Constantine's favour with God; I. 4, 30, 57.

Tyrants. See on 3. 1 above.

12. 3. he had a father. On Constantius I, posthumously known as Chlorus, Eusebius pads out what he had written at

HE 8. 13. 12–13, though there he had also stated that Constantius was the first of the tetrarchs to be deified (13. 12). Constantius rose from a military background to become *praeses* of Dalmatia and praetorian prefect of Maximian in Gaul, before being made Caesar in 293 as a member of the tetrarchy (Fig. 1), and Augustus on 1 May 305 (Barnes, *NE* 4, 35–7; *Origo* 1 repeats the claim of descent from Claudius Gothicus made for the first time in *Pan. Lat.* 7 (6). 2, AD 310). Eusebius goes much further here than in the *HE*, declaring that he was 'on friendly terms with the God over all' (13. 1) and 'extremely attached to what pleases God' (14. 1), and suggesting that Constantine himself was already favourable to Christianity before his father's death (12. 3, though see 27 below). This would seem to confirm Lact., *DMP* 24. 9, which makes Constantine's first act on his accession the ending of persecution (Elliott, 'Conversion' and 'Early Development'), though most scholars in the past have taken 312 to be the date of his conversion. However, it is suggested by a Latin panegyrist that he saw a vision of Apollo in 310 (*Pan. Lat.* 7 (6), 21, dismissed by Barnes, *CE* 36; see for this B. Müller-Rettig, *Der Panegyricus des Jahres 310 auf Konstantin den Grossen* (Stuttgart, 1990)). The treatment of Constantius differs substantially in *Pan. Lat.* 9 (12), AD 313 and 4 (10), AD 321, and the latter introduces a divine sign into its narrative of the battle at the Milvian Bridge, the heavenly troops of Constantius seen coming to Constantine's aid: L'Huillier, *L'Empire des mots*, 247–8.

FIG. 1. Gold medallion from Arras, showing the entry of Constantius Chlorus into London, AD 293. Trustees of the British Museum.

13–18. *Career and character of Constantine's father*

13. 1. this man was the only one. Eusebius claims that Constantius did not carry out the persecutions in his own western part of the Empire, with its centre at Trier; it was important for Christian writers to distance Constantius from the tetrarchic policy, so Lact., *DMP* 8. 7, 'he was different from the others', and 15. 7, 'Constantius, to avoid appearing to disagree with the instructions of his seniors [Diocletian and Maximian], allowed the churches—that is, the walls, which could be restored—to be destroyed, but the true temple of God, which is inside men, he kept unharmed'. Here and at *HE* 8. 13. 13 Eusebius denies that he even destroyed churches. It is true that he had a daughter called Anastasia (a Christian name), and see Eusebius' anecdotes and elaborations below, esp. 17. 2–3; however, in the Latin panegyrics Constantius is presented as a pagan, e.g. 6 (7). 3. 3–4, AD 307; 9 (12). 25, AD 313, and see also Eus., *HE* 8. 13. 12. Elliott, 'Conversion', 421–2, argues for his Christianity.

13. 2. They besieged and ravaged the churches of God. The persecution of Christians began in February (Lact., *DMP* 11–12) or March (Eus., *HE* 8. 2. 4), 303.

13. 3. evil demons. Eusebius, like Christians generally, regards the pagan gods as demons. Originally the terms *daimon* and *daimonion* had the neutral sense of 'divinity' or 'spirit', but acquire evil connotation in Christian circles. See Elaine Pagels, *The Origins of Satan* (Harmondsworth, 1995), and see in particular *SC* 13. 5–6, 15, for an apologetic account of the defeat of these 'gods' by the Christian God; in *PE* demons send oracles and are dispersed by the Gospels. For Eusebius' use of the term see Sirinelli, 201–2, 312–26.

13. 4. having mentioned one or two achievements. Eusebius' earlier account of Constantius was already favourable (*HE* 8. 13. 13–14, and see *Pan. Lat.* 6 (7). 4. 4; 7 (6). 3. 4); now he embellishes it with further anecdotal material, and stresses Constantius's monotheistic piety. In view of the fate of the male descendants of Constantius and Theodora in the bloodbath following Constantine's death in 337, it was also desirable to lay emphasis on Constantius as the perfect father

of Constantine and to avoid mention of the six children of his
second family (Barnes, *NE* 37); see however **17. 3** and **18. 2**
below.

14. Constantius's kindness to his subjects (see also Lib., *Or.*
59.15) is illustrated by a moral tale traced by Winkelmann to
Xen., *Cyrop.* 8. 2. 15–17.

14. 1. the Emperor who then exercised supremacy. Probably Diocletian, and thus referring to Constantius's period as
Caesar. He was made Augustus when Diocletian retired on 1
May 305. Eusebius' stories about Constantius are there to prove
his point, and are quite out of proportion with the rest of the
narrative.

15–16. A story, hardly credible, offered as further 'proof' of
Constantius's unwillingness to persecute, and illustrating the
general statements of 13. 2–3 and *HE* 8. 13. 13; however, 16. 1
might suggest that he did in fact enforce sacrifice. There is a
biblical model for the story in the actions of Jehu in 2 Kings. 10:
18–25.

15. fire and iron, deep sea and every kind of death. For a
catalogue of the sufferings of the martyrs, abbreviated here, see
HE 8. 14. 13.

16. 1. demons. Above, 13. 3.

17. 2–3. Eusebius might appear to claim that before 305
Constantius was Christian himself and converted his wife
Theodora and his children; Constantine makes it more explicit
at II. 49, describing his father as calling on 'the Saviour God'. See
Elliott, 'Conversion' and 'Early Development', for this interpretation. But Eusebius' language is ambiguous (see below on **27**),
and Constantine could well interpret Constantius's call on the
one God as the Christian God. Helena, Constantine's mother,
whom he had married early and presumably divorced (though
some sources claim that she was merely his mistress or con-
cubine, Barnes, *NE* 36), is not mentioned, despite the eulogistic
section about her at *VC* III. 43–7 Eusebius has left in the
reference to Constantine's half-brothers and sisters, despite
writing out the younger Dalmatius at IV. 50, see note *ad loc.*,
and cf. also below, **18. 2**; **21. 2**. If Constantius's family was
infiltrated by Christianity, Eusebius does not know it.

17. 2. the saying. The source is unknown; see p. 22.

17. 3. in all respects a church of God. As Constantine's was later to be (IV. 17). Eusebius had used the idea already of Valerian, *HE* 7. 10. 3, from Dionysius of Alexandria. He imagines the court populated with ministers of God, i.e. clergy, conducting regular Christian services of prayer.

18. 1. Those who were advanced in years. i.e. Diocletian and Maximian, whom Eusebius typically does not name. For a longer account of their retirement in 305, see *HE* 8. 13. 11.

First Augustus. i.e. the senior of the two Augusti (the other was Galerius). Eusebius adds this detail to what he has taken from *HE* in order to support Constantine's claims.

18. 2. For praise of Constantius, cf. **17**. Constantius's children; see above, on **17. 2**; Barnes, 'Panegyric', 99, lists this reference as unlikely after the murders of summer 337, but admits that 'he may well have forgotten to delete the already written sentence'. Eusebius' point is that Constantius was prolific, his colleagues largely childless, and that this is a sign of divine favour.

19–21. Constantine joins his father

19. 1. that ancient prophet of God. Constantine's stay among the other tetrarchs is again (cf. **17. 2**) likened to that of Moses among the Egyptians.

from childhood to youth. For such emphases on Constantine's youthfulness, see above on **5. 1**.

we knew him ourselves as he travelled through the land of Palestine. Eusebius is referring to 301–2, when he apparently saw Constantine travelling by the side of Diocletian; cf. *Oration to the Saints* 16. 2, claiming that Constantine had seen for himself Memphis and Babylon, and see Barnes, *NE* 40.

19. 2–20. 1. physique and bodily height. An ideal Emperor's inner virtue would be reflected in his outward appearance; cf. Eusebius' description of Constantine at the Council of Nicaea (325) at III. 10. 3–4. For references in the Latin panegyrics to imperial strength and vigour, see Smith, 'Public Image of Licinius I', 196–7.

19. 2. rhetorical education. In contrast, *Origo* 2 describes him as having had little education (*litteris minus instructus*), in which it is followed by many modern scholars, who attribute Constantine's alleged weakness in theology to his military background. But the author of the *Oration to the Saints*, and of many other orations, can hardly be described as uneducated, nor would the court of Diocletian at Nicomedia have been uncultured; see also *Epit.* 41. 14, and Barnes, *CE* 47. The theme itself falls under the panegyrical heading of upbringing and formation.

20. 1–2. secret plots . . . safety in flight. Constantine also resembles Moses in having made his escape from the 'tyrants'. It is not improbable that Galerius, the junior Augustus to Constantius after 1 May 305, would have wanted to prevent the latter's son, who had been left out of the settlement, from leaving Nicomedia and joining his father. Constantius is said to have sent a letter to Galerius announcing his illness and asking for his son (Lact., *DMP* 24. 3). However, Eusebius gives a version carefully designed to obscure any sign of ambition on Constantine's part; Lact., *DMP* 24. 5–6, Praxagoras, as reported by Photius, *FGrH*, 219, Aur. Vict., *Caes.*, 40. 2 ff., *Epit.*, 41. 2–3, and Zosimus, 2. 8. 2 ff. all have more colourful stories of Constantine's escape, and *Origo* 3–4 makes him get away on horseback and defeat the Sarmatians, whereupon Galerius does send him to Constantius. For Eusebius it is important to claim that it was God who revealed his danger to Constantine (as also at IV. 47), while his flight resembled that of Moses after killing the Egyptian (Exod. 2: 11–15). However, if God was working for Constantine (20. 2), so was Constantine himself.

21. 1. he arrived . . . at the very moment. A similar story already in Lact., *DMP* 24. 8, though no place is mentioned, and Constantius commends Constantine to his soldiers, not the family. *Pan. Lat.* 6 (7). 7. 1 ff. and *Origo* 4 make it clear that Constantine actually met his father at Bononia (Boulogne), and that they then marched north and campaigned against the Picts in Scotland, Constantius dying only later at York (25 July 306). Of this campaign Lactantius and Eusebius know nothing. Eusebius makes Constantine's first visit to Britain considerably later (see I. 25. 2). Eusebius' deathbed scene is also the more dramatic version; it has Biblical precedents in Gen. 49: 1 (Jacob) and 1 Kings 1: 28–35 (David and Solomon). Constantine's dramatic flight also falls under the rhetorical head of the *celeritas imperatoris* (e.g. *Pan. Lat.* 3 (11). 4. 4, AD 291, of Diocletian and Maximian, 4 (10). 36. 5, AD 321, of Crispus.

21. 2. handed over his part of the Empire by natural succession. The whole passage (21. 2–22. 2) is a much expanded version of *HE* 8. 13. 12–14. Eusebius does even more here to suggest smooth dynastic succession (cf. *Pan. Lat.* 6 (7). 5. 3, AD 307); however, the next few years in practice see Constantine manoeuvring first to gain acceptance and then to detach himself from the tetrarchy. Eusebius avoids these awkward facts, if he knows them, by concentrating on, or even inventing, the details of Constantius' funeral (cf. IV. 70–2 for Constantine's own, also conducted by his son). Proclaimed Augustus at York on 25 July 306, Constantine sent his picture to Galerius, who recognized him, albeit reluctantly, only as Caesar (Lact., *DMP* 25. 1; *Pan. Lat.* 6 (7). 5. 3, attributing the snub to Constantine's modesty). Constantine's first wife was Minervina (Barnes, *NE* 42–3); he was recognized as Augustus by Maximian in 307 with his marriage to the latter's daughter, Fausta. Maximian had returned from exile in support of his son Maxentius, who by late 306 had also proclaimed himself Augustus. The alliance allowed Constantine to claim legitimation against the wishes of Galerius by appealing to the senior emperor (as set forth in *Pan. Lat.* 6 (7) of 307, celebrating his marriage and the alliance; see B. H. Warmington, 'Aspects of Constantinian Propaganda in the Panegyrici Latini', *TAPA* 104 (1974), 371–84; C. E. Nixon, 'Constantinus Oriens Imperator', *Historia*, 42 (1993), 229–46, against Grünewald, *Constantinus*, who regards the panegyric as 'official'). In fact Maximian himself was not at this time recognized formally as Augustus; for these complicated events, omitted or glossed over by Eusebius, see Barnes, *CE* 29–30, *NE* 4–6.

22–4. Constantine declared Emperor

22. 1. his father reigned through him. As Constantine now reigned through his sons (1. 3, IV. 71). Nazarius also claimed the benevolent influence of Constantius on Constantine's reign (*Pan. Lat.* 4 (10), AD 321).

22. 2–23. Constantine is similarly singled out from the other tetrarchs by his legitimate succession at *HE* 8. 13. 13, where it is also said that he was 'in every way wise and very religious'.

23. persecute the churches of God. Similar language of Licinius, below, 56. 1.

I have decided that it is not proper to report the way their lives ended in the present account. See therefore I. 27, 47 for brevity, but contrast I. 57–9 (based on *HE*) and notes, and cf. I. 11. 1 for another stated intention in the *VC* that appears to be subsequently broken. Barnes, 'Panegyric', 99, lists this among the inconsistencies suggestive of revision. Here Eusebius no doubt has in mind that he has in fact omitted the effects of persecution on the persecutors, told in his source, *HE* 8. 13. 10–11.

24. Eusebius concludes the section, whose purpose has been to demonstrate God's unique choice of Constantine to rule. Chs. 22–4 make the transition in the narrative from the lengthy section on Constantius to Constantine, the main subject.

25–41. 2. *Deeds in War I: The Liberation of the West*

Eusebius appears to follow the usual panegyrical order and moves next to deeds in war (*praxeis kata polemon*); see Introduction, § 5.

25. 1. *Constantine settles his father's domain*

25. 1– 2. The provinces ruled by Constantius since 1 May 305 were Gaul, Britain and Spain; however, despite the absence of a chapter division in the manuscripts, 25. 2 seems to suggest that Eusebius did not consider Britain as part of Constantius's 'portion'. The British campaign is not attested elsewhere; Eusebius' source might be Constantine's letters, cf. II. 28. 2 and IV. 9 (where Ocean is mentioned, as at 25. 2).

Eusebius skims over the events of several years (306–12), omitting Constantine's marriage in 307 to Fausta, the daughter of Maximian, and in general his brief and tendentious account ignores completely (or does not know of) the fraught political situation in the Empire; Severus, declared Augustus by Galerius and sent to deal with Maxentius, was defeated and surrendered to Maxentius's father Maximian, who had the title Herculius, at Ravenna (early 307), and was later 'removed' near Rome. It was now that alliance with Constantine seemed a good idea to Maxentius and Maximian, left in open hostility to Galerius in the east, while Constantine saw this as a useful, if temporary, expedient; sooner or later he would need to eliminate Maxentius himself. *Pan. Lat.* 7 (6), addressed to Maximian and Constantine, managed with wonderful coolness to celebrate the alliance, including Constantine's reception into the Herculian line (2. 5; 8. 2), without a mention of Maxentius or Galerius. The latter's military expedition against Maxentius in the autumn of 307 was unsuccessful, and a diplomatic battle began. Constantine's ally, the elderly Maximian, was forced in 308 to seek refuge with Constantine himself by his own son. By the settlement made at the conference of Carnuntum in November 308, held in the presence of both Maximian and Diocletian, Licinius (promoted by Galerius to replace Severus) and Maximin, Caesar since 305, were declared Augusti; Maxentius was excluded, and the job of defeating him given to Licinius (Barnes, *CE* 32 and *NE* 6). But Maxentius managed to retain control of Rome, and Maximian, forced to retire again, took refuge with Constantine; by 310 he had made another bid for the purple, but was handed over to Constantine by the city of Massilia and persuaded to commit suicide. At this point in 310, *Pan. Lat.* 6 (7) (? 1 August) effectively detaches Constantine from the tetrarchy by introducing the idea of his dynastic descent from the third-century Emperor Claudius Gothicus (21–2, and see above), and by attributing to him a vision of Apollo (21), thereby giving him a religious affiliation separate from the tetrarchic and Herculian one; the gods are said to have received Constantius into heaven and welcomed Constantine (for the tendentiousness of the panegyric, see Barnes, *CE* 35–6). But Eusebius may not have had any more detailed information than when he wrote the account in *HE*.

25. Lact., *DMP* 24. 6, famously says that Constantine's first action was to 'restore the Christians to their worship and their God' (trans. Creed). Even if true, this need not mean (despite Elliott, 'Conversion') that he was already actually a Christian; the comment which follows, 'This was the first measure by which he sanctioned the restoration of the holy religion' gives Lactantius' own later interpretation. It is understandable that Eusebius, having denied that Constantius persecuted, makes no mention of such a measure.

25. 2–26. *Constantine observes the plight of Rome*

26. When he then perceived. Eusebius omits all the political events, and represents Constantine as unaware of Maxentius's activities until shortly before his own campaign against him. The idea of the oppression of Rome appears also in *HE* 8. 14. 1–6.

he first gave opportunity. Clearly meant to defend Constantine's apparent delay, suggested by Eusebius' conflation of the chronology of these years, and to cover him from any charges of aggression (a theme taken seriously in the panegyrics; cf. *Pan. Lat.* 4 (10). 8, AD 321, and cf. Lact., *DMP* 43. 4; *Pan. Lat.* 9 (12), AD 313; 4 (10). 9–13, AD 321). Eusebius never gives the titles of Constantine's rivals, and rarely their names (see R. T. Ridley, 'Anonymity in the Vita Constantini', *Byzantion*, 50 (1980), 241–58; Winkelmann, p. liii). This is a general stylistic feature of the work, as of panegyric in general: thus for instance when Pacatus departs from the rule and names Magnus Maximus at *Pan. Lat.* 2 (12). 45. 1–2, it is to considerable rhetorical effect. The account in *HE* 8. 13. 12–15, is not much more detailed, despite mentioning Licinius, Maximin, and (unnamed) Maximian.

27–32. *Constantine seeks divine aid and receives the* labarum

27. 1. magical devices. The whole campaign will be presented as the victory of Christianity over pagan superstition, even though Maxentius too had proclaimed toleration for Christians (*Mart. Pal.* (S) 13. 12–13; *HE* 8. 14. 1; for his policies see D. de Decker, 'La Politique religieuse de Maxence', *Byzantion*, 38 (1968), 472–562). His resort to magic is described at *HE* 8. 14. 5.

he sought a god to aid him. The choice is presented in terms of monotheism versus polytheism, as was apparently also the

case with Constantius (cf. 27. 3, 'his father's God'). Constantine
had not known his father until the latter's deathbed and does not
know the identity of his father's God until he receives the sign
and vision of Christ himself. In this he is like Moses, who is
confronted by the God of his father (Exod. 3: 6) and has to ask
his name (Exod. 3: 13–15); for Eusebius, it is Christ who also
appeared to Moses at the bush (*HE* 1. 2. 10–13). Neither
Constantius nor Constantine is yet aware who the one God is.
See further on **32** below.

27. 3. those who had already campaigned against the tyrant.
These were in fact Severus, Licinius, and Galerius (see above), as
usual unnamed, but Eusebius seems to be thinking only of
Severus and Galerius. Constantine's own philosophical critique
of polytheism can be seen in *Or. ad sanct.* 4. Here Eusebius
attributes to him a doctrine already familiar enough, and biblical
('Herod' in Acts 12: 1–23), that persecutors of Christians come
to a dreadful end. This is Lactantius' theme throughout the *DMP*
and is elaborated by Constantine in his letter of relief to
Christians at *VC* II. 24–27. The delusion represented by faith
in oracles and diviners reappears at *VC* I. 28. and II. 50–1, 54.
Eusebius' version of Severus's death reads more like an account
of an assassination than execution or suicide after capture (for
which see Lact., *DMP* 26. 10–11; *Origo* 4. 10). He does not seem
to have very good information, unless he is simply keeping the
focus on the religious aspects of Constantine's rise (see above on
25. 1–2).

he decided he should venerate his father's God alone.
There was much in common at this time between Christians
and monotheist pagans (Liebeschuetz, 'Religion'), and this does
not mean that Constantius was as yet a Christian. Cf. the
apparently monotheistic prayer which Constantine enjoined on
his army (IV. 19–20, cf. Lact., *DMP* 46. 6, a similar prayer
revealed to Licinius in a dream before his defeat of Maximin, and
many passages in the *Pan. Lat.*). Barnes, *CE* 43, suggests that
Constantine's 'moment of psychological conviction' may have
come only at the consciousness of victory; while this accords with
the narrative of *VC* I. 27–32, see below for some of the problems
with Eusebius' account.

28–32. *The vision of Constantine.*

What follows is probably the most famous passage in the *Life*. Eusebius bases his account of the campaign against Maxentius and the Battle of the Milvian Bridge (28 October 312) on what he had already written at *HE* 9. 9. 2–8. But there, despite the record of Constantine's prayers before the battle and the analogy of Pharaoh's chariots being engulfed in the Red Sea, there is no hint of a vision. He inserts here, more than twenty-five years later, an elaborate story which, he claims, he had heard from the Emperor personally, 'a long time after', and 'confirmed with oaths' (28. 1). It differs in almost all respects from Lactantius' account of the dream experienced by Constantine before the battle of the Milvian Bridge at *DMP* 44, with which legend-writers and historians alike have regularly mixed it up. The versions of the battle in *Pan. Lat.* 9 (12), of 313, and 4 (10), of 321, are couched in religious vocabulary and record signs of divine favour, but these are not Christian (the two panegyrics were also composed eight years apart and differ substantially: see L'Huillier, *L'Empire des mots*, 235–48, with plan on p. 236). For the inscription on the Arch of Constantine (315) see on **40. 2.** But Eusebius' vision as recounted here, like the prayers in *HE* 9. 9. 2, is located before the Italian campaign is launched. In neither work does he recount an eve-of-battle prayer or vision.

Eusebius' information about the west was limited before 325. Though there is no sign that Eusebius had special access to the Emperor at the Council of Nicaea in that year, he might have heard Constantine talking about his conversion and the long-ago battle (cf. Constantine's language at II. 49–54), even perhaps as late as 336, when he was in Constantinople. For his own claims see **I. 1; III. 49; IV. 7. 1.** He also claims to have got the stories about the efficacy of the *labarum* from Constantine (II. 6. 2–9.3, esp. 8. 2, 9. 3). But that does not guarantee their accuracy in either case; even the Council of Nicaea took place thirteen years after the event, and after Constantine's recent victory had transformed the situation. When Eusebius made the final revisions to *HE*, after the victory and before the Council, he did not insert anything about a vision. When he composed the *VC*, however, Eusebius needed a miracle for his portrayal of Constantine, and miracles need authentication. Secular panegyrists commonly claimed special knowledge for their more unlikely stories (cf. *Pan. Lat.* 7 (6). 21, the vision of Apollo in 310; also Claudian claiming to report the dying words of Theodosius about the succession, *III Cos. Hon.* 144–5, and Corippus the dying words of Justinian to similar effect, *Iust.* 4. 337–8; these reported conversations tend to have had no other witnesses). Such accounts typically use vocabulary of 'seeing', and of astonishment: on examples in the panegyrics, see L'Huillier, *L'Empire des mots*, 301. Eusebius makes a similar claim for his report of Licinius' address to his soldiers at II. 5 (see note *ad loc.*), as also for an incident during the campaign of AD 324 (II. 8. 2–9. 3). Furthermore, he admits to having seen the *labarum* only 'somewhat later'; (see below on I. **32. 1**; with I. **30**). The alleged vision of Apollo in 310 allowed Constantine to 'see himself in the visible form of the first princeps, Augustus, with whom Apollo had similarly been associated' (see Nixon and Rodgers, 250 n. 93; Smith, 'Public Image of Licinius I', 187). Here the vision story serves a different though related function by providing the necessary parallel for the story of Moses and the burning bush. God says to Moses 'I am the God of thy father' (Exod. 3: 6, cf. *VC* I. 17. 3–28. 1); both Moses and Constantine are taken by surprise (Acts 7: 31, from Exod. 3: 3; *VC* I. 28. 2), and both ask the name of the God (Exod. 3: 13, *VC* I. 28. 2). The account of the shape of the standard and its manufacture (31) recalls that of the making of the Ark of the Covenant (Exod. 25–7, cf. also below on II. **12**). Finally, like the Ark and the *labarum* (II. 7–9, 16), so too the rod of Moses is stretched out to ensure victory (Exod. 17: 8–13, cf. *VC* IV. 5. 2). For a sceptical view of Eusebius' claims see Leeb, 43–52. Heim, *La Théologie de la victoire*, 92–8, argues that Eusebius left out such manifestations in the *HE* for theological reasons, but it seems more likely that the account is new in the *VC*.

The account has been endlessly discussed. Burckhardt, 271–2, simply omits it from his account of the battle, and later states that 'the familiar miracle . . . must finally be eliminated from the pages of history', and again, 'history cannot take an oath of Constantine the Great too seriously, because, among other things, he had his brother-in-law [Licinius] murdered despite assurances given under oath. Nor is Eusebius beyond having himself invented two-thirds of the story' (p. 296; note that he is no kinder to Lactantius, p. 246); Grégoire, 'Eusèbe' and 'La Vision', argued that the story was a christianization of the miracles told by the Latin panegyrists, by an unknown author, not Eusebius, of the late fourth or early fifth century; the case against such views was best put by Baynes, though signs and wonders were certainly not limited to Christians (see R. MacMullen, 'Constantine and the Miraculous', *GRBS* 9 (1968), 81–96), and the piercing eyes of rulers were associated in panegyric with their capacity to see divine visions (Smith, 'Public Image of Licinius I', 198–9). Elliott, 'Conversion', argues against 312 as a conversion experience on the grounds that Constantine was Christian already, but for the case for development, see Leeb. A rival pagan account of Constantine's conversion also circulated (e.g. Zos. 2. 29, and cf. the satirical version in Julian, *Caes.* 336), whereby he became Christian in the attempt to find forgiveness for the deaths of his son Crispus and his wife Fausta in Italy in 326 (naturally not mentioned by Eusebius), and built Constantinople to get away from the hostility shown to him in Rome; the story is rejected by Sozomen, *HE* 1. 5.

28. 1. As he made these prayers. Eusebius' vision is separated in time from the Battle of the Milvian Bridge; it takes place earlier, 'on a campaign he was conducting somewhere' (28. 2), even before Constantine's campaign against Maxentius began (cf. 32. 3; 37. 2).

a long while after. Perhaps in 336 (see above); but the story may not have been told to Eusebius alone, and so 325 is not ruled out.

the time which followed provided evidence for the truth of what he said. A typical Eusebian apologetic argument.

28. 2. About the time of the midday sun. For the phrase, see also on IV. 64. 1. Constantine sees his vision in the middle of the day, not in a dream. This has led to speculation about some natural astronomical event, like the so-called 'halo phenomenon'. For details and bibliography see Peter Weiss, 'Die Vision Constantins', in J. Bleicken, ed., *Colloquium aus Anlass des 80. Geburtstages von Alfred Heuss* (Frankfurter Althistorische Studien, 13; Frankfurt, 1993), 145–69, who argues that Constantine did see such a phenomenon, but in 310 (cf. *Pan. Lat.* 6

(7). 21. 3–7), and gradually came to identify the *summus deus* of that experience with Christ; on this view, the *labarum* was also the product of his experience in 310, cf. J. J. Hatt, 'La Vision de Constantin au sanctuaire de Grand et l'origine celtique du *labarum*', *Latomus*, 9 (1950), 427–36. Eusebius certainly does not think in such terms.

a cross-shaped trophy formed from light, and a text attached to it which said, 'By this conquer'. Constantine sees a cross. Nothing in the text suggests he sees a *chi-rho* emblem at this point. When Eusebius describes the *labarum* or battle-standard later, the chief shape is the long upright and the cross-piece, making a simple cross. The more detailed and jewelled version, replete with hanging portrait-banner and surmounted with *chi-rho*, is what Eusebius himself had seen, and which he says was an exact replica of what Christ showed to Constantine in a dream (see 29–31 below, which are unambiguous). Historians have created problems by trying to assimilate the vision to what Lactantius writes about the sign given in a dream on the eve of the Milvian Bridge battle (*DMP* 44. 5, with Creed's notes). This was some form of staurogram (a cross with the top looped over) or a *chi-rho*, as on Constantine's helmet on the Ticinum medallions of 315 (see on **31. 1**), to be painted on the shields of the army. Whether the *chi-rho* was already recognized as a Christian sign is not clear: see R. Grigg, 'Constantine the Great and the Cult without Images', *Viator*, 8 (1977), 1–32, at 17–18.

Constantine sees the sign 'resting over the sun', which he continued to commemorate on his coins as Sol Invictus (see Bruun, 'Sol'), whether out of numismatic conservatism (Barnes) or as a sign of solar monotheism. 'Trophy' (*tropaion*) is a favourite word with Eusebius, used both generally and (particularly) of the cross; cf. e.g. 37. 1 where the 'victorious trophy' of Christ is glossed by 'Saviour's sign' or 'saving sign' (*soterion semeion*); the same terminology in *LC*, e.g. 9. 14, 16 (again the two words juxtaposed), and see on IV. 21. It was an idea of long standing (see e.g. Justin, *1 Apol.* 55. 3; Origen, *Jo.* 20. 36). For Eusebius, and in later eastern tradition, the cross represented victory rather than suffering. See further on these equations Storch, 'Trophy'; in application to the *labarum*, *VC* IV. 21; *LC* 6. 21. Eusebius has already in *LC* elevated the 'sign' into a symbolic representation of both the cross and of victory, and uses similarly fluid terminology in the *VC*: see Heim, *La Théologie de la victoire*, 98–105, with bibliography at 103 n. 289. The text 'By this conquer' is clearly part of the heavenly vision, though perhaps originally associated with the dream of 29. The thought is plainly present in the inscription described in 40. 2.

The vision of Constantine had a long subsequent history in later versions, including the Byzantine *Lives*, and in many semi-legendary accounts, especially in connection with the story of the finding of the True Cross (see below on III. 28 ff.). The (lost) late fourth-century church history by Gelasius of Caesarea was an important intermediary for transmitting the *VC* to the church historians of the fifth century and later. See Winkelmann, intro., pp. xix–xxv; S. N. C. Lieu and D. Montserrat, eds., *From Constantine to Julian* (London, 1996), and above, Introduction, § 11.

the whole company of soldiers.   The vision is witnessed by all Constantine's army; numbers suit the public character of the miracle.

on a campaign he was conducting somewhere.   Eusebius implies that this was before he decided to attack Maxentius, while still in Gaul or even Britain. The vision is not connected by Eusebius with the Battle of the Milvian Bridge; indeed, the dream (29. 1), the manufacture of the standard (30), the adoption of Christ as Constantine's God, and the christianizing of the court (31. 1–3) are all placed before the campaign against Maxentius begins (37).

29. 1. the Christ of God appeared to him with the sign.   As well as his vision, Constantine also has a dream, in which Christ himself appears to him together with the cross. He is told to manufacture a copy of what he had seen in the sky. This is the *labarum*, depicted on coins from Constantinople in 327 (*RIC* vii, Constantinople no. 19; Fig. 2), and from Trier and Rome, 336–7, and known to Eusebius from 325 onwards (I. 32. 1, 30), though it is hardly likely that as yet there was the kind of elaborate jewelled version that Eusebius describes. The coin representations do not agree in every detail and there may well have been no standard type; in any case Eusebius describes it in its later form; so also Leeb, 43–52, and see A. Alföldi, ' "Hoc signo victor eris": Beiträge zur Geschichte der Bekehrung Konstantins des Grossen', in T. Klauser and A. Ruecker, eds., *Pisciculi: Festschrift F. Dölger* (Münster, 1939), 1–18, repr. in H. Kraft, ed., *Konstantin der Grosse* (Wege der Forschung, 31; Darmstadt, 1974).

Fig. 2. Constantinople, AD 326–7. *Labarum* piercing a serpent. Trustees of the British Museum.

Lactantius gives a quite different account, and Eusebius' version must be carefully separated from it, though they are often conflated in modern accounts (e.g. *ODB* s.v. Labarum). In Lactantius' version, written not very long after the event, Constantine was told in a dream before the battle by an unidentified voice to mark his soldiers' shields with the 'heavenly sign of God' (Lact., *DMP* 44. 5); he did so, and was victorious. The sign seems to have been some form of the *chi-rho*. Lactantius also reports a dream experienced by Licinius (whom he regards as Christian) before his battle against Maximin, *DMP* 46. 3–6; Licinius was visited by an archangel, who dictated a prayer which was written down, and copies of which were distributed to the army officers (46. 7). But in the *VC*, in an account written much later, the dream of Constantine (recounted by Eusebius alone) and the vision which it follows take place before the campaign has even begun.

Constantine is given a revelation from Christ of a heavenly emblem, and directed to replicate it. Similarly in Exodus Moses is shown a pattern for the Ark of the Covenant and the tabernacle, which he proceeds to copy (Exod. 25–7, 36–9); the pattern was thought of as concretely existing in heaven (see esp. Exod. 25: 9, and the interpretation in Heb. 8: 3–6). Parallels between Constantine's cross-trophy and the Ark of the Covenant may be noted. Painting apotropaic emblems on shields was nothing new: MacMullen, 'Constantine and the Miraculous', 87 (also on the *labarum*).

30. recounted the mysterious communication. Moses too, after receiving instructions from the Lord, speaks to the people (Exod. 35: 4) before summoning the craftsmen in gold and jewels (Exod. 35: 30–36: 1).

the shape of the sign. The overall cross-shape is meant, the *chi-rho* mentioned in 31. 1 not being part of the shape but of the decoration of the *labarum* (*contra* Drake, 'True Cross', 72; the 'sign' mentioned so often in *LC* is also the cross, see above). Cf. 32. 2 below, which makes the point clear.

This was something which the Emperor himself once saw fit to let me set eyes on. Cf. 32. 1, 'That was, however, somewhat later.' Eusebius saw the *labarum* in its established form, as depicted on Constantine's late coins, and here describes what he had seen later (see on **29. 1**, and compare **III. 12**). Even in this form it could be described as cross-shaped, and resembled a military *vexillum*; Firm. Mat., *Err. prof. rel.* 20. 7 refers to it as the *vexillum fidei*.

31. 1. tall pole. Or possibly 'long spear', but the object resembles a flagpole rather than a weapon. It was plated with gold like the ark of God and its carrying-bars in Exod. 25: 10–13.

forming the shape of a cross. The whole structure is cruciform. The fact that the military *vexillum* was cruciform had been noted by Methodius, *Porph.* 1, who claimed that earthly emperors thus used the cross 'for the destruction of wicked habits'. The description of the wreath and the first two letters of the name of Christ point clearly to the later *labarum*, as it was depicted on coins.

These letters the Emperor also used to wear upon his helmet in later times. Like other Christian signs, the *chi-rho* emblem is in fact rare on Constantine's coins, and the early silver medallions of 315 from Ticinum (Pavia) showing the Emperor wearing a high-crested helmet with the Christogram are exceptional (Fig. 3). See P. Bruun, 'The Christian Signs on the Coins of Constantine', *Arctos*, NS 3 (1962), 5–35, against A. Alföldi, 'The

Helmet of Constantine with the Christian Monogram', *JRS* 22 (1932), 9–23; though the form of the *chi-rho* is attested before Constantine, there is no certain Christian use (E. Dinkler, *Signum Crucis* (Tübingen, 1967), 134–5).

Fig. 3. Ticinum, silver medallion of Constantine with *chi-rho*, AD 315. Staatliche Münzsammlung, Munich.

31. 2 From the transverse bar . . . hung suspended a cloth. The general shape was typical of that of a Roman standard, with a symbolic image above a banner. The rich tapestry may have been more true of the specimen observed by Eusebius later; the original was perhaps more utilitarian.

But the upright pole . . . This sentence is difficult to interpret. The portrait or bust of the Emperor is attached to the main shaft of the standard. Eusebius might mean that there was a distinct structure in addition to the monogram and the banner, which held the imperial portrait; however, the portrait should be on the banner itself. Eusebius says the bust was made of gold; perhaps it was hung from the central shaft or cross-piece. The reason for this obscurity may be that after describing the square-shaped banner he deliberately re-emphasizes the very tall upright pole so as to underline the cruciform shape of the whole. The bust is right up 'below the trophy of the cross', i.e. immediately under the crossbar, or, as he says, near the top of the delineating tapestry. Thus the Emperor himself is directly associated with the central point of the cross, with his sons beside him. The manuscripts read *diagraphontos*, 'delineating', whereas editors prefer *diagraphentos*, 'delineated' (either 'just described', or 'decorated with pictures'). In preferring the manuscript reading we assume that Eusebius means to emphasize that the top edge of the banner marks the important line in the design, i.e. the cross-piece.

head-and-shoulders portrait of the Godbeloved Emperor, and likewise of his sons. Eusebius does not say how many sons are depicted. There are three medallions shown on the *Spes publica* coin of 326–7 (Fig. 2) and on the obverse the legend bears the names of Constantine and his sons Constantine and Constantius; by 327, therefore, the name of Crispus had been removed, though it had appeared on the *aes* coinage of 326–7, together with those of the younger Constantine, Constantius, Helena, Fausta, and Constantia (*RIC* vii, 570). If Eusebius had seen a version of the *labarum* in 325 this would have been before the death and *damnatio* of Crispus, which happened in 326.

31. 3. This saving sign. i.e. of the cross (see on **28. 2**).

32. 1. he summoned those expert in his words. Constantine is instructed by bishops or clergy (*mystai* are initiates) as to the meaning of his vision; for the language see also on **III. 25–8; IV. 61. 2–3**. He hears about the Son of God, and of the meaning of the cross, and of his life on earth. Having learnt this from God's own teaching, as he believed (**32. 3**), he decided to read the Scriptures and made Christian clergy his advisers. Eusebius thus demonstrates Constantine's closeness to and dependence upon his clerical advisers; cf. **32. 3** 'he listened attentively'.

Eusebius presents the process as one of preparation of the kind familiar in the Christian catechumenate. The 'convert' is driven by some sign from God to seek instruction from those who know the Scriptures, and learns about Christ and his coming and saving work. Constantine's vision had been an answer to prayer to his father's God; now he learns (perhaps from his father's own courtier-bishops, **17. 3** above) who that God really is. He is even given a detailed account of the divine and human nature of the Son, information usually reserved for the final period of baptismal preparation, and henceforth adopts a pattern of Christian worship ('with all due rites', **32. 3**).

Eusebius summarizes the function of the cross as a token of immortality, 'an abiding trophy of that victory over death which he had once won'. His younger contemporary Athanasius writes of its power to convince men of immortality (*Inc.* 50. 5). While not specifically biblical, the idea originated in the conception that Christ's death and resurrection bring resurrection to mankind (e.g. 1 Cor. 15: 20–2), though the cross is the means of Christ's triumph over human condemnation and 'principalities and powers' in Col. 1: 13–15. Constantine himself presents the death of Christ rather inconspicuously as the climax of his battle to defeat the powers of ignorance and evil (*Or. ad sanct.* 15).

32. 2. Onlybegotten Son. The title for Christ originates in John 1: 18. *Pais* (son) is also scriptural (e.g. Acts 4: 27); it is favoured in Christian liturgical texts, and used by Eusebius of royal offspring (see on **7.** 1 above).

self-accommodation. The life of Jesus is thought of as a heavenly embodiment of the divine Son or Word; 'self-accommodation' (*oikonomia*) is the regular Greek term for what modern theologians refer to loosely as 'the Incarnation'.

33–41. 2. *The campaign against Maxentius*

33–36. *The crimes of Maxentius*

From 33 to 40 Eusebius relies heavily on his earlier version of the defeat of Maxentius in *HE*, particularly 8. 14 (the persecutions by Maxentius and Maximin: *VC* I. 33–6) and 9. 9. 9–11 (Constantine's victory, reproduced with only slight additions in *VC* I. 37–40). The *VC* account begins with the excesses of Maxentius (on his regime see Barnes, *CE* 37–8), necessary to establish him as a persecutor and thereby to justify Constantine's attack, and moves (omitting most of the advance through Italy) to the preparations for the final battle (37), which is described in highly rhetorical fashion (38), and to Constantine's entry into Rome (39), where Eusebius stresses that the Emperor attributes his victory to God and publicly proclaims the victorious cross (39. 3–41. 2).

33. 1. the one who had thus previously seized the imperial city. i.e. Maxentius; cf. below, 47. 1, 49. 1 for similar periphrases (here taken in general terms from *HE* 8. 14. 1).

not to obscure or insignificant persons, but . . . From here the *VC* again picks up *HE* 8. 14. 1–2, expanding on Maxentius's sexual indulgences but suppressing his early favour towards Christians (14. 1), then leaving this passage to be picked up again at 35. 1 below. The language used in 33. 2 of Maxentius's female targets (cf. *Pan. Lat.* 4 (10). 34, AD 321) is used in relation to Maximin at *HE* 8. 14. 14 and of the

tyrants generally at *LC* 7. 7. For the noblewoman's suicide (34)
see *HE* 8. 14. 17; this is a version of the story of Lucretia, and
see Barnes, *CE* 42. Eusebius turns to the end of the *HE*
chapter, returning at 35–6 to where he had left off, and now
using 8. 14. 3–6. Effectively, 33–6 are in part a *cento*, in part a
development, of *HE* 8. 14; see Hall, 'Eusebian Sources', 245–
7, with further detail. For the slaughter of the populace (35. 1)
see Aurel. Victor, *Caes.* 40. 24, cf. Zos. 2. 13, and for
Maxentius's superstitious practices, *Pan. Lat.* 12 (9). 4. 4;
according to Lact., *DMP* 44. 1. 8–9, Maxentius consulted
the Sibylline Oracles. These accusations are part of the stock
in trade of panegyric and its counterpart, invective.

35. 2. thousands were put to death. Hardly 'thousands',
since this seems to refer not to the multitudes mentioned
above but to senators put to death for gain.

37–8. Constantine's victory

**37. Constantine . . . began making every armed preparation
against the tyranny.** We have left Constantine 'on a campaign
somewhere' (28. 1). Of what happened next, Eusebius, using
HE 9. 9. 3, says only that he defeated three armies of Maxentius
and 'advanced to occupy most of the land of Italy' (37. 2); in this
account, Constantine fights the whole campaign under the
patronage of 'God who is in heaven, and his Word, even Jesus
Christ who is the Saviour of all' (*HE* 9. 9. 3). The three battles
took place in Cisalpine Gaul and at Turin and Verona (*Pan. Lat.*
9 (12). 5, 6, 8; also 11 (surrender of Aquileia); 4 (10). 19–26;
Origo 12 (Verona, also depicted on the Arch of Constantine); Zos.
2. 15 (no cities named). Eusebius has been careful to insert the
detail of the cross-shaped *labarum* ('victorious trophy . . . salutary
sign' (*soterion semeion*), not present in the *HE* version). Note that
Constantine took the initiative, as in *HE* 9. 9. 2; in Eutrop. 10. 4
and Aurel. Vict., *Caes.* 40. 16 Maxentius is reluctant to fight,
while in Lact., *DMP* 44. 4 he declares war ostensibly to avenge
his father's death, and Zos. 2. 14–15 has him planning war
before Constantine attacks.

37. 2. sorcery. See on **27** and **33. 1** above.

soldiers and . . . military units. Zos. 2. 15 gives numbers:
90,000 infantry and 8,000 cavalry for Constantine; for Maxentius,

80,000 from Rome and the vicinity, 40,000 Carthaginians, some Sicilians, in total 170,000 infantry and 18,000 cavalry. According to *Pan. Lat.* 9 (12). 3. 3, 5. 1–2 (the earliest account), Maxentius had 100,000 in all, Constantine less than 40,000; he had left some troops on the Rhine, and for his numbers cf. also Lact. *DMP* 44. 2. At 37. 2 Maxentius does not dare to leave the city.

first, second, and third formations. Perhaps the battles at Segusio, Turin, and Verona described in *Pan. Lat.* 9 (12). 5–8, AD 313; 4 (10). 21–2, 25, AD 321. Verona appears to have been a long and difficult encounter.

38. The account is based closely on *HE* 9. 9, but implying more directly that God's providence caused Maxentius to construct his bridge badly (38. 2–3), just as God effectively dragged him out to fight (38. 1). The tale of moral retribution is thereby enhanced. In *Pan. Lat.* 9 (12). 17 the bridge is crowded and Maxentius drowns while trying to cross the river on horseback; in Lact., *DMP* 44. 9 he finds the bridge already broken when he tries to flee; in *Epit.* 40. 6 he is thrown and drowns while crossing a bridge of boats; in Zos. 2. 16. 2–4 the bridge (not of boats) collapses under him, as in *HE*. Cf. also Lib., *Or.* 59. 20, with Maxentius's trick and the same moral. For the differences between *Pan. Lat.* 9 (12), AD 313, and 4 (10), AD 321 see L'Huillier, *L'Empire des mots*, 235–48.

Note that Eusebius introduces the scriptural citations from Exodus and from Psalm 7 (38. 3) with similar phraseology to that used of the Moses story above (see on **12. 2**); it is here taken straight from *HE* 9. 9. 4. The analogy between Constantine and Moses is not explicitly made in either place, but see 39. 1 'the great Servant' (an addition here).

38. 2. the friend of God.   Above, 3. 4.

38. 3. in his cowardice.   Not in *HE* 9. 9, but also introduced at 38. 4; Eusebius thinks the device in the bridge a 'dirty trick'.

38. 4. divine oracles.   Of the Scriptures (Exod. 15: 10), see above on **3. 4**.

38. 5. might be thought thus to have raised the same hymn The hymn is attributed to Constantine personally in 39. 1.

39–41. 2. *Celebrations and monument to victory*

39. 1.   Eusebius adds the direct comparison between Constantine and Moses.

39. 2.   An expanded version of *HE* 9. 9. 9, with more stress on the senators (see Hall, 'Eusebian Sources', 251). For Constantine's dealings with the Senate after his victory cf. *Pan. Lat.* 9 (12). 20, AD 313; his address to the Senate is depicted on the Arch of Constantine (Fig. 4).

39. 2. acclamations.   For a brief introduction to the practice of acclamation in late antiquity see C. M. Roueché, 'Acclamations in the Later Roman Empire: New Evidence from Aphrodisias', *JRS* 74 (1984), 181–99, at 181–8. Constantine himself urged the formal use of acclamations in provincial assemblies (*CTh* 1. 16. 6, AD 331), and *CTh* 7. 20. 2, AD 320, preserves actual acclamations addressed to him.

39. 3–40. 2.   This passage is based on *LC* 9. 8–11 (Winkelmann, 156, and see Hall, 'Eusebian sources', 252–54). The statue described at 40. 2 comes however from *HE* 9. 9. 10. The Latin inscription translated into Greek here is very close to that on the Arch of Constantine, except that the latter, ostensibly set up by the Senate and the Roman people, substitutes the neutral *instinctu divinitatis* for the mention of the 'sign': *quod instinctu divinitatis mentis/magnitudine cum exercitu suo/tam de tyranno quam de omni eius/factione uno tempore iustis/rempublicam ultus est armis* ('since through the instigation of the Divinity and the greatness of his own mind he with his army revenged the state with just arms on one occasion from the tyrant and all his faction'). See N. Hannestad, *Roman Art and Imperial Policy* (Aarhus, 1986), 319–26; the language is highly traditional (cf. Augustus, *Res Gestae* 1: *exercitum . . . per quem rem publicam a dominatione factionis oppressam in libertatem vindicavi*). The same language could apply to conquests over civil enemies or usurpers, as in the *Res Gestae*, or, as applied by Eusebius and others, to the defeat of the persecutors; the inscription is virtually unaltered from *HE* 9. 9. 11, except that the singular 'tyrant' has been replaced, in the light of hindsight, with the more general 'yoke of tyranny'. The Arch was finished quickly; recent excavations have suggested to some that rather than being a new monument, albeit using *spolia*,

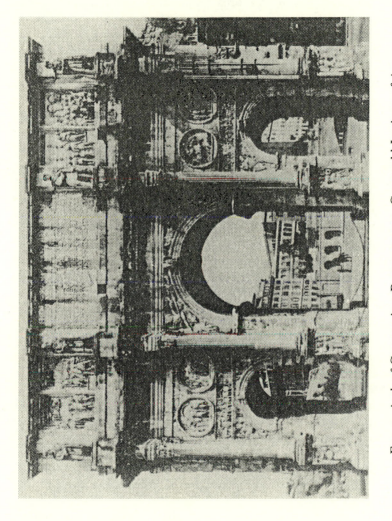

FIG. 4. Arch of Constantine, Rome, AD 315. Courtauld Institute of Art.

the present Arch represents Constantinian additions made to an existing Hadrianic monument: C. Panatella, P. Pensabene, and M. Milella, 'Scavo nel area della Meta Sudans e ricerche sull'arco di Costantino', *Archaeologia Laziale* 12/1, *Quaderni di Archeologia Etrusco-Italica*, 23 (1995), 41–61; see Fig. 4. None the less, the reuse of earlier imperial representations, with recarved heads depicting Constantine and Licinius in two cases in the act of sacrificing, constituted a 'quotation' from the repertoire of imperial success, as indeed do the themes of the new friezes: see P. Pierce, 'The Arch of Constantine: Propaganda and Ideology in Late Roman Art', *Art History*, 12 (1989), 387–418.

The identification of the statue gives rise to problems: Eusebius describes how Constantine was depicted in large size holding in his right hand a cross-shaped standard ('in the shape of a cross', and cf. 41. 1), 'in the middle' of Rome, as a trophy over his enemies, though it is only one of many such images (40. 1): the statue bore a triumphal inscription. The question is whether the surviving colossal head and other fragments in the Musei Capitolini (Fig. 5) come from this statue or from another colossus (see on **IV. 15. 2**); since both the head, which looks to be post-325, and the hands may have been altered or replaced the identification is not impossible (see E. B. Harrison, 'The Constantinian Portrait', *DOP* 21 (1967), 79–96, at 93, and for further discussion, Leeb, 62–9). According to *Pan. Lat.* 12 (9). 25. 4, AD 313, a gold statue was also dedicated to Constantine by the Senate. Over a dozen sculpted images of Constantine survive, in addition to coin portraits: for the development of Constantinian portraiture and its various messages from 306 onwards see Smith, 'Public Image of Licinius I', 185–7, and for its connection with the ideology of imperial panegyric, see pp. 194–202.

41. 1–2.   Eusebius sums up and repeats what he has said already above about Constantine's profession of the cross (see also *LC* 9. 8–9), about the jubilation in Rome (some repetition from 39 above) and about the extent of Constantine's rule and the general happiness (cf. 25. 1 above; *Pan. Lat.* 12 (9). 19). As 22–4 complete 12–24, so 41. 1–2 completes and rounds off 25–40, while simultaneously acting as introduction to the following section about government of the west. Jubilation, happiness, and general prosperity (*felicitas*) are standard themes of imperial panegyric, as is the cheerfulness of the Emperor's own appearance (see Smith, 'Public Image of Licinius I', 197–8).

41. 3–48. *Emperor of the West*

Eusebius interposes between the accounts of the campaigns against Maxentius and Licinius a short section about Constantine's administrative acts following his defeat of Maxentius in 312. Much of this material has already appeared in *HE*, and appears again here in adapted form (Hall, 'Eusebian Sources', 254–9).

FIG. 5. Colossal head of Constantine. Rome, Palazzo dei Conservatori.

41. 3–43. *Generosity to Christians and others*

41. 3. imperial letter. A rescript of settlement, restoring property and exiles and releasing prisoners, in similar terms as the measures recorded after the defeat of Licinius, at II. 20. 2–5 and II. 30–42. Rather than suppose that Eusebius is reporting a measure otherwise unknown, compare in general terms the language of *HE* 10. 5. 2–14 ('Edict of Milan') and 15–17 (letter to Anullinus), whence he has probably developed this passage. 41. 3 does not mention either Christians or persecution as such, nor make any reference to the previous edict of Galerius calling off persecution (311), which Eusebius had reported at *HE* 8. 17.

42. 1–2. Constantine's favours to the Church. This is developed by Eusebius in hindsight, and no doubt in order to reinforce the view he wishes to promote of the Emperor's deference and honour towards bishops (cf. also III. 15; IV. 56); *HE* 10 has nothing about personal meetings or campaigns, nor about enlargement and decoration of church-buildings at this time. Probably Eusebius had no actual information about Constantine's church building in Rome after 312. As above, Eusebius here generalizes from a limited number of known measures mentioned in *HE* 10. 5, together with *VC* II. 24–42 (see below). For Constantine's general programme of church-building see **II. 45. 1.**

table-companions. At III. 15 the dinner given by Constantine to the bishops after the Council of Nicaea is described as though exceptional, but see also **IV. 24** and **46.** The present passage is reminiscent of the generalizations earlier as to the similar favours shown by Constantius Chlorus (above, esp. **17. 3**).

43. Constantine's generosity to his subjects in general ('those outside', i.e. outside the Church, cf. **IV. 24**). For 'grants of land', at 43. 1, compare *CTh* 10. 8. 1, AD 313, though it is not clear that Eusebius had any specific legal source in mind. Again the chapter is highly generalized, and ends with a panegyrical statement on the stock theme of liberality, also depicted on the Arch of Constantine (again at **IV. 1–4**; for Christian charity see also **III. 44** on Helena, and **IV. 44. 2**); the solar imagery at 43. 3, like the conceit of the rejoicing of nature in imperial felicity, also belongs in the context of imperial and tetrarchic panegyric (see MacCormack, *Art and Ceremony*, e.g. 172–3; Liebeschuetz, *Continuity and Change*, 241, with 281–2 on Constantine and Sol); Kloft, *Liberalitas Principis*, 170–7. Ch. 43 interrupts the section on Constantine's favours to the Church, which is resumed at 44. 1.

44–5. *Constantine deals with Church disputes*

Eusebius refers to the quarrel between Donatists and Catholics in Africa (he has given the text of four of Constantine's letters about this in *HE* 10. 5. 15–7. 2), but only in very general terms (44. 1 and 45. 2). A similarly brief mention comes in Constantine's letter to Alexander and Arius at II. 65.

44. 1–2. he convoked councils . . . He did not disdain to be present. Barnes (*CE* 58, *NE* 72, n. 110) takes this to mean that Constantine was himself present at the Council of Arles (AD 314; sources, see Barnes, *NE* 242). However, his presence is not mentioned at *HE* 10. 5. 18–20 and 21–4, which refer to this and to the earlier synod in Rome under Bishop Miltiades, and is more likely to be a retrojection by Eusebius of the circumstances of the Council of Nicaea (325, see III. 6–23; esp. the detail of those present at 44. 2). Significantly, Constantine's urging of peace is a major theme of the account of the latter's antecedents at II. 65–73; synods are mentioned in general terms at II. 65. It is typical of Eusebius to generalize from only one example, as here with 'some were at variance . . . in various places'; similarly, while 'councils' may refer to the synod in Rome and the Council of Arles, it may equally be a broad generalization from the latter alone. Eusebius is an enthusiast for the authority of episcopal synods: see **51** below.

45. 1. gentle voice. The word used (*praos*) is standard in imperial panegyric in Greek, which compliments the mercy (Lat. *clementia*) of the Emperor. Constantine's rebukes, as well as his patience, appear at *HE* 10. 5. 22, and for the likeness to Moses, see on **46** below.

45. 2. those in Africa That is, the Roman province of Africa whose capital was at Carthage.

some evil demon. Cf. **II. 61** for the 'spirit of Envy' as a cause of the dispute over Arius and **IV. 41. 1** referring to Athanasius and the Melitians; at II. 65, as here, Constantine himself uses the imagery of madness and disease of Donatists, but ascribes the schism to persons of 'heedless frivolity'. Here they are described as resentful and perverse, stirred up by 'the evil demon'; their actions will stir up the Emperor's anger against them. Eusebius goes out of his way to play down the seriousness of the Donatist schism (against which Constantine's measures ultimately failed). That Constantine finally left irreconcilable Donatists to the judgement of God is confirmed by Optatus, *App.* 9 and 10 (Stevenson, *NE* 311–12).

46–7. Victories abroad, plots unmasked, and divine favours

46. Though Winkelmann sees a reference to the campaign against the Franks in summer 313 (*Pan. Lat.* 12 (9). 21. 5), this is more likely to be a very generalized statement of the panegyrical theme of Constantine's piety (here to the Christian Church) and the universal *felicitas* and victory which it inevitably brought. *Pietas* (Gk. *eusebeia*) is an indispensable quality of the good ruler, easily adapted for Christian use (Liebeschuetz, *Continuity and Change*, 243); it is applied to Constantine in a pagan context e.g. at *Pan. Lat.* 7 (6). 20. However, there may be biblical touches here too, for instance in 'putting all barbarian nations under his feet' (cf. Ps. 8: 6, 18, 38 and 17: 39; cf. 1 Cor. 15: 27, Heb. 2: 7); Moses is also called *praos*, 'meek' or 'gentle', at Num. 12: 3 (see on **45. 1**).

47. 1. the second of those who had retired from power. This is Maximian, the father of Maxentius, and the passage comes directly from *HE* 8. 13. 15, where it appears in the right chronological order, between the rise of Licinius (308) and Constantine's defeat of Maxentius (312). Here it is placed at the end of Constantine's measures in the west, which seem to follow on from the defeat of Maxentius; however, the context is clearly a general account of plots and conspiracies against Constantine (see below). There are two contemporary and pro-Constantinian versions of Maximian's end: *Pan. Lat.* 6 (7). 14–20 and Lactantius, *DMP* 29. 3–8. Lactantius tells the story in a highly coloured version: after the Conference of Carnuntum (probably November, 308; see Creed, *ad loc.*; Barnes, *NE* 5;

Drake, *In Praise of Constantine*, 19–20), Maximian had tried to trick Constantine, his son-in-law, into limiting the numbers of troops he took to Gaul and spread malicious stories about him, apparently in 310, but Constantine, hearing what was going on, returned and after successfully besieging Maximian at Marseilles, spared him; only after a further plot foiled by Fausta, Maximian's daughter and Constantine's wife, was he given the choice of the manner of his death, and hanged himself (see also on this account Moreau, 367–8).

47. 2. others of the same family. Possibly a reference to Fausta and Crispus, whose mysterious deaths in 326 are otherwise passed over in total silence, but more likely to Bassianus, the husband of Constantine's half-sister Anastasia, who was foiled in a plot with Licinian connections and killed in 315–16 (*Origo*, 14–15; see Barnes, *CE* 66–7); see also **50** below for the general idea.

47. 2. supernatural signs. Eusebius makes the most of the idea behind *HE* 10. 8. 7 'God exposing every deceit and sharp practice to the Godbeloved Emperor', and now claims a plethora of miraculous signs. The Moses typology is also present in the chapter: like Moses, Constantine is called God's 'servant' (47. 2 and 3), and Moses too had received direct revelation and had seen the Lord (Num. 12: 6–8, cf. Num. 12: 3 in 46, above). Constantine is credited now with frequent visions, clearly another generalization (see on **44. 1–2**). He suffers plots from his relatives, as Moses did from Aaron and Miriam. Finally, Num. 12, the passage alluded to here, immediately precedes Moses's preparations for invading the land of Canaan, just as 47 precedes the beginning of the account of Constantine's campaign against Licinius (for all this see Hall, 'Eusebian Sources', 261–2).

48. *Decennalia celebrations*

48. tenth anniversary of his accession. Constantine early counted his *dies imperii* as 25 July 306, the day of his proclamation by the troops, though he did not formally receive the title Augustus until his marriage to Fausta around September 307 (*Pan. Lat.* 7 (6); see Barnes, *NE* 5, with nn.). His Decennalia thus fell in the year July 315 to July 316.

sacrifices without fire and smoke. The Christian liturgy was known as 'the bloodless sacrifice', and Eusebius may mean here that Constantine authorized eucharistic offerings in celebration ('prayers of thanksgiving', *eucharistous euchas*, and cf. the 'due rites' of **32. 3**). More probably, Eusebius alludes to the general view held by philosophers, Jews, and Christians alike that sacrifice should be spiritual rather than physical (notably Porphyry, *De Abstinentia* 2. 24; see generally Frances M. Young, *The Use of Sacrificial Ideas in Greek Christian Writers from the New Testament to John Chrysostom* (Patristic Monograph Series, 51; Philadelphia, 1979)). So Constantine's prayers are without animal sacrifice, which had been opposed in Christianity from the start (see 1 Cor. 8). On Constantine and the prohibition of sacrifice see below on **II. 45; IV. 23, 25.**

49–59. *The Crimes of Licinius*

I. 49–II. 19 recount the campaign against Licinius and his defeat. In the first part, the same ground is covered as in *HE* 10. 8–9, with similar variations and additions as in the previous section. *VC* I. 49. 1–50. 2 is marked by Winkelmann as being expanded from *HE* 10. 8. 2–6. In addition, however, the jubilation of ch. 48 picks up *HE* 10. 8. 1; the 'fierce beast' of 49. 1 recalls *HE* 10. 9. 3, but Eusebius has changed the application of the enemy corresponding to Maxentius (*HE* 8. 14) from Maximin to Licinius. At *HE* 10. 8–9 Licinius gets little space, since this is an addition at the final stage of revision; in the *VC* a much lengthier treatment is required, and space for Maximin is correspondingly reduced (I. 58–9). Contrast Lactantius, *DMP* 43. 1–2; 44. 10–2; 45–7; 49, where Licinius is still Constantine's ally, fighting in the name of the supreme God (46. 3, with his dream of an angel), and his victory over Maximin (313) balances Constantine's defeat of Maxentius. The blackening of Licinius, who in 313 was apparently as pro-Christian as Constantine, began early in order to justify Constantine's aggression against him, and the hasty job done on this by Eusebius in the *HE* is much enhanced in the *VC*. For the process, and for the difficulty inherent in reconstructing Licinius' genuine policies and legislation, see S. Corcoran, 'Hidden from History: The Legislation of Licinius', in Jill Harries and Ian Wood, eds., *The Theodosian Code* (London, 1993), 97–119; see also Fig. 6 (p. 225).

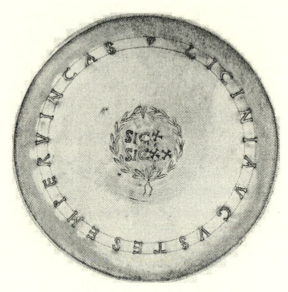

Fɪɢ. 6. Silver dish with inscription of Licinius. Trustees of the British Museum.

49–50. *Breaking faith*

49. 1. the whole Roman domain . . . left in two parts. *HE* had envisaged the orderly division of the Empire as seen in 313, and was only very superficially revised after the defeat of Licinius in 324. At the end of the reign *LC* 1–3, esp. 3. 5–6, has set out a different idea, that of the superiority of monarchy over polyarchy, one Emperor on earth representing one God in heaven; and Eusebius is anxious in the *VC* that the sons of Constantine should maintain unity (above, on the introduction, esp. **I. 3, 5**).

night and day . . . darkness . . . brilliant daylight. Light imagery is used of Constantine's generosity (43. 3) and of the true religion (II. 19. 1).

49. 2. Envy, which hates good. *HE* 10. 8. 2 has both Envy and the evil demon, which appears separately here at 49. 1; cf. **45. 2.**

49. 2. a connection by marriage. Constantine's half-sister Constantia married Licinius at Milan in February 313 (Lact.,

DMP 43. 2, 45. 1; *HE* 10. 8. 4) as part of the agreement then reached between the two Emperors; see also **50. 1.**

50. He therefore waged constant war against his benefactor. See also *HE* 10. 8. 3–5. It was necessary for Constantine's campaign against Licinius to be justified in every possible way; at 49. 2 Licinius' behaviour is associated with envy. Eusebius here plays down the agreement between the two and stresses Constantine's generosity and Licinius' ingratitude.

50. 1. Eusebius suggests that all was in Constantine's gift, even in 313, though it is clear from Lact., *DMP*, and from *HE* 10. 8 that this was by no means the case.

50. 2. God exposed to him the darkly devised plots. See above on **47.**

suddenly breaks the agreement. The account here merely hints at the first clash between Constantine and Licinius at the Battle of Cibalae (316 is the more likely date of this than 314: see Grünewald, *Constantinus*, 109–12), followed by the agreement necessitated by Licinius' tactics and the declaration of the two sons of Constantine and one of Licinius as Caesars (1 March 317); see also on **II. 9. 4.** Lact., *DMP*, does not mention these hostilities, and was therefore probably composed before 315 (Barnes, 'Lactantius'); however, Zos. 2. 18–20 gives a detailed account, laying the blame for treacherousness and conspiracy on Constantine rather than Licinius. Like the *VC* (see Barnes, 'Panegyric', 95), *HE* 10. 8 glosses over these events and moves straight on to the final campaign against Licinius; the reason is to defend Constantine from charges of breaking the accord.

open war . . . . he . . . began a campaign. Cf. *HE* 10. 8. 7–9, on which 50. 2 is closely based. The chronology is left vague in both places, and Eusebius concentrates heavily on Licinius' alleged persecution of Christians, leaving secular aspects of his administration of the east for a hostile summary in 54–5. 49–59 covers the period from 313 to the preliminaries of the campaign in 324, and have expanded the version in *HE* 10. 8–9 by inserting the sections on Licinius' secular policies and on the deaths of Galerius and Maximin. The approach is however dictated more by ideological aims than by chronology; Eusebius wishes to denigrate every aspect of Licinius' rule, in order to establish Constantine as completely justified and his victory as ordained by God. For Licinius' portraits compared with those of Constantine see Smith, 'Public Image of Licinius I', esp. pp. 187–94.

51–4. 1. *Measures against Christians*

Licinius' measures against Christians are based on the account in *HE* 10. 8. 8, 10, 14–19, but with much more emphasis on the attack on bishops, the 'servants of God' (contrast *HE* 10. 8. 8, where he attacks the faithful in general). Eusebius adds and elaborates the point that he forbade synods and meetings (51. 1–2), in clear justification of his own views on the authority of synods. At 52 the bishops are subjected to harassment, exile, and in a few cases to threat of death, whereas in *HE* 10. 8. 14–18 their horrible deaths are told in some detail; this is deferred in *VC* until II. 1. It is claimed that Constantine had bishops about him at court, by implication from the defeat of Maxentius onwards (52, see above on **42. 1**, and cf. **32. 3**). Licinius' sexual crimes (*HE* 10. 8. 13) recall similar accusations against Maximian (Lact., *DMP* 8. 5), Maximin (*HE* 8. 14. 12–17; Lact., *DMP* 38–40), and Maxentius (33–4 above, with *Pan. Lat.* 9 (12), 3.6, 4.4; *HE* 8. 14. 2). The whole is told in a timeless manner which aids the desired impression of the gradual revelation of Licinius' wickedness between 313 and 324, an impression which would have been diminished by an overt treatment of the outflanking of Constantine by Licinius in 316 and their consequent alliance (see on **50. 2**). Eusebius is concerned to discourage the reduction of episcopal influence in the counsels of state after Constantine's death, and especially the setting aside of synodical decisions, as in the case of Athanasius. For the general retrospective blackening of Licinius, and for the latter's legislation in general, see Corcoran, 'Hidden from History', 99; Corcoran, *The Empire of the Tetrarchs: Imperial Pronouncements and Government AD 284–324* (Oxford, 1996), 195, suggesting that Licinius issued an edict or edicts on Christian matters covering the measures recorded in *VC* I. 51. 1 and 53. 1–2. Licinius is already referred to as a 'tyrant' in a Constantinian law of 324 (*CTh* 15. 14. 1).

51. 2. episcopal ordinations. At least three bishops must be present to ordain a new bishop (Nicene Canon 4, 325, reinforcing a long-standing rule; see *HE* 6. 43. 8).

53. Nothing else is known of these measures separating women from men in church contexts. The instruction of candidates for baptism was chiefly done by male clergy, and so would have been impeded.

53. 2. Open-air worship: the opposite policy from that adopted by Constantine's building programme. For Licinius' administration see Barnes, *CE* 69–72.

54. 1. The purging of the army of Christians is described at *HE* 10. 8. 10, though the order has been reversed, with the result that the prayers of the courtiers for the Emperor mentioned there are here ascribed to the soldiers. The 'demons' are the traditional gods. *ILS* 8940 shows troops being compelled to consecrate an annual statue of Sol (Barnes, *CE* 71). Overall in the *VC*, Eusebius gives the impression that the army was much more christianized than seems to have been the case, even considerably later in the fourth century.

54. 2–55. *General policy and character*

54. 2–56. 1. *HE* 10. 8. 11–16 is effectively reproduced word for word, except that the rhetorical figure repeated at 10. 8. 11 and 12 ('unlawful laws') is omitted both times in the *VC* passage, while what *HE* says on land-taxes (10. 8. 12) is somewhat expanded so as to present a more circumstantial account of Licinius' greed, again a stock theme in relation to bad emperors (Constantine in turn is accused of greed by Zos. 2. 38 and by the Anon. *De Rebus Bellicis*, 2); for the theme in *VC* see I. 17; IV. 29–31. The fairness and clemency of Constantine is also contrasted with the cruelty of Licinius by Aurelius Victor, *Caes.* 41, and cf. Lact., *DMP* 50. Conversely, as part of the account of Constantine's liberality *VC* IV. 3 records that he instituted an investigation into unfair land-tax measurement (see also *ILS* 1240–2 for a *peraequator census Gallaeciae*). At 54. 1 and 55. 1 Eusebius uses the rhetorical device of *praeteritio* (the claim to omit, while actually listing the charges), favoured in invective, whose rules generally were the inversion of the rules for panegyric. The allegations of

Licinius' bad character are a case of rhetorical expansion for similar effect. There is no other evidence for his laws on marriage and inheritance (55. 1–2); however, Constantine too was concerned about inheritance (IV. 26). The attack on churches and bishops (56) comes from *HE* 10. 8. 14, followed by *HE* 10. 8. 9 (56. 2).

56–9. *Licinius ignores the fate of Galerius and Maximin*

56. 1. Winkelmann punctuates differently: '. . . and attacks the bishops; whoever he regarded as chiefly opposing him he also reckoned as hostile, the friends. . . .'

56. 2. This passage comes from *HE* 10. 8. 9, and forms a transition to 57–8, which interrupt the narrative and seem to contradict what Eusebius has already said at I. 23. But Eusebius' purpose is made clear in 58. 1 and 59. 1–2: unlike Constantine (I. 27), Licinius did not learn the lessons of experience. There may be an implied lesson here for the sons of Constantine. Eusebius does not attempt to address the recent example of the deaths of Dalmatius and Hannibalianus, but when the time came, these would have had to be explained in a similar manner.

57–9. 2. On Eusebius' accounts of the deaths of Galerius in 311 and of Maximin in 313, see Hall, 'Eusebian Material'. 58. 1–2 is based on *HE* 8. 14. 13–14 (the martyrs under Maximin), a chapter already used for I. 33–6 (Maxentius) and I. 47. 1 (Maximian); see too the parallel in *LC* 7. 7 (closer to *HE*). However, the emphasis here is less on the sufferings of the martyrs than on the cruelty of Maximin. Much is also taken closely from *HE* 8. 16. 3–4, 17. 1 (57) and from 9. 10. 2–15. 4 (58), though with some omissions for brevity; in his account of Maximin, Eusebius omits all that relates to the events of Maximin's hostilities with Licinius and his final defeat (see above on **28. 2** and **49**), but this is likely to be done in order to gloss over the fact that Licinius' victory in 313 was seen by some as directly parallel to Constantine's defeat of Maxentius (so Lactantius, *DMP*, though apparently unknown to Eusebius); further, Eusebius wishes here to emphasize that, far from being on Licinius' side, he had been deliberately misled (II. 4. 2, 4. 2, 11. 2). There are some changes from the model

(*HE* 9. 10. 14) in 58. 4–59. 1 so as to enhance the lesson by making Maximin's illness more public. Maximin's admission of the truth of Christianity (59. 1) is important for the argument of the *VC* as a whole, as is the mention of the 'experience' of God's judgement, for which see also **I. 23, 28; II. 11. 1; III. 55. 5, 58. 1;** in contrast (59. 2), Licinius could have learnt, but did not, from the deaths of Galerius (which he had seen) or of Maximin (of which he knew). The concluding sentence brings back the narrative to Licinius and prepares us for Constantine's campaign against him. The whole passage heightens the folly and wickedness of Licinius, a religious and historical point which perhaps overrides Eusebius' general purpose of silence over the fate of the persecutors (**23**).

BOOK II

1–22. *Deeds in War II: The Victory over Licinius*

1–2. *Licinius attacks the Church*

1. 1–2. Eusebius' chief source is still *HE*. Winkelmann notes the similarity of phraseology at 1. 1 with *HE* 10. 8. 2, also on the deaths of the wicked; the next chapter, *HE* 10. 9. 5, is also to the point (*HE* 10. 9. 6 also at 19. 2 below).

1. 1–2. wild beast, or a twisting snake. For Licinius as a wild beast see *HE* 10. 9. 3; for the snake/serpent image, see on **III. 3** below.

1. 2–3. 2. Derived from *HE* 10. 8. 14–9. 3, almost verbatim, and picking up the reference from the last use at I. 56. 1; the account of Licinius as persecutor, especially of bishops, which he had given nearly fifteen years before, serves Eusebius again for the same purpose. The changes are minor: Eusebius adds the name of Constantine at 1. 2 and 2. 1, expands for clarity at 2. 2, 4, 5 (but abbreviates at 2. 3), makes minor changes at 2. 1, but heightens the wording at 2. 2, omits the summary of Constantine's victory at *HE* 10. 9. 1, but essentially repeats 9. 2–3. Eusebius carefully omits Crispus, who is mentioned at *HE* 10. 9. 4 as stretching out the right hand of salvation together with Constantine, and who still appears on coins as Caesar in 326 (*RIC* vii, Constantinople no. 6). Eusebius returns to *HE* 10. 9. 6

at 19. 2 below, in his account of Constantine's triumph; there is no use of *HE* in the intervening section.

1. 2–2. 1. Amasea in Pontus. There was a bishop at this town on the River Iris as early as 240. The events described here are not otherwise known. In *HE* 10. 8. 14–15 we read 'at Amasea and the other cities of Pontus', and the destruction and closure of church buildings are told as though affecting Pontus only. Here they are apparently told as referring to the whole eastern church. Thus the author of the ancient chapter headings divided before 2. 1, and modern editors follow his interpretation of *VC* here. Departing from his account in *HE*, Eusebius generalizes, probably with no serious historical justification, by adding the words 'by the local officials' (*hegemones*, i.e. the governors in each district).

2. 3. Eusebius describes a persecution of which little is known. That there were banishments of prominent Christians is implied by Constantine's provisions in II. 30–2 below. Their loyalty might well be suspect as Constantine's army approached. But Licinius can hardly even have thought of requiring all citizens to worship the gods, in spite of what Eusebius says.

3–5. *Preparations for a war of religion*

3. 1. he set out to the defence of the oppressed. A blatant attempt to gloss over the fact that Constantine was the aggressor; Eusebius adopts Constantine's own estimate of his mission in attacking Licinius; see **II. 28. 1–19**.

3. 2. the tokens of his hope in God. This refers to the miraculous standard of I. 28–31. The manuscripts add 'by means of the aforementioned standard', deleted as a scribal gloss by editors.

4–5. Constantine's preparations for war are contrasted favourably with Licinius' resort to pagan diviners and oracles, reinforced by Licinius' exhortatory address to his men, reported at 5. 2–4. Unlike Constantine and his father Constantius, Licinius surrounds himself with false prophets who encourage him in his delusions. The passage picks up the theme of Licinius' blindness to true signs (see on I. 57–9. 2). For the resort of Constantine's enemies to magic see on **I. 27. 3**; Maximin is said to have relied on false prophets and oracles in the same way at *HE* 9. 10. 6.

4. 3–4. prophecies.

On oracles see Lane Fox, *Pagans and Christians*, 168–261. The falsity of pagan oracles is a main theme for Eusebius, reappearing e.g. at *LC* 9 where Constantine's victory is said to have proved them wrong. See on **I. 3. 4**, and on **50** below.

5. 2–5. Eusebius claims (5. 5) to have heard about Licinius' speech in 5. 2–4 shortly afterwards from those actually present, though he had not mentioned it at the relevant place in *HE* 10. 9; more probably it is his own invention. He uses the speech to heighten the religious character of the conflict, and makes Licinius himself concede that his defeat will prove Christianity true. Note the contrast with the pro-Christian Licinius presented by Lactantius (see on **I. 28. 2**).

5. 5. The author of the present work. Eusebius uses these or similar words of himself (grammatically plural, 'we who compose this work') at **8. 2** below; cf. **I. 28. 1**; **I. 30**.

6–10. *Licinius' attack repelled by God's aid*

6. 1. Just as Licinius' signs are false, so Constantine's are true. Licinius' subjects see in a vision Constantine's troops marching through the cities as if already victorious. As Eusebius carefully points out (6. 1 fin), this was a sign of what was to come, the counterpart to Licinius' false oracles. Cf. *Pan. Lat.* 4 (10). 14, AD 321, where the orator Nazarius reports the prevailing rumour of heavenly troops of Constantius coming to the aid of his son in 313. Eusebius attributes his knowledge of the vision to hearsay ('they say').

6. 2. It is naturally Licinius who is made the aggressor.

7–9. 3. Miracles attributed to the *labarum*, as allegedly told to Eusebius by Constantine himself (8. 2, 9. 3); cf. **I. 28. 1** and **I. 30**, where he says that the Emperor told him about the making of the *labarum*. It is not impossible that the Emperor spoke to the bishops, including Eusebius, on the origin and miracles of his standard. But that does not mean that the accounts are true.

9.4. When . . . he had won the first battles. Eusebius has often been thought to conflate the two engagements of Constantine and Licinius at Cibalae (316, see below) and Chrysopolis (324); so e.g. J. Vogt, 'Die *Vita Constantini* des Eusebius über den Konflikt zwischen Konstantin und Licinius', *Historia*, 2 (1954), 463–71. The narrative is certainly extremely selective and apologetic, passing over not merely the politics of the years between 313 and 324, but also Constantine's preparations for the war of 324, which were very extensive (see Barnes, *CE* 76). But in II. 6–18 as a whole Eusebius is aware of two campaigns, and seems to distinguish between two first attacks by Licinius and their repulse (6–7) (the 'first battles'), and Constantine's counter-offensive (9. 4–10. 2), after which there is a treaty (11), and a renewed outbreak of hostilities when Licinius breaks it (15–16. 1). The two main confrontations are most likely to be those at Cibalae in Pannonia (*Origo*, 16–18; Zos. 2. 18-1-9; for 316, see e.g. Grünewald, *Constantinus*, 109–12; for 314, *Origo*, 119–23) and the campaign of 324 and the final battle, which took place at Chrysopolis, near Chalcedon (for which see *Origo*, 23–8, and Zos. 2. 22–8); Eusebius fills up the intervening period with a pious account of Constantine's battle techniques. The alternative interpretation would be that he is not referring here to the Cibalae campaign but to the first engagement of 324, which took place near Adrianople in early July (*Origo*, 24; Zos. 2. 22), after which Licinius fled to Byzantium; see however on **12. 1–2.** According to Zosimus, 2. 22. 7, there was great slaughter at Chrysopolis (see below, on **13. 1–2**).

11.1. The same language is used of Licinius' flight as of Maximin at *HE* 9. 10. 6 (see on **4–5** above); thus a passage in the *HE* referring to Licinius' own victory over Maximin (313) is here simply transferred to his defeat by Constantine. Even the notion of an interlude followed by renewed hostilities is to be found in Eusebius' model (*HE* 9. 10. 13–14). Like Maximin, Licinius displays cowardice in the second encounter (16. 1, cf. *HE* 9. 10. 14). Constantine by contrast is depicted as only reluctantly making war, compelled by Licinius' obduracy and renewed resort to sorcerers (11. 1–2). This, together with the divine direction of his military actions (12) and godly mercy to enemies (13), helps to justify Constantine to Eusebius' Christian readers. Many Christians still held to the original pacifism of Christianity, and this may have been intensified by the experiences of persecution of Christians by the state. For imperial actions and military service seen as illegitimate for baptized Christians (though this was by no means a universal view), see J.-M. Hornus, *It is Not Lawful for Me to Fight*, Eng. trans. (Scottdale, 1980), with J. Helgeland, 'Christians in the Roman Army from Marcus Aurelius to Constantine', *ANRW* II. 23. 1 (Berlin, 1979), 724–834; Louis J. Swift, 'War and the Christian Conscience I. The Early Years', *ANRW*. II. 23. 1, pp. 835–68.

12. 1–2. The rest of the narrative, while largely new, consists of little more than religious and moral justification for Constantine. Constantine's prayer tent on the battlefield explicitly (though without naming him) recalls the tent of meeting where Moses, the 'ancient prophet of God' (cf. **I. 12. 1**) regularly met the Lord face to face. The 'divine oracles' are the Scriptures such as Exod. 33: 7–11. The use of the tent is not confined to the campaign against Licinius, but also extends to 'every other occasion on which he was setting out to engage in battle' (cf. 13. 1, 'for a long time past'). Every attack by Constantine is as if prompted by divine revelation after prayer within the tent (12. 2). Scriptural kings are similarly sent into action by specific words from God (e.g. David in 2 Sam. 5: 17–25). 'Organize another campaign' and 'respite' suggest that Eusebius does have in mind the chronological gap between the battles of Cibalae and Chrysopolis.

13. 1–2. Constantine's mercy in war is described as a general principle adopted by him on all occasions, even extending to the practice of buying the lives of the enemy from his own soldiers with payments in gold (13. 2). Barnes, 'Panegyric', 99, marks this as 'a clear insertion', on the grounds that 14. 1 follows on from 12. 2, while 13. 2 contradicts 12. 2. This should not be allowed to obscure the important continuity of thought: the war and all its deaths were defensive, wholly justified, directly commanded by God, and as mercifully conducted as possible. In contrast Zosimus asserts that the slaughter wrought by Constantine at Chrysopolis (September 324) was such that only 30,000 escaped out of an enemy total of 130,000 (2. 26. 3; see also on **9. 4** above), after which Byzantium opened its gates to him. Eusebius perhaps found that an apologia was necessary in the light of prevailing and contrary opinion. One may allow that Constantine believed in his divine mission without accepting Eusebius' specific claims for him here.

14. 1–2.   The same practices are followed also on this occasion; Constantine prepares himself for combat by prayer and ascetic practices.

15–18. *Renewed war and final victory*

15   According to Eusebius Licinius breaks the treaty, as Maximin had done at *HE* 9. 10. 2, and turns back to the pagan gods whom he had admitted to be false (11. 1, cf. *HE* 9. 10. 6 of Maximin). In fact Licinius himself complained of Constantine's breach of his borders: *Origo,* 21.

16. 1.   The *labarum* functions as a totem: Licinius orders his men not only not to do battle against it, but not even to look at it, while Constantine places his faith in the sign (16. 2). On this see Heim, *La Théologie de la victoire,* 98–105.

16. 2–18.   When he sees Licinius breaking the treaty, Constantine embarks on a reluctant but justified attack, defeats the enemy and his gods (the 'demons', 17; see note at **I. 16. 1**), and exacts the penalty due by the laws of war; the terminology of the 'dead' pagan gods is taken direct from *LC* 9. 8.   At IV. 21 similarly Constantine is said to have relied only on the sign, not the accustomed images of pagan gods. As they die Licinius' supporters acknowledge that Constantine's God is the one true God (18; so too Maximin recognizes that his gods are false and confesses the God of the Christians, *HE* 9. 10. 6–12). According to *Origo,* 28–9, and Zosimus, 2. 28, Licinius, besieged by Constantine at Nicomedia, threw himself on the Emperor's mercy, relying on an oath Constantine had sworn to Licinius' wife; Constantine let him go to Thessalonica, but 'not long after broke his oath, as was his custom, and had him hanged' (Zos. 2. 28, trans. Ridley). Eusebius agrees in so far as he makes Constantine kill Licinius and his colleagues by judicial process, not in battle (18).

19. *Victory celebrations*

19. This chapter functions as a transition, beginning with a summary of the fall of Licinius and passing on to the detail of Constantine's decrees and letters, the chief source and content of the remainder of bk. II. Eusebius returns to the *HE* for his starting-point, 19. 1 'now that the evil men were removed' picking up the phraseology used of Maximin at *HE* 9. 11. 1. The main passage used is however 10. 9. 6, the brief account in the *HE* of Licinius' defeat from which Eusebius had departed at *VC* II. 4 (see on 4–5 above). He has in fact simply based his narrative on his earlier version, inserting new material into it and writing out the role of Crispus, the mention of whom at *HE* 10. 9. 6 is replaced here by the explanation of the title 'Victor' (see below). Crispus' role as commander of the naval forces of Constantine was in fact crucial; he won a naval battle himself and was able to destroy Licinius' fleet and gain possession of the straits: *Origo*, 26; Barnes, *CE* 76. For praise of Crispus' achievements before 324 cf. *Pan. Lat.* 4 (10). 36. 3–5, AD 321. In Zosimus' narrative the death of Crispus, attributed to Constantine himself, follows immediately after the account of Constantine's victory (2. 29).

19. 1–2. Eusebius likes to see the unity of the empire under one emperor as a model of the reign of the one God; cf. **22** below, and on the idea of the Empire as one body I. 26, with 49. 1. In his *Martyrs of Palestine* 1. 1, the Christian Procopius quotes *Il.* 2. 204–5 against the multiple sovereignty of the Tetrarchs.

19. 2. **Victor.** Eusebius' statement that the title was taken after the defeat of Licinius, is confirmed by epigraphic evidence (Barnes, *CE* 77).

19. 3. Eusebius returns to *HE* 10. 9. 7, with only minor changes. The mention of Constantine's sons, which includes Crispus at *HE* 10. 9. 7, is not only left in here but even expanded slightly. *HE* 10. 9. 8 refers to the generous and humane decrees of Constantine, and is here much expanded (20–2), leaving *HE* 10. 9. 9, the concluding sentence of the *HE*, aside in order to continue the story in a different and fuller way. Throughout the account of the campaign, however, Eusebius has used *HE* closely, and much of what seems at first sight to be independent material is in fact little more than a reworking or development of what is in the *HE* account. Where there is alteration it can often be understood in terms of his purposes in writing the *VC*. Thus he makes the banning of synods the first as well as the most serious aspect of Licinius' persecution; he takes features of the end of Maximin and attributes them to Licinius, and he emphasizes the empirical element in God's judgements, which are plain for all to see. The sections interposed about Constantine's behaviour on campaign serve above all to persuade us of the Emperor's piety and clemency, and of the efficacy of the *labarum*, while Crispus, whom Constantine was shortly afterwards to have killed, giving rise to adverse pagan explanations of his conversion (see Zos. 2. 29), is written out of the story altogether.

20–2. *Persecution and tyranny ended*
Constantine's measures to benefit Christians: Eusebius expands the brief allusion at *HE* 10. 9. 8 to 'ordinances' immediately following Constantine's victory into a lengthy section explaining them. This section describes the documents which are presented in 23–48; moreover, 23. 1 follows on 19. 3. Pasquali argued that Eusebius cannot have intended both passages to stand in the same work (Barnes, 'Panegyric', 97–8, cf. 100; cf. Pasquali, 'Die Composition', 369 ff.). At 30–41, where the detailed provisions are cited, there is no reference back to the earlier section. Furthermore, 23. 2 refers to two imperial letters, one to the churches and one to those outside, of which Eusebius decides that only the latter is relevant.

Nevertheless, 20–1 illustrates the generosity of Constantine to Christians (as at *HE* 10. 9. 8); in contrast, the letter of 24–42 is cited in order to illustrate 23. 1: 'The Emperor by the power of the Saviour God began to make it plain to everyone who it was that supplied good things to him, and he would insist that he considered him to be the cause of his triumphs, and not himself.' At 23. 2 Eusebius makes it clear why he chooses to quote in full the second of the two letters, so as to preserve the text of the decree, and 'to confirm the truth of our narratives' (the plural could, though it need not, refer back also to 20–1, confirmed by 29–41). The document is cited for the religious confession it contains (24–8 and 42), and for its confirmation of Eusebius' own claims (23. 2). Another possibility is that the letter to the churches referred to in 23. 2 essentially duplicated the provisions of 29–41, and is not therefore cited by Eusebius as such, though it was made the basis of the summary in 20–1, where the point is precisely to do with benefits to Christians. For a further pointer in this direction, see below on 21.

20. 1. as previously among those who occupy the other half of the civilized world. Eusebius virtually admits that he himself had not had access to Constantine's earlier laws relating to Christians between 313–14 and 324; the documents cited in *HE* X all belong to 312–14, whereas all the documents cited in the *VC* postdate the defeat and death of Licinius.

20. 2–21. *HE* 9. 10. 7–11 (the continuation of the passage used above) contains the similar provisions of a law rescinding persecution by Maximin before his death. Eusebius' comment at 9. 10. 12 makes clear the exemplary character of Maximin's recantation, as in the case of Licinius at 18 above.

20. 2. curiales. i.e. decurions, or members of municipal *curiae* (cf. 20. 4, 30. 1), membership of which was conferred by possession of property and which carried heavy financial obligations. Christians who did not qualify had nevertheless been enrolled by ill-wishers.

20. 4. The second option (permanent immunity) seems to go further than what is suggested in 33 below.

21. transferred . . . either by sale or by gift. Since this technical phrase does not appear at the corresponding place in 39, it could be that Eusebius is in fact working from a similar but not identical legal document, rather than merely summarizing that cited below. For the Latin technical terms in the document cited see Pasquali, 'Die Composition', 370–4. For Constantine's legislation of winter 324–5 see *CTh* 15. 14. 1–2, with Barnes, *CE* 208.

22. all those in our part saw before their eyes. It was necessary for Eusebius to repeat these arrangements so as to provide proof of God's dispensation in giving rule to Constantine.

23–43. *Constantine's Confession of God: The Letter to the East*

With the letter of 24–42 Eusebius begins the series of Constantinian documents cited with full quotation in the *VC*. The documents cited are fifteen in all, amounting to a quarter of the whole work (Warmington, 'Sources of Some Constantinian Documents', 94), of which this is by far the longest. Eusebius says that it was issued in both Latin and Greek, and that his copy was signed in the Emperor's own hand (23. 3, cf. II. 47. 2, from his own hand, but translated into Greek; IV. 8, the letter to Shapur, signed by the Emperor in Latin, but translated into Greek for accessibility). Much has been made of alleged adaptations or alterations made to these documents (and see Winkelmann's indices for differences of usage between the documents and the main text, with his intro., p. li and Heikel, pp. lxxi ff.; for the present document see Dörries, *Selbstzeugnis*, 43–6; Corcoran, *Empire of the Tetrarchs*, 315; P. Silli, *Testi Costantiniani nelle fonte letterarie (Materiali per una Palengenesi delle Costituzioni Tardo-Imperiali*, iii (Milan, 1987), no. 16). However, chs. 27 and 28 below, together with the end of 26 and the beginning of 29, have been identified as the text written on the back of P. Lond. 878 (319–20) and not much later than it, thus confirming the authenticity of this document as quoted by Eusebius (A. H. M. Jones and T. C. Skeat, 'Notes on the Genuineness of the Constantinian Documents in Eusebius' *Life of Constantine*', *JEH* 5 (1954), 196–200), and greatly reducing the likelihood that the documents as a group should be regarded as suspect. Though the form of the document is that of a letter, the concluding order for its publication throughout the east (42 fin) shows that it has the force of an imperial edict (see Barnes, *CE* 208–9); though addressed in Eusebius' copy 'to the provincials of Palestine' (23. 3), Eusebius says it was sent to 'every region' (23. 1). This and the other documents in bk. II are well discussed in Pietri, 'Constantin en 324', who also emphasizes the deliberateness of Eusebius' literary intention in including such documents in the *VC*, as he had already done in the *HE*, and the novelty in the context of imperial pronouncements of the sentiments expressed by Constantine (despite recent pagan precedents justifying their religious policies by Galerius and Maximin Daia, see Pietri, 'Constantin en 324', 82 (272)).

23. 2. to the outsiders.   lit. 'to those outside' (sc. the Church). At IV. 24 Constantine declares himself to be the bishop of 'those outside' (see note *ad loc.*).

23. 3.   If Eusebius really had an original copy signed personally by the Emperor, it is an interesting question how he came by it. Warmington ('Sources', 94–7) suggests an imperial notary called Marianus, whose work is described in IV. 44. But see note on **24. 1.**

24–9.   The letter begins with a lengthy introduction setting out how God's judgement can be seen to work in the world: history shows that those who keep God's law prosper, while those who have attacked and persecuted Christians have experienced retribution (25). The sentiment is then repeated (26. 1–2): the faithful may have suffered hardship, but have won greater glory, while the persecutors have been routed; wars have resulted from their actions, but each one individually has received fit punishment, so that they suffer both in this life and after death (27. 1–2). It is God who has applied the saving medicine (28. 1), through the career of Constantine himself, who, starting from Britain, was inspired to restore the divine Law and promote the faith (28. 2), and now has come to the rescue of the east also, confessing his total dependence on God (29. 1). Therefore he, the servant of God, must set about restoring the condition of the faithful in those parts (29. 2–3).

The personal tone, and avowal of commitment to religious duty, are characteristic of Constantine's utterances; cf. the letters to the North African Church preserved in Optatus's *Appendix*. For the theology and sense of his own role expressed here see Pietri, 'Constantin en 324', 83–90 (273–80).

24. 1. Palestine.   Eusebius has the local copy of what was sent to every province; his city of Caesarea was the local metropolis.

24. 2. even more clearly demonstrated.   The general moral superiority of Christianity is confirmed by recent events, i.e. Constantine's victories. In drawing this conclusion for himself Constantine behaves as previous emperors would have done towards their patron gods.

the most dread Law.   Constantine uses the word 'Law' (*nomos*) to mean either the Christian Scriptures (as in 69. 1) or the

Christian religion in general (as in 27. 2; 42). In this he follows other Christian writers, especially Latins like Lactantius ('lex divina', *Inst.* 5. 13. 5; cf. Constantine's letter at Optatus, *App.* 3).

25. all the events of history. The argument that goodness and wickedness meet condign consequences is familiar from the Bible (notably the books of Kings) and from Christian apologetic about the persecutors (notably Lactantius), both of which Constantine would know.

26. Constantine contrasts the faithfulness of martyrs (26. 1) with the cruel folly of their persecutors.

27. harsh wars. Constantine attributes the civil wars to the attack on Christianity. Whatever the truth in Eusebius' portrayal of Licinius as a persecutor (as in II. 1–2 above), it was plainly a part of Constantine's own belief and propaganda in 324–5; see Pietri, 'Constantin en 324', 73–82 (263–72).

27. 2. places of torment below the earth. This is a Greek concept of the afterlife of the wicked (cf. Plut., *Mor.* 2. 567d). In Christianity they rise from the dead for punishment (see Rev. 20: 11–15); see **54** below.

28. 2. Constantine sees his whole career as directed by God to save Christianity ('restore the most dread Law') and to convert people ('the most blessed faith might grow'). Notably, this career begins in Britain, a point which Eusebius himself does not correctly understand, since he does not know that Constantine was first proclaimed there (**I. 25. 2**).

30–42. The measures that now follow are those already described at 20–1, and in the same order: return of exiles and release from curial duties (cf. 20. 2), restoration of their property, release from confinement, prison, and hard labour (20. 3), restoration to military rank (20. 4), release from service in state factories and restoration of noble status (20. 5). Property taken from Christians must be restored, and the property of those killed returned to their rightful heirs, or, if no heir is to be found, to the church in each locality (35–6). Those who have come into possession of such property must hand it back forthwith, and may expect leniency if they comply, but will be treated severely if they do not (37–8). The *fiscus* itself is not exempt from the obligation to restore due property to the churches, and churches are confirmed in their property rights (39) and ownership of martyrs' burial places (40). However, Constantine offers to pardon those who have acquired any such property from the *fiscus* (41). All of these measures would apply not only to any who had been persecuted by Licinius but also to the victims of the earlier persecutions under Maximin Daia and Galerius.

30. 1. curial registers. See on **20. 2.**

37. 2. pardon for this offence. This is the limit of Constantine's generosity. In 313 it was open to those who had acquired Christian property in the sort of circumstances described in 38 below to ask for compensation from the *fiscus*. Constantine is more severe, and more moralistic about acquisitiveness, in this decree. With this we may compare Eusebius' reports in IV. 29. 4–31.

39. . . . to the churches. Either a word or two has fallen out of the text or the phrase should be deleted.

42. The document concludes by repeating the lesson that it is the Christian God who has brought about the end of the persecutors and now enjoins the establishment of correct religious observance. The reference, as earlier in his letters about the Donatists, is to the establishment of the 'divine Law', and the right kind of worship. The tone is forthright and uncompromising (Barnes, *CE* 209–10).

43. the first written communication of the Emperor to us. In fact the first public pronouncement to the eastern provinces, presented by Eusebius as though addressed personally to him.

44–61. 1. *Constantine Promotes the Church and Restrains Paganism*

Eusebius goes on to describe various steps taken by Constantine at once to strengthen the position of the Church.

44–45. 1. *General measures*

44. governors. Eusebius claims that Constantine preferred Christians when appointing provincial governors and prefects; for Christians in office during his reign see D. M. Novak, 'Constantine and the Senate: An Early Phase in the Christianization of the Roman Aristocracy', *Ancient Society*, 10 (1979), 271–310; T. D. Barnes, 'The Religious Affiliations of Consuls and Prefects, 317–361', in id., *From Eusebius to Augustine: Selected Papers 1982–1993* (London, 1994), no. vii; id., 'Statistics and the Conversion of the Roman Aristocracy', *JRS* 85 (1995), 135–47. Table of known provincial governors: Barnes, *NE* ch. 9.

peoples in their various provinces. The Greek term *ethne*, 'peoples', who are 'divided' into administrative units.

those who preferred paganism. An early use of *hellenizein* in its standard fourth-century and later use by Christians to mean 'practise paganism', 'be a pagan'. Note that Eusebius refers to this as a 'law' (see on **24. 2** above).

45. 1. two laws were simultaneously issued. The laws Eusebius mentions have not survived, and the question of whether Constantine in fact forbade sacrifice remains open; if he did, the law was not strongly enforced. 56. 2 and 60. 2 below make it clear that he did not actually ban pagan cult as such, and Libanius claimed later that Constantine put no limitations on it (*Or.* 30. 6; Constantine looted the temples in order to build his own city). However Constantius II alludes to his 'father's law' in a law of 341 forbidding sacrifice (*CTh* 16. 10. 2); see Corcoran, *Empire of the Tetrarchs*, 315–16; Barnes, *CE* 210, 246; id., 'Constantine's Prohibition of Pagan Sacrifice', *AJP* 105 (1984), 69–72; S. Bradbury, 'Constantine and the Problem of Anti-Pagan Legislation in the Fourth Century', *CP* 89 (1994), 120–39. Christian emperors subsequently continued to forbid the 'madness' of sacrifice, and a total ban on sacrifice was part of the anti-pagan legislation of Theodosius I in AD 391–2 (*CTh* 16. 10. 10, 12). Laws of Constantine banned the private use of *haruspices*, outlawed harmful magic and forbade private sacrifice to be used in connection with divination in cases of lightning (*CTh* 9. 16. 1–4, AD 321). An inscription from Hispellum in Umbria (*ILS* 705, AD 333–5) allowed the erection of a new temple to the *gens Flavia*, but laid down restrictions as to the cult that might be celebrated there (see J. Gascou, 'Le rescrit d'Hispellum', *MEFR* 79 (1967), 609–59), and *VC* IV. 16 records that Constantine forbade images of himself to be set up in temples. Eusebius has exaggerated the extent to which Constantine actually proscribed pagan cult (see on **60** below and on **III. 56**, and see H.-U. Wiemer, 'Libanius on

Constantine', *CQ* NS 44 (1994), 522; but see T. D. Barnes, 'Constantine's Prohibition of Pagan Sacrifice', *AJP* 105 (1984), 69–72; 'Christians and Pagans in the Reign of Constantius', *Entretiens Hardt*, 34 (1987), 301–37, at 330) and he may have no further evidence than the two laws which follow. Nevertheless, the Emperor made clear his preference for Christians and his intention to curb certain pagan practices.

45. 2–46. *Church buildings*

45. 1. the other dealt with erecting buildings. Eusebius goes on in 45. 2 to explain the content of the law, which provided for costs of church building to be met out of the imperial treasury (see on **III. 29** for an example). Constantine writes to both provincial governors and to bishops in each province, requiring them to cooperate in the new policy; see **III. 31. 2** for such cooperation in the case of the church of the Holy Sepulchre at Jerusalem.

46. 1–3. Eusebius now includes the circular letter to all bishops which he received in his capacity as bishop of Caesarea. The bishops are ordered to rebuild, restore, or enlarge existing church buildings, and if necessary to build new ones, and to apply for expenses to the civil authorities.

46. 2. that dragon. See on **I. 2** above, and cf. **III. 3. 1**, on the depiction on the imperial palace of Licinius in the guise of a dragon or serpent being pierced and cast down to the deep, beneath a representation of Constantine and his sons.

47–61. 1. *Letter against polytheistic worship*

Like the document at 24–42, this takes the form of a letter to all eastern provinces, justifying the policy now adopted. As with the previous general letter cited (see on **23**), Eusebius reproduces a signed copy, apparently translating it into Greek himself. He comments (47. 2) that reading it is like hearing the very voice of Constantine, and Barnes rightly points out the didactic and prayer-like tone which it adopts (*CE* 210–11). Constantine does not hesitate either to preach to his people or to express his personal aims (48. 2). The letter falls into three parts: introduction (48); account of the recent persecution and its ending (49–54); prayer of thanks and hope for the future (55–60. 2). 'Constantine urges, but does not force, the provincials to abandon paganism and adopt Christianity' (Corcoran, *Empire of the Tetrarchs*, 316).

48. Constantine alleges that, from the point of view of a moral person, the order in the universe demonstrates divine providence and future judgement, even if most people are foolish and do not see it. He follows a familiar Christian argument, already used by St Paul (Rom. 1: 18–20), but even there borrowed from Jewish and Stoic thought (see F. J. Leenhardt, *The Epistle to the Romans: A Commentary*, Eng. trans. (London, 1961), 63). Compare the arguments for God from nature in 57 and 58.

49. 1. only my father. Constantine himself, perhaps Eusebius' source, here makes the exception and the high claims for Constantius recur throughout the *VC*.

50. Apollo at the time declared, it was said. For the falsity of pagan oracles see on 4–5 above, and below, 54. Constantine includes an anecdote about his youth at the court of Diocletian, when Diocletian attempted to discover the meaning of the oracle which he cites (51. 1); hearing that 'the righteous' must be the Christians, he was inspired to renew persecution (52. 2). The oracle (cf. 4. 3–4) comes from the great cult-centre at Delphi, known as the Pythian oracle (54 below), where Apollo spoke through a prophetess, and where there were many tripods (three-legged cauldrons), often of precious materials, given as votive offerings); despite Eusebius' claims, e.g. at *PE* 4. 2. 8, oracular shrines such as Delphi, and Didyma in Caria were still functioning (see P. Athanassiadi, 'The Fate of Oracles in Late Antiquity', *Deltion Christianikès Archaiologikès Etaireias* NS 115 (1991), 271–8). The panegyrist of 310 claimed that Constantine himself had 'seen' Apollo in Gaul (*Pan. Lat.* 6 (7) 21. 4).

51. 1. when I was still just a boy. Constantine refers to himself as *pais*; the date (AD 303) is given by the reference to the renewal of persecution. On the basis of this and other references to him as *iuvenis*, *puer*, or *adulescens*, his birth-date has often been taken to fall in the 280s; however, such terminology can be very elastic, and it was to his advantage to stress his youth and rapid rise. Barnes, *NE* 39–42, argues for a birth-date of 272 or 273, though this would make him *c.* 30 in 303; see also on *VC* I. 19. Constantine refers to the start of persecution in 303 under Diocletian.

52. The effect on Constantine of the violence used during the persecutions under Diocletian and Galerius, and the endurance of the victims, may have been considerable. For Eusebius' version of these events see *HE* 8. 4–13 and *Martyrs of Palestine* 1–8.

53. the barbarians who . . . welcomed the refugees. For the theme of Constantine's universal mission see also **IV. 7, 49–50.**

54. the pits of Acheron. As in **27. 2** Constantine uses the Greek imagery of the underworld as a place of punishment; Acheron is the river of the house of Hades.

Pythian oracles. Both the place and the answer could be called an 'oracle'; see **50** and n.

55. 1–60. 2. Constantine addresses himself to God, to whom he says he has committed himself in love and fear (55. 2). His injunctions to the provincials are cast within this framework in the form of prayers or wishes (56. 1, 59–60). 58 interposes a statement of God's cosmic power. The abrupt change to prayer has one model in the *First Letter of Clement* 59. 2–61, which has some similar themes, and was still regarded as Scripture at this period.

55. 1. your servant. Constantine uses of himself the term which Scripture applies to Moses (see **I. 12. 1, 29. 1**); see Pietri, 'Constantin en 324', 89–90 (279–80). He is not comparing himself to Moses, but the term would encourage Eusebius to do so.

your seal . . . tokens of your merit. The term 'seal' is regularly used for Christian baptism and especially for the sign of the cross there used. 'Tokens of your merit' also refers to the idea of God's saving work through the cross. Such terminology pervades the *LC* in particular. Constantine says he fought all his campaigns under this emblem, and this doubtless influenced Eusebius in making the cross-shaped battle-standard lead the army at the start of the campaign against Maxentius (I. 37. 1).

55. 2. revealed by many tokens. Victories in war were signs which confirmed Constantine's faith in Christ.

your most holy house. i.e. the universal Church.

56. Constantine ostensibly adopts an even-handed attitude to religion; but the permissions are laced with assured commendation of 'holy laws' and 'the shining house of truth', and abuse of 'those in error', 'sanctuaries of falsehood'.

57. Christians hold that the original order of the universe speaks of the Creator; cf. **48.** Constantine argued the point more fully in *Or. ad sanct.* 3.

58. 1. Your power makes us innocent and faithful. Conversion to Christianity is the work of the same God who, he goes on to say, controls the powers of the universe and makes them fruitful.

58. 2. something which they do, even if unseen. The meaning is uncertain. The masculine gender used in this sentence may mean that the false gods, who in Christian thought have real power as invisible *daimones*, would by their conflict with each other injure human life. This fits Constantine's chapter against polytheism in *Or. ad sanct.* 3. The gods can and do hurt people, but the one true God restrains them. But the context in 58. 1 suggests that it is the forces of the physical world that are chiefly in mind, even if personalized in controlling divinities. From Heraclitus onwards, especially in Stoic and some early Christian thought, the function of God and his Word (*logos*) in resolving the conflicting physical and moral opposites is a well-known theme. See e.g. Catherine Osborne, 'Heraclitus', in *From the Beginning to Plato* (Routledge History of Philosophy, 1, ed. C. C. W. Taylor; London, 1997), 88–127; Eric Osborn, *Tertullian, First Theologian of the West* (Cambridge 1998), 65–87.

59. the healing power of medicines. Constantine is fond of the ideas of Christian faith as a cure for moral illness, cf. **28.** 1, and of heresy as disease, III. **64.** Cf. also Opt., *App.* 9 (321)—the 'cure' of the Donatists must be left to God's medicine.

60. 1. Christians are forbidden here to force conversions: the 'contest for immortality' must be voluntarily undertaken.

60. 2. Constantine clearly asserts that customary religion is not forbidden, even if he expresses himself in abusive language ('the agency of darkness'); *contra* T. D. Barnes, 'Constantine's Prohibition of Pagan Sacrifice', *AJP* 105 (1984), 69–72, but see

R. M. Errington, 'Constantine and the Pagans', *GRBS* 29 (1988), 309–18, at 311–12. This is not strictly compatible with the alleged law of 45. 1 (see n.), but may still be Eusebius' source for that statement. Constantine here gives the reasons for sending out this letter, which was perhaps unexpected and (he claims) not strictly necessary: he wishes to make himself clear to all. But he is also responding to criticism by pagans, who imagine that all pagan cult has been abolished: Constantine admits that that would be his preference, but that practicality supervened. His recent decrees have led to abuse: thus he urges concord between pagans and Christians, and resort to prayer rather than over-enthusiastic use of force (56). His policies are not new or revolutionary (as pagans presumably thought, to their dismay); rather, they give to God what is his due (57).

61. 1. like a loud-voiced herald. Cf. I. 4: God set up Constantine as 'a loudvoiced herald of unerring godliness'. Eusebius' own comment that Constantine's purpose in issuing the letter was to dissuade his subjects from paganism and encourage them towards Christianity effectively recognizes the difficulty and disguises the bad relations and abuses to which the legislation seems to have led. The tone of the document cited, which is somewhat defensive, tells against the interpretation which Eusebius puts upon it; compare his fuller interpretation given at **47. 1**.

61. 2–73. *The Disputes in Egypt*

61. 2–62. *The two disputes*

Eusebius opens his account of the religious disputes surrounding Arius and Melitius, which will lead to the narrative of the Council of Nicaea in bk. III, concluding at III. 24. There is a certain blurring of chronology in 61. 2–3. Eusebius suggests that only now does Constantine hear of these disagreements between Christians; the glowing picture of the state of the Christians in 61. 3 naturally refers to what has gone immediately before, thus to late in 324 or early 325 (cf. 'no external terror' . . . 'so newly did serene and deepest peace by God's grace protect the Church'). Eusebius gives no indication of the development of the controversy, just as, typically, he omits to name Arius himself; more details are given by other writers, e.g. Socrates and Sozomen. The trouble begins in Alexandria (61. 4), but has already reached the other provinces (61. 5), where pagans openly mock Christian doctrine in theatres.

The chief documents of the Melitian and Arian disputes are conveniently assembled in Stevenson, *NE* 275–8, 321–37. For the nature of the controversy see briefly S. G. Hall, *Doctrine and Practice in the Early Church* (London, 1991), 121–6. However, much of what later came to be associated with his name is not attributable to Arius himself; moreover, the term 'Arianism', loosely used by modern scholars, implies coherence and system in what was in fact fluid and changing. See R. Williams, *Arius: Heresy and Tradition* (London, 1987); R. P. C. Hanson, *The Search for the Christian Doctrine of God* (Edinburgh, 1988). For schism and heresy as 'disease', cf. **III. 64. 1**, with Optatus, *App.* 9.

61. 3. Envy. Cf. on **I. 45. 2, II. 61. 3; 73** below.

61. 5. disgraceful mockery. Arius himself, a presbyter of the Baukalis church in Alexandria, stirred up popular feeling by composing the *Thalia* (see Stevenson, *NE* 330–2), versified doctrinal statements, which could be sung in the streets or theatres.

62. Eusebius juxtaposes the affair of Arius with that of Melitius ('a previous long-standing issue'; the Melitians are named in the chapter heading), leading later writers, e.g. Soz., *HE* I. 15. 2, to link them; however, the issues were different, since the Melitians, like the Donatists in North Africa, were rigorists in relation to the treatment of defaulters in the persecution of 303–11. Eusebius correctly places the Melitian dispute only in the Egyptian territory, and particularly Thebais, where Coptic monasticism was strongest; indeed, he presents it as between Alexandria and the Egyptian and Thebaic churches. He claims that the Upper Thebaid was divided on both matters (61. 4, 62), and that the controversies had spread to the whole of Libya, while delegations were also being sent to other provinces; the two last sentences of 62 seem to refer to both disputes. Nothing more is said by Eusebius of the early stages of the dispute before Constantine's letter to Alexander and Arius (64–72), nor, of course, of the identity of the supporters of Arius in the other eastern provinces, who included Eusebius himself; much fuller accounts, with names, are given by Socrates and Sozomen. Eusebius' own compromised position at the Council of Nicaea, together with the changed situation in relation to the dispute by the time he composed the *VC*, made his whole account extremely sensitive, and accounts for some, if not all, of his omissions; see further below.

63–73. *Constantine's letter to Alexander and Arius*

63. one of the godly men of his court. This is generally taken to be Ossius, bishop of Cordoba, following Socrates, *HE* 1. 7. 1 (cf. Sozomen, *HE* 1. 16. 5). We have references to his activity in Alexandria in connection with the schism of the presbyter Colluthus (Athanasius, *Apol. sec. (Apol. contra Arianos)*, 74. 4 and 76. 4; Barnes, *NE* 213). B. H. Warmington suggests that it was in fact the notary Marianus ('The Sources of Some Constantinian Documents in Eusebius' Ecclesiastical History and Life of Constantine', *Studia Patristica*, 18/1 (1985), 94–7; see also IV. 44 and n.). The question is complicated by the possibility that the letter of Constantine is not primarily addressed to Alexander and Arius personally, though that is undoubtedly what Eusebius reports, but to the council which met at Antioch in the spring of 325, at which Ossius presided (see Hall, 'Some Constantinian Documents', 87; a different view in R. P. C. Hanson, *The Search for the Christian Doctrine of God* (Edinburgh, 1988), 137). It is not Eusebius' practice to name individuals (see on I. 26), though Ossius is clearly signalled also at III. 7. 1; cf. also below, 73. Constantine is represented as taken by surprise when told about the dispute, which is attributed wholly to the working of Envy (*phthonos*, 61. 3).

famous for his religious confessions. Ossius (or whoever else is meant) was a confessor, i.e. he had been tried or imprisoned for his faith during the persecutions.

64–72. [Letter] to Alexander and Arius. For the document see Opitz, *Urkunden*, 17; Hanson, *Search*, 137–8. Constantine begins by describing his mission as twofold, religious and military. He makes it clear that in his view the peace and prosperity of the Empire depend upon a religious unity pleasing to God. He next recalls his earlier experience with the Donatists in North Africa (66) (which had in fact reached a stalemate: for the sequence of events see Barnes, *NE* ch. 15) and announces his intention of trying to get eastern Christians to settle that dispute after the defeat of Licinius, who had prohibited synods of bishops. This intention had been frustrated by the new dissensions (68). He now proposes himself as arbitrator in this 'small and utterly trivial' matter.

Both Alexander, bishop of Alexandria, and Arius, one of his presbyters, are deemed to have been at fault in pressing this 'futile point of dispute' (69. 1), and their behaviour has resulted in a split between Christians. They should therefore now make peace with each other (69. 2); such matters should not be aired in public and, if they are, are likely to give rise to error (69. 3).

For Constantine, serious matters of doctrine are not at stake (70), and Christians should not be seen to quarrel over 'small and quite minute points' (71. 1), but should be like philosophers and agree to disagree (71. 2). The present quarrelling is vulgar and childish (71. 3), even a temptation by the devil (71. 4).

The Emperor attempts to use his own influence, aided by God, to bring the parties together (71. 4) and repeatedly states that the point of difference is slight and unimportant, and that divine Providence, the nature of the Law and reverence for God are not in dispute (72. 6–8); it is not clear from this on the other hand what the 'small matters' actually were. Constantine expresses personal pain, and asks Alexander and Arius and their supporters to be reconciled for his sake (72. 1), much as he had earlier appealed to the Donatists not to interfere with his sacred duty as Emperor (Optatus, *App.* 9); the news had caused him to change his plan of visiting the east from Nicomedia, though he implies that he will come after all if the matter is settled (72. 2–3).

Eusebius alone reports this letter, despite his own involvement in the dispute which led to his condemnation at Antioch (see above) and change of allegiance at Nicaea. He constantly emphasizes the Emperor's conciliatory approach and his efforts at mediation (see on the Donatist controversy at **I. 45**). Stronger language is reserved for earlier heresies and schisms, not contemporary ones (e.g. III. 63–6). However, in a later letter to Arius not included by Eusebius, Constantine uses the violent language of invective, describing Arius as a wild animal 'wearing the mask of simplicity' and making a series of quasi-hysterical threats againt him and his followers (Opitz, *Urkunden*, 33, AD 332 or 333; see Barnes, *CE* 233).

66. send some of you. These words are one of several indications that the real audience addressed was not Alexander and Arius personally, but an assembly of bishops, perhaps that at Antioch early in 325 (see **63**).

67. reared . . . in oriental nurseries. The Christian faith began in Palestine, part of the imperial diocese Oriens, and spread chiefly through Antioch.

69. you Alexander . . . you, Arius. If the letter is primarily to a council at Antioch, Constantine may suppose the originators of the dispute to be present (though see Hanson, *Search*, 149), or may apostrophize them for vividness; these words may account for the heading of the letter as Eusebius reports it (63–4 above). Constantine's account of the origins of Arianism is very early, and less tendentious than Alexander's letters. Alexander tests his Alexandrian presbyters, each of whom governed a whole congregation in the city, on their interpretation of a scriptural text ('a certain passage from what is written in the Law'). Much of the dispute turned on the interpretation of texts such as Prov. 8: 22 (LXX), where the divine wisdom says 'the Lord created me', which Arians took to prove that the divine Son was himself created by the Father. The consequence was formal mutual excommunication: 'fellowship was repudiated'; see Alexander's letters (Socrates, *HE* I. 6. 4–13; Theodoret, *HE* I. 4. 5–9; conveniently in Stevenson, *NE* 322–34, 328–9).

69. 2. some sort of gymnastic exercise. To argue about the nature of Christ's preexistence and similar topics might be a suitable rhetorical exercise, or even a game, for schoolboys. Constantine's own exasperation with refined philosophical argument shows through in what follows (69. 3).

71. 1. It is here again apparent that an assembly of bishops, not two individuals, is being addressed.

71. 2. Philosophy was usually learnt in one school with a traditional basis. What Constantine here asserts about unanimity in fundamentals was not always true.

72. 2. my intention was to press on eastward. This is easier to understand, especially in combination with 67 above, if addressed to an assembly in Antioch, the capital of the diocese of Oriens, than in Alexandria. Scholars differ as to whether Constantine actually went to Antioch at this time: cf. Barnes, *NE* 212; Lane Fox, *Pagans and Christians*, 635–62; Hall, 'Some Constantinian Documents'.

73. the one who cooperated. i.e. Ossius, who adds further arguments to those of Constantine. These words assume that the article *ho* has dropped out before *ou* at line 4 of p. 79 in Winkelmann's edition. Without the correction the subject of the verb is Constantine, which makes no sense. The person referred to is plainly the same as was described in 63; see **63** and cf. Hall, 'Some Constantinian Documents', 87.

BOOK III

1–3. *Constantine Superior to the Tyrants through Piety*

Eusebius turns from the problems outlined at the end of bk. II to Constantine's constructive settlement of religious affairs, which occupies most of bk. III. The first sentence summarizes II. 61. 2–3, and might possibly have belonged to the end of that book rather than the beginning of this; see Winkelmann, p. lv. Eusebius then summarizes Constantine's pro-Christian policies, first by contrasting him with the tyrants (1. 1–7) and then by describing the public exhibition of his Christianity in word and sign (1. 8–3. 3). The remainder of the book sets out Eusebius' view of the universal settlement achieved by the Council of Nicaea, the programme of church building, the resolution of further conflicts in the Church, and the suppression of heresy.

In making the transition (already begun at the end of bk. II) from his account of victory over Licinius and settlement of church affairs to that of the divisions within the Church itself, Eusebius has to take care to preserve Constantine's own reputation as the bringer of ecclesiastical peace, which will be a strong element in his account of the Council of Nicaea (III. 4–24). He does this in two ways: by ascribing all division to the work of Envy, thus removing blame from individuals while emphasizing Constantine's own distress (III. 1, cf. II. 61. 2–3), and by returning to the theme of the contrast between Constantine and the tyrants from whom he had delivered the Empire (III. 1. 1–7), following it with an emphatic assertion of Constantine's novel achievement and proclamation of Christianity (1. 8–3. 3). This then serves as the introduction to the account of the Council of Nicaea, which immediately follows.

1. 1. Envy, the hater of the good. Similarly the division between Donatists and others in North Africa is ascribed to the envy of 'some evil demon' (I. 45. 2–3), and the crimes of Licinius to 'Envy, which hates good' (I. 49. 2). Eusebius has already used the idea in relation to Arius and Melitius at II. 61. 2 (Envy provoked dissension between bishops so as to disrupt the general peace and happiness), and in the closing sentence of bk II. Cf. *V. Ant.* 5. 1, 'the envious devil, hater of the good' (on the term *misokalos* see G. Bartelink, '*Misokalos*, epithète du diable', *Vig. Christ.* 12 (1958), 37–44).

1. 1. The Emperor, . . . dear to God, certainly did not neglect his responsibilities. By various apologetic devices Eusebius preserves his image of Constantine as bringer of peace and distances him from responsibility for ecclesiastical disharmony: cf. I. 45. 3 (in the Emperor's view, Donatists are to be pitied rather than punished, and present no threat to himself; thus he is not roused to anger—contrast Opt., *App.* V); II. 61. 2, 53, III. 4 (he hears of dissension with shock and dismay).

doing all the things opposite to those crimes committed . . . by the tyrants. l. 2–7 takes the form of a recapitulation of the wickednesses of the persecutors in the form of a rhetorical comparison with the virtue of Constantine, a standard encomiastic technique (see on **I. 7–8**, and cf. I. 5. 2, Constantine compared with the persecutors; 10. 2, compared with Nero and others). The language, and the balancing clauses, make this a highly rhetorical passage. As at I. 42–45. 1, Eusebius moves from Constantine's favour towards Christians at a particular moment in his reign to general statements covering the whole of it. The comparison (seen as an interruption in the narrative by Barnes, 'Panegyric', 100) begins with general statements, moving to Constantine's recent rulings on property (1. 2); gifts to and promotion of Christians (1. 3, cf. IV. 1, also an encomiastic passage); restoration and building of churches (1. 4, a topic to be covered later in bk. III); copying of the Scriptures (cf. IV. 36); synods (for the generalizing plural cf.

I. 44. 1 and II. 66; for the entertainment of bishops cf. III. 15. 1–2); destruction of temples (but only the most notorious, cf. III. 55–8); honour to the memorials of martyrs (1. 6, possibly referring to the Roman churches associated with martyr-cult, but Constantinople itself was dedicated to 'the God of the martyrs', III. 48. 1, and see Barnes, *CE* 222 for possible commemoration by Constantine of a local martyr); Christians at court (1. 6, cf. IV. 18. 1); generosity (1. 7, cf. IV. 1, 28); mercy in the courts (cf. IV. 2, 26, though there contrasting Constantine's improvement on ancestral law rather than, as here, its restoration).

1.7. Tantalus. In mythology he was notorious for greed, and appropriately punished in Hades.

1.8–2.2. Constantine as proclaimer of God is a theme derived in part from the Emperor himself (II. 28. 2), and also used in the preface (cf. I. 5. 2, 8. 3), and esp. at IV. 14–39. For God's choice and promotion of Constantine (1. 8), cf. I. 4–6, here enhanced by emphasis on the novelty of a Christian Emperor.

2.2. marking his face with the Saviour's sign. For Christians making the sign of the cross cf. e.g. *V. Ant.* 13. 5, 78. 5; F. Dölger, *Sphragis* (Paderborn, 1911), 171 ff.

3.1–3. A painting in encaustic (i.e. using hot wax, 3. 2, 3. 3) over the entrance to the palace. It showed the Saviour's, or 'saving', sign (3. 1) above the heads of Constantine and his sons (3. 2), and below, a serpent (Isa. 27: 1, cf. Ps. 90: 13) being pierced by a weapon (3. 2) and cast down into the depths of the sea. This was presumably in Constantinople, and therefore probably on the Chalke, or Bronze Door, if this was in fact built by Constantine; cf. C. Mango, *The Brazen House: A Study of the Vestibule of the Imperial Palace of Constantinople* (Copenhagen, 1959), 22–4, discussing this passage, which is also included in his *The Art of the Byzantine Empire 312–1453* (Englewood Cliffs, NJ, 1972, repr. 1986), 15–16. Typically, neither the iconography nor the scriptural parallel are entirely straightforward. The picture could be taken to represent a cross, with separate busts of Constantine and his sons, and below, a writhing serpent; but since on the coins of 327–37 there are depictions of the *labarum* piercing a serpent (e.g. the follis of 327, *RIC* vii, Constantinople, no. 19, on which see Bruun, 'Christian Signs', 21–2, and cf. Fig. 2, p. 209) it is more likely that this is also what is meant here, in which case this description too is projected back from the period after the Council of Nicaea, itself yet to be described.

3. 1. 'dragon' and 'crooked serpent'. Eusebius thinks of Isa. 27: 1. The serpent represents both the devil (cf. 3. 2, 'the invisible enemy of the human race') and Constantine's own vanquished enemy, Licinius (cf. II. 2, 46. 2, 'that dragon'). For Eusebius, the image confirms the truth of prophecy (3. 3); in order to emphasize the point he makes it twice, first citing individual terms from the verse in Isaiah (3. 1), then quoting it in full (3. 3). The picture is thus a 'true representation in pictorial art' (3. 3.); cf. on I. 10. 1 for the *VC* itself as a 'verbal portrait', and cf. note on III. 15. 2 below. Leeb, 51, points to the earliest appearance of Christ in such a pose, on a sarcophagus of 310.

3. 2. his own feet and those of his sons. Mango, *Brazen House*, 23, says 'two', but the number of Constantine's sons is not explicitly stated; for the number represented on the *labarum*, see on I. 31. 2. At the dramatic date of the narrative, i.e. immediately before the Council of Nicaea, Constantine had four sons, Crispus' death falling in 326; if, as seems likely, the *labarum* in its final form was not in fact manufactured until later (see I. 30, with 32.1), the number intended here will have been three. The mention of feet suggests a typical *calcatio* scene (so A. Grabar, *L'Empereur dans l'art byzantin* (Paris, 1936), 44), in which case the serpent is a new introduction, but is perhaps rather an example of loose writing by Eusebius.

4–24. *The Council of Nicaea*

Eusebius' is the only continuous contemporary account of the Council, of which no *Acta* survive, though some twenty canons do, dealing with matters of church discipline, provincial authority, and settlement after the ending of persecution (Stevenson, *NE* 338–47). Allusions to the Council can be found in the writings of Athanasius, who attended it as a deacon (*De decretis Nicaenae synodi*, 19–20; *Ep. ad episcopos Africae*, 5–6), but they are partial and incomplete; descriptions are also found in the later church historians, but their starting-point is the account in the *VC*. Since Eusebius' account is extremely selective, and since the other evidence is sometimes contradictory, it follows that we are badly informed about this crucial event in the history of the Church. It cannot have been easy for Eusebius to write about the Council in the context of the *VC*, since his own role in the Council lacked integrity (see below); this was especially the case if he was writing so much later, when the Council's decision to exile Arius had been overturned, and its defenders, Athanasius and Marcellus, themselves exiled (see on **IV. 41–2**). With the return of these exiles after Constantine's death, and while Eusebius was still working on the *VC*, he was drawn into renewed opposition to their position (see Cameron, 'Construction'; Barnes, *CE* 263–5). Against this, the Council of Nicaea had probably been the first occasion on which Eusebius had met the Emperor, and he had clearly been immensely impressed, whether by the man himself (see on **10** below) or by the occasion and the opportunities it afforded; this shows clearly in his account, which he treats as a set-piece, while adopting the familiar method of passing over its awkward features as far as possible in silence. The preparations for the meeting, the appearance of the Emperor, and his condescension to the bishops, are given as much or more attention as the actual proceedings, which are described only briefly and in very general terms; at the same time, the preliminaries discreditable to Eusebius are simply omitted. More broadly, in accordance with the general techniques of the *VC*, the account is presented less as a comprehensive record of the event than in terms of imperial eulogy; this explains both its brevity and the particular themes which Eusebius has chosen to emphasize. III. 4 is seen by Barnes as an insertion by the editor of the *VC* ('Panegyric', 100).

The immediately preceding Council of Antioch, at which Eusebius himself had been condemned for Arian sympathies, is entirely omitted; see below, 6–9, and see Hanson, *Search*, 146–7; Stevenson, *NE* 334–7.

4–9. *The calling of the Council*

Chs. 4–5 establish the three major topics of disagreement: the disputes centred on Arius, Melitius, and the date of Easter. Some arguments have been set out already in Constantine's letter to Alexander and Arius (II. 63–72), but this attempt at reconciliation by the Emperor was a failure (5. 3). This fact, and

Constantine's observation that the churches are divided over Easter, is now said to have led him directly to summon the meeting at Nicaea (5. 3). Eusebius thus omits all the complicated antecedents to the Council (see below, on **6–9**), and ascribes the initiative and the credit to the Emperor alone.

4. Envy dreadfully agitating the churches. For the role of Envy and the disputes see **II. 61. 2–62** and **III. 1**. Again Eusebius does not make clear the issues in dispute, any more than he names those who were condemned at Nicaea. His account of the proceedings (13–14 below) is brief and evasive, concentrating on the Emperor's ability to produce harmony within the Church and quickly passing to the more congenial theme of the Vicennalia celebrations. Recent scholarship on Arius and on the general questions involved emphasizes the range of positions taken, and the probable lack of a clearly defined 'Arian' position at this date. The Council of Nicaea produced the formula which attempted to define the relation of the Son to the Father, and which was to form the basis of the Nicene Creed, and exiled Arius himself and a few others. However, its effect was rather to crystallize something that could be labelled 'Arianism' than to condemn an existing sect. Little remains of Arius's own writings (see Hanson, *Search*, 5–15), and much of what passes for the history of Arianism derives from the caricatured statements of its later opponents: see the works referred to on **II. 61–72**, with R. Williams, 'Does it Make Sense to speak of Pre-Nicene Orthodoxy?', in Williams, ed., *The Making of Orthodoxy: Essays in Honour of Henry Chadwick* (Cambridge, 1989), 1–23. The fact that Eusebius himself was deeply implicated in the matter and inclined towards the side of Arius is a major element in shaping his account. For a brief discussion of the issues and of the antecedents of the Council, see Hall, *Doctrine and Practice*, 121–8.

daring to insult the images of the Emperor. Damaging or knocking over imperial images was a standard manifestation of popular unrest, a famous example being that of the so-called 'Riot of the Statues' at Antioch in 387. But according to Eusebius, this did not anger Constantine so much as distress him (see above on **1. 1**, with I. 45. 3; according to the conventions of imperial encomium, emperors were expected to maintain a dignified calm, and not to manifest unseemly anger). Eusebius does not locate these disorders, and has already said that the effects of the disputes were widespread (II. 61. 4–62). Alexandria was often prone to public disorder, but what Eusebius says here goes beyond anything else in the early evidence. Bishop Alexander criticizes the Arians for greed, false accusations against other clergy in court, and the disgrace of young women preaching their doctrines (see Theodoret, *HE* 1. 4. 36, Stevenson, *NE* 328–9).

5. 1. the disagreement over the Feast of the Saviour. i.e. the long-standing dispute over the date of Easter. It suited Eusebius to pass as smoothly as possible over the theological issues discussed at Nicaea, laying emphasis on the matter of settling an agreed date for Easter. But it was just as necessary for the latter issue to be settled, if the Church was to be united under Constantine's protection (cf. 19. 1), and the problems were hardly less complex. Eusebius represents them here in cursory form: it was a matter of whether to follow Jewish practice or 'the exact time of the season' (5. 1; cf. also Constantine's letter, 19. 1). He does not discuss the problems surrounding the fixing of the equinox, or the less significant divergence of practice between Rome and Alexandria. For his own position (cf. *HE* 5. 24), see on **18. 1** below.

The Feast of Passover (Hebrew *Pesach*, Aramaic and Greek *Pascha*) was fixed by the lunar month Nisan, originally the first month of the year (Exod. 12: 2; the fundamental Passover law is Exod. 12: 1–36). It was observed by an evening meal on the fourteenth day, i.e. the night when the moon was full, with a roasted lamb from the Temple at Jerusalem (until the latter's destruction in AD 70), and a festival week in which no leavened bread was consumed. The New Year (which later and modern Jewish calendars fix in autumn) was then fixed by the spring equinox (now 21 March). Problems had already arisen before Christian times about which moon was the first of the year, in view of the problem of reconciling lunar and solar years, for which intercalation of an extra month was regularly required; this was done by adding a second month Adar to the normal one which preceded Nisan. At Alexandria this need was computed in advance by using astronomical tables; according to Eusebius, following the Christian Anatolius (*HE* 7. 32. 16–19), the Jewish philosopher Aristoboulus and his predecessors argued the matter astronomically. Others at Qumran, and apparently also the so-called Therapeutae in Egypt, devised a strictly solar calendar with fixed months of thirty days each (see Annie Jaubert, *La Date de la Cêne: Calendrier biblique et liturgie chrétienne* (Paris, 1957), Eng. tr. *The Date of the Last Supper* (New York, 1965); J. van Goudoever, *Jewish and Christian Calendars* (Leiden, 1961)). At some time (perhaps at the Synod of Jabneh, AD 90), the rabbis adopted a more rustic observational method of deciding whether spring had come (according to the signs of growth in plants and shrubs), or whether an extra Adar must be intercalated before the Passover month of Nisan.

Christians inherited the problem. Those of them who kept Pascha did so to commemorate the death and rising of Christ, who according to the Gospels had been executed at the Passover, either on 15 Nisan (Matthew, Mark, Luke), or 14 Nisan (John). Christians regarded the Old Testament narratives of the sacrifice of the Passover lamb and the escape of Israel from Egypt as types or models of salvation through Christ's death and resurrection. They observed it by a fast (originally one or two days, but later extended to six or forty days), which concluded with a feast. About AD 190 there was a dispute between the Roman bishop Victor and the churches round Ephesus (Eus., *HE* 5. 23–4). The Asiatic churches broke their fast on 14 Nisan (hence they were termed Quartodecimans, 'Fourteenthers'), the Romans and others always on a Sunday, the custom which prevailed, perhaps because of a desire to be distinguished from the Jews. According to earlier scholars (and recently B. Lohse, *Das Passafest der Quartodecimaner* (Gütersloh, 1953)), this was the issue debated and decided at Nicaea (see III. 14, 18–20 below). More probably by Constantine's time all ended the fast on the Sunday following 15 Nisan; the divergence lay in how 14/15 Nisan was fixed (so first L. Duchesne, 'La Question de la Pâque au Concile de Nicée', *RQH* 28 (1880); for recent discussion see V. Grumel, 'Le Problème de la date pascale au IIIe et IVe siècles', *REB* 18 (1960), 163–78; Giuseppe Visonà, 'Ostern/Osterfest/Osterpredigt I', *TRE* 25 (1995), 517–30.

5. 1. follow the practice of the Jews. Christians who followed Jewish practice (predominantly in Syria and Mesopotamia) relied on the local Jewish community to determine Passover, and began and ended their paschal fast accordingly, beginning their 'holy week' before Passover and ending it the Sunday following. In many years the same full moon and Easter date would be observed as in other churches; but when a difference did occur, it would be a whole moon (four weeks) earlier or later.

the exact time of the season. The remainder (listed by Constantine, 19. 1 below) observed the equinox and the full moon that followed it with astronomical precision. Eusebius elsewhere reports the paschal computations of Hippolytus (fl. Rome, *c.*200–20; see *HE* 6. 22) and Dionysius of Alexandria (247–8 to 264–5; *HE* 7. 20), both of whom used an eight-year cycle, though he reports the former as sixteen years (see *HE*, tr. Lawlor and Oulton, ii, 209–10); more accurately, Anatolius, an Alexandrian who became bishop of Laodicea in Syria *c.*269, worked out a nineteen-year cycle (*HE* 7. 32. 13–19). At the eastern Council of Serdica of 343 (in fact meeting at Philippopolis), a table was produced to demonstrate that the Jews had also adopted a nineteen-year cycle, but one determined by the moon which began in the Roman month March, not by the equinox, so that Passover often fell between 14 March and the equinox of 21 March (E. Schwartz, 'Christliche und jüdische Ostertafeln', *AGWG. PH* 8/6 (1905), 121–5; Grumel, 'Le Problème de la date pascale', 173–5). There were further residual problems (not mentioned by Eusebius) about the precise fixing of the equinox (which Anatolius got wrong, unless the text is corrupt, and which Rome dated to 25 March), and divergence between Roman and Alexandrian practice, for Roman dating, even though coinciding for much of the time with that of Alexandria, was determined rather by the need to finish Lent before the *dies natalis urbis Romae* (21 April), and by the entry of the sun into the first zodiacal sign, Aries, on 20 March. Constantine's letter similarly assumes that there were only two systems, the Jewish and the Christian (19. 1).

5. 2. divine ordinances. The rules had been laid down in Exod. 12 (cf. Constantine's words at 18. 5 below). But whichever way was correct, one or the other party was in flagrant breach, some still fasting while others relaxed in the fifty days of Eastertide (cf. 18. 6 below).

5. 3. the letter . . . to those in Alexandria. See II. 63–73.

6–9. A eulogistic description of the excitement of the bishops as they gather. With a smooth transition, Eusebius describes the summoning of the Council of Nicaea by Constantine; he omits the immediate antecedents (except in the general statements at 4 above; see Barnes, *CE* 212–14), including his own role in them, and in particular his own condemnation at a synod at Antioch held late in 324 or early in 325, and presided over by Ossius (on which see H. Chadwick, 'Ossius of Cordova and the Presidency of the Council of Antioch, 325', *JThS* NS 9 (1958), 292–304). This synod in a synodical letter preserved in Syriac, which is our only evidence for it (Opitz, *Urkunden*, 18, 19; Stevenson, *NE* 334–7), adopted an anti-Arian creed and excommunicated Bishops Eusebius of Caesarea, Theodotus of Laodicea, and Narcissus of Neronias, who persisted in their disagreement pending a further council to be held at Ancyra. Lane Fox, *Pagans and Christians*, 643–4, suggests that Constantine himself delivered his *Oration to the Saints* on Good Friday of 325 at the end of the Council, but for other views on its date see e.g. T. D. Barnes, 'The Emperor Constantine's Good Friday Sermon', *JThS* NS 27 (1976), 414–23; H. A. Drake, 'Suggestions of Date in Constantine's *Oration to the Saints*', *AJP* 106 (1985), 335–49. Eusebius also omits Constantine's subsequent change of venue from Ancyra to Nicaea (see Constantine's letter of invitation to the bishops: Opitz, *Urkunden*, 20, Stevenson, *NE* 338; for the views of Marcellus, bishop of Ancyra, later to be exiled for his defence of Nicaea and attacked by Eusebius of Caesarea in his *Contra Marcellum*, see Hall, *Doctrine and Practice*, 127–8; political reasons in the aftermath of the murder of Licinius are adduced by Barnes, *CE* 214). Eusebius presents the calling of the Council as smoothly as he can, so as to reduce the impression of serious division and not to obscure the image of the victorious Constantine.

6. 1. a world-wide Council. The term 'world-wide', 'ecumenical' is applied for the first time to this Council, distinguishing it from the many other synods held before and after it; see H. Chadwick, 'The Origin of the Title "Oecumenical Council"', *JThS* NS 23 (1972), 132–5. Thus Nicaea came to be regarded as the first of the ecumenical councils recognized by both east and west. For recent discussion of the Council, with bibliography, see

C. Brennecke, 'Nicäa I', *TRE* 24 (1994), 429–41; Colm Luibéid, *The Council of Nicaea* (Galway, 1982)

right to use the public post. Constantine had already offered these facilities to bishops attending the Council of Arles in 314; see Opt., *App.* 3; Eus., *HE* 10. 5. 21–4 = Opitz, *Urkunden*, 14–15.

A city was also designated which was appropriate for the Council. See above for Constantine's intervention. His letter recommended Nicaea for its greater proximity for western bishops, its favourable climate, and his own intention to attend. The name Nicaea (*Nikaia*) appropriately signifies 'victorious'.

6. 2. No doubt Eusebius' enthusiasm, expressed in his (literally) flowery language, was perfectly genuine; see on **10** and **15** below. 'Priests' (*hiereis*) here as usual at this time means 'bishops'.

7. 1. From all the churches. Attendance was in fact somewhat uneven, in that there were far more bishops attending from the east and the Balkans than from the west (see Hanson, *Search*, 156–7). They included confessors who had suffered in the persecution, and the bishop of Alexandria, at least, was accompanied by his deacon, Athanasius, later to be famous as one of the greatest defenders of Nicene orthodoxy; see Barnes, *CE* 214–15. Eusebius' description is reproduced by Socrates, *HE* 1. 8, to which Socrates then adds further details, including that of the attendance of the confessors, and of laymen skilled in debating; other names are given by Sozomen, *HE* 1. 17. The style of Eusebius' account recalls the panegyrical topos of universal submission, for which see IV. 7, 14; this is made explicit at 7. 2 below.

the very famous one i.e. Ossius of Cordoba (see on **II. 63**).

7. 2. the one in charge of the imperial city. i.e. Sylvester, the bishop of Rome (given as Julius by Sozomen, *HE* 1. 17).

8. The Council is also a fulfilment of the statements in Acts 2: 1–13, a rare explicit New Testament citation in the *VC*.

In the present band the number of bishops exceeded 250. About 300: Athan., *Hist. Arian.* 66; Socrates, *HE* 1. 8 says 'over three hundred', Sozomen, *HE* 1. 17, 320. Theodoret, *HE* 1. 8. 1 reports 270 (from Eustathius of Antioch). The number 318 (that of the servants of Abraham in Gen. 14: 14) was soon generally accepted; however the number of surviving subscriptions to the Creed is smaller than Eusebius' 250: see H. Gelzer, H. Hilgenfeld, O. Cuntz, *Patrum Nicaenorum Nomina* (Leipzig, 1898). For recent discussion see Brennecke, 'Nicäa I', 431.

many other attendants. These included laymen, according to Socrates (see above), and even pagans (Gelasius of Caesarea, fr. 13, but see F. Winkelmann, 'Charakter und Bedeutung der *Kirchengeschichte* des Gelasios von Kaisareia', *Polychronia: Festschrift F. Dölger*, i, *Byz. Forsch.* 1 (1966), 346–85, at 347). Eusebius emphasizes rather the clerical nature of the gathering.

9. word of wisdom   This biblical phrase (1 Cor. 12: 8) here means 'theological knowledge'.

meals should be generously provided.   Not only did Constantine call the Council, provide transport, and participate himself (see below), but he even provided a meal service; this made the Council very different from ordinary ecclesiastical synods.

10–14. *The proceedings of the Council.*
Apart from the brief description in 13, Eusebius gives no account of the debate (which occupied much of June and July 325), concentrating instead on the Emperor's personal appearance (10. 1–5) and his address (12. 1–5); on his account see also Hanson, *Search*, 157–63. In contrast, Eusebius explained and defended himself in some detail to his own church at Caesarea (Stevenson, *NE* 344–7).

10. 1.   The Council meets in the main hall of the imperial palace at Nicaea. Special seating has been provided for those attending, and a small gold chair for the Emperor (10. 5). Eusebius emphasizes the lack of military escort, evidently the normal accompaniment of the Emperor (10. 2, cf. 15. 2 below), and lays most stress on Constantine's physical appearance and dress, 'like some heavenly angel of God' (10. 3–5); while the language used of Constantine's demeanour at 10. 4 recalls the terminology of imperial panegyric, for which see R. R. R. Smith, 'Public Image of Licinius I', *JRS* 87 (1997), 194–202. Eusebius underlines his effect by emphasizing that on this occasion Constantine's demeanour was one of extreme modesty (cf. 10.

4, his eyes are cast down, unlike the usual *fulgor oculorum* which is a hallmark of the imperial gaze; see Smith, 'Public Image', 198–200, used of Constantine himself at *Pan. Lat.* 7 (6). 9. 5, AD 307; 7 (6). 17. 1, AD 310; 9 (12). 19. 6, AD 313), and stresses his spiritual as well as his physical beauty. Similarly, Antony's physical condition when he died, like that of Moses at the end of his life, is taken as proof of his holiness (*V. Ant.* 93. 1–2, cf. Deut. 34: 7).

Apart from the utility of this emphasis for his presentation of the Council, it is also likely that this was the first occasion on which Eusebius had met the Emperor personally, and that he was genuinely impressed by the experience; this would also have been a very suitable occasion for the presentation to the Emperor of the final version of the *HE*, hastily revised after Constantine's recent defeat of Licinius (Hall, *Doctrine and Practice*, 128–9). Eusebius omits important facts. One of the matters considered by the Council was his own theological position. He had, probably in self-defence, tendered a creed of his own, but finally accepted the formula of Nicaea and subsequently needed to explain his dramatic change of heart to his congregation at Caesarea in a letter in which he laid particular stress on the intervention of the Emperor. This explanation of the Council's proceedings and his own role in it by Eusebius is of prime importance for understanding what actually went on, and what the *VC* deliberately does not tell us (Opitz, *Urkunden* 22; Stevenson, *NE* 344–7; Socr., *HE* 1. 8; Barnes, *CE* 215–17; Hall, *Doctrine and Practice*, 128–33; Hanson, *Search*, 159).

11. The bishop who was first in the row on the right. The chapter-heading calls him Eusebius, i.e. Eusebius of Nicomedia, despite Sozomen's identification with Eusebius of Caesarea (*HE* 1. 19); for the view that it was Ossius who presided see T. D. Barnes, 'Emperor and Bishops, A. D. 324–44: Some Problems', *American Journal of Ancient History*, 3 (1978), 53–75, at 56–7.

a rhythmical speech.   i.e. a rhetorical encomion.

a speech somewhat like this.   Constantine spoke in Latin, his speech being translated by an interpreter (13. 1), though he intervened in the actual debate in Greek (13. 2). For Constantine's Greek cf. IV. 8, 32, 35 (with C. Ando, 'Pagan Apologetics and Christian Intolerance', *Journal of Early Christian Studies*, 4/2 (1996), 180; Lane Fox, *Pagans and Christians*, 629–30). Eusebius does not claim to be translating himself, or to be reproducing Constantine's exact phraseology, as with some of the documents cited. The speech itself echoes the sentiments already attributed to Constantine when he heard of the division within the Church; the tone is highly conciliatory, in tune with Eusebius' emphasis on the Emperor's calm and eirenic role (cf. 'in a soft and gentle voice'). Gelasius of Cyzicus, *HE* 2. 7. 1–41, reports the text of another speech reputedly given by Constantine when opening the Council, but this is probably not genuine (see C. T. H. R. Ehrhardt, 'Constantinian Documents in Gelasius of Cyzicus, Ecclesiastical History', *JbAC* 23 (1980), 48–57).

13. 1–2. This short section contains all that is said about the proceedings of the Council; again the emphasis is on the Emperor, in particular his role as conciliator. Nothing whatever is said as to the content of the dispute, the formula arrived at or the addition of the term *homoousios*, elsewhere attributed by Eusebius to Constantine himself (see above). Sozomen later justified such omission on prudential grounds, as being unsuitable for the uninitiated (*HE* I. 20; contrast Socr., *HE* I. 8).

14. the Faith prevailed . . . and the same timing for the Festival of the Saviour was agreed. i.e. the two points at issue, the doctrinal matter and the date of Easter. Neither is spelled out here; Constantine's letter (17–20) explains the Easter issue, though not that of the Creed, which again receives very summary mention (17. 2). There is no reference here as in II. 62 and III. 4 to the Melitian schism, which was certainly one of the main issues resolved: see the letter in Socrates, *HE* I. 9. 1–14 (Stevenson, *NE* 347–9).

general decisions . . . ratified in writing. The bishops present were required to subscribe to the Creed, on which see Hanson, *Search*, 163–72. Eusebius himself did so, as did the vast majority, though only after detailed exposition and discussion of how it was to be interpreted. However, Arius and two of his supporters did not, and were exiled (see below, with Barnes, *CE* 216–17; for the signing procedure, Athan., *Hist. Ar.* 42. 3; Philostorg., *HE* I. 9a; Hanson, *Search*, 162). This is deliberately obscured by Eusebius' use of the term 'unanimous'. No records survive of the proceedings of the Council, and apparently none were kept. Eusebius makes no mention of the canons of Nicaea which concerned general issues of church discipline and matters such as the status of Rome, Antioch, Alexandria, and Jerusalem (Stevenson, *NE* 338–47). The aftermath of the Council was by no means as tidy as Eusebius suggests: he makes no mention of the deposition of Theognis of Nicaea and the same Eusebius of Nicomedia who had pronounced the Emperor's eulogy (11 above; cf. Stevenson, *NE* 351–3; Socr., *HE*. I. 8 (Constantine's disappointment with Eusebius of Nicomedia); Soz., *HE* I. 21; Gelasius, *HE* 3. app. 1, and see below). It was the same Eusebius of Nicomedia who was later to baptize the Emperor (see on **IV. 61. 2–3**).

held a victory-feast to God. It is not clear whether this is the same as the the banquet described in the next chapter.

15. *Vicennalia celebrations*

Eusebius gives a remarkable description of how Constantine entertained the bishops after the Council, celebrating his Vicennalia, which began on 25 July 325. He conveys the tremendous impression which this event evidently made on him and on the others invited. Bishops were not merely admitted to the imperial palace, but dined there as the guests of the Emperor; Eusebius is moved to make a bold visual comparison with Christ's kingdom in heaven, and to refer to what was happening as being unreal, using a Homeric phrase, 'dream, not fact' (*Od.* 19. 547).

16–20. *Constantine's report to the churches*

The Council's decisions were made known by synodal letters and by letters from the Emperor, of which Eusebius records only one; the other imperial letters were sent to the church of Alexandria, and dealt with the credal formulation (Socr., *HE* 1. 9. 17–25 = Stevenson, *NE* 350–1, Opitz, *Urkunden*, 25), and to that of Nicomedia, on the exile of Eusebius of Nicomedia and Theognis of Nicaea (Optiz, *Urkunden*, 20, 27), while this one (17. 1–20. 2 below, cf. Socr., *HE* 1. 9. 32–46, Theod., *HE* 1. 9) concentrates on the Easter question (see A. di Berardino,

'L'imperatore Costantino e la celebrazione della Pasqua', in G. Bonamente and F. Fusco, eds., *Costantino il Grande dall'antichità all'umanesimo*, (Macerata, 1992), 363–84, at 377). The Council reported to the church of Alexandria and to Christians in Egypt and Libya the condemnation of Arius, as of Theonas and Secundus, both of Libya, the judgement against the Melitians (effectively omitted by Eusebius, who is also silent on the Novatians) and the decision to keep Easter according to the practice of Rome and Alexandria, not with the Jews (Socr., *HE* I. 9. 1–14, Stevenson, *NE* 347–50).

Unlike his introduction to Constantine's speech made at the Council (11 above), Eusebius here claims to include the actual document, 'as if on an inscription'.

17. 1–20. 2. Constantine's letter about the date of Easter, cf. Opitz, *Urkunden* 26. The opening paragraph (17. 1–2) consists of an explanation and justification for the Council taking as its starting-point Constantine's own religious duty rather than the Church's existing divisions; for similar justification cf. the letters addressed to the church of Africa in connection with the Donatist dispute, cf. Opt., *App.* 5, and on the present letter Dörries, *Selbstzeugnis*, 66–8. It has been argued that it was an addition (Pasquali, 'Die Composition', 377–8), but it fits logically here, although Eusebius has made a letter to the easterns about the paschal controversy serve as a general letter (cf. 'to the churches', see on **18. 6** below) covering the decisions of the Council as a whole.

In 18. 1–20. 1 Constantine describes the differing practice in relation to the date of Easter, expresses his own views, and orders all churches to follow the decision of the Council (20. 1). Constantine took a personal interest in the issue, addressing a letter to Eusebius on the subject and responding to the latter's (lost) treatise with another, which Eusebius reproduces below (IV. 34–5). More prominence is given here to the need to distinguish the Christian festival from the Jewish Passover (18. 2–4, 19. 1, cf. **5. 1–2**: some eastern churches still fix Easter 'with the Jews') than to division between Christian churches themselves (18. 5–6, 19. 1), although for the west at least that had already been the subject of the first canon of the Council of Arles, 314 (CCSL 148. 9; Stevenson, *NE* 293). Constantine uses strong language about the Jews (18. 2–4, 19. 1): for discussion see G. Stemberger, *Juden und Christen im heiligen Land* (Munich, 1987), 45–6; Berardino, 'L'imperatore Costantino', 379–80. The letter thus brings to bear a variety of arguments for its acceptance: unanimous agreement at Nicaea, theological argument directed against the Jews, the Emperor's own personal authority and that of God, through the decision of the Council (Berardino, 'L'imperatore Costantino', 382). Constantine seems to believe that the correct system went back to Jesus himself (18. 3, 5).

17. 2.   Constantine states his view of the character of an episcopal council: it constitutes the spiritual arm of the state and a court which takes the needful 'decision' on disputed issues. It is also divinely authorized (see 20. 1). The references to 'points' and 'topics' and to the 'difference of opinion or dispute about the faith' allude to the doctrinal issues discussed, but are not elaborated further. Constantine's attendance was strictly uncanonical; he therefore emphasizes that he attends as a fellow Christian ('your fellow-servant'), as in II. 72. 1; III. 24. 1.

18. 1.   On the Easter or paschal controversy see 5. 1–2. Canon 1 of the Council of Arles (314) decreed that Easter should be kept on a single day notified by the bishop of Rome. Eusebius' account of the controversy in an earlier period at *HE* 5. 24, is written from the point of view of the Asian churches, which were in dispute over this matter with Rome; for his apparent change of heart see William L. Petersen, 'Eusebius and the Paschal Controversy', in Harold W. Attridge and G. Hata, eds., *Eusebius, Christianity and Judaism* (Studia Post-Biblica, 42; Leiden, 1992), 311–25.

festival, from which we have acquired our hope of immortality.   Probably a reference to the salvation brought by the passion of Christ, but the reference could be to baptism, which almost invariably took place at Easter.

one system and declared principle.   Since Jewish dates were probably not uniform, much local variation occurred.

18. 3. received from the Saviour.   Divine authority is claimed for the Roman/Alexandrian system.

18. 4. observe the Pascha a second time in the same year.   The meaning is uncertain. The usual explanation is that if the feast is kept after the equinox in one year and before the equinox in the next, that makes two feasts in one solar year. But Constantine's words may refer to diversity of dates leading some people to keep the feast twice, a month apart, in the same spring. John Chrysostom in 386–7 at Antioch attacked the Protopaschites, 'those who fast the first Pascha'. There he speaks for the decision taken by the Council of Nicaea, which had changed the ancient practice of Antioch. It is quite possible that all his vilification of the Jews in the set of homilies against the Jews (*PG* 49, 843–942), of which the attack on the Protopaschites is one, are determined by a crisis among Christians about the keeping of Easter, and some of them may have celebrated twice. Notice the symbolic importance of a single, unitary feast, stressed in the following sections, 18. 5–6.

The Jews were generally held responsible by Christians for the crucifixion of Jesus, rather than the Romans (see already 1 Thess. 2: 14–15; Matt. 27: 22–6; John 11: 47–50). Their act is called parricide, literally 'father-killing', perhaps in a generalized sense as with the Latin *parricidium.*

18. 5. The Church's unity requires a simultaneous celebration: the festival is in Christ's purpose one, just as the Church is one. The 'day of our liberation' is also the day . . . of his holy passion, i.e. the feast of Easter at the end of the Paschal fast, the separate commemoration of Good Friday being a later development. The Church is 'cherished by one Spirit, that is, by the divine will', apparently a reference to the Holy Spirit in the Church, identified with God's will. The need to find a single formula for Easter observance is linked to fundamental theology. See note on **20. 1**; Dörries, *Selbstzeugnis*, 374.

18. 6. your Holiness. . . . 19. 1 your Good Sense . . . your Intelligence. The honorific titles imply that the bishops are addressed; the form is in each case plural. The heading of the letter as given at 17. 1 is 'to the churches', and it concludes with a farewell to the Emperor's 'dear brothers' (20. 2); it is concerned with the churches of Cilicia, Syria, and Mesopotamia whose practice followed that of the Jews (Athan., *Letter to the African Bishops* 2, *PG* 26, 1032; *De synod.* 5; see Berardino, 'L'imperatore Costantino', 370; the synodal letter to Egypt mentions simply 'eastern brothers': Socr., *HE* 1. 9; Stevenson, *NE* 349; Theod.,

HE 1. 9), but Eusebius says it was sent to 'each of the provinces' (20. 3). The body of the letter is addressed in the plural to bishops, or more probably metropolitan bishops, who are enjoined to make the contents known to 'our beloved brothers' (20. 2) and to ensure that the Council's decision is carried out. Probably disingenuously, Constantine represents the decision as unanimous, and glosses over (if he was aware of it) any disagreement as to the date of the festival elsewhere, for instance between Rome and Alexandria (19. 1–2). However, the exact date was not prescribed; the matter was a difficult one and uniformity of practice was not attained so easily (Berardino, 'L'imperatore Costantino'; Barnes, *CE* 217).

19. 1.   The repetitive and incoherent structure of this paragraph betrays Constantine's concern. Constantine has 'personally given his word' to persuade the reluctant and absent churches.

with one harmonious will.   No distinction is drawn between Roman and Alexandrian practice, and the equinox is not mentioned; perhaps Constantine had seen a table of agreed dates, which expected no discrepancy before 343 (Schwartz, *Christliche und jüdische Ostertafeln*, 24–5). Rome comes first, and Alexandria is not mentioned apart from Egypt and Libya. The appearance of Cilicia is surprising, since it retained the Jewish dating along with Syria and Mesopotamia (Huber, *Passa und Ostern*, 69–70).

Jewish perjury.   Killing Jesus, whom they should have recognized as their Lord, is considered an act of treason.

20. 1.   Constantine asserts the widely held Christian belief that bishops in council speak with inspired divine authority; see Socrates, *HE* 1. 19. 24, Stevenson, *NE* 350 (Constantine writes to the Alexandrians about the Council) and cf. also Optatus, *App.* 5.

20. 2. when I come, as I have long desired.   This passage shows that the letter was addressed principally to Antioch and the churches associated with it, and that Constantine had not yet made the visit indicated in **II. 72.** 2–3. Similarly he had said that he would go to Africa and enforce the judgements against the Donatists (Opt., *App.* 7); he never made either journey, though after the defeat of Licinius at Chrysopolis he had gone as far east as Antioch, and possibly as far as Palestine (so E. D. Hunt, *Holy Land Pilgrimage in the Later Roman Empire A. D. 312–460* (Oxford, 1982), 6, and cf. above **II. 72. 2**).

The clergy are expected to communicate the Council's decision to the laity ('our beloved brothers').

devilish savagery. i.e. the regime of Licinius, who had probably been killed with his son just before the Council met (Barnes, *CE* 214).

20. 3. Eusebius says the same letter is sent to each province, though see on **17. 1**.

21–2. *The bishops dismissed*

Eusebius reports a final exhortatory address by Constantine to the bishops attending the Council. Despite his professed deference to their decisions (6. 1, and cf. Opt., *App.* 5), the Emperor does not hesitate now to lecture the bishops on their behaviour towards one another, or to reinforce his admonitions to the Council with letters to those who had not attended and gifts to their congregations, in celebration of his Vicennalia (22). However, the moral and spiritual exhortations may owe more to the pastoral ideals of the elderly Eusebius than to any actual words of the Emperor. Note the similarities with the letter to Alexander and Arius (**II. 64–72**). Eusebius has already quoted one of Constantine's letters from the Council at **III. 17–20**.

23–4. *Further conciliatory negotiations and letters*

All was not quite so smooth and unanimous as Eusebius or Constantine would have liked; some matters dragged on. The canons of Nicaea, ignored by Eusebius, may have been produced by a continuing committee (Hall, *Doctrine and Practice*, 134). By 327 or 328, Arius and Euzoius were restored, followed by Eusebius and Theognis, apparently by a second 'Council of Nicaea', if this is what Eusebius is referring to (see Barnes, 'Emperor and Bishops'); R. Lorenz, 'Das Problem der Nachsynode von Nicäa', *Zeitschr. f. Kirchengesch.* 90 (1979), 22–40, with Socr., *HE* 1. 14. 1–2, Soz., *HE* 2. 16. 1–2). The arguments for such a 'second session' are rebutted by Colm Luibhéid, 'The

Alleged Second Session of the Council of Nicaea', *JEH* 34 (1983), 165–74, who points out that in III. 23 Eusebius is describing the controversy over the Melitian settlement ('the Egyptians alone'), not negotiations over Arius or his supporters. There are further complications in Alexandria, like the rise to the bishopric of Athanasius (cf. Barnes, *CE* 229–30), as well as the Emperor's own change of policy towards favouring Eusebius of Nicomedia and other supporters of Arius, and the encouragement given by canon 7 of Nicaea to the see of Jerusalem in competition with the metropolitan status of Eusebius' own see of Caesarea (see further below). Not surprisingly, Eusebius glosses over the Emperor's awkward change of mind and presents the aftermath of Nicaea solely in terms of Constantine's extreme concern for the Church's unity and welfare.

24. 2. there may be an opportunity to assemble these in a special collection. An ambition that remained unfulfilled, but which demonstrates Eusebius' commitment to making available Constantine's letters as a general principle.

25–47. 3. *Buildings on Three Most Sacred Sites*

The rest of bk. III is occupied by a lengthy account of church-building in Palestine, and of measures taken against pagan temples and heretics and schismatics. Imperial *munificentia* traditionally showed itself in building, not least religious building, and Augustus in the *Res Gestae* makes much of his restoration of temples (*RG* 20–1).

Eusebius moves straight from the account of the Council of Nicaea and its aftermath to the excavation and discovery of the tomb of Jesus, without finishing his account of Constantine's Vicennalia, which ended on 25 July 326. This is understandable. In the spring of 326 Constantine travelled to Italy in order to hold the rest of the celebrations in Rome, but before he entered Rome itself on 15 July 326, his eldest son Crispus had been executed on the Emperor's orders at Pola, and his wife Fausta committed suicide soon after (for these mysterious events, see Barnes, *CE* 220–1). Whatever the true reason behind Crispus' death, Eusebius does not wish to mention it, and has already written Crispus out of the narrative of Constantine's defeat of Licinius, in which he had in fact played a significant part. The elevation of Constantine's mother Helena and her journey to Palestine, which soon followed (i.e. in 326–7, not 324–5 as suggested by S. Borgehammar, *How the Holy Cross was Found: From Event to Medieval Legend* (Stockholm, 1991), 137–40), were probably stimulated by these events, a connection which is broken in the narrative arrangement in *VC* III. There are thus several reasons, besides the limited and local range of Eusebius' information, why so much space should have been given to Constantine's church buildings in the *VC*; for this aspect and for the *VC* in the context of Latin imperial panegyric, see also S. MacCormack, 'Latin Prose Panegyrics: Tradition and Discontinuity in the Later Roman Empire', *REA* 22 (1976), 29–77. It is worth noting that the foundation and inauguration of Constantinople are not treated as such in the *VC*, though one might have expected an extensive account; instead, Eusebius gives the city only brief reference (III. 48–9, but in the general context of church-building). In this context, too, the lengthy account of church-building in Palestine is all the more striking. Constantine's building in the Holy Land is discussed by Hunt, *Holy Land Pilgrimage*, 6–27; see also id., 'Constantine and Jerusalem', *JEH* 48 (1997), 405–24; on the literary evidence see esp. E. Wistrand, *Konstantins Kirche am heiligen Grab in Jerusalem nach den ältesten literarischen Zeugnissen* (Göteborg, 1952).

25–8. *Excavation of the Holy Sepulchre*

Eusebius gives pride of place to the discovery of the burial cave of Christ, which he relates in the form of a set-piece and regards as a demonstration of God's favour to Constantine (25. 1, 26. 6); he had himself personally taken part in the dedication of the church of the Holy Sepulchre in 335, and one of the speeches he then delivered survives (see **IV. 46**). The extant *SC* (trans. Drake, *In Praise of Constantine*) is philosophical and theoretical in tone, but there too Eusebius refers to the sepulchre as a witness to Christ's resurrection (18. 3); the *SC* also functions as an apologia for Constantine's church-building policy.

VC III. 25–40 has been much discussed of late, with recent emphasis, supported also from the *SC*, on the view that Eusebius' theology, following in the tradition of Origen, distanced him from concentrating on the physical sites of the Gospel narrative, on the cross as a physical object and indeed from relics in general. See for this view Drake, 'True Cross', esp. 15 ff.; P. Walker, *Holy City, Holy Places?* (Oxford, 1990), 122–30; A. Lassus, 'L'Empereur Constantin, Eusèbe et les lieux saints', *Rev. de l'hist. des religions*, 171 (1967), 135–44; for criticism of Walker, see Leeb, 91–2. It is also argued that rivalry between his own see of Caesarea and the rise of that of Jerusalem was a motive for a certain reticence (so Z. Rubin, 'Church of the Holy Sepulchre and the Conflict between the Sees of Caesarea and Jerusalem', *Jerusalem Cathedra*, 2 (1982), 79–105), and further suggested by several scholars that the idea of excavating for the sites of the crucifixion (but see further below) and resurrection had been agreed in private between Constantine and Macarius of Jerusalem when the latter attended the Council of Nicaea: see recently Peter Walker, 'Jerusalem and the Holy Land in the Fourth Century', in A. O'Mahony, ed., with G. Gunner and K. Hintlian, *The Christian Heritage in the Holy Land* (London, 1995), 22–34, at 25 and Hunt, 'Constantine and Jerusalem', 410–12; see M. Biddle, *Tomb of Christ* (Stroud, 1999), 65 and further on 29 below.

However, the amount of space and emphasis given by Eusebius to the discovery and the building of the church remain striking, and Walker admits that his account 'brims with excitement'; there is nothing in the text itself to suggest hostility or suspicion on his part. The actual importance of his account in contributing to the sacralization of the Christian holy sites both in Jerusalem and outside is well brought out by R. Wilken, *Land Called Holy* (New Haven, 1992), 88–100 (cf. esp. 90 'In the midst of his Life of Constantine Eusebius has inserted a book of signs, but unlike the signs in the Gospel of John, which were miracles, those in Eusebius' book are *places*', and see p. 291 n. 27).

The discovery is told in terms of God's inspiration and favour to Constantine. Wilken, *Land Called Holy*, 88–90, draws attention to a number of features of Eusebius' account: sacral vocabulary ('holy' places); language of pollution and purification (26. 3, 6); emphasis on the site as a 'cave' (not in the New Testament; see below); the 'surprise' of the discovery (28: yet Constantine knew where to order the excavation, 25; see below); the cave described as itself a sign and testimony (*martyrion*, 28); see also R. L. Wilken, 'Eusebius and the Christian Holy Land', in Attridge and Hata, eds., *Eusebius, Christianity and Judaism*, 736–60. Before Constantine, little attention had been paid by Christians to Jerusalem and the holy places, which were covered over by the Roman city of Aelia Capitolina (AD 135), and a pagan temple built over or near the sepulchre: see e.g. Stemberger, *Juden und Christen im heiligen Land*, 51. Eusebius had written of the ruined Jewish Temple himself at *DE* 406c, cf. 273d. M. Biddle, 'Tomb of Christ: Sources, Methods and a New Approach', in K. Painter, ed., *'Churches Built in Ancient Times': Studies in Early Christian Archaeology* (London, 1994), 73–147, at 93–100, cautiously concludes that before 135 there was a local tradition which identified the spot and identified the tomb as a rock-cut cave, and see Biddle, *Tomb of Christ*, 53–64. Cf. Eus., *Onomast.* 74. 19– 21, where Golgotha is placed 'in Aelia to the north of Mt. Sion'; for Eusebius' insistence on the site of Jesus's tomb as a cave, see Walker, *Holy City, Holy Places*, 189, 268–9. Walker, 'Jerusalem and the Holy Land', 26, admits that 'Eusebius' fondness for caves is slightly puzzling'; Joan Taylor, *Christians and Holy Places: The Myth of Jewish-Christian Origins* (Oxford, 1993), 89–112, 136–7, argues against veneration of the holy places before Constantine, denies that mystic caves were venerated by Jewish Christians (though they were by pagans) and considers the tomb site unlikely to be authentic. See however J. E. Taylor, 'Golgotha: A Reconsideration of the Evidence for the Sites of Jesus' Crucifixion and Burial', *New Testament Studies*, 44 (1998), 180– 203 and Biddle, *Tomb of Christ*, 70, arguing against A. J. Wharton, 'The Baptistery of the Holy Sepulchre at Jerusalem and the Politics of Sacred Landscape', *DOP* 46 (1992), 313–25, at 322 (based on Taylor, *Christians and Holy Places*, 120).

Taylor, *Christians and Holy Places*, 141, argues that Constantine wanted to build a shrine to the sign, i.e. the cross, and only then found the supposed tomb site; that, however, is not what Eusebius plainly says. Eusebius' account establishes the sites themselves as proof of the events, both in the amount of space given to them and by his emotive and highly theological language, much of which is also the language of mysteries and initiation (see E. Yarnold, 'Who Planned the Churches at the Christian Holy Places in the Holy Land?', *Studia Patristica*, 18 (1985), 105–9, and see on **43**; for this language in *LC* (e.g. pref., 5–6), see Calderone, 'Eusebio', 7, and see Taylor, *Christians and Holy Places*, 147–8). Similar language and ideas can be found in *LC* 9. 15–17, cf. 16 'on the very site of the evidence for salvation', a passage in which he also expresses the idea of the three holy caves of the nativity, burial, and ascension of Christ; Eusebius' idea of places as proofs: Wilken, 'Eusebius and the Christian Holy Land', 746–7.

26. 1. the whole tribe of demons. i.e. the pagan gods, see on **I. 16.** Taylor's argument, *Christians and the Holy Places*, 339, is that Constantine was not so much aiming at honouring known holy places as replacing pagan cult centres with Christian ones.

the angel . . . had rolled away the stone. Eusebius recalls New Testament texts, Matt. 28: 2–3 and Luke 24: 5. Cyril of Jerusalem claimed that the stone and traces of the garden were still to be seen when he wrote in 348 or 350 (*Catech.* 10. 19, see Walker, *Holy City, Holy Places*, 270, with Biddle, 'Tomb of Christ', 101–2; *Tomb of Christ*, 65–6, here following Walker, and supposing that Cyril may have been present 'as a boy' when the cave was uncovered). Part of the original stone is traditionally believed to be preserved at the entrance to the tomb, enclosed in a central altar (Biddle, 'Tomb of Christ', 137), but Eusebius seems to be writing metaphorically here.

26. 2. this very cave of the Saviour. One of the three mystical caves referred to by Eusebius in *LC* (see above, and for the nativity and the ascension, below, 41–3); for his association of caves with holiness, an idea shared by Porphyry, see Wilken, *Land Called Holy*, 89; 'Eusebius and the Christian Holy Land', 743–4, with Yarnold, 'Who Planned the Churches?', 106. Caves are associated with initiation (Walker, *Holy City, Holy Places*, 191 and n., draws attention to Eusebius' vocabulary without seeing its apologetic significance). On the rock-site, see also Hunt, *Holy Land Pilgrimage*, 10–11, pointing out that the rock itself must have been cut away (so Cyril, *Catech.* 13. 35); Eus., *Theoph.* 3. 61 says that one could see the rock containing the tomb, with only one cavern within it. Biddle, 'Tomb of Christ', 102; *Tomb of Christ*, 69–70, is prepared to suppose that the present 'free-standing feature' represents the original rock of the tomb that was found, though this is not necessarily the tomb of the Gospels, cut away and embellished by Constantine with columns (below, 34). As with the building of St Peter's on the Vatican, the position of the rock here imposed severe limits on the builders and dictated the orientation of the complex, which looked west towards the tomb.

26. 3. a terrible and truly genuine tomb, one for souls . . . a gloomy sanctuary to the impure demon of Aphrodite. With heavy irony Eusebius refers to a temple built on the spot, a real tomb for those who believed in it (cf. his references to cult images as 'dead idols', 26. 3 and elsewhere); the builders of the temple acted in ignorance of God's plan; recent discussion and earlier bibliography on the site, with comments on Eusebius' interpretation, in Biddle, 'Tomb of Christ', 96–103; id., *Tomb of Christ*, 58–69; Shimon Gibson and Joan Taylor, *Beneath the Church of the Holy Sepulchre Jerusalem: The Archaeology and Early History of Traditional Golgotha* (Palestine Exploration Fund Monographs, series maior, 1; London, 1994), 68–9, 71; Walker, *Holy City, Holy Places*, 242–4, Rubin, 'Church of the Holy Sepulchre', n. 21; see also e.g. Drake, 'True Cross', 4.

J. Patrich, 'The Early Church of the Holy Sepulchre in the Light of Excavations and Restoration', in Y. Tsafrir, ed., *Ancient Churches Revealed* (Jerusalem, 1993), 101–17, at 102–5, discusses the results of excavations undertaken in the 1970s and early 1980s which revealed earlier structures, concluding however (p. 105) that 'in any matter relating to the site and its buildings in Roman times we are more ignorant than otherwise', but asserting that the 'intensive contruction by Constantine destroyed large portions of the former buildings, as Eusebius' writings and the few remains that have come to light in excavations testify'. It suited Eusebius that the temple should be a temple of Venus/Aphrodite, but Jerome, *Ep.* 58. 3 seems to say rather that there was a statue of Jupiter at the site of the resurrection and one of Venus on the site of the crucifixion, i.e. on the alleged Rock of Calvary (see Stemberger, *Juden und Christen*, 54–5; J. Wilkinson, *Jerusalem Pilgrims before the Crusades* (Warminster, 1977), 82–3), though the coins of Aelia Capitolina show two temples of *Tyche* (Biddle, *Tomb of Christ*, 56–7, with discussion of the position of the camp of the Tenth Legion). Biddle comments (*Tomb of Christ*, 58) that 'what Eusebius has to say about the excavations and what was revealed may be broadly correct, even if economical'.

26. 3. dead idols . . . polluted altars. Gibson and Taylor, *Beneath the Church*, 69, 71, take this as implying a number of statues, not just one, and indeed a complex of shrines, but the plural is typical of Eusebius' writing on pagan shrines; cf. e.g. below, 54–8.

26. 5–28. Constantine alone is inspired by God to reveal the site.

26. 7–27. The temple is demolished. The terms 'fraud' and 'error' refer to the falsity of the religion represented. Constantine orders that all the rubble and wood is to be removed and dumped a long way away, the site dug to a great depth and the earth and stones also removed to a place far away. The purpose is to remove the pollution of pagan worship (cf. 'demonic bloodshed', i.e. sacrifices). The church will thus be one of the 'trophies raised by him over the demons everywhere on earth' (*LC* 9. 5). Eusebius has a clear interest in claiming discontinuity between the temple and the church; however, as one might expect, Hadrianic materials were reused in the Constantinian construction (Gibson and Taylor, *Beneath the Church*, 67–8). Golgotha and the tomb were both inside the Third Wall of Herod Agrippa (AD 41–4), though said to be outside the city wall in the Gospel accounts.

28. The site is revealed, 'against all expectation', like 'a representation of the Saviour's return to life'. The surprise is surely in some sense a rhetorical device on Eusebius' part; it does not necessarily mean that the site itself had not been identified (see above, on **25–8**), though an actual tomb had not been visible. But the discovery of the rock-cut cave is both a proof of the resurrection and an imitation and reminder of Christ's death and rising again. Eusebius ends by repeating the idea: the site of the sepulchre testifies 'by facts louder than any voice to the Resurrection of the Saviour'. The word *gnorisma* ('evidence') in Constantine's letter to Macarius (**III. 30. 1**) should be taken in this sense, to refer to the cave/tomb, rather than to the True Cross (cf. Leeb, 91); cf. the comment of Wilken, *Land Called Holy*, 90, cited on **25–8** above.

The use of the term *gnorisma* by Constantine may have

suggested Eusebius' language here. He focuses on places, not relics, and while it is perfectly possible that some wood fragments should have been 'discovered', perhaps in the area of the *martyrion* (so Walker, 'Jerusalem and the Holy Land', 25; Gibson and Taylor, *Beneath the Church*, 83, rightly pointing out that the wood later described 'cannot have been a large piece', let alone three complete crosses as later believed), if so, we do not know when, and there is no place in this narrative for a dramatic finding of the True Cross (so also Wilken); it is not mentioned by the Pilgrim of Bordeaux, who visited the site in 333, and the first references come twenty years later in Cyril of Jerusalem. Despite that, Drake ('True Cross', after Rubin, 'Church of the Holy Sepulchre', 82–5, followed by Walker, *Holy City, Holy Places*, 244–5; see also J. W. Drijvers, *Helena Augusta* (Leiden, 1992), 83–8) argues that the story of its finding has been deliberately omitted by Eusebius. Likewise Hunt, 'Constantine and Jerusalem', 413, claims that Eusebius has 'misrepresented' both the topography of the site and the Emperor's intentions, on the grounds that 'it seems clear' that the basilica 'was as much the church of the Cross as it was of the Holy Sepulchre'; ironically, he goes on (414–15) to argue that the phraseology of Constantine's letter refers to 'a composite consisting of both Tomb and Calvary', and against Rubin that *gnorisma* (for which see on 30. 1 below) does not necessarily refer to the wood of the cross itself.

Arguments based on the idea of deliberate omission are dangerous where Eusebius is concerned. Although it is true that Cyril of Jerusalem has a little more to say on the rock-cave itself (Biddle, 'Tomb of Christ', 101; cf. Walker, *Holy City, Holy Places*, 270–1), Eusebius is very prone to omissions of detail. Note that while later generations universally ascribed the supposed discovery of the True Cross to Helena, her name was attached to the story only later, whether in Jerusalem itself or by Ambrose in his funeral oration for Theodosius I in 395 (*De obitu Theod.*, CSEL 73, 40 ff.); recent discussion: Stemberger, *Juden und Christen*, 56; Borgehammar, *Holy Cross*; S. Heid, 'Der Ursprung der Helenalegendes im Pilgerbetrieb Jerusalems', *JbAC* 32 (1989), 41–71; Drijvers, *Helena Augusta*, 131–45. Later church historians grafted together material from the *VC* and an account of the finding of the cross (Borgehammar, *Holy Cross*, 19 ff.). Its finding under Constantine, though not necessarily by Helena, is accepted by Taylor, *Christians and the Holy Places*, 136–42 and H. Heinen, 'Helena, Konstantin und die Überlieferung der Kreuzesauffindung im 4. Jahrhundert', in E. Aretz *et al.*, eds., *Der heilige Rock zu Trier: Studien zur Geschichte und Verehrung der Tunika Christi* (Trier, 1995), 83–117. Borgehammar, *Holy Cross*, 126–7, is even inclined to ascribe it to Helena; in contrast, Wharton, 'Baptistery of the Holy Sepulchre', 323, concludes that the cross is more likely to have been 'found' after Eusebius wrote, like the ring of Solomon and the phial of oil allegedly used in anointing Old Testament kings that Egeria saw in the Holy Sepulchre in 384 (*It. Eg.* 37), not to mention the reed, sponge, lance and other objects referred to in later accounts (see on this Gibson and Taylor, *Beneath the Church*, 79); so also Hunt, 'Constantine and Jerusalem', 415.

28. Testimony. The word used is *martyrion*, not with reference to the architectural form of a *martyrium*, or to its later usage as a term for the basilica (see below, with Walker, *Holy City, Holy Places*, 268 n.) but to its function as 'proving' the event of the resurrection (see on **25–8** above, with **30. 2** 'the evidence of this miracle', **30. 4** 'pledge (*pistis*) of the Saviour's passion', and cf. *LC* 9. 16; *SC* 18. 3; Wilken, 'Eusebius and the Christian Holy Land', 746–7). The term was indeed later applied to the basilica, e.g. by Egeria, *It.* 30. 1, and see on **31. 3**, **33. 1**, and **40** below; the usage is discussed by Cyril of Jerusalem, *Catech.* 14. 10. After Eusebius it also became a standard architectural term. For Eusebius' terminology for church buildings, and use of the term *martyrion*, see G. J. M. Bartelink, '"Maison de prière" comme dénomination de l'église en tant qu'édifice, en particulier chez Eusèbe de Césarée', *REG* 84 (1971), 101–18; R. Ousterhout, 'The Temple, the Sepulchre and the *Martyrion* of the Saviour', *Gesta*, 29 (1990), 44–53, at 50–1.

29–40. *The church of the Holy Sepulchre*
Eusebius prefaces his account of the actual building complex (33–40) by describing Constantine's instructions to those in charge, and quoting his letter to Bishop Macarius of Jerusalem; cf. also his letter to Macarius about the site of Mamre, **III. 52–3. 3** below.

29. 2. He instructed those who governed the eastern provinces . . . and the bishop of the church who then presided in

Jerusalem. Constantine expects provincial governors to assist bishops in this official church-building, just as he expected them to make it possible for bishops to travel to church councils (cf. his letters in relation to the Council of Arles, AD 314, Eus., *HE* 10. 5. 2 1–24; Opt. *App.* 3 = Soden, *Urkunden*, 14). The tone of Constantine's instructions is very typical: see Cyril Mango, *Byzantine Architecture* (New York, 1976), 58–9.

The boost given to the status of the see of Jerusalem by canon 7 of Nicaea (the bishop of Aelia 'should have his proper honour, saving to the metropolis (Caesarea) the honour peculiar to it') may have been connected with the planned building (cf. 29. 1, 'as if he had intended this for a long time'); the Emperor is credited with the whole inspiration for the scheme, though it could have been put to him at Nicaea or elsewhere (see above, 25–8). In accordance with his usual practice, Eusebius does not himself name Macarius, although the name is given in the heading to the letter, and Rubin ('Church of the Holy Sepulchre', 88) is surely wrong to deduce rivalry from the omission; for a parallel cf. e.g. Eusebius' failure to name Eusebius of Nicomedia in connection with the Council of Nicaea (above, **III. 11**, and see below on Mamre); he also praises Ossius of Cordoba and Marianus the notarius without naming them, e.g. **II. 63** and **IV. 44**.

30. 1. evidence of his most sacred passion. According to Rubin, 'Church of the Holy Sepulchre', 83, 'a contemporary reader would hardly have applied these terms to anything but the True Cross', but see above on **28**. The phrase *gnorisma . . . tou pathous* does differ from most of Eusebius' references to 'testimony', 'evidence', proof', etc. in this context, in that it associates it with the passion rather than with salvation, i.e. with the crucifixion rather than the resurrection. However, if taken in Rubin's sense it would be a sole allusion to the True Cross in the passage, and Constantine's letter would have to be understood as referring to something quite other than the general thrust of Eusebius' long description (as Hunt indeed admits, 'Constantine and Jerusalem', 413). In his main account Eusebius focuses on the cave-tomb, and not on Golgotha, and the political arguments adduced for such omission of the cross and concerned with the rivalry between the sees of Caesarea and Jerusalem would apply equally to the cave of the resurrection, on which he does lavish so much space. As Wilken argues ('Eusebius and the Christian Holy Land', 745–55), Eusebius has moved since he wrote *DE*, and since these discoveries, to a new understanding of the importance of the holy places. His narrative, with its elaborate insistence on the three caves, and his stress on victory and salvation, leads him to emphasize the resurrection rather than the death of Christ, which was in any case the eastern understanding. *Gnorisma*, if taken to refer to the cross, would have interrupted this theme and required some explanation from Eusebius. Had the supposed True Cross in fact been discovered during these excavations, Eusebius was quite capable of referring to it. It is probably also of significance that he refers to it in the *LC* in symbolic rather than material terms. That which has been hidden (30. 1) is more probably the cave, the subject of chs. 25–8 and the reason for Constantine's letter; *contra*, Taylor, *Christians and the Holy Places*, 136. Even if Eusebius places the emphasis on resurrection, while Constantine himself thought rather of 'a mystery-site connected with the death of Christ' (so Yarnold, 'Who Planned the Churches?' 108), it does not follow that *gnorisma* here has to refer to the True Cross itself. For the suggestion that Constantine's original intention was to provide a cathedral for Jerusalem, rather than a monument enshrining the cave or the cross, see Wharton, 'Baptistery of the Holy Sepulchre', 322–33, and in Annabel Jane Wharton, *Refiguring the Postclassical City. Dura Europos, Jerash, Jerusalem and Ravenna* (Cambridge, 1995), 85–100, but see Biddle, 'Tomb of Christ', 103; *Tomb of Christ*, 90; and now Taylor, 'Golgotha'.

the enemy of the whole republic. i.e. Licinius.

30. 2–4. In the preamble to his instructions, Constantine, like Eusebius, is preoccupied with the idea of 'proofs' of the Christian faith.

31. 1. your . . . Good Sense. cf. above, **19. 1.** The responsibility for the building is to lie with the bishop, who is to be assisted by the civil administration by the supply of craftsmen, labourers, and materials.

31. 2. Dracillianus. Dracillianus was *vicarius Orientis* with the rank of *illustris*; he is known also from *CTh* 2. 33. 1 and 16. 5. 1, of 326, see Barnes, *NE* 141, 246. The governor of Palestine who would have received the Emperor's instructions to supply work-men and materials to Macarius is not named.

31. 3. columns or marble. It is interesting that Constantine distinguishes between materials available locally and marble, whether as ready-made or reused columns or in raw state, which may need to be supplied from further afield. Constantine's letter apparently envisages only a basilica of typical kind, though more splendid. It does not differentiate between tomb and crucifixion site; Golgotha is not mentioned, nor is there mention of a *martyrion*, in the technical architectural sense.

32. 1. the vault of the basilica. The reference seems to be to the roof, or rather, ceiling, of the proposed basilica, and as to whether or not it should be in the coffered style found in several contemporary and later basilicas (e.g. Trier, S. Maria Maggiore), and if so, decorated with gold; see 40 below. The first church of St Peter's in Rome and other Constantinian churches there, e.g. the Lateran basilica, were of similar type. Eusebius uses the Latin term *lakonarios*, otherwise unattested in Greek (cf. the Latin *lacunar*).

33. 1. New Jerusalem was built . . . facing the famous Jerusalem of old. It is difficult to see this as compatible with the view that Eusebius was ambivalent about the possible elevation of Jerusalem over Caesarea (Rubin, 'Church of the Holy Sepulchre', 88 ff; see on **25–8** above). He makes, probably for the first time, the obvious point, ubiquitous in later Christian polemic against Jews, that a 'new' Christian 'Jerusalem' had now been built to excel the old Jerusalem, the city of the Jews, which had been destroyed. More particularly, 'facing' (*antiprosopos*) must refer to the location of the church complex, 'facing' the Jewish Temple across the valley (it can hardly be said to 'face' the city as such); Eusebius uses the term 'Jerusalem of old' to stand for the site of the Jewish Temple, symbolically and actually destroyed, and repeats the notion of 'facing' it in the opening of the next sentence ('opposite'). For the symbolism see Wharton, *Refiguring the Postclassical City*, 85–100. It is worthy of note that it is the building itself which is described as the 'new Jerusalem' and identified with that spoken of by the prophets ('perhaps that fresh new Jerusalem proclaimed in prophetic oracles'; cf. Rev. 3: 12, 21. 2; the allusion has already been developed at *LC* 9. 15, *SC*

1. 2; see Wilken, *Land Called Holy*, 96, 'Eusebius and the Christian Holy Land', 749–50). Eusebius does not here go on, as he had done earlier, to refer to the destroyed Temple, or to the texts held by Christians to deny that it could ever be rebuilt (Matt. 24: 1–2, with Dan. 9: 27); nevertheless, the thought sufficiently explains why Constantine and all later Christian emperors chose to leave the site of the ruined Temple to speak for itself rather than building Christian buildings on it. For further discussion of the place of Jerusalem in the thought of Origen and Eusebius see R. Wilken, *John Chrysostom and the Jews* (Berkeley and Los Angeles, 1983), 135–8, and *Land Called Holy*, 93–7.

at the very Testimony to the Saviour.   It is less obvious what Eusebius means by 'at' (*kata*), or indeed, by *martyrion* here. However, he has so far used *martyrion* in its basic sense of 'witness', 'testimony', to refer to the burial-site, i.e. the cave (see above, and see on **30. 1**), and the same usage seems to be guaranteed here by the addition of *soterion* ('of the Saviour', or 'saving'), an epithet which he frequently attaches to the terms 'sign' (*semeion*) or trophy (*tropaion*). 'At' seems to have a weak meaning of 'near', or simply 'over', 'on the site of'. The complications arise in connection with the interpretation of the first stage of the complex as a whole, which seems to have been composed of three main components, the basilica, the inner court, and the structure over the actual cave of the resurrection; there was also a large atrium in front of the basilica, with steps leading from the *cardo* or main street, as shown on the Madaba map (Fig. 7). Eusebius' overall description is notoriously difficult to understand, as well as being incomplete, and different interpretations have been put forward; for summaries of the problems see Patrich, 'Early Church of the Holy Sepulchre', 105–12; Ousterhout, 'The Temple, the Sepulchre and the *Martyrion* of the Saviour'. The rotunda over the tomb, later known as the Anastasis, seems not to have been built when the church was dedicated or when Eusebius wrote this passage (so C. Coüasnon, *The Church of the Holy Sepulchre in Jerusalem* (Oxford, 1974), 15, and see e.g. Gibson and Taylor, *Beneath the Church*, 77; Hunt, *Holy Land Pilgrimage*, 11; Rubin, 'Church of the Holy Sepulchre', 81; Walker, *Holy City, Holy Places*, 251, with

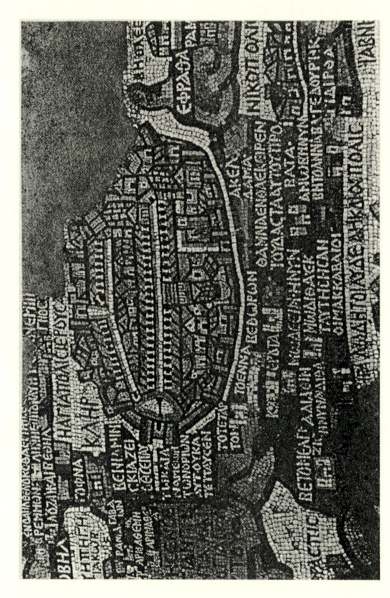

FIG. 7. Mosaic map from Madaba, Jordan, 6th century, showing church of Holy Sepulchre. Courtesy of Fr M. Piccirillo.

earlier bibliography, but *contra*, V. C. Corbo, *Il Santo Sepolchro di Gerusalemme* (Jerusalem, 1981)). Eusebius has little to say about this part of the complex, whereas he describes the basilica in some detail, see H. Kühnel, *From the Earthly to the Heavenly Jerusalem. Representations of the Holy City in Christian Art of the First Millennium* (Rome-Freiburg-Wien, 1987), 81). Recent study has shed more light on the Constantinian structure over the tomb (known later as the Edicule, cf. the *aedicula* over the tomb of St Peter in Rome): it contains the remains of earlier *aediculae* and of an original rock-cut tomb, see Biddle, *Tomb of Christ*, 65–72, 109–19, and see below on **34**; Lucy-Anne Hunt, 'Artistic and Cultural Inter-Relations between the Christian Communities at the Holy Sepulchre in the 12th Century', in A. O'Mahony, ed., *The Christian Heritage in the Holy Land* (London, 1995), 57–96, at 68. Rubin, 'Church of the Holy Sepulchre', points out that at *VC* III. 28, 33, and 40 the term *martyrion* is used to refer to the whole building as it was in Eusebius' day, though he does not make the additional point that it is also used by him in its literal sense of 'proof' or 'testimony'. Later, confusingly enough, 'Martyrion' came to denote the basilica (Hunt, *Holy Land Pilgrimage*, 13 and n.); for ingenious suggestions as to how and when this may have happened, see Rubin, 'Church of the Holy Sepulchre', 84, Walker, *Holy City, Holy Places*, 268 n. Constantine's basilica (the Martyrion) was largely destroyed by the Caliph al-Hakim in AD 1009 (Biddle, *Tomb of Christ*, 72), after which the rotunda was rebuilt and developed by Constantine IX Monomachos, AD 1042–8 (though see Biddle, *Tomb of Christ*, 73–81, for Michael IV, 1034–41), with emphasis on the liturgical commemoration of the scenes of Christ's passion.

33. 3–39. Eusebius' account, which is of great importance as the only contemporary source except for the account of the Pilgrim of Bordeaux (above), distinguishes three elements: the construction over the cave (33. 3), a large space open to the air (34–5), and the basilica (36. 1) with no mention of the cross. The problem for scholars attempting to reconstruct the Constantinian complex has been that of reconciling what Eusebius says with what is known of the later buildings; the possible dangers inherent in this approach are well put by Rubin, 'Church of the Holy Sepulchre', app. I, with earlier references. Gibson and Taylor,

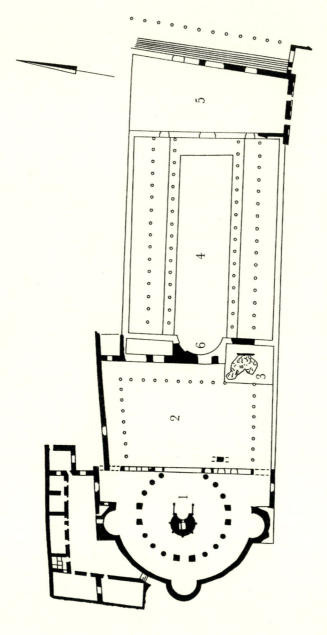

FIG. 8. Constantine's complex at the Holy Sepulchre, Jerusalem, with the Rotunda of the Anastasis (the Resurrection) as completed in the later 4th century. (1) Tomb of Christ, with Edicule over it; (2) Inner court; (3) Rock of Calvary; (4) *Martyrion*, or basilica; (5) Atrium; (6) Dome or 'hemisphere'. Drawn by Steven Ashley. Courtesy of Professor M. Biddle.

Beneath the Church, 73–4, offer a translation of 34–9 with notes, but unfortunately they have not used Winkelmann's essential critical text. See also Fig. 8 (from Biddle, *Tomb of Christ*, fig. 63).

There is a large bibliography on the nature of the Constantinian building, for which the evidence of Eusebius is of key importance, though it needs to be assessed in relation to recent archaeological discoveries. The reader also needs a guide through the frequent differences of interpretation and indeed of reporting Eusebius. Modern discussions are unfortunately by no means all reliable. The most important recent study is by Biddle; see also Corbo, *Il Santo Sepolchro*; Coüasnon, *Church of the Holy Sepulchre*; L. H. Vincent and F. M. Abel, *Jérusalem Nouvelle* (Paris, 1914); Ousterhout, 'The Temple, the Sepulchre and the *Martyrion* of the Saviour'. For a guide, see Walker, *Holy City, Holy Places*, 247–52. The church is depicted on the sixth-century Madaba mosaic map and in the early fifth-century apse mosaic in Santa Pudenziana in Rome.

33. 3. As the principal item.   Eusebius writes of 'beautifying' the cave itself with a memorial (*mnema*). His language, metaphorical as usual, is difficult to press (in what sense does the memorial 'comprise' (*periechon*) the 'trophies' of the resurrection?). But he seems to be referring to a construction, with columns (34), rather than a substantial building over and around the tomb, that is to the Edicule, not the later rotunda. He lays most emphasis on the tomb-site, but mainly goes on to describe the basilica, which was not over the tomb. For his description of the tomb, and comparison with that of Cyril (*mnema*) see Walker, *Holy City, Holy Places*, 265–75; Biddle, *Tomb of Christ*, 45, 47. Eusebius may be describing the original Edicule.

34. superb columns.   These may be the columns of the Edicule around the rock of the actual tomb: for detailed discussion, see Biddle, 'Tomb of Christ', esp. 73–92, 101–5; *Tomb of Christ*, 68–9. The Anastasis rotunda was built over this construction, which itself had a conical roof. For the subsequent history of the Edicule see Biddle, *Tomb of Christ*, 70–3, and for the early visual evidence, ibid. 22–8.

35. large space wide open to the fresh air.   Between the tomb and the basilica was a court, to be distinguished from the outer

atrium through which the basilica was entered; cf. 39 below.
Eusebius makes no mention of the rock of Golgotha in the south-
east corner.

36 the royal temple.   Cf. 38 'royal house', i.e. the basilica, to
the east of the tomb. The interior was decorated with marble
slabs on the walls, as in Justinian's S. Sophia in Constantinople
and many earlier buildings. There was a coffered ceiling
decorated with gold (36. 2). In 37 the description of the basilica
continues. It is a classic five-aisled design: each side of the nave
was a double row of columns, with an upper and a lower range,
and there were three doors at the east end, while at the west end
was an apse or dome (*hemisphairion*, 38; cf. *It. Eger.* 46. 5 *absida*
and see below), with twelve columns representing the twelve
apostles. In front of the east end, where the doors opened, was
the atrium proper, and beyond that, a fine entrance portico to the
whole complex (39); see for discussion Ousterhout, 'The
Temple, the Sepulchre and the *Martyrion* of the Saviour' and
Fig. 8.

38. hemisphere.   Or as Gibson and Taylor have, 'a dome
which has been extended to the highest part of the royal
house'; this would have to be a dome over the basilica (which
is very unlikely), not the Anastasis rotunda, or a ciborium over
the altar in the apse, see their comment, *Beneath the Church*, 74.
See also Kühnel, *Earthly to Heavenly Jerusalem*, 82–3, with
A. Piganiol, 'L'Hémispherion et l'omphalos des lieux saints',
Cahiers archéologiques, 1 (1945), 7–14; J. G. Davies, 'Eusebius'
Description of the Martyrium at Jerusalem', *AJA* 61 (1957),
171–3. All interpretations are controversial.

**40. This then was the shrine which the Emperor raised as a
manifest testimony.**   It is not immediately clear whether the
'shrine', and thus the 'testimony', refers to the whole complex, or
just to the basilica described in 36–8. The description of the
whole complex ends with a generalized conclusion about the
magnificence of its decoration. But major problems remain.
Probably Eusebius does not mention the rotunda because it
was constructed later (see above), though the later dating of the
dome of the rotunda depends wholly on negative evidence,
namely the silence of Eusebius, the Bordeaux Pilgrim, and
Cyril. But nor does Eusebius make any mention either here or

in the *LC* or *SC* of the rock identified as Golgotha and incorporated into the court in front of the tomb, in sharp contrast to Cyril of Jerusalem, in whose *Catechetical Orations* Golgotha plays a prominent part; see Hunt, *Holy Land Pilgrimage*, 12. It has been supposed that Constantine erected a monumental or jewelled cross on Golgotha, but this is unlikely (see C. Milner, ' "Lignum Vitae" or "Crux Gemmata"? The Cross of Golgotha in the Early Byzantine Period', *BMGS* 20 (1996), 77–99). Walker, *Holy City, Holy Places*, 252–60, explains the omission of Golgotha here in terms of Eusebius' theological preference for the revelation of immortality through the resurrection over the death of Christ on the cross; this, he argues, is why he focuses on the cave-tomb, and fails to mention the place of the crucifixion altogether. The same argument is used by Walker, following Drake, 'True Cross', to explain his silence about the finding of the cross, though he had in fact mentioned the site of Golgotha in his *Onomastikon* (74). The suggestion that the rock of Golgotha was cut away and exposed after the first building operations (J. Jeremias, 'Wo lag Golgotha und das Heilige Grab?', *Angelos*, 1 (Leipzig, 1926), 141–73, at 159) is dismissed by Walker as implausible (*Holy City, Holy Places*, 253 n. 46). The Bordeaux Pilgrim in 333 refers to the *monticulus Golgotha* as being very near the tomb (see Rubin, 'Church of the Holy Sepulchre', 85, and on the exposed Rock of Calvary, Gibson and Taylor, *Beneath the Church*, 80). For criticism of Walker see Leeb, 91–2. It is better to regard Eusebius' account as incomplete; he also omits the baptistery, which had also already been mentioned in 333 by the Bordeaux Pilgrim (ed. Geyer and Cuntz, *CCSL* 175 (1965), 1–26); cf. Wharton, 'Baptistery of the Holy Sepulchre', 314–15.

41–43. 4. *Churches at Bethlehem and the Ascension*

The other two 'mystic caves' are those of the nativity and that now identified as associated with the ascension, on the Mount of Olives (41. 1; for Eusebius' insistence on the three caves, allegedly developed by him in the context of rivalry with Macarius, see Walker, *Holy City, Holy Places*, 188–94, and see above on **26. 2**). The two churches built on these sites, at Bethlehem and on the Mount of Olives (the Eleona church), are attributed to Constantine's mother, Helena (cf. 43. 1, 'She immediately consecrated'; 43. 3, 'the Emperor's mother erected on the Mount of Olives . . . she raised the sacred house of the church', 43. 4). But the buildings are also Constantinian (41. 1, 2; 43. 2, 4), and it is the Emperor who provides the resources (43. 4, 'her son providing her with the right arm of imperial authority'). There then follows (43. 5–47. 3) a brief notice of Helena's death, and a lengthy eulogy, which interrupts the general section on Constantine's church-building (resumed at 47. 4 with reference to Constantinople).

The role of Helena, the reasons for her journey and her later association with the finding of the True Cross have been much discussed: see esp. Drijvers, *Helena Augusta*; Hunt, *Holy Land Pilgrimage*, 28–49; 'Constantine and Jerusalem'; Borgehammar, *Holy Cross*. She certainly provided a powerful model for later pilgrimages and journeys by imperial women to the Holy Land (see J. W. Drijvers, 'Helena Augusta: Exemplary Christian Empress', *Studia Patristica*, 24 (1993), 85–90), though it is less certain that her own journey should in fact be termed a pilgrimage; for the view that it was an imperial progress (see on **42. 1** and **44** below), see Kenneth G. Holum, 'Hadrian and St. Helena: Imperial Travel and the Origins of the Christian Holy Land Pilgrimage', in R. Ousterhout, ed., *The Blessings of Pilgrimage* (Urbana, Ill., 1990), 66–81.

41. 1. the cave of the first divine manifestation. Since the second-century *Protevangelion of James* 17. 3–18. 1, the birthplace of Jesus was believed to be a cave at Bethlehem (see J. K. Elliott, ed., *The Apocryphal New Testament* (Oxford, 1993), 49, 64).

41. 2–42. 2. Eusebius needs to explain why Helena is suddenly introduced: the two churches at Bethlehem and on the Mount of Olives became in a sense memorials to the Empress, who died shortly after her visit to the east (43. 5), and in Constantine's presence (46. 2), probably in 327 (so Barnes, *NE* 9 n. 40, with *CE* 221; her coins continued to be issued until 329). Her Christian zeal is emphasized, and there is naturally no mention of any connection with the deaths of Crispus and Fausta in 326, also omitted in the *VC* (above, **25–47. 3**); Helena's influence was seen in those events by pagan writers (e.g. *Epit. de Caesaribus* 41. 12; Zos. 2. 29. 2, correctly, according to Barnes, *CE* 220–1), and Constantine's need for penance, if only vicarious, was also inferred (Zosimus, and cf. Julian, *Caes.*), or for public distraction (see Barnes, *CE* 221). Eusebius gives the public explanation for her journey (Hunt, *Holy Land Pilgrimage*, 33). Though he has not previously given her a role in the presentation of Constantine's background (a striking fact in relation to the space devoted to Constantine's father Constantius), he now stresses her Christian faith (*contra*, Zon. 13. 1. 5, referring to the period before 312), and attributes her conversion to Constantine himself (47. 2).

42. 1. when she made it her business. The journey is ascribed to Helena's own prompting, motivated by the desire to give thanks for Constantine and her grandsons the Caesars. After the death of Crispus there were two Caesars, namely Constantine II and Constantius; Constans is attested as Caesar only in 333.

though old. According to **46** below she was 80 when she died.

wondrous land. See Wilken, 'Eusebius and the Christian Holy Land', 754–5, who discerns in the phrase the beginnings of the conception of the Christian Holy Land.

to inspect with imperial concern the eastern provinces with their communities and peoples. The object of the journey was not therefore solely to make a pilgrimage to the holy places or to build churches in Palestine; see Hunt, *Holy Land Pilgrimage*, 33–6. See further on **44–5** below.

42. 2. she accorded suitable adoration to the footsteps of the Saviour. Eusebius cites Ps. 132 (131): 7 as referring to Bethlehem. He had already cited both this and the previous verse in *DE*; for discussion, and for the later use of Psalm 132 (131): 6–7 by Cyril and Jerome, see Walker, *Holy City, Holy Places*, 180–1, 183; Hunt, 'Constantine and Jerusalem', 418. Opinions as to the correct exegesis of the passage differed (Walker, pp. 180, 183 n. 47).

43. 1. Bethlehem. Though the present church of the Nativity at Bethlehem is Justinianic, traces of the fourth-century building survive (see B. Bagatti, *Gli antichi edifici sacri di Betlemme* (Jerusalem, 1952), esp. 16–21). It seems to have been a large basilica, with an octagonal structure at the apse-end functioning as a martyrium enclosing the actual cave, and approached, like the basilica of the Holy Sepulchre, by a very large colonnaded atrium or forecourt. For bibliography see Hunt, *Holy Land Pilgrimage*, 15, and see R. Krautheimer, *Early Christian and Byzantine Architecture* (Harmondsworth, 1975), 60–2. The basilica was seen by the Bordeaux Pilgrim in 333.

43. 3. the monument to the journey into heaven of the Saviour of the Universe. Though Eusebius associates the cave on the Mount of Olives with the ascension (41. 1), by the 380s Egeria considered the ascension to have taken place elsewhere (though nearby), on a site soon commemorated by the church known as the Imbomon (see Walker, *Holy City, Holy Places*, 201–2, and on Eusebius' understanding of the Mount of Olives, 199–213). Helena's church is that known as the 'Eleona' (A. Ovadiah, *Corpus of the Byzantine Churches in the Holy Land*, Eng. trans. (Bonn, 1970), 71–82), planned in a form similar to the church at Bethlehem.

43. 3. a true report maintains that in that cave the Saviour of the Universe initiated the members of his guild in ineffable mysteries. The cave was also associated with Jesus' apocalyptic discourse recorded at Matt. 24: 4–25, an identification which Eusebius confirms; *DE*. 6. 18. 23 refers both to the discourse and to the ascension. Eusebius uses vocabulary associated with the mysteries; see also on **25–8** above. At *Theoph*. 4. 18 Eusebius locates Jesus' utterance about the permanent ruin of the Temple, which is found at Matt. 24: 2, as delivered not on the Mount but 'around the Temple' (Walker, *Holy City, Holy Places*, 204). There was some awkwardness in taking a cave as the actual scene of the ascension, and Eusebius' terminology has led to differing views as to Helena's foundation: for discussion, see ibid. 204–5, 209–13.

43. 4–47. 3. *The death of the Empress Helena*

Eusebius devotes a long section to describing and eulogizing the activities of Helena, though only in relation to the last years of her life.

43. 5. the very portal of old age. A Homeric expression (*Il.* 22. 60).

44–45. Helena's progress through the eastern provinces is described in generalizing encomiastic style, but Eusebius leaves

no doubt of its imperial nature: she distributes largesse and
gives donatives to the soldiers as well as performing acts of
Christian charity and making gifts to churches (see Hunt, *Holy
Land Pilgrimage*, 35–7; 'Constantine and Jerusalem', 417;
Drijvers, 'Helena Augusta: Exemplary Christian Empress'). She
failed however to receive due deference in at least one case, that of
Bishop Eustathius of Antioch: see H. Chadwick, 'The Fall of
Eustathius of Antioch', *JThS* NS 49 (1948), 27–35. As Hunt
remarks, Eusebius' words in 44 recall the terms of Constantine's
letter dealing with Christians in the east after the defeat of
Licinius (II. 24–42, esp. 30–1). With the phrase 'the wonderful
woman' at the end of 45, Eusebius describes Helena in exactly
the terms conventionally used of their subjects by later hagio-
graphers; cf. also 'thrice-blessed' at **46. 2**.

46. 2–47. 3   Great emphasis is laid by Eusebius on Helena's
death. Though Eusebius gives no detail (47. 1), being generally
ill–informed on Constantine's Roman buildings, she was
buried (cf. *Lib. Pont.* I. 182) in a porphyry sarcophagus in a
mausoleum on the Via Labicana in Rome which Constantine
had constructed perhaps for himself, together with the basilica
of SS. Marcellino e Pietro: see Drijvers, *Helena Augusta*, 74–5.
Eusebius is more interested in presenting Helena in such a
way as to enhance Constantine's own piety and sense of
family, no doubt in order to counteract the events of 326:
thus when he attributes Helena's Christianity to her son (47. 2),
it is as proof of the latter's piety towards his mother (cf. also
47. 3). With the words 'she seemed to him to have been a
disciple of the common Saviour from the first' he suggests a
retrojection of her Christian faith in much the same way as he
had enhanced the piety of Constantius Chlorus; later church
historians asserted that she had brought Constantine up as a
Christian, e.g. Theod., *HE* 1.18. There is of course no
mention of Helena's dubious origin (even Ambrose, *De obitu
Theod.* 42 could refer to her as a *stabularia*, 'inn-keeper' or
perhaps 'barmaid'), her presumed rejection by Constantius in
favour of Theodora, daughter of Maximian (see Barnes, *NE*
36) or her birth-place according to later sources (Drepanum on
the gulf of Nicomedia, said to have been refounded as
Helenopolis by Constantine; see Cyril Mango, 'The Empress

Helena, Helenopolis, Pylae', *Travaux et mémoires*, 12 (1994), 143–58). Her acclamation as Augusta is included, together with the reference to her official coinage (47. 2), on which she is shown wearing the diadem, as further proof of Constantine's favour; a date of 8 November 324 (to coincide with the raising of Constantine's son Constantius to the rank of Caesar) is proposed for the imperial title by P. Bruun, *RIC* 7. 69, and Latin inscriptions from the west record her as the mother of Constantine and grandmother of the Caesars, as at 42. 1 and 46. 1: see Drijvers, *Helena Augusta*, 43–54, with Hunt, *Holy Land Pilgrimage*, 31–2, on statues and honours received by her in the west, 324–6. But Eusebius' claim that Constantine gave her control over the imperial treasuries (47. 3) no doubt relates specifically to her eastern journey rather than suggesting that she now had equal status with him in the Empire. Despite their apparent detail, the general emphasis of Eusebius' chapters on Helena is to confirm Eusebius in his omission of the Emperor's stay in Italy and Rome in 326, and of the painful events which occurred there, to amplify the account of his religious patronage in Jerusalem and its surroundings, and to display the family piety of an emperor who had only recently been implicated in the deaths of his eldest son and his own wife. There is no mention of the later and ubiquitous legend of Helena as finder of the True Cross. Nor is she connected with the building or the excavation at the Holy Sepulchre, which are both wholly attributed to the initiative of Constantine himself; deliberate omission would contrast sharply with the care which Eusebius takes both to delineate what Helena did in the Holy Land, and to ensure that Constantine receives credit even for this. A different view is offered by Rubin, 'Church of the Holy Sepulchre', 86–7, 92, who supposes a connection between Helena and Macarius unwelcome to Eusebius, and argues that Eusebius has consciously written Helena out of the account of the Holy Sepulchre. If however Helena was really 'not entirely palatable' (ibid. 92), some explanation has to be found for the unusual and encomiastic emphasis which Eusebius gives to her, especially at 43–7.

47. 1. the imperial city.   i.e. Rome.

47. 4–53. *Other Churches Built*

The account of church-building in Palestine is interrupted by reference to Constantinople (47. 4–49) and by a chapter referring to Nicomedia and Antioch (50), after which Eusebius records the founding of the church at Mamre and inserts a further letter from Constantine to Macarius and the bishops of Palestine (51–3).

47. 4–49. *Constantinople*

Although Eusebius himself delivered his Tricennalian Oration before Constantine in Constantinople, and preserves much anecdotal material about his stay in bk. IV (see Drake, 'Genesis'), he does not describe the city in any detail, and it should be noted that it appears here in the context of Christian benefactions (see however also **III. 3.** 1–3, **54.** 3; **IV. 36**). As usual, he is apt to generalize (48. 1, cf. 47. 4 'newly built churches' throughout the provinces). Of the 'very many places of worship' and 'very large martyr-shrines', both inside and outside the city, Constantine is with certainty associated with few, apart from his own mausoleum, linked to the church of the Holy Apostles (see on **IV. 58–60**, unfortunately with a lacuna in the text). Socrates attributes S. Irene to him (*HE* 1. 16), and he may have been responsible for the large basilica to the local martyr Mocius, outside the city wall (referred to by Soz., *HE* 8. 17. 5, see Barnes, *CE* 222) and a church of Acacius inside the Constantinian wall (Socr., *HE* 6. 23); see C. A. Mango, *Le Développement urbain de Constantinople (IVᵉ–VIIᵉ siècles)* (Paris, 1985), 35–6; G. Dagron, *Naissance d'une capitale: Constantinople et ses institutions de 330 à 451* (Paris, 1984), 388–9. As Dagron remarks (p. 389), the 'Christian capital' of Constantine's creation was not so much Constantinople as Jerusalem. Eusebius is not interested in mentioning here the secular and indeed imperial buildings by which Constantine transformed the existing town of Byzantium, and which included a main street and a forum with a great statue (Mango, *Le Développement*, 23–34), though he has mentioned the palace earlier for its representation of Christian imperial victory (**III. 3** above, and see below). In contrast to Eusebius' praises, Zosimus emphasizes the haste and shoddiness of the buildings

(II. 2); pagans criticize Constantine's expenditure on Constantinople and the consequent neglect of city councils (Lib., *Or.* 49. 2, with 30. 6; see H.-U. Wiemer, 'Libanius on Constantine', *CQ* NS 44 (1994), 518–19).

48. 2. a city bearing his own name. Cf. *Origo*, 30, 'he renamed Byzantium after himself Constantinople [i.e. the city of Constantine] in memory of his great victory'.

he saw fit to purge it of all idol-worship. In contrast Zosimus writes of Constantine building two new temples there, to Rhea and to Fortuna Romae (2. 31); see also Malal., 324 Bonn, with Dagron, *Naissance*, 373–7; Mango, *Le Développement*, 34–6. Short of deporting all the existing inhabitants what Eusebius suggests would have been impossible, nor could the majority of the many new inhabitants encouraged to settle there by the offer of grain distribution and other measures (Zos. 2. 31–2) have been Christian. Even if we discount Philostorg., *HE* 2. 17, on the alleged worship given to Constantine's own statue in Constantinople (accepted by R. MacMullen, *Christianity and Paganism in the Fourth to Eighth Centuries* (New Haven, 1997), 34), Aurel. Vict. says that there were statues of the imperial family in Rome and a priesthood established in Africa (*Caes.* 40. 28).

nowhere in it appeared those images of the supposed gods. Lib., *Or.* 30. 6 says that Constantine despoiled temples in order to build Constantinople, and was punished for it (30. 37). For the pagan statues removed by him to Constantinople and used to decorate the Hippodrome and Senate House see *Chron. Pasch.* 528–9 and see on **54. 2** below.

49. emblems of the Good Shepherd, evident signs to those who start from the divine oracles. The good shepherd (John 10: 11) was a motif shared with pagans. Eusebius may be putting a Christian interpretation on pagan statuary, as here in the case of groups depicting a man with lions (for the story see Dan. 6). For discussion and for the meaning of *symbola* (cf. IV. 45) see R. Grigg, 'Constantine the Great and the Cult without Images', *Viator*, 8 (1977), 4.

the royal quarters of the imperial palace. Eusebius seems to be writing from personal knowledge. Little is known with certainty of the Constantinian phase of the imperial palace: see

Mango, *Le Développement*, 26; *Brazen House*, 22–3, and see on
III. 3; **IV. 22**, with *LC* 9. 11.

a protection for his Empire. Eusebius presents the cross
explicitly as a talisman (so rightly Drake, 'True Cross', 17–19,
though his remarks as to the cross-shaped structure of the
Church of the Holy Apostles at p. 20 are mistaken: see on
IV. 58–60).

50. *Nicomedia and Antioch*

a very large and splendid church. The previous church at
Nicomedia, the capital of Bithynia, and tetrarchic capital, had
been burnt by order of Diocletian at the start of the persecution
in 303 (Lact., *DMP* 12); its replacement was thus an appropriate
demonstration of Constantine's triumph.

**50. 2. The most pre-eminent cities . . . the metropolis of the
Orient.** The so-called Golden Octagon at Antioch is presented
as being one among many such churches built in provincial
capitals. The church, which does not survive, but which was of
considerable architectural importance, is depicted in a floor
mosaic from Yakto, Antioch, and seems to have adjoined the
palace on the Orontes island (Krautheimer, *Early Christian and
Byzantine Architecture*, 79–80); it was dedicated by Constantius II
(see G. A. Downey, *A History of Antioch in Syria* (Princeton, 1961),
342–5).

51–3. *Mamre*

In his survey of church-building Eusebius now returns to the
subject of Palestine and the church built at the oak of Mamre,
near Hebron, where Abraham received his three divine visitors
(Gen. 18: 1–33), and thus the site of another theophany; since
the building activity here involved destroying an existing temple,
the account also serves to connect this section with what follows.
The procedure adopted by Constantine is similar to that
described by Eusebius for the Holy Sepulchre: the Emperor
writes both to Macarius and the other bishops of Palestine and to
the civil authorities (51. 2, cf. 53. 2), instructing them to
cooperate. The *comes* Acacius (53. 2) is to clear the area of

pagan statues and worship, and then consult the bishops about building a church on the site. Eusebius can include a copy of the Emperor's letter of instructions because he was a recipient of it himself (51. 2 'he also dispatched to the author of the present history a reasoned admonition, a copy which I should, I think, add to the present work'). Though the letter is addressed by name to Macarius, it is also sent to the other bishops including himself (52. 1), and Eusebius accepts joint responsibility for Constantine's rebuke (51. 2 'he took us to task'); Rubin, 'Church of the Holy Sepulchre', 88, unnecessarily sees this as further indication of Eusebius' hostility to Macarius. Constantine had been told of the pagan worship on the site in letters from Eutropia, the mother of Fausta (52. 1), who evidently also visited Palestine; Rubin, 'Church of the Holy Sepulchre', 90, places her visit between the defeat of Licinius and the Council of Nicaea (see also Walker, *Holy City, Holy Places*, 276), and the reference to her here becomes more comfortable if the visit took place before the death of her daughter Fausta in 326. Rubin ingeniously argues that Eusebius deliberately includes the letter so as to expose his rival Macarius, who, however, was soon to assume the role of guide to Constantine's own mother Helena ('Church of the Holy Sepulchre', 88–91, accepted by Walker, *Holy City, Holy Places*, 276 n.); it seems more likely that he includes the letter in order to make his dossier of Constantinian documents as complete as possible. Macarius is not named by Eusebius, but this is in accordance with his normal practice (see e.g. on **IV. 61. 2–3**). Constantine's letter is placed out of chronological context here, which serves to reduce the importance of Eutropia (below, on **52. 1–53. 3**). The church itself followed a form now familiar in general terms: a large basilica with an atrium, in this case surrounding the well, the altar of Abraham, and the oak-tree (Hunt, *Holy Land Pilgrimage*, 15, with earlier bibliography; Ovadiah, *Corpus of Byzantine Churches*, 131–3).

52–53. 3. For Constantine's letter to Macarius and the other bishops of Palestine (cf. Soz., *HE* 2. 3. 6). Constantine's mother-in-law (**52. 1**) Eutropia, mother of Fausta and wife of Maximian, is said to have brought back an unfavourable report of the condition of the site of Mamre. The theophany at Mamre (Gen. 18: 1–20, esp. 18–19) was held to be the first manifestation of the Logos, and the passage is used by Justin, *Dial. with Trypho*, 56, and had already been mentioned by Eusebius at *DE* 5. 9. 5–8, where he alludes to an image of the three visitors on the oak, and *HE* 1. 2. 7–8; later the scene was interpreted as pointing to the Trinity. For Eutropia see Hunt, 'Constantine and Jerusalem', 416.

52. sacrilegious abominations. The language is very Eusebian, cf. e.g. *LC* 8, and cf. also *SC* 13.

53. 2. Acacius. Constantine has instructed Acacius the *comes* (*PLRE* i, Acacius 4, cf. below 62. 1, otherwise unknown) to destroy all signs of pagan cult, and to build a basilica, which Macarius and the bishops of Phoenice are to design; any further desecration is to be notified to the Emperor at once by letter.

53. 3–4. Constantine ends with a forthright lesson in biblical geography for Macarius and the bishops.

54–8 *Pagan Temples*

54. *Removal of valuables*

Constantine's demolition of temples is more extravagantly described at *LC* 8, and cf. also Eun. *VS* 461, but according to Zos. 2. 31 there were new temples even in Constantinople, and cf. Malal., 324 Bonn (see above on **48. 2**); Constantine himself affirmed toleration after his defeat of Licinius (II. 56). The extent to which he actually despoiled or demolished temples is difficult to establish: Libanius, *Or.* 30, *Pro templis*, AD 388–91, corroborates the despolation, while claiming that cult itself was permitted, but see further on **IV. 23**. Jones, *LRE* 108, accepts that the Constantinian introduction of the gold *solidus* was made possible by the confiscation of temple treasures, but the sources for the confiscation and the monetary and economic reforms alike are tendentious (e.g. Anon., *De Rebus Bellicis* 2); significantly, Zosimus, our best, albeit very hostile, source for Constantine's secular and economic policies, makes no mention of temple treasures in this context.

54. 2. the sacred bronze figures . . . he displayed to all the public. Constantine removed cult statues from major temples and put them on show in Constantinople; they included the

Pythian and Sminthian Apollos, the tripods and Serpent Column from Delphi and the Heliconian Muses. These and other images were placed in the public places of Constantinople, including the Hippodrome and the palace, allegedly so that the citizens could laugh scornfully (54. 3) at their ignominious fate. Eusebius has to work hard, and draw on all his linguistic resources, to turn Constantine's beautification of his city with famous statues of antiquity ('un décor de statues', Dagron, *Naissance*, 36, 89, see also 373–76; 'civic display', S. Bassett, 'The Antiquities in the Hippodrome of Constantinople', *DOP* 45 (1991), 87–96; T. F. Madden, 'The Serpent Column of Delphi in Constantinople; Placement, Purposes and Mutations', *BMGS* 16 (1992), 111–45) into an anti-pagan gesture.

For Eusebius' satirical theme of Christian mockery of pagan gods and their images see *HE* 10. 4. 16; *LC* 8. 1–3, 8; *SC* 17. 13, and for criticism of the broader conclusions often drawn from this passage about Christian attitudes to pagan statuary see John Curran, 'Moving Statues in Late Antique Rome: Problems of Perspective', *Art History*, 17 (1994), 46–58. The statues remained on the *spina* of the Hippodrome until 1204 (Alan Cameron, *Porphyrius the Charioteer* (Oxford, 1973), 180–7; it was already in the sixth century 'packed with the statuary of 1000 years', p. 184). During the Byzantine period the statues were often misunderstood and suspected of magical or dangerous properties: see C. Mango, 'Antique Statuary and the Byzantine Beholder', *DOP* 17 (1963), 55–75; Liz James, ' "Pray not to Fall into Temptation and be on your Guard": Antique Statues in Byzantine Constantinople', *Gesta*, 35 (1996), 12–20. The remains of the Serpent Column can still be seen on the site of the Hippodrome in Istanbul today, and the four horses of Lysippus on the façade of San Marco, Venice.

54. 3. Another fate awaited the golden statues. *LC* 8. 4 similarly distinguishes between precious metal, melted down for reuse, and the 'heroes fashioned of bronze' which were carted away. Eusebius' standard rhetorical technique, faced with a necessary mention of pagan cult, is to resort to heavy sarcasm and scorn (54. 4); he reuses his earlier, highly apologetic, description from the *LC* (8. 1–7): in a reversal of the recent persecution of Christians, the pagan priests are ordered amid

Christian laughter to bring out their gods; no troops or force are needed, only one or two of his intimates (*gnorimoi*, 54. 5, cf. IV. 29. 4, 68. 1). The whole account is rhetorical and lacking in detail; despite the reference to 'communities and nations', 'city by city and country by country' (54. 6), no individual place or image is actually named, and Eusebius even resorts to a Homeric allusion referring to Constantine (54. 7, *LC* 8. 4, cf. *Od*. 4. 242).

55. *The shrine at Aphaca demolished*

The borrowing from *LC* 8. 4–7 continues throughout the chapter, except that here Eusebius names the site, Aphaca (55. 2), which Constantine had personally visited (55. 5). Each of these sites was, however, like Mamre, a special case (Lane Fox, *Pagans and Christians*, 671), whether the site of sacred prostitution like Aphaca and Heliopolis, or with particularly sensitive recent associations, like Aigai.

55. 5–56. *The temple of Asclepius in Cilicia demolished*

Eusebius omits the end of the section in *LC* (8. 9), adding instead two other examples, the first being that of the temple of Asclepius at Aigai in Cilicia. This was associated with the pagan sage Apollonius of Tyana, who had been the subject of a recent work by the pagan Hierocles of which Eusebius himself composed a refutation, the *Contra Hieroclem*: according to Philostratus's *Life of Apollonius of Tyana*, 1. 7, Apollonius had turned the temple into a 'holy Lyceum and Academy'. Like that of Apollo, the cult of Asclepius was booming in Greece and Asia Minor (other principal centres were Epidaurus and Pergamum) in the second and third centuries (see Lane Fox, *Pagans and Christians*, ch. 5; R. MacMullen, *Paganism in the Roman Empire* (New Haven, 1981), 28–34). Eusebius chooses his examples with care, but despite his claims, Aigai continued to function (Zon. 13. 12, referring to Julian in 352; Lib., *Ep*. 695. 2, 1342; Libanius blames Constantius II for its destruction, cf. *Or*. 30. 6, 37–9; 62. 4, 350, see Wiemer, 'Libanius on Constantine', 523–4; P. Petit therefore claimed that the reference in *VC* was a later interpolation, 'Libanius et la Vita Constantini', *Historia*, 1 (1950), 579–80; *contra*, F. Vittinghof, 'Eusebius als Verfasser der VC', *RhM* 96

(1953), 361–4). Similarly the oracle of Apollo at Didyma continued to function, although Eusebius claims that it was silent (*PE* 4. 2. 8; cf. 5. 17 on the end of oracles, with Barnes, *CE* 175–6, 179; P. Athanassiadi, 'The Fate of Oracles in Late Antiquity', *Delt. Chr. Archaiol. Etair.* NS 115 (1991), 271–8; it was a question of competition between pagans and Christians as to the authority of divine pronouncements.

56. 1. saviour and healer . . . those who slept near him, and sometimes healed the diseases . . . Eusebius does not deny that visions of the god and healings took place, but he sees them as demonic deception to keep souls from the saving truth. Asclepius was, like Apollonius, an obvious analogue for Jesus. His cures were brought about by incubation (sleeping in or near the temple) and dreams; thus he can be associated in Eusebius' mind with pagan oracles. The shrine of Asclepius at Epidaurus was described by Pausanias (2. 27. 1–3), and by Aelius Aristides in his *Sacred Tales*, and that at Pergamum by the sophist Polemo (Philostratus, *Lives*, 1. 25. 4), and the dreams and cures are recorded in many inscriptions and ex-votos.

56. 2. the vaunted wonder of the noble philosophers. i.e. Apollonius and his devotees.

the one who . . . could find no spell to protect himself. The inability of pagan gods to defend themselves is also the theme of *LC* 9 (cf. 9. 4 'not even Pythian Apollo himself, nor any other of the higher demons . . .'). Asclepius is named by Eusebius in company with Apollo at *SC* 13. 4.

57. General campaign against idolatry

57. 1–2. laughed and mocked . . . bones and dry skulls from dead bodies. cf. 54. 2, 3, and in general *SC* 13. Pagans attacked the Christian cult of relics on similar grounds (*SC* 11. 3).

58. The shrine of Aphrodite at Heliopolis demolished

Despite Constantine's actions (advocacy of chastity in a personal letter, 58. 2, cf. on **IV. 26. 2–5**, and the establishment of a church there, 58. 3), Heliopolis (Baalbek), with its great temple of Zeus, long remained a pagan centre, and was still a place of alleged pagan activity in the late sixth century. Phoenicia is singled out by Eusebius for its excessive pagan practices (*SC* 13. 7, where Heliopolis is also mentioned).

The claims made by Eusebius in III. 54–8 should be treated with caution. He gives few specific examples, twists his material to give it an apologetic meaning, and embeds his statements within a context of highly coloured and tendentious rhetoric. Though Eusebius can cite a few apparently parallel cases (see on **IV.** 25) it is going too far to claim (Barnes, *CE* 248) that the behaviour attributed to Constantine here 'should be presumed typical'; on the contrary, the destruction of temples is hard to demonstrate on a large scale before the reign of Theodosius I (see Curran, 'Moving Statues', 53–4, of Rome).

59–66. *Church Disputes Settled*

59–63. *Constantine's letters about Antioch*

As usual, Eusebius introduces the topic of disputes within the church with a reference to the spirit of Envy (cf. on **III.** 1. 1; **IV.** 41). The trouble at Antioch centred on its bishop Eustathius, a supporter of Nicaea exiled *c.* 328 or before (cf. Chadwick, 'Fall of Eustathius'; Barnes, 'Emperor and Bishops', 59–60); Eusebius himself was closely involved, having been attacked by Eustathius, and retaliated with counter-accusations (Socr., *HE* 1. 23. 8–24. 1), as well as presiding at the council which deposed him, but this is not revealed in the disingenuous account in the *VC*. Somewhat transparently, Eusebius includes three letters from the Emperor, one of them to himself (61. 1–3), omitting, he says, others which would have revealed the actual issues under dispute and in which Constantine attempted to mediate (59. 4–5); he thus passes over the truth, which was that Eustathius was likely to be reinstated (Barnes, *CE* 228). The letters make it clear that the Emperor had offered Eusebius the see, and that he had refused it; they demonstrate Constantine's earnest involvement with church affairs, and his Christian instruction (59. 4, cf. also 58. 2, 63. 3), though a deeper reason for including them is also self-promotion and self-defence on the part of Eusebius.

59. 3. the one who caused the sedition.   i.e. Eustathius.

60. Constantine's letter to the laity commends Eusebius of Caesarea for his 'learning and integrity' (60. 3) but proceeds to warn the congregation at Antioch that it must not poach a bishop from elsewhere; Eusebius duly took the point and declined (61. 1–2, 62. 1). A second council chose Constantine's nominee, Euphronius of Caesarea in Cappadocia (62. 2).

62. 1. For Acacius the *comes* see above, 53. 2. Theodotus, bishop of Laodicea, was apparently presiding. He and Narcissus of Neronias in Cilicia were those who with Eusebius himself were temporarily dismissed at the anti-Arian synod of Antioch in 325, but now returned to favour. It is no surprise that they wanted Eusebius to become bishop of Antioch. Theodorus was bishop of Tarsus, Alpheius of Apamea in Syria Secunda. Aetius is an unknown bishop; he can hardly be the eminent Neo-Arian theologian of that name (so Winkelmann, index, s.v.), for the latter was not even ordained deacon until at earliest 355.

63–5. *Suppression of sects*

For Constantine's decree against schismatics and heretics (64–5) see S. G. Hall, 'The Sects under Constantine', in W. J. Shields and Diana Wood, eds., *Voluntary Religion* (Studies in Church History, 23; Oxford, 1986), 1–13, and Øyving Norderval, 'Kaiser Konstantins Edikt gegen die Häretiker und Schismatiker (*Vita Constantini* III. 64–65)', *Symbolae Osloenses*, 70 (1995), 95–115. The decree is dated to 324 by Barnes, *CE* 224, so as to antedate the sympathy of Constantine for the Novatianists displayed at Nicaea (Socrates, *HE* 1. 10, cf. canon 8); it is dated to 325–6 by Norderval so as to fall between the Council of Nicaea and a decree permitting Novatianists to keep long-standing properties, dated to 25 September 326 (*CTh* 16. 5. 2 = P. R. Coleman-Norton, *Roman State and Christian Church* (London, 1966) i. 158). Eusebius however here places it after Nicaea and the troubles at Antioch, and may be right. Sects as well as the imperial church may have benefited from the lifting of persecution, and to some extent from privileges and exemptions granted to churches (cf. *CTh* 16. 5. 1, inhibiting such reliefs). The complaint about the long period of destructiveness (65. 1) suggests some lapse of time and led Hall to propose 328–30 as the true date, with a reversal of

policy on Novatianism. Earlier, Constantine had seemed to hold
that doctrinal disputes were of minor importance (*VC* II. 68. 2,
70–71. 3), but the canons of Nicaea concerned themselves with
the practical question of the treatment of heretics and schismatics
including Paulians (19) and Novatianists (8). Here Constantine's
language is violent; dissident groups are to have their churches
confiscated and are forbidden to hold meetings (65. 1); instead
they should join the Catholic Church (65. 2). Arguing for a
change of heart from a previously 'eirenic' policy: H. A. Drake,
'Lambs into Lions', *Past and Present*, 153 (1996), 29–30.

63. 2. under a cloak of sanctity.   Strict ecclesiastical discipline
was the rule for Novatians and Cataphrygians, sexual continence
and dietary abstinence for Valentinians and Marcionites. The
sects also had their saints, which made them even more
poisonous in Eusebius' eyes.

63. 3. An order to the provincial governors.   Eusebius
implies another decree, conceivably that of 1 September 326
(*CTh* 16. 5. 1, see above).

64. 1. Novatians, or Cathari, 'Pure ones', cf. Hall, *Doctrine and
Practice*, 88–9. This group renounced the main Church in the
250s because of the slackening of penitential rules under persecution, though they did not differ in doctrine. Eusebius regarded
them as a major threat, and may even have added them at the
head of the list in view of Constantine's favourable treatment of
them in 325 and 326 (see above). **Valentinians:** once a large
school among the so-called 'gnostics', whose inventive intellectu-
alism derived from Valentinus (mid-second-century; cf. Hall,
Doctrine and Practice, 39–45). **Marcionites:** followers of Marcion
(cf. ibid., 37–9), probably an earlier second-century figure.
Paulians: continuing followers of Paul of Samosata, the bishop
of Antioch condemned for heresy about 268 and finally ejected in
272 (ibid. 110–11). **Cataphrygians:** also called Phrygians or
Montanists, see ibid. 46–7, a second-century charismatic and
puritan sect deriving from Phrygia. It is notable that these are all
old-established groups. The contemporary divisions, Donatism,
Arianism, and Melitianism, were perhaps rather regarded as
splits within the Catholic body which were capable of reconciliation. Constantine sees heresy as diverting believers from the true
Church and thus making the healthy sick.

64. 3. The crimes done among you. It was usual to list all kinds of horrors as the work of heretics. But even without specific atrocities like cannibalism and incest, the sects were held to have committed the crime of traducing the imperial Catholic Church, which was to them erroneous and diabolic. Their personal virtues would only aggravate the offence by making their ideas seem plausible.

65. The ban on meetings and confiscation of buildings, including private houses used for meetings, are typical repressive measures like those of the persecutors which Constantine tries to correct. Since all the sects (except perhaps the Paulians) continued active, they cannot have been thoroughly enforced.

66. Eusebius concludes bk. III with his own comments on the letter and its effects, and presumably writes from personal experience of the difficulty of enforcing a genuine change of heart in compulsory converts.

66. 1. the books of these persons. The books of these groups were also to be 'hunted out' (66. 1), though this is not mentioned in the text as he has just given it, or in the law of 1 September 326; it may have been done on the initiative of zealous bishops. Constantine later ordered the burning of books by Arius and the anti-Christian Porphyry (Socrates, *HE* 1. 9. 30–1), and the practice has a long history among Christians (cf. Acts 19: 18–19).

Despite his intemperate language ('wild beasts', 'wolves'), Eusebius admits that many did join the Church, though some may have done so for the wrong reasons (see Ando, 'Pagan Apologetics and Christian Intolerance', 201); those not separated by doctrine were treated more generously (66. 3).

The book ends with a flourish: unity is restored, thanks to Constantine. Barnes, 'Panegyric', 115, sees in the praise of Constantine's offer of readmission a veiled allusion to the restoration of Arius and Euzoius.

BOOK IV

1–14. *The Prosperous Empire*

As the chronological progression draws nearer to Constantine's last years and the time of writing, bk. IV returns at first to a more conventionally panegyrical treatment (for the arrangement of the book as a whole see Drake, 'Genesis', esp. 25–6). Eusebius wishes to demonstrate first that the Christian monarchy established by Constantine has brought all the benefits to the Empire that pagan panegyrists claimed for pious pagan emperors, and which are made for Constantine by the Latin panegyrists, e.g. *Pan. Lat.* 4 (10) 35–6, AD 321. The claims are conventional, as are the accusations levelled against him in the contrasting account in Zos. 2. 38, based on Eunapius (see Barnes, *CE* 255–6).

1–4. *Philanthropy*

Despite his expressed intentions (I. 11. 1), Eusebius turns briefly first to secular matters, which also feature in the anecdotal material later in bk. IV. The order of topics (generosity; senatorial order; Goths and Sarmatians) is the same as in *Origo*, 30–2, which may raise the possibility of a common source, containing also the text of the letter to Shapur.

1. 1–2. he would honour each one of those known to him with special promotions. Eusebius wishes to illustrate Constantine's generosity (*liberalitas, philanthropia*: see Kloft, *Liberalitas Principis*, 172), but also points, though without explaining it explicitly, to a much more significant development, the enlargement of the senatorial order. The opposite view, according to which Constantine is blamed for greed, extravagance, and prodigality, is to be found in the pagan tradition: Aur. Vict. 40. 15 (but for his clemency cf. 41. 4), Julian, *Or.* 1. 6. 8b, with *Caes.* 335b, *Or.* 7. 22, 228a, Anon. *De Rebus Bellicis* 2. 1, Amm. Marc. 16. 8. 12, *Epit. de Caes.* 41. 16, Zos. 2. 38. 1 (see on **2–4**). Constantine needed to win supporters and conciliate by promotions or other means those who had backed Licinius (see Peter Heather, 'New Men for New Constantines', in P. Magdalino, ed., *New Constantines* (Aldershot, 1994), 11–33, at 15, on this passage, and see on **IV. 29–33** below). Eusebius describes the normal working of the imperial patronage system, But even he admits that Constantine's excessive benevolence or favouritism towards his friends earned him criticism (**IV. 31, 54**).

1. 2. some were appointed *comites* . . . Constantine formalized the order of imperial *comites* and divided them into three grades; these and other innovations in rank and titulature laid the foundations for the development of a highly structured late Roman bureaucracy (Jones, *LRE*, 103–6; C. Kelly, in *CAH* 13, 138–83; Heather, ibid. 184–210).

many thousands more shared honours as *clarissimi*. Eusebius makes sweeping claims for the scale of Constantine's bestowal of senatorial rank. But even if exaggerated, this extension of senatorial status (for which see also *Pan. Lat.* 4 (10). 35, AD 321), which allowed the re-entry of the Roman senatorial families into the government, besides admitting easterners and provincials to the order, laid the foundation for a major development during the late Empire (Heather, 'New Men'; Jones, *LRE* 106–7, 523–62; Barnes, *CE* 257). Eusebius does not state (as implied by Heather, 'New Men', 16) that Constantine founded a senate at Constantinople; according to *Origo*, 30, Constantine did so, though he called its members only *clari*, not *clarissimi*; see also Soz., *HE* 2. 3. 6. But Zos. 3. 11. 3 attributes it to Julian; Dagron, *Naissance*, 120–4, esp. 122, argues that the senate of Constantinople in Constantine's day was less a separate creation than the group of those who followed him or whom he established there, and to whom he gave senatorial status if they did not already have it (cf. also Zos. 2. 31. 3 on Constantine's establishment of houses for senators who accompanied him). The numbers were still small in Themistius' day, but rose dramatically by the end of the century (Jones, *LRE* 527). Like the senate itself, the Senate House at Constantinople was inevitably also attributed to Constantine, the founder (see Mango, *Le Développement*, 29, 33, 35; 'The Development of Constantinople as an Urban Centre', *Studies on Constantinople* (Aldershot, 1993), 1, at 124), though it is not mentioned in the *VC* and does not feature in Zosimus' list of Constantinian monumental buildings at 2. 30–1.

in order to promote more persons the Emperor contrived different distinctions. See Heather, 'New Men', for this increase in the size of the administration, the growth of which was to be one of the main features of the late Roman state. Nazarius, *Pan. Lat.* 4 (10). 35. 2, AD 321, praises Constantine for admitting the flower of the provincials to the Roman senate, but

Ammianus later thought that the reform went against ancient tradition and established order (21. 10. 8).

2. He removed a fourth part of the annual tax charged on land. For this and for the rest of the passage see Barnes, *CE* 255, 257–8; Aur. Vict., *Caes.* 40–1, confirms Constantine's granting of tax privileges, whereas Zos. 2. 38 paints a black picture of his new taxes, the *chrysargyron* and the *follis senatorius*, and of the oppressiveness of his regime in financial matters (cf. Lib., *Or.* 2. 38. 1). In financial as in administrative matters, it is difficult to put together a consistent picture from the tendentious and very incomplete literary accounts (Barnes, *CE* 255–8; Eusebius does not mention the *collatio lustralis*, a new tax much criticized in the pagan sources, Zos. 2. 38. 1); nevertheless, though partial, Eusebius' comments offer important contemporary evidence. Constantine's extravagance ('generosity', according to favourable accounts) is a constant theme in pagan critique: Julian, *Caes.* 335b; *Epitome de Caes.* 41. 6; Ammianus 16. 8. 12; it is contrasted with Licinius' *parsimonia* at *Epit.* 41. 3: see Wiemer, 'Libanius on Constantine', 520.

3. adjustment officers (*peraequatores*). These were officials appointed to deal with census adjustments or reassessments.

4. anyone who had stood before such an Emperor . . . As Drake has pointed out ('Genesis'), several details included in bk. IV suggest personal observation or information, quite possibly when Eusebius was in Constantinople for Constantine's Tricennalia in 336; see further below on **IV. 7.**

5–6. *Foreign relations I: Pacification of Goths and Sarmatians* Despite his intention expressed at I. 11 to exclude military affairs, Eusebius now turns to the conventional panegyrical theme of the Emperor as bringer of peace, if need be by military victory; Constantine brings the lawless tribes to civilized order, so that their individual members pass from bestiality to Roman freedom. Eusebius' claims about these dealings with former enemies and Constantine's mission to demonstrate the faith (cf. Rufinus, *HE* 10. 8), are confirmed by Constantine's letter to the Council of Tyre (Athanasius, *Apol. contra Arianos*, 86. 10–11; Gelasius, *HE* 3. 18. 1–13), and cf. Lib., *Or.* 59. 29, 39. For Constantine's treaty with the Goths (332), their federate status and his relations with them see Peter Heather, *Goths and Romans*

332–489 (Oxford, 1991), 107–15; *contra* Eusebius, both Julian and Themistius state that payments were still made (Heather, 'New Men', 109, 114, and on the evidence of Jordanes, 108–9). Constantine claimed victory and in 335–6 took the title Dacicus Maximus (Heather, 'New Men', 108–9; Barnes, 'Victories', 151).

7. Foreign relations II: Foreign tributes

constant diplomatic visitors . . . we ourselves were once present. Constantine receives embassies and gifts from the Blemmyes, India, and Ethiopia (see also IV. 50, ambassadors from India). The scene replicates a triumphal motif from imperial art, yet Eusebius claims that he was there and saw it himself; see Drake, 'Genesis', 26; B. H. Warmington, 'Virgil, Eusebius of Caesarea and an Imperial Ceremony', in C. Deroux, ed., *Studies in Latin Literature and History*, iv (Brussels, 1986), 451–60. Barnes, *CE* 253, suggests that this occasion was the culmination of Constantine's Tricennalia and that Eusebius probably saw the scene in the Hippodrome. Other indications of autopsy in bk. IV are at 33, 45, 46 (speeches made by Eusebius himself); possibly 49 (wedding of Constantius II, see Drake, 'Genesis'), 48 (the reaction of Constantine to excessive praise), 30 (his rebuke to an official for greed). Drake argues that Eusebius was already planning the work and collecting material in Constantinople in summer 336, and that he may have stayed in the capital until after Easter 337, bk. IV (of which Easter is 'an important sub-theme', Drake, 'Genesis', 29; see also the details of observation at IV. 22, 55, 56) being completed in draft by the end of the year (Drake, 'Genesis', 30–1); in Drake's view, Eusebius asked permission to write the *VC* late in 335 when he repeated for the Emperor the speech he had delivered on the Holy Sepulchre at Jerusalem (IV. 33)—the reaction was cool but he received encouragement for the project after his speech on the Emperor's Tricennalia delivered before him in 336 (Drake, 'Genesis', 30).

Eusebius' presentation of Constantine receiving gifts from eastern envoys, a theme taken up again in IV. 50, is seen as part of a sense of universal mission by G. Fowden ('The Last Days of Constantine: Oppositional Versions and their Influence', *JRS* 84 (1994), 146–70; cf. his *Empire to Commonwealth: Con-*

sequences of Monotheism in Late Antiquity (Cambridge, 1993), chs. 4 and 5), who also suspects ('Last Days of Constantine', 149) that **IV. 50**, referring to 'ambassadors from India' bearing gifts of jewels, may allude to a certain Metrodorus, referred to as a philosopher and traveller in several later sources. IV. 14. 1, with **IV. 50**, at least shows that Eusebius himself wanted to stress universal rule. But the theme is both a literary topos (cf. Warmington, 'Virgil', comparing it with the scene on the shield of Aeneas at *Aen.* 8. 720–31) and a regular theme in late antique imperial art, and Eusebius had himself already used similar ideas at *VC* I. 8; Eusebius thus drew on 'the most venerable clichés of military glory' (Warmington, 'Virgil', 458), though generally stressing the pacificatory more than the bellicose (ibid. 459).

8–14. 1. *Foreign relations III: Peace with Persia*

See Fowden, 'Last Days of Constantine', 146–53; T. D. Barnes, 'Constantine and the Christians of Persia', *JRS* 75 (1985), 126–36. Again the subject is taken up later in bk. IV, with an account of Constantine's final expedition (56, cut off by a lacuna in the text; see Fowden, 'Last Days of Constantine', 147). Here Eusebius places Constantine's dealings with Persia within the panegyrical topos of universal peace and in an apologetic context of Christian universalism. The date of this letter, perhaps sent in response to an Iranian initiative, falls between 324 and 337 (Fowden, 'Last Days of Constantine', 148 n. 11; Barnes, 'Constantine and Christians of Persia', 131–2 ('shortly after October, 324').

8–13. Constantine's letter to Shapur: the genuineness of this, which differs in some ways from the other documents cited (see below), is still commonly doubted: see e.g. A. D. Lee, *Information and Frontiers: Roman Foreign Relations in Late Antiquity* (Cambridge, 1993), 37; F. G. B. Millar, 'Emperors, Frontiers and Foreign Relations, 31 BC to AD 378', *Britannia*, 13 (1982), 1–25, at 2. For the tone ('deliberately aphoristic, allusive and indirect'), see Barnes, *CE* 258–9; 'Constantine and Christians of Persia', 131. Constantine none the less makes clear his claim to patronage over Shapur's Christian subjects (13); furthermore, Armenia had become Christian officially in 314, and Iberia became so about 330. In 324–5 the Latin poet Publilius Optatianus Porfyrius suggested that Constantine was already planning a Persian invasion (*Carm.* 18. 4). The politeness of this letter was a temporary diplomatic expedient: in 337 Constantine did plan the invasion, with a full panoply of religious propaganda to accompany it (for Eusebius' version, which differs from some later ones, see on **IV. 56** and see Fowden, *Empire to Commonwealth*, 93–7; Constantine as crusader: ibid. 96). For Constantine's sense of mission, see also **II. 28**, exemplified in his conquests from the Atlantic to the east.

8. This document also is in circulation among us, written by the Emperor personally in Latin . . . For Eusebius' claim to have a personal copy, cf. **II. 23, 47**. He may well have obtained it in Constantinople in 336 (so Drake, 'Genesis', 28); for Marianus the notary as a possible source see Warmington, 'Sources of Some Constantinian Documents', who takes *pheretai . . . par'* to mean 'is cited (or described) to' rather than 'is in circulation among', which is the more natural understanding. Taken with the absence of a heading or introductory greeting such as we have with every other letter of Constantine in Eusebius' account, this may suggest that Eusebius has this document from a secondary history or source. It is difficult to believe that even Constantine could have begun his letter to Shapur without some other remarks, before embarking on his religious history and advice. Either Eusebius, or his source, has omitted the opening. This is the only letter included by Eusebius on a secular theme, though Constantine's wish to protect the Christians of Persia was sufficient reason for Eusebius to include it. According to Barnes, 'Panegyric', 100, 'Eusebius intended this letter to follow those quoted in II. 24–60'.

9. this cult. The abruptness of the description suggests that Christianity has already been mentioned in the letter.

whose sign my army . . . carries on its shoulders. This is the miraculous standard of I. 28–32. Eusebius uses the same phrase of its bearers in II. 8. 1; 9. 1.

from these men. Constantine attributes his success to the prayers of the Christians. The whole passage conveys a veiled warning to Shapur that an anti-Christian policy will lead to conflict.

10. 1. abominable blood and foul hateful odours. i.e. animal sacrifice. One might suppose that here Constantine appeals to the common ground of Persian Zoroastrianism and Christian cult in rejecting such rites.

11. 2. that one, who was driven from these parts by divine wrath. Constantine clinches his familiar argument about the fate of the persecutors (see e.g. **II.** 54) with reference to Valerian, Emperor from 253. Valerian turned against the Christian Church (Eus., *HE* 7. 10. 1–4). He was defeated and captured by Shapur I in 260, an event recorded by Shapur in a great inscription and depicted on rock reliefs at Naqs-i-Rustam; Christian sources, e.g. Lact., *DMP* 5, recounted with satisfaction his ignominious treatment and his death after being flayed alive. For references see Dodgeon and Lieu, 57–65, with notes.

14. 2–39. *Constantine's Sanctity*

A variety of illustrations follow, designed to demonstrate the holiness and piety of the Emperor; to pagan critics, of course, Constantine was an example of impiety to the old gods (Jul., *Caes.*, 336b).

14. 2–16. *Personal piety*

15. 1. he had his own portrait so depicted on the gold coinage. A well-known gold medallion from Siscia dating from the Vicennalia (326–7) shows Constantine's head in this pose wearing a diadem, his head thrown back and his eyes raised as if to heaven (*RIC* vii, Siscia no. 206; cf. Fig. 9); in fact, though Eusebius does not say so, the type recalled depictions of Alexander the Great, also a deliberate choice from 325 onwards (see Smith, 'Public image of Licinius I', 187, and cf. Leeb, 57–62; H. P. L'Orange, *Likeness and Icon: Selected Studies in Classical and Early Mediaeval Art* (Odense, 1973), 85). For the idea expressed metaphorically, see *LC* 3. 5.

15. 2. he was portrayed standing up . . . in a posture of prayer. For the colossal statue of Constantine (Fig. 5) of which the head and arm and leg pieces are in the Musei Capitolini (cortile) see K. Fittschen and P. Zanker, *Katalog der römischen Porträts in den Capitolinischen Museen und in . . . alteren Sammlungen* (Mainz am Rhein, 1993–5), 2 vols., i, Text, pp. 147–52; Tafeln Tf. 149, nos. 120–1 and Tf. 151–42; Smith, 'Public Image of Licinius I', 185–6, for extant full-length statues; it may have been a reused statue of Maxentius. Eusebius shows an unusual awareness of the importance of visual representation (cf. **I. 40; III. 3; IV. 73**), even if he puts it to apologetic uses.

16. Such was the way he would have himself depicted. See on **15. 1.**

by law he forbade images of himself to be set up in idol-shrines. This seems to be contradicted by the Hispellum inscription from late in the reign (*ILS* 705= *ILCV* I.5, trans. Coleman-Norton and Bourne, no. 306; see on **II. 45**, and on statues, **III. 48. 2**), which permitted a temple to be erected in honour of the Flavian family, and games to be held. However, the decree explicitly requires that 'it should not be polluted by any contagion of the deceits of superstition'. This is taken by Dörries, *Constantine the Great*, 182–3; *Selbstzeugnis*, 209–11, 339, to imply secularization of the imperial cult, but the latter certainly continued (see Averil Cameron, 'Herrscherkult III. Altkirche ab Konstantin', *TRE* 15/1–2 (1986), 253–5). For the limited role of legislation in bringing about Christianization see David Hunt, 'Christianising the Roman Empire: The Evidence of the Code', in Jill Harries and Ian Wood, eds., *The Theodosian Code* (London, 1993), 143–60, at 157–60.

Fig. 9. Siscia, gold medallion of Constantine with uplifted head, AD 326. Trustees of the British Museum.

17–21. *Staff and military personnel*

Constantine's palace was like a church; he would read the Scriptures and pray with members of the imperial household. Constantine's scriptural study and inspiration: **I. 32. 3; II. 12. 1.**

in the manner of a church of God. Eusebius' assumptions about the nature of a church are interesting: it spends its time in studying and interpreting the Bible, and in 'lawful' prayers (that is, orthodox and in conformity with the regular daily practice of the churches). Such study and devotion may well be generally true of Constantine, even if here exaggerated; cf. **I. 32. 3; II. 12. 1.**

divinely inspired oracles. cf. **I. 3. 4; II. 12. 1; IV. 43. 3.**

18. 2. He therefore decreed . . . rest on the days named after the Saviour. In March 321 Constantine banned legal and similar business on 'the venerable day of the Sun', while encouraging agricultural work to take advantage of the weather (*CJ* 3. 12. 2). Four months later, acts of emancipation of children and manumission of slaves, which could now be carried out in churches, were also exempted from the ban (*CTh* 2. 8. 1; cf. Stevenson, *NE* 319). Neither text uses the Christian term 'the Lord's Day', as Eusebius implies. This passage repeats *LC* 9. 10, and cf. also *SC* 17. 14, with a very similar presentation of Constantine's role as Christian monarch (see Barnes, *CE* 249–50).

. . . the days of the Sabbath. Winkelmann, following Valesius, adds a word and reads ⟨*pro*⟩ *tou sabbatou*, 'the days *before* the Sabbath', on the basis of the fact that Sozomen later adapts this passage and makes it refer to resting from legal transactions on Fridays as well as Sundays, in honour of the crucifixion of Jesus on that day (Soz., *HE* 1. 8. 11–12; note *ten pro tes hebdomes*). There is no other record, however, of rest prescribed on Friday, the Christian fast-day, though various exemptions down to Justinian in the sixth century relieved Jews of prosecution on the Sabbath. It is better to keep the unanimous manuscript reading and assume that Constantine repeated this exemption for Jews in some form, and that Eusebius gives it a Christian interpretation, just as he interprets the legislation about the pagan day of the Sun as explicitly Christian. In contemporary Christian exegesis the rest of Jesus in the tomb on the Saturday between his crucifixion and his resurrection was taken as a fulfilment of the Sabbath law and God's own Sabbath rest (Exod. 20: 7); see further Hall, 'Some Constantinian Documents', 100–2.

18. 3. he taught all the military. Eusebius particularly stresses Constantine's measures on the army, though the surviving fragments of legislation are not so limited. Soldiers who are Christian are given time off to worship on Sundays; those who are not are required to join in prayer.

19–20. 2. he gave order in a second decree. Constantine legislates that non-Christian soldiers should be required to join in a common prayer every Sunday, for which the wording is here given (20. 1); Eusebius refers to this instruction in more general terms at *LC* 9. 10. The phrase 'just outside the city' suggests that Eusebius knows this only of the Constantinople garrison, and this fits the description of Constantine's sermonizing to the troops. Eusebius does not mind leaving the impression that it was universal in the army. The day (*dies solis*), the hands extended to heaven, and the address to God chiefly in terms of victories won indicate the cult of Sol Invictus, prominent both on Constantine's coinage and in features of the vision of I. 28. Eusebius tries to excuse this to his Christian readers by emphasizing that Constantine pointed the troops beyond heaven (and the sun), 'extending their mental vision yet higher to the heavenly King', who should be regarded as the true giver of victory. The prayer resembles that used by Licinius and his army in the campaign against Maximin Daia, said by Lactantius to have been dictated to him by an angel on the night before the battle, after which it was taken down and copies were distributed (*DMP* 46–7); it has been argued that both prayers had their origin in the meeting of Constantine and Licinius at Milan (A. Piganiol, *Mélanges Grégoire* (1950), 515). For Constantine's attempts to ensure the loyalty of the army in these ways see R. MacMullen, *Christianizing the Roman Empire AD 100–400* (New Haven, 1984), 44–6; a generation or more later, soldiers allegedly still remembered Constantine's harangues (ibid. 46, citing Theodoret, *HE* 4. 1. 4).

20. 2–21. Eusebius concludes his section on Constantine's Christian mission to his troops. The 'saving trophy' to be marked on their shields and carried before the army must be some form of cross. It might however have been a version of the *chi-rho*, like that used on the shields at the Milvian Bridge in Lactantius's account: see **I.** **28–31**, and for reliance on images of the gods by Constantine's enemies, **II.** 16. Grigg, 'Constantine the Great and the Cult without Images', 21, points out the looseness of Eusebius' term, 'sign', which might mean cross, christogram, or *chi-rho*.

22–3 *Domestic religion*

2. 21–2. On days of the Feast of the Saviour. Constantine kept enthusiastically the fast before and the feast of Easter. This culminates in the lighting of candles (22. 2) during the night of Easter Eve, and these are kept burning till dawn in honour of the resurrection. Eusebius may have seen this himself at Constantinople in 337 (Drake, 'Genesis', 29). The feast was of great importance to the Church and we may believe that Constantine turned it into a public holiday; his concern for its unanimous observance appears in the letter of III. 17–20; cf. also the exchange of **IV.** **34–5**, and his death at Eastertide, **IV. 60.** 5; 64.

23–5. *Christianity promoted and idolatry suppressed*

For the order and construction of this ('messy') passage see Barnes, 'Panegyric', 100.

23. every form of sacrifice banned. Cf. notes to **25.** 1 'in successive laws and ordinances he prohibited everyone from sacrificing to idols', and **II. 45**, also referring to a law forbidding sacrifice. Constantine's law forbidding sacrifice has not survived; see on **II. 45**. For the temple which he allowed to be erected to the Gens Flavia at Hispellum see on **16** above. Libanius, *Or.* 30, *Pro templis* (AD 388–91), claims that unlike Constantius II, Constantine had not disallowed pagan practices, cf. also Them., *Or.* 5. 70d–71a, calling Jovian a new Constantine for his religious toleration. But these sources are also tendentious: the extent to which Constantine did attempt to suppress pagan worship is therefore disputed (see, esp. on the interpretation of *VC* II. 48–60, T. D. Barnes, 'Constantine's Prohibition of Pagan

Sacrifice', *AJPh* 105 (1984), 69–72, with R. Errington, 'Constantine and the Pagans', *GRBS* 29 (1988), 309–18; S. Bradbury, 'Constantine and the Problem of Anti-Pagan Legislation in the Fourth Century', *CP* 89 (1994), 120–39). For his legislation on magic and divination (25. 1) cf. *CTh* 9. 16. 3 (318); 16. 1 (320), with 16. 2 (319). As in the conclusion of *SC* (16. 13–14), Eusebius links Constantine's measures against pagan cult with his positive prescription of Christian study and observance (see Barnes, *CE* 249); the Emperor bans sacrifice, magic, and idolatry, and encourages Christian worship by ordaining that Christian festivals be celebrated and Sundays kept holy.

reverence the Lord's Day. Eusebius has already paraphrased this enactment at length (above, **18–19**).

24. a bishop . . . over those outside. Constantine's alleged description of himself is one of the most famous and puzzling statements in the *VC*; see Winkelmann, 'Authentizitätsproblem', 236–38; D. de Decker and G. Dupuis-Masay, 'L' "Épiscopat" de l'empereur Constantin', *Byzantion*, 50 (1980), 118–57; J. Straub, *Regeneratio Imperii* (Darmstadt, 1972), 119–34, 134–59. The reference is surely to those outside the Church, though Fowden, *Empire to Commonwealth*, 91 n., takes it as a statement about mission, i.e. as referring to other peoples; otherwise 'the laity': see G. Dagron, *Empereur et prêtre: Étude sur le 'césaropapisme' byzantin* (Paris, 1996), 146–7. IV. 24 and 44 ('like a universal Bishop') regarded as interpolations: W. Seston, 'Constantine as bishop', *JRS* 37 (1947), 128–9. Both passages have given rise to speculation about their supposed implications for church-state relations. But the sentiment in each case fits with the theory expressed in *LC*, and here the remark is made in the context of a dinner-party (for Constantine entertaining bishops cf. also **III. 15. 1**; **IV. 46**), and as a kind of aside; while it does express both the Emperor's sense of mission and his way of acting, perhaps it should none the less not be taken too seriously (so Barnes, *CE* 270).

25. 1. gladiatorial combat. Constantine's general policy towards pagan worship had been set out in 324: qualified toleration, combined with official disapproval (Barnes, *CE* 211–12; cf. *CTh* 15. 12. 1, AD 325). In practical terms, he proceeded more by pursuing well-chosen examples of deplorable pagan practice than by attempting universal suppression; and though successive Christian emperors forbade gladiatorial games, neither they nor sacrifices could be legislated out of existence.

25. 2–3. With Constantine's measure against homosexual priests in Egypt compare **II. 55. 3.** Eusebius gloats over the sequel: the Nile rose even higher than before, as though a way had been prepared for it by the removal of pollution. See MacMullen, *Christianizing the Roman Empire*, 50, on this passage: Eusebius wrote 'no doubt with the text of the decree before his eyes'; on the basis of this and similar measures, 'the Empire had never had on the throne a man given to such bloodthirsty violence as Constantine. He could hardly control the tone of his proclamations.' *Pace* MacMullen, Eusebius does not actually say that the priests were slaughtered; at **III. 55** they are converted by the spectacle of the demolition of the temple. Admittedly the language is violent (cf. also on **III. 65**), but this is the style of all late Roman legislation from Diocletian on.

26–8. *Legislation and public charity*

26. 1. Eusebius has mentioned the 'countless' innovations in Constantine's legislation, and will now go on to his reforms of earlier laws. For a brief survey of his social legislation, emphasizing its piecemeal nature, see Liebeschuetz, *Continuity and Change*, 295–6.

2. 62–5. Ancient laws. Constantine's repeal of the Augustan marriage laws (*CTh* 8. 16. 1, AD 320), part of a general edict *ad populum* on the family and marriage, of which seven fragments survive, is presented by Eusebius solely in Christian terms (Barnes, *CE* 52); in fact it was more probably designed to please the wealthier classes and the senatorial aristocracy. Eusebius has selected this item from a much wider mass of legislation on marriage and family, which is not in total to be seen in Christianizing terms; other fragments from the law are listed by Barnes, *NE* 74 and in *Codex Theodosianus*, ed. T. Mommsen and P. Meyer (Berlin, 1905), i, pp. ccix–ccxiv, with a full list of the surviving fragments of Constantine's legislation on marriage and family in J. Evans-Grubbs, *Law and Family in Late Antiquity: The Emperor Constantine's Marriage*

Legislation (Oxford, 1995), app. I. See also ead., 'Constantine and Imperial Legislation on the Family', in Jill Harries and Ian Wood, eds., *The Theodosian Code* (London, 1993), 120–42, at 122–6. It is possible in this instance to compare what actually survives directly with how it is represented by Eusebius; see Evans-Grubbs, 'Abduction Marriage in Antiquity: A Law of Constantine (*CTh* IX. 24. 1) and its Social Context', *JRS* 79 (1989), 59–83, esp. 75–6; *Law and Family*, esp. 128–30. In 321 the Latin panegyrist Nazarius interpreted the legislation in terms of a restoration of morality (*Pan. Lat.* 4 (10). 38), with no special reference to Christianity, and Constantine's measures in connection with marriage were certainly much broader in their scope than that would suggest (see in general J. Beaucamp, *Le Statut de la femme à Byzance (4ᵉ–7ᵉ siècle)*, i (Paris, 1990), e.g. at 284–5). Severe legislation on adultery and divorce followed the events in Constantine's own family in 326 (Piganiol, *L'Empire chrétien*, 35–6 and for a list and discussion see Evans-Grubbs, *Law and the Family*, app. II; on *CTh* 3. 16. 1, AD 331, see 'Constantine and Imperial Legislation', 127–30).

Eusebius attributes the repeal of the Augustan legislation (apparently still in force in the early fourth century, cf. *Pan. Lat.* 6 (7). 2. 4, AD 307) to Constantine's desire for 'sacred justice', and suggests that the Emperor's prime motive was to remove penalties from those who had adopted a life of celibacy, 'through a passion for philosophy' (26. 3). Eusebius uses the Platonic terminology already current in Christian contexts; according to Piganiol, *L'Empereur Constantin*, 123–5, therefore, the law of 320 is to be explained in terms of Constantine's respect for philosophy, Christian or pagan. But the term seems to be an example of *philosophia* as specifically Christian 'asceticism', a common usage in the fourth century (Lampe, s.v., B5 and see below, 28. 1). Eusebius is a witness to the Christian ideal of virginity, and to developing monasticism; clerical celibacy was already an issue (cf. Canons of Elvira, 33; Ancyra, 10; Neocaesarea, 1, and for its discussion at Nicaea, not mentioned by Eusebius, Socr., *HE* 1. 11; Soz., *HE* 1. 23); the same concern is attributed to Constantine himself at 28. 1, 'he would all but worship God's choir of those sanctified in perpetual virginity'. But relatively few Christian celibates would have been affected by the Augustan laws, as they were mainly aimed at the socially prominent upper classes. The passage offers a clear indication of Eusebius' general methods; the effect is certainly one-sided. Thus he cites the law of 320 (cf. also *CJ* 6. 23. 15, on inheritances, dated to 339 in the MSS but in fact also part of the law of 320) as exemplifying Constantine's fairness and clemency (for which see Aur. Vict., *Caes.* 41. 4, 17), and praises Constantine for rectifying the defects of the original laws and using reason to make them more righteous. Admittedly he is not trying to give a complete picture of Constantine's legislation as a whole, but as Corcoran points out, he had criticized Licinius in the *HE* for bringing in very similar legislation (*HE* 10. 8. 11–12, cf. Corcoran, 'Hidden from History', 102); in fact Constantine's law of 320 was strictly speaking issued in the names of both emperors, however much Constantine (and Eusebius) tried later to separate the Constantinian from the Licinian (see Corcoran, 'Hidden from History', 103). Sozomen, *HE* 1. 9. 3–4, seems to know more about the Augustan legislation than Eusebius, and is more explicit as to Constantine's motives in repealing it; writing a century later, however, he is not necessarily more reliable.

While it did coincide with the main growth of Christian asceticism, the real importance of the removal of the Augustan constraints on inheritance was probably more strictly economic, for, combined with Constantine's enactment relating to legacies to the Church (*CTh* 16. 2. 4, AD 321), it opened the way for people to remain unmarried and to leave their property to the Church.

26. 5. for those near death ancient laws prescribed. Constantine's change is described in the context of Christianizing measures (cf. also 27) and is to be read as intended to prevent the circumvention of donations to the Church (see above); *CTh* 16. 2. 4 places a strong emphasis on the sanctity of a man's dying wish.

27. 1. no Christian was to be a slave to Jews. cf. *CTh* 16. 9. 1, Sirm. Const. 4 (AD 335), with a range of earlier laws, beginning in 315, regulating the condition of Jews (*CTh* 16. 8. 1–5); see Barnes, *CE* 252, 270, emphasizing the harshness of Constantine's attitude (as evinced in Eusebius' phraseology here), and on the dates of the legislation, 392 n. 74. Constantine's abolition of crucifixion and prohibition of branding on the face the image of the divine (see Barnes, *CE* 51) had a similar thrust. Cf. Aur. Vict.

41, with J. P. Callu, 'Du châtiment dans la cité', *EFR* 79 (1984), 313–59, especially 358 ff.

27. 2. Synodical rulings are to be given the imperial seal, so as to place the judgements of bishops above the wishes of governors. No such law survives, but the sentiment is typical of Constantine's exaggerated respect for bishops, claimed already e.g. in his letter to the Council of Arles, Optatus, *App.* 5 (AD 314). Eusebius does not refer here to Constantine's measures on episcopal jurisdiction (cf. Barnes, *CE* 51), but cf. Sozomen, *HE* 1. 9. 5 and see Hunt, 'Christianising the Roman Empire', and in general J. Gaudemet, *L'Église dans l'empire romain* (Paris, 1958).

27. 3–28. 1. Constantine established a grain distribution for the citizens of Constantinople, on the model of Rome (Dagron, *Naissance*, 530–5; J. Durliat, *De la ville antique à la ville byzantine: Le Problème des subsistances* (Rome, 1990)), but Eusebius' theme here is rather that of Christian charity. He stresses Constantine's generosity, especially to Christian celibates; cf. 'godly philosophy', 28. 1 (see on **26. 2–5**). 27. 3 is simply resumptive (cf. 26. 1), but in 28 Eusebius emphasizes Constantine's positive enthusiasm for Christian charity and Christian piety.

29–33. *Speaking and listening*

Eusebius provides a remarkable picture of Constantine as preacher, speaker, and listener (see Fowden, *Empire to Commonwealth*, 87). The Emperor, he claims, spent much time and care on personally preparing his speeches, and thought it his duty to expound the Christian principles on which his rule was based. Eusebius describes this activity as *philosophia*, which might however move into the field of *theologia* (29. 2). By the 'multitudes' who flocked to hear him (29. 2), Eusebius seems to mean the members of the court (*gnorimoi*, 29. 4), some of whom are made to feel ashamed by the Emperor's castigation. The Emperor did not spare them from detailed rebuke (29. 4), and told them that he must give an account to God not only of his own, but also of their activities (for Constantine's sense of responsibility cf. Opt., *App.* 3. 314).

Eusebius is naturally most interested in Constantine's style as a preacher, starting with his extreme reverence when speaking of

God (29. 2), and moving to his attacks on polytheism and his advocacy of the Christian God and the divine plan of salvation (29. 3). He then proceeded to criticize the personal shortcomings of his hearers (29. 4), warning them that they would have to face divine judgement (cf. also **IV. 55**).

For once Eusebius ventures a more personal note: the audience claimed to support the Emperor's views, and applauded him, but made no changes in their own conduct (29. 5). In the anecdote that follows (30. 1), surely based on personal experience, Constantine noticed this too, and retaliated, though still without effect (30. 2). Finally, Eusebius claims that the Emperor's clemency was a matter of complaint (31, see on **IV. 1. 1–2** above); this is claimed as a later interpolation by J. Seidl, 'Eine Kritik an Kaiser Konstantin in der *Vita Constantini* des Euseb', in E. Chr. von Suttner and C. Palock, eds., *Wegzeichen: Festgaben zum 60. Geburtstag von H. M. Biedermann* (Das östliche Christentum, 25; Würzburg, 1971), 83–94, but cf. III. 66. Eusebius drops his accustomed panegyrical mode and seemingly lets us see the awkwardnesses of life at the Constantinian court; writing from the standpoint of the rule of Constantine's sons, he allows for the possibility of a somewhat stricter regime.

29. 2. initiating the audience. For the language of initiation, above, 22. 1; below, 34, 35. 1, 61. 2–3.

32. Constantine's speeches: usually composed in Latin (cf. the letter to Shapur, II. 9) and professionally translated. The document at II. 48–60 is similarly translated by Eusebius (II. 47. 2). At Nicaea Constantine's speech was given in Latin and translated, though he conversed there in Greek too (III. 13). Eusebius promises to append to the *VC* a speech translated from Latin into Greek and entitled 'to the assembly of saints', usually identified with the surviving *Oration to the Saints* (see Introduction, p. 51), which includes all the features described in 29. 2–5.

33. 1–2. Eusebius' speech on the church of the Holy Sepulchre in Jerusalem, which Constantine allowed him to deliver in his own presence; Eusebius describes the rapt attention with which the Emperor received it, insisting on standing, adding his own pertinent comments and approval of its theology and refusing to sit down, or to allow Eusebius to break off or shorten it. See on

IV. 46, where Eusebius seems to describe a speech significantly different in content from the present one. Drake, 'Genesis', 22–5, suggests that the descriptive material about the site there mentioned, but not in *SC*, was later removed by Eusebius and used instead for the appropriate part of *VC* III. 25–40; another possibility (Barnes, 'Two Speeches'; *CE* 266) is that *SC* (chs. 11–18 of the hybrid speech that is preserved with the *VC*) is in fact a further speech by Eusebius on the same subject, and indeed Eusebius says at IV. 45 that he delivered several. The dedication of the church had taken place in September 335, and the recitation of the speech probably belongs to late autumn that year.

34–7. *Letters on Christian topics*

Letters between Eusebius and the Emperor; for the changes of subject, see Barnes, 'Panegyric', 100–1. Eusebius includes the text of two letters which he had himself received: at 35. 1–2, the Emperor's reply to a treatise which Eusebius had addressed to him on the meaning of Pascha, and at 36. 1–3 a request from Constantine to Eusebius for fifty copies of the Scriptures for Constantinople. It is reasonable to suppose that they belong in the same chronological context, i.e. after Eusebius' return to Caesarea late in 335 (33. 2).

35. Eusebius' treatise on Pascha, translated from Greek into Latin for the Emperor (35. 3), and explaining the differences of opinion about the festival (35. 1), is lost; Constantine claims to have read it himself, and to have ordered copies to be made as Eusebius wished. He urges Eusebius to write more such works. We do not know which dispute about the Pascha is in mind. It could still be that explained in the notes to **III. 5** and **III. 35–6**, which the Nicene decisions did not wholly settle. The reference here to 'its beneficial and painful bringing to fulfilment' could have subtle reference to recent developments in Jerusalem. The claimed discovery of the True Cross, which Eusebius does not mention, went with the beginnings of the cult of the death of Christ on Good Friday. Eusebius continues to regard the Pascha as a single feast in which the suffering of Christ is subsumed in his resurrection. It is not impossible that rumblings of this disagreement between Caesarea and Jerusalem underlay both this correspondence and the speeches about the Holy Sepulchre described in 33.

36. In the second letter Constantine requests that Eusebius oversee the production of fifty copies of the Scriptures for Constantinople, with leather bindings, the materials to be provided by the governor, together with two vehicles for their safe transport in the care of one of Eusebius' deacons. For another letter (on the see of Antioch) addressed by Constantine to Eusebius personally see **III. 61.** According to Barnes, *CE* 267, the tone now is respectful, but not intimate; however, the letters included here do signify a closer relationship between the two, while the request for copies points to the known Biblical scholarship of Eusebius and to an active scriptorium at Caesarea (Barnes, *CE* 124–5). The number does not mean that there were fifty churches in Constantinople at this date (Mango, *Le Développement*, 34–6, cf. **III. 48** for exaggeration by Eusebius).

37. threes and fours. These words probably mean only that he sent them three or four volumes at a time (see Barnes, *CE* 345 n. 139), but could imply three- and four-volume sets. The whole Bible could not be bound in a single codex, if the writing were of a size to read in church.

37–9. *Conversion of cities*

37–8. Heikel spotted that there must be a lacuna in the text here, in the middle of 37. An alternative would be to see the later part of 37 as belonging after 38, stating the evidence for the information given in 38. If so the dislocation could go back as far as hasty compilation by Eusebius himself.

37. Maiuma, the harbour-city of Gaza in Palestine, was given the status of a city and renamed Constantia after Constantine's sister, itself later becoming an episcopal see; *TIR Judaea and Palestina*, 175. However, Julian reversed this change (Soz., *HE* 5.3), and paganism was by no means suppressed in the area. Gaza remained a cosmopolitan city even after the destruction of the temple of Zeus Marnas in the early fifth century, for which see the *Life* of Porphyry of Gaza by Mark the Deacon, ed. H. Grégoire and M. A. Kugener, *Marc le diacre: Vie de Porphyre*,

évêque de Gaza (Paris, 1930). Sozomen, *HE* 2. 5 places this and
the case of Constantine in Phoenicia in the context of the general
suppression of idolatry and destruction of shrines mentioned at
VC III. 55–8, but without being able to add further named
examples, Eusebius too having resorted to sweeping generalization at this point (39. 2). An inscription records that Orcistus in
Phrygia similarly received city-status, at their request, in the light
of the Christianity of its inhabitants (*MAMA* vii. 305).

39. 3. Eusebius signals the end of a section and moves on to an
account of the last part of the reign.

40–52. *Final Achievements*

40–52. 3. *The Tricennalia and promotion of sons*

Only now in the body of the text does Eusebius come to the
subject of Constantine's sons and successors, and he does so in
an elaborate and forced conceit, likening them to the Trinity and
linking their respective promotions to the dates of Constantine's
anniversaries. In fact, though, Constantine II was born on 7
August 316 and proclaimed Caesar 1 March 317; Constantius
was proclaimed Caesar 8 November 324 and Constans on 25
December 333 (see Barnes, *NE* 44–5, 8). Constantine's eldest
son Crispus, Caesar in 317 and killed in 326, is not mentioned.

The year of Constantine's Tricennalia ended on 25 July 336.
For Eusebius' own movements during 335–6, and his visits to
Constantinople, see Drake, 'Genesis'.

41–2. *The Council at Tyre*

There is little in Eusebius' brief notice to explain why the
Council was summoned, or what was the point under dispute;
most of the space is given to the text of a letter from Constantine
summoning the Council, and the name of Athanasius, condemned by the Council and exiled by Constantine on 7
November, is not mentioned. Much of the reason for this
highly tendentious treatment lies in Eusebius' own involvement
in the ecclesiastical politics of 335–6 (see below).

41. Eusebius places the Council of Tyre (the metropolis of
Phoenicia, 41. 3–4) between the beginning of Constantine's

Tricennalia (25 July 335) and the dedication of the Holy
Sepulchre at Jerusalem (13–20 September); the bishops were
to proceed there from the Council, having settled their disputes
(41. 2). Constantine summons the Council after Envy has cast a
shadow over the general happiness (41. 1; see on **III. 1. 1, 59**). As
with the account of the Council of Nicaea, the true reason for
calling it (Athanasius' quarrel with the Melitians) is left unstated,
as is any suggestion that Athanasius was exiled for upholding the
decisions taken at Nicaea or that Constantine had agreed to the
reinstatement of Arius himself. Much had preceded the Council,
including Constantine's dispatch of a vitriolic letter to Arius in
332 when the latter was showing impatience at Athanasius'
continued intransigence (Barnes, *CE* 232–3); however, by 335
Arius was finally readmitted, with Constantine's agreement, by
the Council of Jerusalem (see on **43. 3** below, and cf. Barnes, *CE*
233–9; Norderval, 'Emperor Constantine and Arius', 135–43).

Eusebius himself was deeply involved in these events. After
Constantine's death Athanasius and the other exiled bishops
were allowed to return, with the result that while Eusebius was
writing the *VC* there was a real danger that Constantine's policy
in his later years, which Eusebius strongly supported, might be
undone; see Cameron, 'Construction'. He himself had gone on a
delegation to Constantine in Constantinople to persuade him to
accept the condemnation of Athanasius by the Council of Tyre
(Athanasius, *Apol. sec.* 9, 87; Sozomen, *HE* 1. 35). Here, to
include Constantine's letter summoning the council, while
omitting altogether both the reasons behind it and the complicated manœuvres which followed it, was a bold and disingenuous way of reminding his audience that Athanasius had indeed
been exiled. Athanasius gave a highly tendentious account of
these events in his *Apology against the Arians* (*Apol. sec.*) (Barnes,
Athanasius, 25–33), on which Socr., *HE* 1. 27–35 and Soz.,
HE 2. 25–8 depend. The disputed chronology of the Council
and the confrontation of Athanasius and Constantine in Constantinople, together with the meeting in Jerusalem and the
arrival of the bishops in the capital, depends also on the Syriac
Index to Athanasius' *Festal Letters* (ed. SC 317; Paris, 1985),
73 ff.); see Barnes, 'Emperors and Bishops'; H. A. Drake,
'Athanasius's First Exile', *GRBS* 27 (1986), 193–204; Hanson,
Search, 259–65.

41. Envy. See I. 49. 2, and note on **II. 60.**

41. 2. Eusebius portrays the Council of Tyre as a mere preliminary to the Council of Jerusalem, which is the greatest to date (47). This is not supported by Constantine's letter to the bishops at Tyre (42), nor by the other evidence, but suits Eusebius' own preoccupations; see Hunt, 'Constantine and Jerusalem', 419.

mean demon Cf. **I. 45. 2–3.**

41. 3. the divine Law forbids. See Matt. 5: 23–4.

42. Constantine's letter to the Council cited by Eusebius merely summons the synod and is included to impress the audience with the idea of the Emperor's concern for the peace of the Church; it is almost as bland as Eusebius' narrative. Contrast the highly emotional letter of Constantine cited by Athanasius, *Apol. sec.* 36, and repeated by Socr. 1. 34 and Soz. 2. 28, where the Emperor describes how Athanasius had stopped him in the middle of the road and demanded a hearing; after this, Socrates says (1. 35), some bishops went to Constantinople and produced a further charge against Athanasius. These were sensational events, in which Eusebius played a prominent role himself, but he has simply glided over them.

42. 3. Dionysius He was a former governor of Phoenice, and now apparently *consularis Syriae* (*PLRE* i, 259). His mission includes summoning Athanasius, who says he was reluctant to attend until constrained by his letter (*Ap. Sec.* 71. 2).

with a particular eye to good order. From Athanasius' viewpoint his enemies were given an armed guard (ibid.).

43–8. *The assembly in Jerusalem*

The Council of Tyre was followed by the assembly in Jerusalem and dedication of the church, after which Eusebius went to Constantinople and was present when Constantine himself exiled Athanasius on 7 November. All the more reason, when Constantine's sons were pursuing a conciliatory policy towards the exiles, for Eusebius' deliberate care in presentation. He gives the dedication ceremony a full literary treatment, highlighting his own role and the speeches he wrote for the occasion (45–6).

43. 3. Eusebius struggles to justify his view of the meeting in Jerusalem as a significant world-wide gathering. His rhetorical convention forbids names, but even so he can indicate only one metropolitan, presumably Alexander of Thessalonica. The young Pannonians are probably Ursacius of Singidunum and Valens of Mursa, who had been present at Tyre. The others cannot be readily identified, even the solitary scholar from Persia, and must have been comparatively minor bishops. They were apparently supporters of the current imperial theology, and directed the Alexandrian and Egyptian churches to reinstate Arius and his associates (Athan., *Syn.* 21).

44. the one in charge of all these things, a man close to the Emperor. Named as Marianus the notary in the *kephalaia* to this passage and by Soz., *HE* 1. 26, who says he had delivered Constantine's letter to the Council of Tyre (see *PLRE* i, Marianus 2); Warmington, 'Some Constantinian Documents', 95, also compares the phraseology of *VC* II. 63 and 73 (on the letter to Alexander and Arius), and suggests that Marianus, who receives 'more fulsome praise than any other individual in the *Life* except members of the dynasty', was Eusebius' source for the letters to Shapur and to Alexander and Arius, and possibly for other documents in addition. Like the Council of Nicaea, the festival of the dedication is made the occasion for banquets and a high level of imperial display and largesse (defended by Eusebius at *SC* 11. 3); Hunt, 'Constantine and Jerusalem', 419–21.

45–6. It is clear that numerous orations (45. 1–2) were delivered, including several by Eusebius himself (45. 3), and that their content, including that of Eusebius' own addresses, varied considerably. Cf. Hunt, 'Constantine and Jerusalem', 420 'this was indisputably an occasion of state'; as Nicaea had coincided with Constantine's Vicennalia, so his Tricennalia was celebrated at Jerusalem. The content of the present *SC* (chs. 11–18 of what has been passed down in the MSS as the *Tricennalian Oration, LC*), cannot be reconciled with Eusebius' description of his speech in 46, which seems to suggest a far more precisely descriptive account; see also on **IV. 32** and see Drake, *In Praise of Constantine*, 35–45; Barnes, 'Panegyric', 101, suggesting that the wrong speech was appended by the editor of the *VC*. But the mention here of 'works of art' and 'offerings' does not fit the passage on the church in *VC* III (see on **IV. 33. 1–2**), and he tells us clearly enough that there were several speeches, apparently differing from each other.

45. 2. disclosing hidden meanings This implies divining Christian truths in the Scriptures by allegorical and typological interpretation, in this case texts understood to refer to the buildings being dedicated (cf. III. 33. 2). The priests with less literary skill 'propitiated God with bloodless sacrifices' (a phrase regularly used to describe the eucharist or mass), as well as with other rites and prayers.

45. 3. symbolic rites. For the meaning of *symbolois* (rites, liturgy) and for the looseness of Eusebius' terminology, see Grigg, 'Constantine and the Cult without Images', 4–5.

46. the Emperor's works of art and large number of offerings. See Grigg, 'Constantine and the Cult without Images', for the question of whether Constantine's churches had figural decoration or statuary, as is claimed e.g. of the Lateran basilica in Rome in the later *Liber Pontificalis*.

he dined with the bishops present. cf. III. **15** (Nicaea, explicitly recalled at 47); **IV. 24.** Eusebius claims that Constantine enjoyed his performance, though he cannot quote actual words; cf. **IV. 33** above. The chapter interrupts the context of the Council (Barnes, 'Panegyric', 101, also claiming that the opening of 47 refers back to 45).

47. Eusebius compares the meetings of bishops at Nicaea and at Jerusalem, one connected with the Vicennalia of Constantine, the other with his Tricennalia, and one with victory, the other with peace. His elevation of these two synods as symbols of Constantine's success in bringing peace to the Church is wholly artificial. Various other councils are ignored, and the continuing and growing controversies between Athanasius and most of the eastern Church made to seem insignificant. Moreover, the decision taken at Jerusalem about Arius was in complete reversal of the events which followed the Council of Nicaea, something which the disingenuous account of Eusebius does its best to obscure.

48. He was annoyed on hearing these words. Another personal touch (above, on **IV. 7**).

49–50. *The universal Empire*

The marriage of Constantius (his second son after Constantine II, Crispus being omitted) to a daughter of Julius Constantius, see Barnes, *NE* 45; the identity of Constantine II's wife is unknown. A glimpse is given of the domestic life of the imperial family, again accompanied by imperial largesse.

50. For the embassy from India see on **IV.** 7 of which this is a doublet. The incident illustrates Constantine's universal rule, from Britain to the far east; the domestic happiness of ch. 49 is extended to the whole world in ch. 50.

51–2. 3. *Sons prepared for succession*

Eusebius reports that Constantine 'divided the government of the whole Empire among his three sons' (51. 1). Though the chronological indicator is vague ('now that he was in control of both ends of the entire inhabited world'), Eusebius refers to 335, when Constantine made a constitutional settlement, obviously with the succession in mind; see Grünewald, *Constantinus*, 150–3. The true picture was less clearcut than he presents it here: while *VC* IV. 51 speaks only of the three (*sic*) sons of Constantine, *Origo*, 35, makes it clear that they shared their power with Dalmatius, son of Flavius Dalmatius, consul 333, and grandson of Constantius Chlorus, declared Caesar on 18 September 335, and his brother Hannibalianus, who was made 'king of kings and of the Pontic peoples' and given Constantine's daughter Constantina in marriage. In addition to the areas designated for the sons of Constantine, Dalmatius was assigned the *ripa Gothica* (*Origo*, 35; for commentary see König, *ad loc.*); see also Eusebius himself at *LC* 3. 4, where he refers to Constantine metaphorically yoking the 'four Caesars' to his quadriga. It is unlikely that the three princes alone received the retinue mentioned at 51. 3, and indeed a praetorian prefect attached to Dalmatius may be indicated by a North African inscription (*AE* (1925), 72; see Barnes, *NE* 134–6; G. Dagron and D. Feissel, 'Inscriptions inédites du Musée d'Antioche', *Travaux et mémoires,* 9 (1985), 421–61). Hannibalianus and both Dalmatii were among those killed at Constantinople in 337 (Zosimus, 3. 40. 3; Julian, *Ep. ad*

Ath. 270c); thus Eusebius had good reason to do as he did earlier in the case of Crispus, and in this case to cover up both the extent to which they had been honoured by Constantine and the guilt attaching to Constantius II. The technique of omission is standard in political panegyric (in line with the official practice of *damnatio memoriae*); cf. Libanius, *Or.* 59 (344–5), where Constantine II is likewise unmentioned; see Wiemer, 'Libanius on Constantine', 513. Eusebius eulogizes Constantine's sons with an unctuous passage about their upbringing and the careful Christian training they had received from their father (cf. the similar treatment given at *VC* I. 13–18 to Constantius Chlorus, and cf. also Lib., *Or.* 59. 17–47, where Wiemer, 'Libanius on Constantine', sees the *VC* as a possible source, though the emphasis is secular). Eusebius takes care to say that the princes were receptive to this instruction (**52. 2**), and treats them as equal, although Constans was younger than his brothers (born in 320 or 323; Barnes, *NE* 45) and had been declared Caesar only on 25 December 333. The effect is to enhance the image of Constantine effectively ruling through his sons which opens and closes the work (**I. 1. 3; IV. 71. 2**; see also Grünewald, *Constantinus*, 160, and cf. *LC* 3. 4), and indirectly to promote Eusebius' view of how they should themselves rule. This passage at least must postdate summer 337, and antedate 340 when Constantine II was killed (Zos. 2. 41).

52. 3. even of the highest officials. Eusebius still finds the adherence of such men to Christianity somewhat remarkable.

52. 4–73. *Baptism and Death*

52. 4–55. *Constantine's physical health and faith in immortality*

Eusebius praises in turn Constantine's physical, spiritual and mental qualities. He was physically fit up to the time of his death, which according to most of the narrative sources fell when he was 64 or 65 (53; discussion: Barnes, *NE* 39–42); at I. 8 Eusebius says the Emperor lived twice as long as Alexander, and began his reign at about the age when Alexander died. For Constantine's physical appearance at the Council of Nicaea see *VC* III. 10. 3–4. Eusebius goes on (54. 1–3) to remark on his generosity and kindness, for which he was sometimes criticized (cf. also **IV. 31**), testifying directly to his personal observation (54. 2); Constantine's *clementia*: Lib., *Or.* 19. 19; 20. 24. Constantine had detractors: he was even held by Eusebius himself to be too tolerant of rapacity in his officials, and, interestingly, too trusting of people who deceitfully professed Christianity (54. 2–3; see Ando, 'Pagan Apologetics and Christian Intolerance', 201). Eusebius' assertion that such people were soon punished by God (55. 1) suggests that these were well-known figures. Dalmatius and Hannibalianus and their associates, who perished in the massacre of 337, might be meant, but we cannot tell. Pasquali, 'Die Composition', 383, followed by Barnes, 'Panegyric', 101, saw this as related to the restoration of Athanasius from exile by Constantine's sons; Barnes further suspects the first sentence of 55 as an editorial connection.

55. 1. to the very end he continued to compose speeches. Constantine's enthusiasm for instructing his subjects is one of the strongest impressions left of him by the *VC* (see 28–32 and cf. **III. 12**). Before he died he even delivered a kind of funeral oration (55. 2) in which he discoursed on the immortality of the soul and on divine punishment. Again Eusebius suggests that there were particular targets—not just pagans, but some among his own inner circle; he does not draw any Platonic or other parallels. Constantine turned to a pagan philosopher present and directly asked for his opinion. According to Athanasius, Antony, too, felt his death coming and discoursed to his monks (*V. Ant.* 89–91); he had also debated at length with pagan philosophers.

56–7. Preparations for war against Persia

According to *Origo*, 35, Constantine died *in suburbano Constantinopolitano villa publica* near to Nicomedia while making ready an expedition against Persia. The text of *VC* breaks off at 56. 3 with a lacuna of half a page and resumes in the midst of Eusebius' description of Constantine's mausoleum (see below). The Geneva edition of 1612 has a supplement, printed in Winkelmann's *apparatus* and translated here, which may be no more than an expansion of the *kephalaion*, according to which Constantine took bishops with him on the expedition, and a tent made like a church, received a Persian embassy, and took part with the rest in the Easter vigil.

For the sources, motives, and chronology of the Persian expedition see Barnes, 'Constantine and Christians of Persia', esp. 133–4; Constantine had already responded to Persian aggressive moves by 336 and was making the expedition ready in 337 when he died at Nicomedia on 22 May, whereupon Shapur invaded Mesopotamia. The *gloria exercitus* issues of the end of the reign no doubt relate to these plans (Fig. 10 and see Grünewald, *Constantinus*, 159). Fowden's version ('Last Days of Constantine', 146–53; cf. *Empire to Commonwealth*, 94–7) is more highly coloured: finding it a problem that Eusebius turned so quickly to another topic, he suspects that the text of Eusebius has been bowdlerized by later generations wishing to save Constantine's reputation against a possible charge of war-mongering; indeed, Gelasius of Cyzicus claims that Constantine abandoned the campaign out of concern for the Christians of Iran (*HE* 3. 10. 26–7). But this is to underestimate Eusebius' skill in dealing with awkward material, which is amply attested in this book and earlier in the *VC*; he was well enough practised, in particular, at disguising a war of aggression as a religious campaign. Libanius, *Or.* 59. 126 understandably gives different, i.e. non-religious, motives, and the later church historians (Ruf., *HE* 10. 12; Philost., *HE* 2. 16; Socr., *HE* 1. 39; Soz., *HE* 2. 34. 21; Theod., *HE* 1. 32) omit or play down the Iranian campaign for their own reasons, but Fowden's suggestion ('Last Days of Constantine', 152) that someone from this circle deliberately removed the offending passage from Eusebius' text is not convincing. It is true that the transition in the *VC* from Iranian

Fɪɢ. 10. (*a*) Nicomedia, ᴀᴅ 336–7, *gloria exercitus* type, obv. (*b*) Same, rev. Trustees of the British Museum.

campaign to mausoleum seems awkward, but Eusebius had to move on to the baptism, death, and funeral of Constantine, and a description of his mausoleum does not seem out of place.

The lacuna in the text of half a page recorded (as the chapter headings indicate) how Constantine took bishops with him, and his prayer-tent, and (57) how he received a Persian embassy and kept night vigil with others at Easter. Fowden, 'Last Days of Constantine', 147, argues that Socrates, *HE* 1. 18 reflects part of the missing passage.

58–60. *The shrine of the Apostles*

The accustomed vagueness of Eusebius' language in this passage, combined with the fact that it follows immediately on from a lacuna in the text, makes it difficult to be sure what he is describing. Certainly there has been some earlier description; the first words of 58 do not at present read like the opening of a new section, and later in the fourth century, *c.*380, Gregory of Nazianzus refers in a poem to the building as cruciform (*PG* 37. 1258); does Eusebius describe a church as well as a mausoleum, or only the latter, in which case we would have to assume that the church was built later, probably under Constantius II? Scholars have put much weight on the use of the word 'shrine' (*neon*) at 58. 1 as indicating a church, and cf. **70. 2** below, but C. Mango has recently concluded, against, e.g. Krautheimer, *Early Christian and Byzantine Architecture*, 72–3, that the description as we have it is only of a mausoleum (*martyrion* according to the Greek chapter heading) ('Constantine's Mausoleum and the Translation of Relics', *BZ* 83 (1990), 51–61, with earlier bibliography, esp. 55–9, with translation of this passage at 55); *doma* and *domation* seem to mean simply 'building', 'room' (so Mango). Others, e.g. Leeb, 93–120, suppose that only a church is described; see further below, and see also Bonamente, 'Apoteosi', 118, cited on 71–3.

The passage is characteristic of Eusebius' descriptions of churches (see on the Holy Sepulchre, III. 29–40, the church at Antioch, III. 50, and cf. his panegyric on the church at Tyre, *HE* 10. 4. 2–71, esp. 37–45, all of which which closely resemble the description here). The present building has a gilded coffered ceiling (58, cf. **III. 32**, and on **36**) and is decorated with 'various stones', probably marble; it is set in a porticoed quadrangular court with many rooms for practical purposes (59). This may seem indicative of a basilica; however, Leeb, 93–120, and cf. 'Zum Ursprung des Kaiserbildes im Kreuz', *JÖB* 41 (1991), 1–14, argues, against Mango, that the building described is a cruciform church (see also Krautheimer, *Early Christian and Byzantine Architecture*, 72–3), and that *domation* refers to a construction round the tomb similar to the edicule over the tomb of Christ in the church of the Holy Sepulchre (see on **III. 34**).

For the argument of G. Downey, 'The Builder of the Original Church of the Apostles at Constantinople: A Contribution to the Criticism of the Vita Constantini Attributed to Eusebius', *DOP* 6 (1951), 53–80, that chs. 58–60 and 70–1 are interpolations, see Winkelmann, 'Authentizitätsproblem', 238–9.

60. 1. to perpetuate . . . the memory of our Saviour's Apostles. There is no suggestion here of two buildings. Eusebius goes on to reveal Constantine's intention—this was to be his own mausoleum, where prayers would be said on his behalf, and he might 'after death partake in the invocation' (*prosrhesis*, on which see Mango) 'of the Apostles', and *therefore* (60. 2, *sic*) he gave instructions for services also to be held there and set up a central altar. This sounds like a circular *martyrion* (memorial), although that term is applied by Eusebius equally to basilicas (above, on **III. 33**); only one construction is being described, see esp. Mango, 'Constantine's Mausoleum', 57; so also Leeb, though critical of Mango. It is typical of Eusebius to suggest, however implausibly, that no one knew Constantine's real intention; he likewise stresses the element of surprise in the discovery of the cave of the Holy Sepulchre (**III. 28**). Both are instances of a conventional panegyrical device designed to cast more glory on Constantine.

60. 2. his own remains. *skenos*: earthly dwelling, tabernacle, i.e. the body.

60. 3. he erected twelve repositories. *thekas*: 'coffins' (Mango, 'Constantine's Mausoleum'). For the meaning and intention see further Mango, 59–60, with P. Grierson, 'The Tombs and Obits of the Byzantine Emperors', *DOP* 16 (1962), 1–63, at 5. Constantine's sarcophagus (*larnax*) was in the middle, surrounded by those of the Apostles, perhaps with effigies and inscriptions (so Mango, 'Constantine's Mausoleum', 55). In this tomb Constantine was later buried (IV. 70–1); his son Constantius II was buried beside him in 361. For the translation of the relics of SS. Timothy, Luke, and Andrew in 356 and 357, and for the later history of the mausoleum see Mango, 'Constantine's Mausoleum', 56. The arrangement whereby Constantine's tomb stood in the middle of those of the Apostles, thereby implying an identification of himself with Christ (so also Leeb, 103–10, 115; Krautheimer, *Early Christian and Byzantine Architecture*, 'its connotation was that of the heroon-martyrium of the Emperor himself; where he rested in the sign of the cross'), may seem to us to be in bad taste, but nothing suggests that Eusebius felt the same (*contra*, Mango, 'Constantine's Mausoleum', 59–60 and cf. **IV. 71**); the Apostles are treated as if they are the divine *comites* of the Emperor, while what survives of Eusebius' description of the mausoleum with its porticoed atrium indeed recalls the church of the Holy Sepulchre at Jerusalem. Finally, the construction claims a status for Constantinople rival to that of Rome as being under apostolic protection, even if not an apostolic foundation (though in fact Timothy and Luke were only 'second-generation apostles', Mango, 'Constantine's Mausoleum', 59).

60. 5. Constantine's final illness comes upon him as he completes the Easter celebration.

61–4. *Illness, baptism, and death*

There is no mention here of Constantine's being on campaign; the narrative implies that he went to the hot baths in Constantinople and then to Helenopolis, on the south of the Gulf of Izmit, as soon as he became ill on Easter Day, and from there had proceeded as far as the outskirts of Nicomedia when he 'called together the bishops' (61.3) and was baptized. Eusebius does not here connect the Emperor's movements with his Persian plans which had been interrupted by the festival of Easter (see above for the lacuna at ch. 57), but there seems no reason to suspect deliberate tampering with the text or to suppose that Eusebius himself is hiding something (Fowden, 'Last Days of Constantine', 147–9; 150–1 'Eusebius was obliged to fudge the narrative at IV. 57'; 152 'this expurgation of Eusebius'; cf. also

Empire to Commonwealth, 97). Indeed, the chapter heading to the missing ch. 57 indicates that Persian envoys had arrived shortly before Easter, and Socr., *HE* 1. 18. 12, probably drawing on Eusebius, suggests that agreement was reached on the strength of the 'fear' they felt before the Emperor. See Richard Burgess, '*AXYPΩN* or *ΠΡΟΑΣΤΕΙΟΝ*. The location and circumstances of Constantine's death', *JThS*, NS 50 (1999), 153–61.

61. 1. hot water baths of his city. Eusebius makes Constantine fall ill on Easter Day; he then visits the baths in Constantinople, from where he proceeds to Helenopolis and thence to Nicomedia, near which city he is baptized. *Pace* Fowden, 'Last Days of Constantine', 147, Eusebius does not say that Constantine went to the Pythia Therma, hot baths at Helenopolis.

61. 1. the city named after his mother. Helenopolis in Bithynia, formerly Drepanum, said to be Helena's birth-place by Procopius, *Aed.* 5. 2. 1–5 and much developed by Justinian. Drepanum was associated with the martyr Lucian (cf. 'chapel of the martyrs') and renamed after Helena by Constantine: Jerome, *Chron.*, *Chron. Min.* 1. 450; see Drijvers, *Helena Augusta*, 10–11. For its importance as a cult-centre under Constantine and Constantius II, see H. C. Brennecke, *Lucian von Antiochien*, *TRE* 21 (1991), 474–9.

61. 2–3. Constantine becomes a catechumen and seeks baptism. The language throughout cc. 61–4 is that of initiation: cf. the references to purification, secrets, seals, rebirth, brightness, and ascent (see on **III. 25–8, 26. 2**); for the baptismal ceremonies and the fourth-century texts see E. Yarnold, *The Awe-Inspiring Rites of Initiation*, 2nd edn. (Edinburgh, 1991). The Emperor died at Pentecost (64), the last day of the Easter festival, 22 May 337, after his baptism. It was usual to be baptized at the Easter vigil, after intensive preparation during Lent, preceded by a catechumenate often of three years in duration. Constantine's decision was by these standards precipitate, but for Eusebius it was sufficiently remarkable that he should have made it (62. 4); the instruction in doctrine and scripture reported in I. 32 might be thought to have covered the ground whether that account is historical or not. In fact, infant baptism was not yet the norm, and a decision to be baptized was taken very seriously and involved much solemn preparation, so that despite what has often been imagined, Constantine's late baptism carries no implication that the Emperor was unsure of his faith. Nor is it surprising (*pace* Fowden, 'Last Days of Constantine', 153) either that he was baptized by Eusebius of Nicomedia or that Eusebius is not named here; Eusebius, bishop of Nicomedia, became bishop of Constantinople soon after Constantine's death and was already the highly influential leader of the pro-Arian group to which Eusebius of Caesarea also belonged (see above, on **IV**. **41–2**), while it is standard practice for Eusebius of Caesarea as for other panegyrists to leave even major figures unnamed (see above on **IV**. **43**. **3**; Eusebius of Nicomedia is also unnamed in the account of the Council of Nicaea at **III**. **11**. **1**, and cf. **7**. **2**). On the other hand, it is interesting (Burgess, 'Date and circumstances'), that the army and various military commanders are present (63.2; 65. 2; 66. 1).

The baptism of Constantine became the subject of legends and apocryphal accounts, and was soon relocated in Rome and ascribed to Pope Sylvester, eventually becoming the basis of the medieval 'Donation of Constantine';· the *Actus Sylvestri* version was known to John Malalas (sixth century.) and can be traced to the late fourth or early fifth century, see Dagron, *Empereur et prêtre*, 156–8; Lieu and Montserrat, *From Constantine to Julian*, 27–8, Fowden, 'Last Days of Constantine', 153–70 (although the early stages of the transmission are likely to be more complex than the stemma at 166 implies).

61. 3. making confession. It was usual for a baptismal candidate to confess sins, either generally or with particulars (Yarnold, *Awe-Inspiring Rites*, 15–16). The 'laying-on of hands' at this stage in proceedings is not otherwise paralleled; it could signify remission of sins, or a welcome into the fellowship of those awaiting imminent baptism. When 'he called together the bishops' it may be that those assembled for his campaign are in mind (see **57**).

61. 3. the suburbs of Nicomedia. According to *Origo*, 35, Constantine died 'in a suburban villa of Constantinople'; the rest of the tradition, including Orosius, 7. 28, 31 (and cf. e.g. Eutrop. 10. 8. 2; Jerome, *Chron.*, AD 337) refer to a *villa publica* near Nicomedia. The term *proasteion* used by Eusebius might perhaps be translated 'suburban villa'. The place is named as

Acyron or Achyron (e.g. Aurel. Vict., 41. 16, Jerome, *Chron.*, AD 337); see further Burgess, 'Date and circumstances'.

62. 1. Constantine announces to the bishops his desire for baptism ('the seal that brings immortality'), which he says he had once hoped to receive in the River Jordan (an ambition whose presumption attracts no criticism from Eusebius); it is now likely to be a deathbed baptism, but if the Emperor lives, he is ready to change his way of life (62. 3). This change involves attaching himself to the intimacy of the worship he is now allowed to join, and accepting moral standards, which certainly for many Christians, and perhaps even for Eusebius, were not thought compatible with the military and civil duties and worldly commitments of an emperor. But Constantine did not survive and we cannot rely on the historicity of his reported words.

62. 4. they in their turn performing the customary rites . . . These would include anointings, exorcism, triple immersion in water, and laying-on of hands. Eusebius does not go into detail; he is more interested in making the comment which follows about Constantine's extraordinary innovation in being the first emperor to seek baptism. There is no precise detail there either; rather, as so often elsewhere, Eusebius projects onto Constantine his own interpretation. Similarly Corippus (see on chs. 65–7 below) devotes his rhetorical art to Justinian's funeral procession and mourners rather than to the actual burial.

62. 5. he put on bright imperial clothes which shone like the light. Constantine dresses in white as was usual for a Christian initiate in the days following baptism, and rests on a white couch; he has given up the imperial purple as a sign of his new status, and says that those who do not share it are to be pitied. Eusebius does not claim a direct source for Constantine's final words, but he does have circumstantial detail. The Emperor receives the soldiers and officers (63. 2), who are bewailing their imminent loss in formal acclamations ('wished him extension of life'), and urges them to take the same step. Constantine and acclamations: see C. M. Roueché, 'Acclamations in the Later Roman Empire: New Evidence from Aphrodisias', *JRS* 74 (1984), 181–99, at 186.

63. 3. he made disposition of his property. The 'Romans living in the imperial city' (Rome, rather than Constantinople, seems to be meant; cf. 69. 1) are singled out for special grants, while Constantine hands over the Empire to his sons like an inheritance. The account of Constantine's death in Socrates, *HE* 1. 39–40 was influential on later writers; it is partly, but not completely, dependent on the *VC*, and Socrates' version of Constantine's will (*HE* 1. 39. 3) comes from Rufinus, *HE* 10. 12; see Burgess, 'Date and circumstances', for full discussion of this and later variant traditions about Constantine's death.

64. 1. Each of these events. Constantine's illness, preparation and baptism fall in the seven weeks between Easter and Pentecost, and his death on the day of Pentecost itself (64. 2); for Eusebius, 'Pentecost' is the whole of this period. Constantine is 'taken up to his God' as Christ also ascended to heaven (64. 1); at the same time, however, his ascent is a traditional theme in the funerary rites for pagan emperors (see on **73** below).

about the time of the midday sun. The same portentous circumlocution is used of Constantine's vision of the cross (**I. 28. 2**). Eusebius himself seems to respect the symbolism which enables Constantine to reconcile the cult of the sun with the Christian faith (cf. also **IV. 19–20** and Introduction, p. 45).

he bequeathed to mortals . . . Constantine's mortal remains are left behind, while he unites his soul to God. Eusebius then concludes the section with dignified brevity, marking a transition to the necessary description of the mourning, funeral, and succession.

65–7. *Mourning and lying-in-state*

Eusebius describes the mourning of the soldiers and people in conventionally panegyrical terms; in a scene that is the antithesis of rejoicing and *adventus*, all orders and all ages weep and lament for the Emperor, invoking him in traditional terminology as saviour and benefactor, while in addition the soldiers mourn him as their good shepherd. For similar terminology applied to the worship of the soldiers to God, inspired by Constantine, cf. *LC* 8. 10; the terms themselves, including the motif of the good shepherd, are found in Hellenistic kingship theory (Baynes, 'Eusebius' Christian Empire', 171), but the extravagance of the scene and the choice of detail are typical of imperial panegyric (e.g. Corippus, *In laudem Iustini* 3. 41–61, the funeral of

Justinian, an account with many similar elements). As befits an emperor, it is the military who mourn first, and who escort his body (66. 1), and the description of what follows (66–72) preserves traditional motifs from imperial funerals even while attempting to give them a Christian significance (see the analysis in MacCormack, *Art and Ceremony*, 117–21); for Constantine, see P. Franchi dei Cavalieri, 'I funerali e il sepolcro di Costantino Magno', *MEFR* 29 (1916–17), 205–61.

Constantine's body, laid in a golden coffin and wrapped in the imperial purple he had ostentatiously renounced (62. 5), is taken under escort to Constantinople to lie in state in the imperial palace (66. 1), adorned with the diadem and honoured by perpetual vigil, receiving the same formal and official homage from the soldiers as when he was alive (67. 1); first the army, then the senate and the people pay their respects in turn. It is however the soldiers who take the decisions (67. 2); the lying-in-state 'went on for a long time', while everyone waited, no doubt with some trepidation, to see what Constantine's sons would do (Constantius had in fact already arrived; see Barnes, *CE* 261). Eusebius improbably claims that no previous emperor had received such honours (67. 3, cf. MacCormack, *Art and Ceremony*, 118).

68–73. *Succession and funeral*

The immediate aftermath of Constantine's death was politically highly sensitive, and Eusebius' main objective, especially writing with hindsight, was to make the succession seem smooth and inevitable (see on **71–3**, and cf. **I. 1–11**; **IV. 51–2**). He therefore tries to emphasize the uniqueness of the transition and of Constantine's continued influence (67. 3; 68. 2; for the latter point see MacCormack, *Art and Ceremony*, 118–19), and presents the succession as a matter of natural inheritance (IV. 51. 1, 63. 3, and by implication also 67. 2; 68. 2). He further glosses over any tension between Roman (pagan) *consecratio* and Christian burial at Constantinople (see on **69. 1**). The account here should be compared with the similar treatment of that of Constantine's own succession on the death of his father Constantius Chlorus at I. 20–2, on which see MacCormack, *Art and Ceremony*, 116.

68. 2. all the troops everywhere . . . By a fiction of election, albeit military, the three sons of Constantine, already Caesars, are designated as successors; while no mention is made of other claimants (see on **IV. 51–52. 3**), the fact that there is need for a decision at all, even a fictional one, conveys a sense of uncertainty. There was an obvious danger that civil war between them would break out immediately.

68. 3. Soon they saw fit . . . Eusebius telescopes the chronology. Constantine's three sons were not declared Augusti until 9 September 337 (*Chron. Min.* 1. 235), after the removal of their rivals (Zosimus 2. 40); the three met in Pannonia and arrived at a (temporary) settlement and division of the Empire (Julian, *Orat.* 1. 19a; for the chronology see T. D. Barnes, 'Imperial Chronology, AD 337–350', *Phoenix*, 34 (1980), 160–6). The first to be eliminated was Constantine II (340; Zosimus 2. 41). See R. Klein, 'Die Kämpfe um die Nachfolge nach dem Tod Constantinus des Großen', *BF* 6 (1979), 101–50. The reference to Augusti is not necessarily a sign of different redactions (so Winkelmann, pp. lv–lvi, reporting Pasquali).

announcing their individual votes and voices to each other in writing. While military support was essential for imperial succession, it seems unlikely that it happened on this occasion in the way that Eusebius claims.

69. 1. the inhabitants of the imperial city. Eusebius describes the reception of the news in Rome ('the imperial city', distinguished from Constantinople, 'the city named after the Emperor', e.g. 66. 1), whose citizens hoped that Constantine would be buried there; according to Aur. Vict., *Caes.* 41. 18, they were seriously upset by the slight; cf. *Epit.* 41. 17, *Origo*, 6. 35. Senate and people mourned and praised Constantine, honouring him with portraits and expressing hopes that his sons would become emperors. Constantine depicted in heaven: see on **15. 2** above and **73** below; similarly, *Pan. Lat.* 6 (7). 7. 3, AD 310, imagines his father Constantius being received among the gods and with the hand of Jupiter extended to him (discussion, MacCormack, *Art and Ceremony*, 119–21).

Rome would have been the normal setting for the ceremony of *consecratio* of a dead emperor, conferred by the Roman Senate (see G. Bonamente, 'Apoteosi e imperatori cristiani', in

G. Bonamente and A. Nestori, eds., *I cristiani e l'impero nel IV secolo* (Macerata, 1988), 107–42, at 108; see below on **71–3**, with earlier bibliography); the pictures Eusebius describes are the *imagines* commemorating such an event. But on this occasion there was no body and no pyre, and the Emperor was laid to rest in his Christian mausoleum at Constantinople. Constantine's funeral marks a major departure from tradition (so also Grünewald, *Constantinus*, 162 and see on **71–3**). Eusebius' smooth phraseology makes it hard to know how much if any of the traditional Roman ceremonial took place (Bonamente, 'Apoteosi', 110–11); he may be discreetly passing over an actual pagan ceremony or suggesting that the traditional forms were on this occasion refused. The usual *consecratio* coins were none the less issued (see P. Bruun, 'The Consecration Coins of Constantine the Great', *Arctos*, NS 1 (1954), 19–31; Fig. 11) and Constantine was granted the traditional title *divus* (see on **73**).

Baths and markets were closed. i.e. a *iustitium* was declared.

70. But those here . . . Eusebius moves swiftly from Rome to Constantinople and writes as if he was there himself. Constantius II (without his brothers) conducts the funeral procession, again under close military escort; the body of Constantine is taken to his mausoleum and laid there.

70. 2. the new Emperor Constantius. Eusebius pre-empts his status; he was not Augustus for several months (above, on

FIG. 11. (*a*) *Consecratio* coin of Constantine, obv., Constantine with veiled head. (*b*) Rev., with chariot ascending to heaven and hand of God descending. Byzantine Collection, Dumbarton Oaks, Washington, DC.

68. 2). Constantius had seized the initiative, honouring his father 'with his presence', while his brothers were still dangerously absent.

71–3. Constantine's funeral (for which Eusebius is our only source) and its relation to earlier imperial funerals have often been discussed: see MacCormack, *Art and Ceremony*, 119–21; A. Kaniuth, *Die Beisetzung Konstantins des Grossen: Untersuchungen zur religiösen Haltung des Kaisers* (Breslau, 1941); S. Calderone, 'Teologia, succesione dinastica e consecratio in età constantiniana', *Le Culte des souverains dans l'Empire romain* (Entretiens Hardt, 19; Geneva, 1973), 215–61; J. Arce, *Funus Imperatorum: Los funerales de los emperadores romanos* (Madrid, 1988), 159–68, with bibliography; Dagron, *Empereur et prêtre*, 148–54.

The ceremonial in Constantinople falls into two stages: a lying-in-state in the palace (66–7; this may have lasted for some time), and then a procession from the palace to the mausoleum (70) followed by a Christian service (71; see Simon Price, 'From Noble Funerals to Divine Cult: The Consecration of Roman Emperors', in David Cannadine and Simon Price, eds., *Rituals of Royalty: Power and Ceremonial in Traditional Societies* (Cambridge, 1987), 56–105, at 100–1 and see on **69. 1**). Constantine was inhumed, probably the first emperor to be treated in this way after death; accordingly there was no place for the funeral pyre, which had been accorded primary importance in the ceremonial until the tetrarchic period (see Price, 'Noble Funerals', 98). Constantius and the soldiers withdraw before the Christian funeral service begins, with the Emperor's body placed on a high dais. As he desired (71. 2), he is accorded burial together with the memorials to the Apostles, in what became known as a *depositio ad sanctos*, so that his remains can be seen being included in their invocation (*prosrhema*, cf. on **60. 1**; for the nature of the worship offered in connection with Constantine's tomb see Bonamente, 'Apoteosi', 130–1). He is gathered in to the people of God and shares in worship and prayers, holding on to the Empire even after his death and directing it, still with his imperial titles, as if he has been brought back to life. This is Eusebius' strongest claim for Constantine's continued influence after his death. In the preface the Emperor is depicted as looking down from his place with God in heaven

(**I. 1. 2**), yet influencing his sons in every part of the world (**I. 1. 1**). The traditionally Roman military funeral has given way to a Christian one, and the dead Emperor's apotheosis comes near to becoming a Christian resurrection. The service itself is not described (see on Constantine's baptism, **62.** 4), though the terminology ('obsequies', 70. 2; 'ministers of God', 'divine worship', 71. 1) is fully Christian; Eusebius wants to point a lesson to those surviving, namely that Constantine was not really dead, but continued to live and reign. However, even though he was called *divus* on coins and elsewhere (Bonamente, 'Apoteosi', 111 and see below), Constantine has received a Christian funeral and his apotheosis is a spiritual one (Arce, *Funus Imperatorum*, 163–4, 128; Bonamente, 'Apoteosi', 113–16). Eusebius goes further in ch. 72, explicitly likening Constantine to Christ, without quite saying that he rose again (see on **64.** 1 above); the phoenix, included only to be rejected by Eusebius as a true comparison, and taking the place played by the eagle of Jupiter on traditional *consecratio* issues, was taken by Christians as a symbol of resurrection (first in 1 Clement 26: 1) as well as signifying the rising of the sun and the continuity of imperial power through the succession (so in Corippus, *In laudem Iustini* 1. 349–55 with refs. at Cameron *ad loc.*).

71. 2. his end bestowed the Empire. Eusebius continues to bend the true chronology.

73. Constantine was shown posthumously on coins with head veiled and with the legend *divus* or *divo*, and on the reverse as rising in a four-horse chariot, with a hand being extended from heaven (Fig. 11). There is much discussion of the religious significance of these issues: see Grünewald, *Constantinus*, 159–62; L. Koep, 'Die Konsekrationsmünzen Kaiser Konstantins und ihre religionspolitische bedeutung', *JbAC* 1 (1958), 94–104; MacCormack, *Art and Ceremony*, 122–4; Calderone, 'Teologia, succesione dinastica e consecratio'; Arce, *Funus Imperatorum*, 166–7; L. Schumacher, *Gnomon*, 61 (1989), 527–8; F. Dvornik, *Early Christian and Byzantine Political Philosophy* (Washington, DC, 1966), ii. 649–50; L. Cracco Ruggini, 'Apoteosi e politica senatoria nel IV s. d. C.: Il dittico dei Symmachi al British Museum', *Rivista storica italiana*, 89 (1977), 425–89; Bonamente, 'Apoteosi'. They may date only from the period after September 337 (see Bonamente, 'Apoteosi', 126–7, but see Grünewald, *Constantinus*, 161). But Constantine was called *divus* on inscriptions both before and after 9 September 337, and laws continued to be issued in his name, e.g. *CTh* 13. 4. 2, 2 August 337); an official interregnum was politically undesirable. The iconography of the coins belongs in the repertoire of (pagan) imperial *consecratio* issues; the veiled emperor recalls his special status with the gods, while the quadriga and the hand extended from above convey the idea of apotheosis (earlier parallels: MacCormack, *Art and Ceremony*, 122–4; Constantius Chlorus: see above on **69.** 1, with *Pan. Lat.* 7 (6). 14. 3, AD 307, Constantius ascending in a chariot led by the sun). Eastern issues of Constantine: Bruun, 'Consecration coins', Koep, 'Die Konsekrationsmünzen'; Bonamente, 'Apoteosi', 123–7. Both the quadriga and the hand of God motifs lent themselves easily to Christian use, the former also being associated with the ascent of Elijah and succession of Elisha (2 Kgs. 2: 9–14; see MacCormack, *Art and Ceremony*, 124–6) and the hand of God being transferred to scenes of the ascension of Christ. Eusebius does not here point out the meaning of the iconography in his characteristically heavy-fisted way; nor is it necessary to believe that he had in mind an actual *consecratio* (so Grünewald, *Constantinus*, against Arce and others), though Constantine was the last emperor for whom *consecratio* coins were to be issued. The representation of Constantine in heaven attributed to Rome by Eusebius (**69.** 1) can be paralleled, though not so clearly, in earlier imperial art, and the same motif was used of Christ (MacCormack, *Art and Ceremony*, 127–30). Eusebius has fused and adapted pagan and Christian funeral imagery in the particular context of imperial apotheosis and succession. However, while it is tempting to suppose that he has consciously and carefully adapted traditional elements to a new Christian use ('a dividing line, a watershed', MacCormack, *Art and Ceremony*, 131; later Christianized imperial funerals: ibid. 132–4; cf. also Calderone, 'Teologia politica', Christian innovation rather than the deliberate ambiguity seen by Seeck and others), his main purpose in the *VC* is to smooth everything into a harmonious religious and political message. He may be recording in ch. 73 what seemed to him a somewhat awkward fact, and for that reason to be presenting it unadorned. On the other hand his account does point, unsurprisingly, to a mixture of traditional, i.e. pagan, elements and Christian ones.

74–5. *Conclusion: The Unique Emperor*

The final paragraph returns to Eusebius' general themes: Constantine ended persecution, and was the first Christian Emperor, the destroyer of idolatry, the undaunted herald of Christ and champion of the Church. No other, whether Greek, barbarian, or Roman, has been his equal.

BIBLIOGRAPHY

ALFÖLDI, A., ' "Hoc signo victor eris": Beiträge zur Geschichte der Bekehrung Konstantins des Grossen', in T. Klauser and A. Ruecker, eds., *Pisciculi. Festschrift F. Dölger* (Münster, 1939), 1–18, repr. in H. Kraft, ed., *Konstantin der Grosse* (Wege der Forschung, 31; Darmstadt, 1974).

ANDO, CLIFFORD, 'Pagan Apologetics and Christian Intolerance in the Ages of Themistius and Augustine', *Journal of Early Christian Studies*, 4/2 (1996), 171–207.

ARCE, J., *Funus Imperatorum: Los funerales de los emperadores romanos* (Madrid, 1988).

ARETZ, E., *et al.*, eds., *Der heilige Rock zu Trier: Studien zur Geschichte und Verehrung der Tunika Christi* (Trier, 1995).

ATHANASSIADI, P., 'The Fate of Oracles in Late Antiquity', *Deltion Christianikès Archaiologikès Etaireias*, NS 115 (1991), 271–8.

ATTRIDGE, HAROLD W. and HATA, G., eds., *Eusebius, Christianity and Judaism* (Studia Post-Biblica, 42; Leiden, 1992).

BAGATTI, B., *Gli antichi edifici sacri di Betlemme* (Jerusalem, 1952).

BARCELÓ, P. A., 'Die Religionspolitik Kaiser Constantins des Grossen vor den Schlacht an der Milvischen Brücke (312)', *Hermes*, 116 (1988), 76–94.

BARNES, T. D., 'Publilius Optatianus Porfyrius', *AJP* 96 (1975), 173–86.

—— 'The Emperor Constantine's Good Friday Sermon', *JThS* NS 27 (1976), 414–23.

—— 'The Victories of Constantine', *Zeitschrift für Papyrologie und Epigraphik* 20 (1976), 149–55.

—— 'Two Speeches by Eusebius', *GRBS* 18 (1977), 341–5.

—— 'Emperor and Bishops, A. D. 324–344: Some Problems', *American Journal of Ancient History*, 3 (1978), 53–75.

—— 'Imperial Chronology, AD 337–350', *Phoenix*, 34 (1980), 160–6.

—— 'Constantine's Prohibition of Pagan Sacrifice', *AJP* 105 (1984), 69–72.

—— 'Constantine and the Christians of Persia', *JRS* 75 (1985), 126–36.

—— 'The Conversion of Constantine', *Classical Views*, NS 5 (1985), 371–91.

—— 'Christians and Pagans in the Reign of Constantius', *Entretiens Hardt*, 34 (1987), 301–37.

—— 'Jerome and the *Origo Constantini imperatoris*', *Phoenix*, 43 (1989), 158–61.

BARNES, T. D., *Athanasius and Constantius: Theology and Politics in the Constantinian Empire* (Cambridge, Mass., 1993).

—— 'The Religious Affiliations of Consuls and Prefects, 317–361', in *From Eusebius to Augustine: Selected Papers 1982–1993* (London, 1994), no. vii.

—— 'Statistics and the Conversion of the Roman Aristocracy', *JRS* 85 (1995), 135–47.

BARTELINK, G. J. M., '*Misokalos*, epithète du diable', *Vigiliae Christianae* 12 (1958), 37–44.

—— ' "Maison de prière" comme dénomination de l'église en tant qu'édifice, en particulier chez Eusèbe de Césarée', *REG* 84 (1971), 101–18.

BASSETT, S., 'The Antiquities in the Hippodrome of Constantinople', *DOP* 45 (1991), 87–96.

BEAUCAMP, J., *Le Statut de la femme à Byzance (4ᵉ–7ᵉ siècle)*, i (Paris, 1990).

BERARDINO, A. DI, 'L'imperatore Costantino e la celebrazione della Pasqua', in Bonamente and Fusco, eds., *Costantino il Grande dall'antichità all'umanesimo, Macerata, 18–20 Dicembre, 1990* (Macerata, 1992), 363–84.

BERKHOF, T., *Die Theologie des Eusebius von Caesarea* (Amsterdam, 1939).

BERGER, A., *Untersuchungen zu den Patria Konstantinupoleos* (Poikila Byzantina, 8; Bonn, 1988).

BIDDLE, M., 'The Tomb of Christ: Sources, Methods and a New Approach', in K. Painter, ed., *'Churches Built in Ancient Times': Studies in Early Christian Archaeology* (London, 1994), 73–147.

—— *The Tomb of Christ* (Stroud, 1999).

BONAMENTE, G., 'Apoteosi e imperatori cristiani', in G. Bonamente and A. Nestori, eds., *I cristiani e l'impero nel IV secolo* (Macerata, 1988), 107–42.

—— and FUSCO, F., eds., *Costantino il Grande dall'antichità all'umanesimo, Macerata, 18–20 Dec. 1990* (Macerata, 1992).

—— and NESTORI, A., eds., *I cristiani e l'impero nel IV secolo* (Macerata, 1988).

BORGEHAMMAR, S., *How the Holy Cross was Found: From Event to Medieval Legend* (Stockholm, 1991).

BRADBURY, S., 'Constantine and the Problem of Anti-Pagan Legislation in the Fourth Century', *CP* 89 (1994), 120–39.

BRENNECKE, H. C., 'Nicäa', *TRE* 24 (1994), 429–41.

BRETT, E. T., 'Early Constantine Legends: A Study in Propaganda', *Byzantine Studies*, 10 (1983/4), 52–70.

BRUBAKER, LESLIE, 'To Legitimize an Emperor: Constantine and

Visual Authority in the Eighth and Ninth Centuries', in P. Magdalino, ed., *New Constantines* (Aldershot, 1994), 139–58.

BRUUN, P., 'The Consecration Coins of Constantine the Great', *Arctos*, NS 1 (1954), 19–31.

BURGESS, R. W., 'The Dates and Editions of Eusebius's *Chronici Canones* and *Historia Ecclesiastica*', *JThS* NS 48 (1997), 471–504.

CALDERONE, S., 'Teologia, succesione dinastica e consecratio in età constantiniana', *Le Culte des souverains dans l'Empire romain* (Entretiens Hardt, 19; Geneva, 1973), 215–61.

—— 'Il pensiero politico di Eusebio di Cesarea', in G. Bonamente and A. Nestori, eds., *I cristiani e l'impero nel IV secolo* (Macerata, 1988), 45–54.

CAMERON, AVERIL, *Flavius Cresconius Corippus, In laudem Iustini Augusti minoris libri IV*, text, translation, introduction and commentary (London, 1976).

—— 'Constantinus Christianus', *JRS* 73 (1983), 184–90.

—— 'Eusebius of Caesarea and the Rethinking of History', in E. Gabba, ed., *Tria Corda: Scritti in onore di Arnaldo Momigliano* (Como, 1983), 71–88.

—— *Christianity and the Rhetoric of Empire* (Berkeley and Los Angeles, 1991).

—— and HERRIN, JUDITH, *et al.*, eds., *Constantinople in the Early Eighth Century. The Parastaseis Syntomoi Chronikai* (Leiden, 1984).

CANNADINE, DAVID and PRICE, SIMON, eds., *Rituals of Royalty: Power and Ceremonial in Traditional Societies* (Cambridge, 1987).

CHADWICK, H., 'The Fall of Eustathius of Antioch', *JThS* NS 49 (1948), 27–35.

—— 'Ossius of Cordova and the Presidency of the Council of Antioch, 325', *JThS* NS 9 (1958), 292–304.

—— 'The Origin of the Title "Oecumenical Council"', *JThS* NS 23 (1972), 132–5.

CHESNUT, G., *The First Christian Histories* (Théologie historique, 46; Paris, 1977).

CORBO, V. C., *Il Santo Sepolchro di Gerusalemme. Aspetti archeologici dalle origine al periodo crociato*, i–iii (Jerusalem, 1981).

CORCORAN, S., 'Hidden from History: The Legislation of Licinius', in Jill Harries and Ian Wood, eds., *The Theodosian Code* (London, 1993), 97–119.

—— *The Empire of the Tetrarchs: Imperial Pronouncements and Government AD 284–324* (Oxford, 1996).

COÜASNON, C., *The Church of the Holy Sepulchre* (Oxford, 1974).

COWDREY, H. J., 'Eleventh-Century Reformers' Views of Constantine', *BF* 24 (1997), 63–91.

Cox, Patricia, *Biography in Late Antiquity: A Quest for the Holy Man* (Berkeley and Los Angeles, 1983).

Curran, John, 'Moving Statues in Late Antique Rome: Problems of Perspective', *Art History*, 17 (1994), 46–58.

Dagron, G., *Naissance d'une capitale; Constantinople et ses institutions de 330 à 451* (Paris, 1984).

—— and Feissel, D., 'Inscriptions inédites du Musée d'Antioche', *Travaux et Mémoires*, 9 (1985), 421–61.

—— *Empereur et prêtre: Étude sur le 'césaropapisme' byzantin* (Paris, 1996).

Davies, J. G., 'Eusebius's Description of the Martyrium at Jerusalem', *AJA* 61 (1957), 171–3.

De Decker, D., 'La Politique religieuse de Maxence', *Byzantion*, 38 (1968), 472–562.

Dinkler, E., *Signum Crucis* (Tübingen, 1967).

Dölger, F., *Sphragis* (Paderborn, 1911).

Downey, G., 'The Builder of the Original Church of the Apostles at Constantinople: A Contribution to the Criticism of the Vita Constantini Attributed to Eusebius', *DOP* 6 (1951), 53–80.

—— *A History of Antioch in Syria from Seleucus to the Arab Conquest* (Princeton, 1961).

Drake, H. A., rev. of Barnes, *CE*, *AJP* 103 (1982), 462–6.

—— 'Suggestions of Date in Constantine's *Oration to the Saints*', *AJP* 106 (1985), 335–49.

—— 'Athanasius's First Exile', *GRBS* 27 (1986), 193–204.

—— 'Constantine and Consensus', *Church History*, 64 (1995), 1–15.

—— 'Lambs into Lions: Explaining Early Christian Intolerance', *Past and Present*, 153 (1996), 3–36.

Drijvers, J. W., *Helena Augusta: The Mother of Constantine the Great and the Legend of her Finding of the True Cross* (Leiden, 1992).

—— 'Helena Augusta: Exemplary Christian Empress', *Studia Patristica*, 24 (1993), 85–90.

Droge, A., *Homer or Moses? Early Christian Interpretations of the History of Culture* (HUT 26; Tübingen, 1989).

Duchesne, L., 'La Question de la Pâque au Concile de Nicée', *RQH* 28 (1880).

Durliat, J., *De la ville antique à la ville byzantine: Le Problème de subsistances* (Rome, 1990).

Dvornik, F., *Early Christian and Byzantine Political Philosophy: Origins and Background*, i–ii (Washington, DC, 1966).

Ehrhardt, C., 'Constantinian Documents in Gelasius of Cyzicus, *Ecclesiastical History*', *JbAC* 23 (1980), 48–57.

Elliott, J. K., ed., *The Apocryphal New Testament* (Oxford, 1993).

ELLIOTT, T. G., 'The Language of Constantine's Propaganda', *TAPA* 120 (1990), 349–53.

—— 'Eusebian Frauds in the Vita Constantini', *Phoenix*, 45 (1991), 162–71.

—— *The Christianity of Constantine the Great* (Scranton, Pa., 1996).

EPSTEIN, ANNABEL WHARTON, 'The Rebuilding and Redecoration of the Holy Apostles in Constantinople: A Reconsideration', *GRBS* 23 (1982), 79–92 (see also WHARTON).

ERRINGTON, R. M., 'Constantine and the Pagans', *GRBS* 29 (1988), 309–18.

EVANS-GRUBBS, J., 'Abduction Marriage in Antiquity: A Law of Constantine (*CTh* IX. 24. 1) and its Social Context', *JRS* 79 (1989), 59–83.

—— 'Constantine and Imperial Legislation on the Family', in Jill Harries and Ian Wood, eds., *The Theodosian Code* (London, 1993), 120–42.

—— *Law and Family in Late Antiquity. The Emperor Constantine's Marriage Legislation* (Oxford, 1995).

FITTSCHEN, K. and ZANKER, P., *Katalog der römischen Porträts in den Capitolinischen Museen und in den alteren . . . Sammlungen* (Mainz am Rhein, 1993–5), 2 vols.

FOWDEN, GARTH, *Empire to Commonwealth: Consequences of Monotheism in Late Antiquity* (Cambridge, 1993).

—— 'The Last Days of Constantine: Oppositional Versions and their Influence', *JRS* 84 (1994), 146–70.

FRANCHI DEI CAVALIERI, P., 'I funerali e il sepolcro di Costantino Magno', *MEFR* 29 (1916–17), 205–61.

GAGER, J. G., *Moses in Greco-Roman Paganism* (New York, 1972).

GASCOU, J., 'Le Rescrit d'Hispellum', *MEFR* 79 (1967), 609–59.

GAUDEMET, J., *L'Église dans l'empire romain* (Paris, 1958).

GELZER, H., HILGENFELD, H., CUNTZ, O., *Patrum Nicaenorum Nomina* (Leipzig, 1898).

GERO, S., 'The True Image of Christ: Eusebius's Letter to Constantia Reconsidered', *JThS* ns 32 (1981), 460–70.

GIBSON, SHIMON and TAYLOR, JOAN, *Beneath the Church of the Holy Sepulchre Jerusalem: The Archaeology and Early History of Traditional Golgotha* (Palestine Exploration Fund Monograph, series maior, 1; London, 1994).

GRABAR, A., *L'Empereur dans l'art byzantin* (Paris, 1936).

GRIERSON, P., 'The Tombs and Obits of the Byzantine Emperors', *DOP* 16 (1962), 1–63.

GRIGG, R., 'Constantine the Great and the Cult without Images', *Viator*, 8 (1977), 1–32.

GRUMEL, V., 'Le Problème de la date pascale au IIIe et IVe siècles', *Revista eclésiastica brasileira* 18 (1960), 163–78.

HÄGG, T., and ROUSSEAU, PHILIP, eds., *Greek Biography and Panegyrics in Late Antiquity* (Berkeley and Los Angeles, forthcoming).

HALL, S. G., 'The Origins of Easter', *Studia Patristica*, 15 (1984), 554–67.

—— *Doctrine and Practice in the Early Church* (London, 1991).

—— 'Some Constantinian Documents in the *Vita Constantini*', in S. N. C. Lieu and D. Montserrat, eds., *Constantine* (London, 1998), 86–103.

—— The Sects under Constantine', in W. J. Shields and D. Wood, eds., *Voluntary Religion* (Studies in Church History, 23; Oxford, 1986), 1–13.

HANNESTAD, N., *Roman Art and Imperial Policy* (Aarhus, 1986).

HANSON, R. P. C., *The Search for the Christian Doctrine of God* (Edinburgh, 1988).

HARL, M., 'Les Trois Quarantaines de Moïse', *REG* 80 (1967), 407–12.

—— 'Moïse figure de l'évêque dans l'Eloge de Basile de Grégoire de Nysse', in Spira, ed., *The Biographical Works of Gregory of Nyssa* (Philadelphia, 1984), 71–120.

HARRIES, JILL, and WOOD, IAN, eds., *The Theodosian Code* (London, 1993).

HARRISON, E. B., 'The Constantinian Portrait', *DOP* 21 (1967), 79–96.

HEATHER, PETER, 'New Men for New Constantines', in P. Magdalino, ed., *New Constantines* (Aldershot, 1994), 11–33.

HEID, S., 'Der Ursprung der Helenalegendes im Pilgerbetrieb Jerusalems', *JbAC* 32 (1989), 41–71.

HEIM, F., *La Théologie de la victoire de Constantin à Théodose* (Théologie historique, 89; Paris, 1992).

HEINEN, H. 'Helena, Konstantin und die Überlieferung der Kreuzesauffindung im 4. Jahrhundert', in E. Aretz et al., eds., *Der heilige Rock zu Trier* (Trier, 1995), 83–117.

HELGELAND, J., 'Christians in the Roman Army from Marcus Aurelius to Constantine', *ANRW* II. 23. 1 (Berlin, 1979), 724–834.

HOLLERICH, M., 'The Comparison of Moses and Constantine in Eusebius of Caesarea's *Life of Constantine*', *Studia Patristica*, 19 (1989), 80–95.

HOLUM, KENNETH G., 'Hadrian and St. Helena: Imperial Travel and the Origins of Christian Holy Land Pilgrimage', in R. Ousterhout, *The Blessings of Pilgrimage* (Urbana, Ill., 1990), 66–81.

HORNUS, J.-M., *It is Not Lawful for Me to Fight*, Eng. trans. (Scottdale, 1980).

HUBER, W., *Passa und Ostern* (BZNW 35; Berlin, 1969).

HUNT, E. D., *Holy Land Pilgrimage in the Later Roman Empire A. D. 312–460* (Oxford, 1982).

—— 'Christianising the Roman Empire: The Evidence of the Code', in Jill Harries and Ian Wood, eds., *The Theodosian Code* (London, 1993), 143–60.

—— 'Constantine and Jerusalem', *JEH* 48 (1997), 405–24.

HUNT, LUCY-ANNE, 'Artistic and Cultural Inter-Relations between the Christian Communities at the Holy Sepulchre in the 12th Century', in A. O'Mahony, ed., *The Christian Heritage in the Holy Land* (London, 1995), 57–96.

JAMES, LIZ, ' "Pray not to Fall into Temptation and be on your Guard": Antique Statues in Byzantine Constantinople', *Gesta*, 35 (1996), 12–20.

JAUBERT, ANNIE, *La Date de la Cêne. Calendrier biblique et liturgie chrétienne* (Paris, 1957), Eng. trans., *The Date of the Last Supper* (New York, 1965).

JEREMIAS, J., 'Wo lag Golgotha und das Heilige Grab?', *Angelos*, 1 (Leipzig, 1926), 141–73.

JONES, A. H. M., and SKEAT, T. C., 'Notes on the Genuineness of the Constantinian Documents in Eusebius' *Life of Constantine*', *JEH* 5 (1954), 196–200.

KANIUTH, A., *Die Beisetzung Konstantins des Grossen: Untersuchungen zur religiösen Haltung des Kaisers* (Breslau, 1941).

KAZHDAN, A., 'Constantin imaginaire': Byzantine Legends of the Ninth Century about Constantine the Great', *Byzantion*, 57 (1987), 196–250.

KEE, A., *Constantine Versus Christ* (London, 1962).

KEIL, V., *Quellensammlung zur Religionspolitik Konstantins des Grossen*, Texte zur Forschung, 54 (Darmstadt, 1989).

KERESZTZES, P., *Constantine: A Great Christian Monarch and Apostle* (Amsterdam, 1981).

KLAUSER, TH., and RUECKER, A., eds., *Pisciculi: Festschrift F. Dölger. Antike und Christentum*, Ergänzungsband, 1; Münster, 1939).

KLEIN, R., 'Die Kämpfe um die Nachfolge nach dem Tod Constantinus des Großen', *BF* 6 (1979), 101–50.

KLOFT, H., *Liberalitas Principis: Herkunft und Bedeutung. Studien zur Prinzipatsideologie* (Kölner historische Abhandlungen, 18; Cologne, 1970).

KOEP, L., 'Die Konsekrationsmünzen Kaiser Konstantins und ihre religionspolitische Bedeutung', *JbAC* 1 (1958), 94–104.

KRAFT, H., 'Kaiser Konstantins religiöse Entwicklung', *Beiträge zur historischen Theologie*, 20 (1955), 160–201.

KRAFT, H., ed., *Konstantin der Grosse* (Wege der Forschung, 31; Darmstadt, 1974).

KRAUTHEIMER, R., *Early Christian and Byzantine Architecture*, 2nd rev. edn. (Harmondsworth, 1975).

KÜHNEL, H., *From the Earthly to the Heavenly Jerusalem: Representations of the Holy City in Christian Art of the First Millenium* (Römische Quartalschrift Supp. 42; Rome, Freiburg, and Vienna, 1987).

LASSUS, A., 'L'Empereur Constantin, Eusèbe et les lieux saints', *Rev. de l'hist. des religions*, 171 (1967), 135–44.

LEE, A. D., *Information and Frontiers: Roman Foreign Relations in Late Antiquity* (Cambridge, 1993).

LEEB, R., 'Zum Ursprung des Kaiserbildes im Kreuz', *Jahrbuch der Österreichischen Byzantinistik* 41 (1991), 1–14.

—— *Konstantin und Christus: Die Verchristlichung der imperialen Repräsentation unter Konstantin dem Grossen als Spiegel seiner Kirchenpolitik uns seines Selbstverständnisses als christlicher Kaiser* (Arbeiten z. Kirchengeschichte, 58; Berlin, 1992).

LEENHARDT, FRANZ J., *The Epistle to the Romans. A Commentary*, Eng. trans. (London, 1961).

LIEU, SAMUEL N. C., and MONTSERRAT, DOMINIC, eds., *From Constantine to Julian: Pagan and Byzantine Views: A Source History* (London, 1996).

—— and —— eds., in conjunction with Bill Leadbetter, and Mark Vermes, *Constantine: History, Historiography and Legend* (London, 1998).

L'HUILLIER, M.-C., *L'Empire des mots: Orateurs gaulois et empereurs romains, 3ᵉ et 4ᵉ siècles* (Paris, 1992).

LINDER, A., 'The Myth of Constantine the Great in the West: Sources and Hagiographic Commemoration', *Studi Medievali*, 3rd ser. 16 (1975), 43–95.

LOHSE, B., *Das Passafest der Quartodecimaner* (BFChTh. M. 54; Gütersloh, 1953).

L'ORANGE, H. P., *Likeness and Icon: Selected Studies in Classical and Early Mediaeval Art* (Odense, 1973).

LORENZ, R., 'Das Problem der Nachsynode von Nicäa', *Zeitschr. f. Kirchengesch.* 90 (1979), 22–40.

LOUTH, A., 'The Date of Eusebius' *Historia Ecclesiastica*', *JThS* NS 41 (1990), 111–23.

LUIBHEÍD, COLM, *The Council of Nicaea* (Galway, 1982).

—— 'The Alleged Second Session of the Council of Nicaea', *JEH* 34 (1983), 165–74.

MACMULLEN, R., *Constantine* (New York, 1969).

—— *Christianizing the Roman Empire* AD 300–400 (New Haven and London, 1984).

—— 'Constantine and the Miraculous', *GRBS* 9 (1968), 81–96.
—— *Christianity and Paganism in the Fourth to Eighth Centuries* (New Haven, 1997).
MADDEN, T. F., 'The Serpent Column of Delphi in Constantinople: Placement, Purposes and Mutations', *BMGS* 16 (1992), 111–45.
MAGDALINO, P., ed., *New Constantines* (Aldershot, 1994).
MANGO, CYRIL, *The Art of the Byzantine Empire 312–1453* (Englewood Cliffs, NJ, 1972, repr. 1986).
—— *The Brazen House: A Study of the Vestibule of the Imperial Palace of Constantinople* (Copenhagen, 1959).
—— 'Antique Statuary and the Byzantine Beholder', *DOP* 17 (1963), 55–7.
—— *Byzantine Architecture* (New York, 1976).
—— *Le Développement urbain de Constantinople (IVᵉ–VIIᵉ siècles)* (Paris, 1985).
—— *Studies on Constantinople* (Aldershot, 1993).
—— 'Constantine's Mausoleum and the Translation of Relics', *Byzantinische Zeitschrift* 83 (1990), 51–61.
—— 'The Empress Helena, Helenopolis, Pylae', *Travaux et mémoires,* 12 (1994), 143–58.
MAUSE, M., *Die Darstellung des Kaisers in der lateinischen Panegyrik* (Palingenesia, 50; Stuttgart, 1994).
MILLAR, F. G. B., 'Emperors, Frontiers and Foreign Relations, 31 BC to AD 378', *Britannia,* 13 (1982), 1–25.
MILNER, CHRISTINE, ' "Lignum Vitae" or "Crux Gemmata"? The Cross of Golgotha in the Early Byzantine Period', *BMGS* 20 (1996), 77–99.
MOREAU, J., 'Zum Problem der Vita Constantini', *Historia,* 4 (1955), 234–45.
—— 'Eusebius von Caesarea', *Reallexikon für Antike und Christentum* 6 (Stuttgart, 1966), 1052–88.
MORTLEY, RAOUL, *The Idea of Universal History from Hellenistic Philosophy to Early Christian Historiography* (Lewiston, NY, 1996).
MÜLLER-RETTIG, B., *Der Panegyricus des Jahres 310 auf Konstantin den Grossen* (Stuttgart, 1990).
MURRAY, SR. CHARLES, 'Art and the Early Church', *JThS* NS 28 (1977), 303–45.
NIXON, C. E. V., 'Constantinus Oriens Imperator: Propaganda and Panegyric. On Reading Panegyric 7 [307]', *Historia,* 42 (1993), 229–46.
NORDERVAL, ØYVING, 'Kaiser Konstantins Edikt gegen die Häretiker und Schismatiker (*Vita Constantini* III. 64–65)', *Symbolae Osloenses,* 70 (1995), 95–115.

NORDERVAL, ØYVING, 'The Emperor Constantine and Arius: Unity in the Church and Unity in the Empire', *Studia Theologica*, 42 (1988), 113–50.

NOVAK, D. M., 'Constantine and the Senate: An Early Phase in the Christianization of the Roman Aristocracy', *Ancient Society*, 10 (1979), 271–310.

O'MAHONEY, A., ed., with G. GUNNER and K. HINTLIAN, *The Christian Heritage in the Holy Land* (London, 1995).

OUSTERHOUT, R.,'The Temple, the Sepulchre and the *Martyrion* of the Saviour', *Gesta*, 29/1 (1990), 44–53.

—— ed., *The Blessings of Pilgrimage* (Urbana, Ill., 1990).

OVADIAH, A., *Corpus of the Byzantine Churches in the Holy Land*, Eng. trans. (Bonn, 1970).

PAGELS, ELAINE, *The Origins of Satan* (Harmondsworth, 1995).

PATRICH, J., 'The Early Church of the Holy Sepulchre in the Light of Excavations and Restoration', in Y. Tsafrir, ed., *Ancient Churches Revealed* (Jerusalem, 1993), 101–17.

PETERSEN, WILLIAM L., 'Eusebius and the Paschal Controversy', in H. W. Attridge and G. Hata, eds., *Eusebius, Christianity and Judaism* (Studia Post-Biblica, 42; Leiden, 1992), 311–25.

PETIT, P., 'Libanius et la Vita Constantini', *Historia* 1 (1950), 562–80.

PIERCE, P., 'The Arch of Constantine: Propaganda and Ideology in Late Roman Art', *Art History*, 12 (1989), 387–418.

PIETRI, CHARLES, 'Constantin en 324. Propagande et théologie impériales d'après les documents de la *Vita Constantini*', in *Crise et redressement dans les provinces européennes de l'Empire (milieu du IIIe-milieu du IVe siècle ap. J.C.) Actes du colloque de Strasbourg (décembre 1981)* (Strasbourg, 1983), 63–90 (repr. C. Pietri, *Christiana Respublica: Éléments d'une enquête sur le christianisme antique*, Collection de l'École française de Rome, 234, i–iii (Paris, 1998), i, 253–80.

PIGANIOL, A., *L'Empereur Constantin* (Paris, 1932).

—— *L'Empire chrétien*, 2nd edn. (Paris, 1972).

—— 'Sur quelques passages de la Vita Constantini', *Annuaire de l'Institut de Philologie et d'Histoire Orientales*, 10 (*Mélanges Grégoire*) (1950), 513–18.

—— 'L'Hémispherion et l'omphalos des lieux saints', *Cahiers archéologiques*, 1 (1945), 7–14.

PRICE, S. R. F., 'From Noble Funerals to Divine Cult: The Consecration of Roman Emperors', in David Cannadine and Simon Price, eds., *Rituals of Royalty* (Cambridge, 1987), 56–105.

RIDLEY, R. T., 'Anonymity in the Vita Constantini', *Byzantion*, 50 (1980), 241–58.

RODGERS, B. SAYLOR, 'Constantine's Pagan Vision', *Byzantion*, 50 (1980), 259–78.

—— 'Divine Insinuation in the Panegyrici Latini', *Historia*, 25 (1986), 69–99.

—— 'The Metamorphosis of Constantine', *Classical Quarterly* NS 39 (1989), 233–46.

ROUECHÉ, C. M., 'Acclamations in the Later Roman Empire: New Evidence from Aphrodisias', *JRS* 74 (1984), 181–99.

RUBIN, Z., 'The Church of the Holy Sepulchre and the Conflict between the Sees of Caesarea and Jerusalem', *Jerusalem Cathedra*, 2 (1982), 79–105.

RUGGINI, L. CRACCO, 'Apoteosi e politica senatoria nel IV s. d. C.: Il dittico dei Symmachi al British Museum', *Rivista storica italiana*, 89 (1977), 425–89.

RUHBACH, G., *Apologetik und Geschichte: Untersuchungen zur Theologie Eusebs von Caesarea*, Diss. Theol. (Heidelberg, 1962).

RUSSELL, D. A., and WILSON, N. G., eds., *Menander Rhetor* (Oxford, 1981).

SCHWARTZ, E., 'Christliche und jüdische Ostertafeln', *AGWG. PH* NS 8/6 (1905), 121–5.

SANSTERRE, J.-M., 'Eusèbe de Césarée et la naissance de la théorie "césaropapiste"', *Byzantion*, 42 (1972), 131–95, 532–94.

SEIDL, J., 'Eine Kritik an Kaiser Konstantin in der *Vita Constantini* des Euseb', in E. Chr. von Suttner and C. Palock, eds., *Wegzeichen: Festgaben zum 60. Geburtstag von H. M. Biedermann* (Das ostliche Christentum, 25; Würzburg, 1971), 83–94.

SESTON, W., 'Constantine as Bishop', *JRS* 37 (1947), 128–9.

SHIELDS, W. J., and WOOD, DIANA, eds., *Voluntary Religion*, Studies in Church History, 23 (Oxford, 1986).

SILLI, P., *Testi Costantiniani nelle fonte letterarie: Materiali per una Palengenesi delle Costituzioni Tardo-Imperiali*, iii (Milan, 1987).

SMITH, R. R. R., 'The Public Image of Licinius I: Portrait Sculpture and Imperial Ideology in the Early Fourth Century', *JRS* 87 (1997), 170–202.

SPIRA, A., ed., *The Biographical Works of Gregory of Nyssa*. Proccedings of the Fifth International Colloquium on Gregory of Nyssa (Mainz, 6–10 Sept. 1982), Patristic Monograph Series, 12 (Philadelphia, 1984).

STEMBERGER, G., *Juden und Christen im heiligen Land: Palastina unter Konstantin und Theodosius* (Munich, 1987).

STRAUB, J., *Regeneratio Imperii* (Darmstadt, 1972).

SWAIN, S., and EDWARDS, M., eds., *Portraits: Biographical Representation in the Greek and Latin Literature of the Roman Empire* (Oxford, 1997).

362　BIBLIOGRAPHY

SWIFT, L. J., 'War and the Christian Conscience I. The Early Years', *ANRW* II.23.1 (Berlin, 1979), 835–68.

TAYLOR, JOAN E., *Christians and Holy Places. The Myth of Jewish-Christian Origins* (Oxford, 1993).

—— 'Golgotha: a Reconsideration of the Evidence for the Sites of Jesus' Crucifixion and Burial', *New Testament Studies* 44 (1998), 180–203.

TSAFRIR, Y., ed., *Ancient Churches Revealed* (Jerusalem, 1993).

VAN ESBROEK, M., 'Legends about Constantine in Armenian', *Classical Armenian Culture* (Chico, Calif., 1982), 79–101.

VAN GOUDOEVER, J., *Jewish and Christian Calendars* (Leiden, 1961).

VINCENT, L. H., and ABEL, F. M., *Jérusalem Nouvelle* (Paris, 1914).

VISONÀ, G., 'Ostern/Osterfest/Osterpredigt I', *TRE* 25 (1995), 517–30.

VITTINGHOF, F., 'Eusebius als Verfasser der VC', *RhM* NS 96 (1953), 361–4.

VOGT, J., 'Die *Vita Constantini* des Eusebius über den Konflikt zwischen Konstantin und Licinius', *Historia*, 2 (1954), 463–71.

—— *Constantin der Grosse und seine Zeit* (Munich, 2nd edn., 1960).

—— 'Constantinus der Grosse', *Reallexikon für Antike und Christentum* 3 (1956), 306–79.

VON HAEHLING, R., *Die Religionszugehörigkeit der hohen Amtsträger der römischen Reiches von Constantins I. bis zum Ende der theodosianischen Dynastie*, Antiquitas 3. Reihe 23 (Bonn, 1972).

WALKER, PETER, *Holy City, Holy Places? Christian Attitudes to the Holy Land in the Fourth Century* (Oxford, 1990).

—— 'Jerusalem and the Holy Land in the Fourth Century', in O'Mahony, ed., *The Christian Heritage in the Holy Land*, 22–34.

WALLACE-HADRILL, D. S., *Eusebius of Caesarea* (London, 1960).

WARMINGTON, B. H., 'Aspects of Constantinian Propaganda in the Panegyrici Latini', *TAPA* 104 (1974), 371–84.

—— 'The Sources of Some Constantinian Documents in Eusebius' Ecclesiastical History and Life of Constantine', *Studia Patristica*, 18/1 (1986), 93–8.

—— 'Virgil, Eusebius of Caesarea and an Imperial Ceremony', in C. Deroux, ed., *Studies in Latin Literature and History*, iv (Brussels, 1986), 451–60.

—— 'Eusebius of Caesarea's Versions of Constantine's Laws in the Codes', *Studia Patristica*, 24 (1993), 201–7.

WEISS, PETER, 'Die Vision Constantins', in J. Bleicken, ed., *Colloquium aus Anlass des 80. Geburtstages von Alfred Heuss* (Frankfurter Althistorische Studien, 13; Frankfurt, 1993), 145–69.

WEITZMANN, K., ed., *The Age of Spirituality: Late Antique and Early*

Christian Art, Third to Seventh Century (New York, Metropolitan Museum, 1979).

WHARTON, ANNABEL JANE, 'The Baptistery of the Holy Sepulchre at Jerusalem and the Politics of Sacred Landscape', *DOP* 46 (1992), 313–25.

—— *Refiguring the Postclassical City: Dura Europos, Jerash, Jerusalem and Ravenna* (Cambridge, 1995).

WIEMER, H.-U., 'Libanius on Constantine', *Classical Quarterly* NS 44 (1994), 511–24.

WILKEN, R., *John Chrysostom and the Jews: Rhetoric and Reality in the Late Fourth Century* (Berkeley and Los Angeles, 1983).

—— *The Land Called Holy: Palestine in Christian History and Thought* (New Haven, 1992).

—— 'Eusebius and the Christian Holy Land', in Attridge and Hata, eds., *Eusebius, Christianity and Judaism*, 736–60.

WILKINSON, J., *Jerusalem Pilgrims before the Crusades* (Warminster, 1977).

WILLIAMS, R., *Arius: Heresy and Tradition* (London, 1987).

WILSON, ANNA, 'Biographical Models: the Constantinian Period and Beyond', in Lieu *et al.*, eds., *Constantine: History, Historiography and legend* (London, 1998), 107–35.

WINKELMANN, F., 'Die Beurteilung des Eusebius von Cäsarea und seiner Vita Constantini im griechischen Osten', in J. Irmscher, ed. *Byzantinische Beiträge* (Berlin, 1964), 91–119.

—— *Untersuchungen zur Kirchengeschichte des Gelasios von Kaisareia* (Berlin, 1966).

—— 'Ein Ordnungsversuch der griechischen hagiographischen Konstantinviten und ihrer Überlieferung', in J. Irmscher and P. Nagel, eds., *Studia Byzantina* ii (Berliner Byzantinische Arbeiten, 44; Berlin, 1973), 267–8.

—— 'Die älteste erhaltene griechische hagiographische Vita Konstantins und Helenas (BHG Nr. 365z, 366, 366a)', in J. Dummer, ed., *Texte und Textkritik* (TU 133; Berlin, 1987), 623–3.

—— 'Charakter und Bedeutung der *Kirchengeschichte* des Gelasios von Kaisareia', *Polychronia: Festschrift F. Dölger*, i, *Byz. Forsch.* 1 (1966), 346–85.

WISTRAND, E., *Konstantins Kirche am heiligen Grab in Jerusalem nach den ältesten literarischen Zeugnissen* (Göteborg, 1952).

YARNOLD, E., 'Who Planned the Churches at the Christian Holy Places in the Holy Land?', *Studia Patristica*, 18 (1985), 105–9.

—— *The Awe-Inspiring Rites of Initiation*, 2nd edn. (Edinburgh, 1991).

INDEX